Managing Information Services

Managing Information Services:

A Transformational Approach

JO BRYSON

ASHGATE

Published by
Ashgate Publishing Limited
Gower House
Croft Road
Aldershot
Hampshire GU11 3HR
England

Ashgate Publishing Company
Suite 420
101 Cherry Street
Burlington, VT 05401-4405
USA

Ashgate website: http://www.ashgate.com

British Library Cataloguing in Publication Data
Bryson, Jo, 1950–
   Managing information services : a transformational
   approach. – New ed.
   1. Information services – Management
   I. Title
   025.5'2'068

Library of Congress Cataloging-in-Publication Data
Bryson, Jo, 1950–
   Managing information services : a transformational approach / by Jo
   Bryson. — 2nd ed.
      p. cm.
   Includes index.
   ISBN 0-7546-4631-9 (hardback) -- ISBN 0-7546-4634-3 (pbk.)
   1. Information resources management--Handbooks, manuals, etc. 2. Corporate
libraries--Administration--Handbooks, manuals, etc. 3. Information services--
Management--Handbooks, manuals etc. I. Title.

   T58.64.B795 2006
   658.4'038011--dc22

                                                                2006005844

ISBN-10: 0 7546 4631 9 (Hbk)
ISBN-10: 0 7546 4634 3 (Pbk)

ISBN-13: 978 0 7546 4631 0 (Hbk)
ISBN-13: 978 0 7546 4634 1 (Pbk)

Printed and bound in Great Britain by MPG Books Ltd, Bodmin, Cornwall.

Contents

List of Figures

Preface

There are three kinds of organizations: those who make things happen, those who watch things happen; and those who wonder what's happened.

Anonymous

This book has been written with the view to positioning and making things happen in a challenging and changing world. It is a management handbook for people working in information services in small to medium sized organizations, and a management textbook for students in information services, librarianship, records management and information and communications technology (ICT).

Organizations, project managers and individuals take a journey of life, along the path of which challenges and opportunities are encountered. *Managing information services: A transformational approach* has been written to equip them for this journey with the view to shifting mindsets and strategically positioning and transforming information services so that they are on the pathway to a promising future. Continuing with this analogy, organizations and individuals have to map out their future direction and be ready to take up the challenges, to create and successfully manage opportunities, and to make the right decisions in rapidly changing business and societal environments as dilemmas are presented along the way.

Managing information services: A transformational approach focuses on managing information services in dynamic environments where information is critical to maintaining organizational competitiveness through customer satisfaction and retention, increased productivity and performance, and financial viability. The underlying philosophy is that anything is possible, and solutions can be found for even the most exceptional and extraordinary circumstances. Common themes that reoccur throughout the book include:

- the need for transformational leadership that involves vision, personal energy and commitment, instilling a passion for what can be possible in the future;
- encouraging others to succeed beyond their dreams by creating an inspiring environment, sharing enthusiasm and generating the desire to excel;
- challenging environments can be turned into opportunities; especially where the information service has been energized from within;
- rethinking information services so that they are dynamic and have the flexibility to withstand strategic shocks and cope with changing circumstances;
- vitality, quality and innovation are tools that can be used to enable products and service offerings to exceed customer expectations; and
- engaging in change and unlocking ideas are successful positioning strategies to create the next advantage ahead of others.

The book is the second edition of *Managing information services: An integrated approach* by the same author. Where the first edition, brought together the disciplines of librarianship, records management and archives, information systems, computing and telecommunications to promote an integrated approach, this book extends the concept to other establishments. It explores the idea that institutions such as art galleries and museums have similar cultural and social capital business drivers, and whilst each of these institutions has traditionally been managed as silos, they could do more. Rethinking service delivery away from the traditional siloed institutional, professional and media focus that can be found in libraries, art galleries and museums towards an integrated multimedia approach could deliver a richer citizen centric experience.

Managing information services: A transformational approach adopts the reality that information services exist in a market space, rather than the traditional market place. This is a global, connected and always on environment where multi-channel service delivery is required to meet different customer needs and expectations. It is also a world where seeking competitive advantage and managing change is not good enough. Successful organizations need continually to invent the next advantage, using bright ideas, information, knowledge, creativity and innovation to do so. They must also build individual and organizational capability to create and engage in change.

It is with this background that the information services manager must:

- manage in a dynamic environment;
- plan and manage for transformation;
- create the right corporate environment;
- transform the corporate environment;
- manage themselves and others;
- ensure effective governance and accountability; and
- position to excel in service delivery.

The concept of the parent organization is used throughout the book. This refers to the corporate environment in which the information service operates. It may be the local government authority, government department, private sector organization, research centre or academic institution. It is an important concept as the environment of the parent organization often shapes the environment of the information service. Within this environment, the information services manager plays a role in transforming the information service as well as contributing to and working with executive management to transform the parent organization. Many of the topics are scalable in terms of understanding the management issues at different levels within the parent organization. For example, they can be used for reference to assist in the day-to-day management activities of the information service. They can also be used to provide an understanding of the wider organizational management issues that occur in the parent organization.

PART I – MANAGING IN A DYNAMIC ENVIRONMENT

1. Introduction to management
2. Strategic influences

PART II – PLANNING AND MANAGING FOR TRANSFORMATION

3. Strategic planning
4. Human resource management
5. Knowledge and information management
6. Technology and strategic asset management
7. Financial management

PART III – CREATING THE RIGHT CORPORATE ENVIRONMENT

8. Corporate culture
9. Politics
10. Policy making
11. Innovation and creativity

PART IV – TRANSFORMING THE CORPORATE ENVIRONMENT

12. Leadership
13. Engaging in change
14. Group dynamics and team building
15. Motivation
16 Conflict management
17. Negotiation

PART V – MANAGING YOURSELF AND OTHERS

18. Personal communication and networking
19. Stress management
20. Career planning and personal development
21. Managing expertise and generation gaps

MANAGING INFORMATION SERVICES: A TRANSFORMATIONAL APPROACH

EPILOGUE

Achieving the transformation - the final strategy

PART VI – GOVERNANCE AND ACCOUNTABILITY

22. Corporate governance
23. Accountability and influence
24. Encouraging transparency
25. Measuring benefits and performance
26. Risk management
27. Security
28. Outsourcing

PART VII – POSITIONING TO EXCEL IN SERVICE DELIVERY

29. Competitive strategies
30. Corporate image
31. Ensuring service quality

Figure P0.1   Managing information services: a transformational approach

Orientation

Part I, *Managing in a Dynamic Environment*, provides an introduction to management and its importance in transforming organizations in the knowledge age. It considers twelve new mindsets and approaches needed to effect transformation and provides background to the challenges of managing in the knowledge age. It describes the various managerial roles, the levels of management that can be found in organizations and their managerial skills. The second chapter provides context to the transformation change that is taking place in the environment in which information services operate. It considers the drivers of change and the strategic influences being felt in both the internal and external environment, and addresses the different techniques for future proofing organizations.

Part II, *Planning and Managing for Transformation*, provides an integrated approach to strategic and scenario planning, as well as the specifics of planning and managing human resources, knowledge and information, technology and other strategic assets and finance. Whilst there is a chapter devoted to each of the resources, the underlying approach is that they are planned as an integral part of the strategic planning process.

Creating the right corporate environment in which transformational change occurs is the theme of Part III of the book, *Creating the Right Corporate Environment*. There are chapters on developing and managing a strong, ethical and high-performance corporate culture, such that it is able to sustain flexibility, innovation and transformational change; on the nature of politics and political behaviour from both an individual and organizational perspective; on strategies for developing policy to ensure that individual interests are managed for the greater good and that individuals within the organization are moving forward in the same direction; and on creating an innovative environment that is the basis for ensuring that the organization is equipped to think differently, turn risks into opportunities and secure new advantages ahead of others.

Having established the foundation for the future of the information service and created the right corporate environment, the information services manager must now use their leadership and interpersonal skills to transform the organization. Part IV of the book, *Transforming the Corporate Environment*, considers the skills and attributes required to effect transformational change. The chapter on leadership considers leadership skills, attributes and styles as well as how to measure leadership effectiveness. The chapter on change management is titled *Engaging in Change*, which reflects the theme of building and shaping an organizational capacity to think differently, to be innovative, to create and embrace change, and in developing ownership and commitment to action where change is energized from within. Linked to the leadership and change theme is the ability to build teamwork to achieve outcomes as a group of people rather than as individuals. The abilities to motivate people, manage and resolve conflict and negotiate win-win outcomes are all necessary elements of good leadership in transforming organizations. Chapters on each of these are included in Part IV of the book.

Part V, *Managing Yourself and Others*, concentrates on managing the well-being of the people who work in the information service as well as the manager. It includes chapters on personal communication and networking, stress management, career planning and personal development, as well as managing diversity brought about by different expertise and generation groups. Each chapter contains strategies that can be used at the personal level and at the organizational level.

The theme for Part VI is effecting good corporate *Governance and Accountability* and brings a new dimension to the book. It includes a new chapter on corporate governance principles, ethics, codes of conduct, and managing for sustainability and different forms of capital. Power, influence and authority are now brought together and considered in a chapter on accountability. Decision making is regarded as part of encouraging transparency in organizations and a section is included on understanding perceptions and intuition. The chapter on measuring benefits and performance addresses how to evaluate and realize benefits, to enhance the return on investment through adding value, price for services, as well as strategies for measuring and evaluating performance.

The competitive global environment is introducing new risks for organizations. Risk factors increasingly involve security, including information security, physical security and the security of the organization's image. All of which can have financial, political, competitive, legal, human or technological impacts. Many organizations are outsourcing as a means of managing risk and enabling them to concentrate on their core business. With this in mind, risk management, security and outsourcing make up the remaining chapters in Part VI.

The final and most important outcome of the managerial value chain is the enabling of product and service delivery. Part VII, *Positioning to Excel in Service Delivery*, deals with defining and managing the end products and services that result from all of the other activities in the book. It contains chapters on strategic marketing strategies to increase the competitiveness of the information service and its parent organization, managing the corporate image and ensuring service quality. These ensure that services and products are delivered in multi-channel environments that meet the needs of customers.

The *Epilogue* brings all of the parts of the book together in explaining the transformational approach.

Acknowledgments

This book builds upon a rich source of ideas that have accumulated from over thirty years of experience that has taken me on a journey from managing large public library systems, to lecturing in information service management to my present role in setting the strategic direction for ICT for a state government. This journey has been in the public and private sectors and academic institutions. It has taken place at local, national and international levels. I have learnt a great deal from my interactions with my team members, managers, peers, students, colleagues and friends that have been part of this journey over the years. Some of this has been what not to do, as well as what to do. There are too many people to thank individually, but you know who you are and I am grateful for the opportunity to have shared moments in my working life with you all.

Ideas have also come from general management and information management books and journals that I have read over the years. I appreciate the time that others have spent in documenting their wisdom and knowledge so that individuals like me could share it.

Finally, I wish to thank my husband, Dr Vic Fazakerley, for his support and constructive feedback on the book's contents, Professor Nick Moore who encouraged me to write the very first text book, and the editorial and other staff at Ashgate Publishing who have provided support and encouragement over the years.

In closing, I have written the book to share my passion for information services and to give something back to those working in these disciplines, so that they may inspire others and excel in challenging environments.

Jo Bryson
Perth, Western Australia
January 2006

Managing in a Dynamic Environment

The theme for Part I is managing in an unpredictable and increasingly complex environment; where survival and success are often founded on creating the next advantage through transformational change, which requires an unprecedented measure of cleverness, ingenuity and flexibility on the part of the manager. Managers need to foresee and make sense of threats in a global knowledge-based economy and society, whilst being highly creative and inventive in seeking out new opportunities. Their role has been likened to dancing on a moving carpet.

To put this in context, Chapter 1 explores a number of challenges facing management today. It explains some of the skills, mindsets and roles of managers that are necessary to meet these challenges and the levels of management. Whilst organizational structures have flattened, three levels of management can still be found in organizations. These are the executive, mid-level management and line management. Each of these levels has a different role and uses different skills. New mindsets and approaches to management are also required in the knowledge age that differ from the organizational skills of the past. By understanding these different requirements, a clearer picture is gained about how management skills, mindsets, tasks and roles help the organization achieve its desired future and outcomes.

The environment in which information services operate is undergoing transformational change. Chapter 2 describes different techniques for future proofing organizations by considering concepts of possibilities and probabilities and introducing the reader to some of the drivers of change and transformation in the external environment. Chapter 2 explains the major strategic influences in the external environment that impact upon information services and organizations. In addition, it addresses complexity in the environment and identifies the internal environmental characteristics that are most likely to be found in successful organizations.

PLANNING AND MANAGING FOR TRANSFORMATION

CREATING THE RIGHT CORPORATE ENVIRONMENT

TRANSFORMING THE CORPORATE ENVIRONMENT

MANAGING YOURSELF AND OTHERS

MANAGING IN A DYNAMIC ENVIRONMENT

PART I – MANAGING IN A DYNAMIC ENVIRONMENT

1. **Introduction to management**
   The challenges of the knowledge age; Management – a transformational approach: New mindsets and approaches; Levels of management

2. **Strategic influences**
   The context of environments; Future proofing for tomorrow; The drivers of change and transformation; Strategic influences in the external environment; Strategic influences in the internal environment

EPILOGUE

POSITIONING TO EXCEL IN SERVICE DELIVERY

GOVERNANCE AND ACCOUNTABILITY

Figure PI.1   Managing in a dynamic environment

1 *Introduction to Management*

The challenges of the knowledge age

In the last two hundred years, Western societies have transitioned through economies and societies first based on agriculture, then on industry and now, knowledge. The magnitude of these changes is such that they are called revolutions and each one has challenged the way in which people work, think, live and communicate. The knowledge age differs little in its impact, its ability to present challenges and the associated requirement to rethink economies, societies and lifestyles from its previous counterparts. However, a key difference between the knowledge age and the previous two ages is that the former were built on knowing how and knowing what. The knowledge age is founded on knowing who and why. It is also an age where the market environment is no longer solely a physical presence as per the market place; it is increasingly a virtual presence, or market space. It is a learning age where an understanding of trends and possibilities goes hand in hand with identifying the inconceivable and making choices or preferences as to where to position for the future.

The knowledge age is also a time in which organizations face major uncertainty about the future and sudden strategic shocks in a global environment. These sudden, unprecedented shocks may originate from the other side of the world, but their effect is still profound. Creative and making the connections thinking is needed to envisage what these unprecedented risks and extraordinary shocks may be, and how best to prepare organizations to withstand them in the event of their happening.

In this environment, new business thinking and new business practices are not just restricted to technology savvy organizations or the information and communications technology (ICT) sectors. All organizations have to think and act in new ways to:

- develop new business opportunities and advantage;
- transform and rejuvenate existing products and services; and
- prepare for sudden, unprecedented shocks.

In the knowledge age, the most important business assets are not the tangible assets of the past. Intangible assets such as knowledge, expertise, innovation and branding are the new business enablers. In addition, knowledge and know-how are the key enablers for individual and organizational competitiveness, to manage risk and to service customer needs. This requires transformational change, shifts in thinking, and different patterns of investment (in time and money) in knowledge, innovation and human capital.

Within organizations different models of learning and investment in knowledge are taking place. People are now looking further than the traditional and explicit sources of knowledge and information to meet their needs. Progressive organizations recognized that their imagination, creativity and consequential business advantage are predicated on educated and skilled people who can create, share, and use knowledge well.

It is now generally recognized that the abilities to create, share and use knowledge are key factors in the creation of wealth and high-value employment, in stimulating creativity and in improving the quality of life. The importance of sharing knowledge, learning and creativity goes beyond the work place. Community engagement, collaboration and participation in decision making, being the hallmarks of progressive governments, are all predicated on knowledge, know-how, knowing who and knowing why. Sustainability and diversity in lifestyle, the economy, the environment and in cultures are also dependent on creative and innovative thinking, the sharing of knowledge and collaboration, and breaking down silos of institutions. In these environments, the opportunity exists for information services to become valuable centres for living, learning, growing and connecting people.

The knowledge age and its incumbent technologies have raised expectations in service delivery, requiring organizations to transform the way in which products and services are delivered. Successful organizations now focus on relationships rather than transactions in service delivery. Mobile and other electronic delivery mechanisms make possible the availability and delivery of services and information 24x7 to any place, mobile and global. Customers expect to see seamless services across multiple channels that are tailored to need; being customer centric rather than organization or discipline centric. For libraries, information services and other cultural institutions this means having a multi-institutionalized and multi-disciplined collaborative approach to service delivery. It also means managing a range of flexible and integrated channels for service delivery.

To illustrate this, Parker et al (2005, p. 176) quotes Troll (2002) on the future of libraries.

As libraries struggle with the fallout of the digital age, they must find a creative way to remain relevant to the twentieth century user who has the ability and means of finding vast amounts of information without setting foot in a brick and mortar library. ... The freely accessible information on the web, in conjunction with the escalating costs of library materials, threatens the traditional mission of libraries to create and sustain large, self-sufficient collections for their patrons.

Alongside these challenges, new advantages and opportunities are arising that draw upon the skills and expertise of information workers. Large companies are developing and implementing sophisticated knowledge management systems to capture, store and disseminate much-needed information gathered from their internal and external environment.

The funding base for many information services is also being challenged. A whole generation of people are about to retire from the work place or move to part-time employment, with a commensurate loss of an income-related tax base, which is a traditional source of funding for many information services. At the same time the knowledge age is placing greater demand for knowledge and information. New mechanisms are needed for managing in this environment; especially in ensuring the sustainability of services in an era of decreasing financial contributions. This means making smarter decisions. To manage this environment, managers need to:

- plan for transformation;
- create the right corporate environment;
- transform the environment to meet new environmental conditions and needs;
- manage themselves and enable others to achieve the goals of the organization;
- ensure an appropriate level of governance and accountability; and
- position the organization to excel in service delivery.

There are also growing expectations that organizations will take a responsible attitude to social and environmental sustainability in their management of capital, resources and the environment, in their family-friendly work practices, and in their relationships with the community.

Management – a transformational approach

The increasingly sophisticated expectations and knowledge-based activities described above are some of the drivers for transformational change in libraries and information services. Libraries and information services managers have the unique and dual responsibilities for planning and managing their own corporate intelligence, knowledge and information, as well as facilitating access and disseminating knowledge and information to others to assist them to predict the future, facilitate decision making, create new products and for life-long learning and personal development. Those supporting business and corporate environments, research and development institutions will be at the forefront of transformational change as their abilities to offer new information and services and exploit new opportunities in ICT will be critical to the survival and success of their parent organization.

It is also in this environment that the information services manager assumes a significant leadership and change management role in understanding and preparing for the challenges of tomorrow. This is not just significant for the library or information service, but also for the whole organization or community that the library or information service serves. This leadership and change management role requires new mindsets and perspectives, capabilities, skills and aptitudes.

First and foremost, the managers have to inspire others; building and sharing a vision for the future of the information service. As well as painting a picture that describes what the future services may look like, good managers exhibit leadership and build total commitment, enabling everyone to personally identify with and own the vision, working as a team to achieve it. In inspiring others and in creating the common identity amongst individuals, managers will use communicating, networking, motivating and leadership skills.

The vision cannot be achieved just by focusing upon individuals and the internal or corporate environment. The manager must also focus upon the relativity of the information service to its existing and potential competitors in the external environment. This requires skills in competitive positioning, image building and politics.

Many activities involve teams where the members have a diversity of skills and backgrounds. Achieving outcomes through group activities requires a different set of management and leadership skills to those needed in dealing with individuals as group behaviours differ from individual behaviours. Individuals also behave differently in groups to the way they do by themselves. Good managers recognize this and manage group activities accordingly.

Business transformation is often critical for the survival of organizations in changing and competitive environments. Business transformation requires rethinking the role of the organization and repositioning it for the future. The change can be quick and far reaching, realigning operations and relationships both internally and externally. Managers who introduce business transformation as a strategic tool must have a very clear vision of the future position of the parent organization amongst its competitors.

Survival in a competitive environment also relies upon profitability and productivity. This is achieved through the effective management of knowledge and information, people, finances and technology resources. In addition to these, risk, quality, and customer and stakeholder interfaces have also to be managed.

New mindsets and approaches

Transformational management uses more than a set of skills. It requires a different approach incorporating an open mindset and perspective, and different skills and aptitudes. It embraces a way of thinking, an attitude and behavioural style that is global and innovative. Whilst strategic thinking, technical, interpersonal, knowledge enabling, conceptual and analytical skills are still used, they are applied with a different mindset; for it is personal drive and initiative, a passion and an openness of mind that makes a difference. Those that really transform organizations incite a passion in others, build an organizational capability to view adversity as a challenge, and look for new opportunities in fast-changing environments.

Of the twelve mindsets and approaches that follow, not all will be used in equal proportions across the organization. Managers at different levels will draw on different mindsets and may apply them differently. All twelve mindsets will be used by executive management as role models as well as strategically in setting the direction for the future, whilst at the team manager level the mindsets will be used with a more operational focus.

CREATING AND SHARING THE VISION

The ability to create and share a vision is the most important executive management and leadership role, whose responsibility lies in positioning the organization in the future. It involves the ability to have a mental picture of different future scenarios and to visualize the library, its organization and community in a preferred future space. Strategic thinking skills are also necessary in order to capitalize on these ideas through opportunity and innovation. Together, these visionary and strategic thinking skills are used to shape the destiny of the organization. They are used in setting the strategic focus for the organization and in visualizing future possibilities. Strategic thinking skills are used to bring together and consider the implications, interdependencies and possibilities of a huge range of issues.

Both an external perspective and an entrepreneurial flair are needed to envisage probabilities and opportunities, identify issues and determine trends ahead of others. In shaping thinking and translating action into activities, mid-level managers need to take into account the impact of changing environments, and new technical and service delivery possibilities. Good judgment, intelligence and commonsense are required to make the right call and to manage the many varied and sometimes competing issues.

Strategic thinking skills also include inspiring a sense of purpose and direction for others, and encouraging people to think beyond their traditional boundaries to a very different future. Management success in this area is heavily reliant on innovative thinking and the ability to enthuse others. Advocacy and championing are also important roles in developing an understanding in others of the organization's vision, purpose, value and usefulness.

HAVING A GLOBAL PERSPECTIVE

The increasing global focus on external contexts and stakeholder relationships in the knowledge and information environment is driving the need for a global perspective. Whilst information has historically been sourced globally, service delivery has tended to be localized. Multinational corporations, international collaboration in approaches to research and development and universal access now means that service delivery spans continents with its associated management and technical implications for libraries and information centres.

Having a global perspective or mindset entails the ability to look worldwide for opportunities and threats, being prepared to seek answers from elsewhere, delivering services to portable devices any time, any place, considering best practices in service delivery that have worked in another place, being comfortable in managing multicultural environments, being open to ideas and having a global view of the library and information service market.

BUILDING AN ORGANIZATIONAL CAPACITY TO CREATE AND EMBRACE CHANGE

To succeed in rapidly changing environments, libraries and information services must seize opportunities quickly, rapidly redesigning their information products and services to assist the organization to meet changing customer needs and finding new ways of doing things cost effectively. All levels of management are involved in creating and leading a productive and dynamic work environment that can face new issues and rapidly changing priorities on an almost daily basis. This includes developing the right organizational and individual capabilities to embrace and endure strategic change. Skills need to be developed where people are extremely adaptable and enthusiastic about work, can think innovatively and critically, learn quickly and be immediately responsive to external influences.

Strategic change management skills also include devising and implementing strategies to reshape and implement the future, and being able to clarify and minimize uncertainties for others. Managers with good change management skills display resilience to pressure, can remain focused on the tasks and outcomes, and demonstrate personal courage and coping skills in times of adversity.

DRIVING ORGANIZATIONAL RENEWAL

Linked to the previous skill is the need to keep reinventing or renewing the organization. This is for two reasons: as organizations grow, they follow a path that reaches a peak; this is the point at which the organization must renew itself to achieve even greater outcomes and success, and to avert decline. Secondly, in a competitive world, organizations need to keep inventing the next advantage that puts them ahead.

Renewal can come in many forms: in new ways of thinking or doing things differently to achieve greater productivity, in developing new products or services, or taking a different perspective of risks and turning these into opportunities.

EXPLOITING TECHNOLOGY FOR BUSINESS OUTCOMES

The ability to use equipment such as personal computers, hand-held and wireless devices, and servers, as well as a knowledge of sources of information, software and information systems are fundamental skills required of people at all levels of the organization. These skills are developed on the job or through formal education and training programmes. However, using technology as a tool or catalyst for transformational change requires more.

Keeping in tune with technology advances and exploiting these for customer-centric service delivery in the always on, anywhere, any time environment is an executive management responsibility. It is a business not a technology issue. Mobile commerce and other connectivity solutions are redefining service delivery by providing customized services to a variety of hand-held devices, any time, any place. Customer relationship management tools, new web-enabling technologies and wireless-based telephony are also driving change and executive management must understand the business implications and opportunities of each emerging technology.

BUILDING INTELLIGENT AND LEARNING ORGANIZATIONS

In order to manage change, successful organizations and communities need to be intelligent or learning organizations. Intelligent organizations value individual intelligence and knowledge and enable people to share and exploit their knowledge for personal, organizational and community success. Learning organizations institutionalize training and development as an essential component of implementing a corporate memory system. The learning of new skills and the finding out of new things are regarded as an ongoing part of the work process. In these settings, the need for knowledge-enabling skills at all levels of management has increased as corporate and individual knowledge and intelligence are recognized as strategic and critical assets for a knowledge-enabled organization.

Managers in libraries and information centres can play a significant role in creating and building intelligent organizations and communities. Executive managers have a critical role in creating and leading a knowledge-intensive culture and focusing on strategies that support organizational learning and knowledge creation. They actively demonstrate an understanding of the value of and are visibly committed to enabling the knowing how, what, who and why through training and skills development, knowledge and information management, and knowledge-sharing practices and processes.

Whilst some knowledge and information comes from published and unpublished sources, the more strategic knowledge and information is obtained through intelligence gathering, building personal networks with customers, distributors, suppliers, past and present employees, consultants and business contacts. This means executive and mid-level management giving more attention to creating, managing and valuing the interpersonal and institutional relationships and norms that an organization has internally and with the external environment. One example is building cooperation and trust that add value and which shape the quality and quantity of its interactions. Some knowledge and information will require skills in interpretation and intuition, with the end requirement to evaluate and sometimes integrate diverse opinions in order to form a rich picture of the internal and external forces that will influence and shape the future of the information service.

MANAGING THE POLITICAL AGENDA

To move ideas forward, managers must know how to get things done within the parent organization, how to lobby and constructively use their persuasive skills and power to drive the change. This requires them to interpret correctly the political environment, to 'open doors', to identify supporters and sponsors, and quickly to build networks, commitment and support. Political skills include demonstrating astuteness in acting on intuition and making judgments on emerging or complex issues of a political nature. It includes anticipating events or being able to deal with matters before they become damaging issues.

The boundary-spanning role of senior executives means that they continually identify and take action to minimize the effect that external political influences can have on their organization. They ensure the smooth running of the organization, allowing their people to get on with their job of achieving their required targets and outcomes without being hindered by unconstructive external pressures.

CREATING CREATIVE ENVIRONMENTS

A creative environment is fostered through leadership and management skills and mindsets that support and actively encourage people to think differently and bring their creative ideas to work. It is based on the philosophy that everyone has the capacities to solve problems in unique ways, to conceive bright ideas, and to use entrepreneurial thinking, but many are discouraged from doing so. The management role is to unlock or free up know-how, talents, skills and expertise in people so that they can be used for everyone's benefit.

Developing creative and innovative thinking is an activity that should be employed at all levels of management. Senior management need themselves to be innovative in their thinking, whilst building and demonstrating their commitment to a corporate culture that values ideas generation, open communication and entrepreneurial thinking. They also need to sustain this commitment through their actions year after year; championing their cause, motivating and preparing others to accept innovation and change readily.

EFFECTING ETHICS AND INTEGRITY

Much more attention is now being placed on the corporate responsibility to act ethically and with integrity, with public and social accountability and the pursuit of excellence, all of which includes concepts of legitimacy, fairness and ethics. Whilst each individual has a personal and professional responsibility to act ethically and with integrity, executive management has a responsibility to set and ensure compliance with ethical standards and demonstrate by example issues such as honesty, fairness and equity, respect and integrity, and accountability. Such standards should define what is right and wrong in terms of the conduct of individuals and how those in a position to materially influence the operations of the information service should operate.

Senior executives also have responsibilities for establishing management oversight roles and putting the correct systems, practices, procedures and corporate culture in place to support accountability and the capacity to make the right decisions throughout all levels of management. It is far more than requiring managers to comply with legal and regulatory regimes.

BUILDING PRODUCTIVE RELATIONSHIPS

With the greater emphasis on building a better understanding of the external environment and customer-centric services, relationship building skills are becoming increasingly important. Relationship building and interpersonal skills are used by all levels of managers in interacting with people, internal and external to the organization. They are used to maintain a network of contacts and relationships through which the organization's objectives are achieved. Interpersonal skills are also used to communicate the vision both internally and externally, in negotiating, lobbying and in promoting the organization to stakeholders.

Interpersonal skills are used to cultivate productive working relationships and partnerships with a diverse range of stakeholders. Executive managers utilize their interpersonal and relationship building skills in their boundary-spanning role. This includes networking to obtain information about competitors and other developments in the external environment, in building trust and nurturing relationships with others, and in getting people to cooperate and collaborate with each other.

Relationship building and interpersonal skills include being able to listen to other viewpoints, to understand and adapt the desired message to meet the needs of different audiences, and to build a rapport with people. They also embrace the abilities to negotiate and put forward viewpoints in a persuasive manner where there is a contest of ideas and disparate views. Mid-level managers use these skills in liaising between executive and first line management, in discussing needs and delegating, in guiding and mentoring people, and, in translating policies into actions.

Line managers use their skills in understanding and motivating others, both individually and in teams. Good relationship and interpersonal skills are important in creating an environment in which tasks are effectively and happily accomplished.

INSTILLING A PASSION

Instilling passion into organizations is part of the visionary mindset and talent of a good leader. In shaping and driving the strategic directions for the organization, effective executives demonstrate a passion for what they believe the organization can achieve and instil this in others, whilst having the capacity to remain focused on strategic outcomes in turbulent and changing environments. Passion is also a necessity for other levels of management where their role is also to exhibit a strong personal drive and create enthusiasm in those around them. Managers that have passion also demonstrate a natural eagerness for results and dedication to the achievements of the organization that ignites keenness in other team members.

Leaders and managers that instil passion are self-motivated, decisive and have a flair for getting things done in extraordinary circumstances and for stimulating others to achieve individual and corporate success. Demonstrating Type A characteristics, they are highly energetic and enthusiastic people, usually with a strong innovative capacity. They possess a strong commitment to personal achievement and in getting others to achieve, especially in areas where there are competing demands and multiple agendas.

STRIVING FOR EXCELLENCE AND QUALITY

Striving for excellence and service quality in the design and delivery of customer-centric services and products takes a similar drive and commitment to instilling a passion in the workplace. However design and delivery are only part of the equation. Of equal importance is the customer relationship management, service experience and service support that encourages the continual use of the service or product. A holistic approach is necessary that instils excellence and quality into the culture and psyche of the organization; extending through every step of the value chain and throughout the complete life cycle of the customer interface. Ensuring an organizational commitment to excellence and quality requires a mindset and attitude that values and distinguishes perfection and attention to detail, and which is translated into activities, processes and procedures at all levels of the organization.

Levels of management

The following provides a brief introduction to levels of management and their roles that are typical in organizations today. Changing organizational structures mean less mid-level managers. The traditional triangle shape is flattening, with the mid-level and line management strata being replaced with flexible teams and team leaders in a star or networked arrangement.

Levels of management also exist within multiple structures. For example, the information service can also be a service delivery unit within a larger entity, the parent organization. Whilst the information services manager would hold the executive management position for the information service, they may or may not be a member of the executive team within the parent organization.

EXECUTIVE MANAGEMENT

The executive management team reports directly to the Chief Executive, who may also be given titles such as President or Director General. The executive team comprises the most senior members of the organization. The information services manager or Chief Information Officer may be part of the executive team. To reach and maintain this level of management requires strong personal drive and initiative. With responsibilities for creating and sharing the vision and for building an organizational capacity to embrace change, they need strong strategic and organizational change management skills, as well as personal passion.

The executive is responsible for positioning the organization in the external environment. This requires sound political, relationship building and interpersonal skills. Theirs is a boundary-spanning role. They are the interface between the organization and major stakeholders, those who have a stake or strategic interest in the organization. They interact with external organizations by lobbying and negotiating on issues that have an impact on the organization's business strategies. They spend time troubleshooting and managing the political environment.

Managers at this level spend a considerable amount of time with their executive peers in the industry and stakeholders such as Board members, suppliers, and to a lesser extent their employees. Most of their work is verbal and is often reactive. They receive short snatches of information that they have to piece together to anticipate the future and chart the way forward; keeping the organization ahead of its competitors and determining the changes that are advantageous to the organization. These intelligence-gathering exercises are not just for their own benefit. In an age where survival and success rely upon knowledge and ideas to create new and innovative offerings and make the right decisions in an uncertain environment, executive managers also need first-class knowledge-enabling skills and a strong commitment to knowledge sharing so that others can also make use of their knowledge and information.

In differentiating the organization from others executive managers need a sound understanding of how technology can be exploited for business outcomes and the mindset and ability to create a creative environment. Understanding that a corporate commitment to excellence and quality and ethics and integrity within the organization must come from the top, they demonstrate through their management activities and personal actions their awareness and binding obligation to these outcomes.

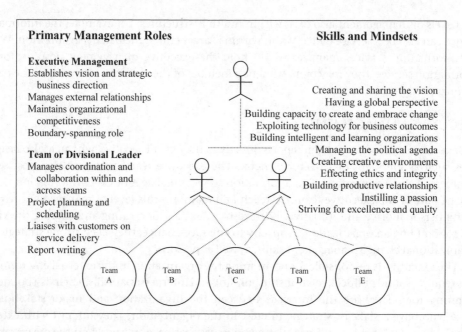

Figure 1.1   Levels of management – roles and mindsets

MID-LEVEL MANAGEMENT

This level of management is rapidly merging with line management as organizations move to more streamlined and matrix management structures. In the example of Figure 1.1 mid-level and line management have been totally integrated. Traditionally mid-level managers have ultimate responsibility for specific service areas; these may also be known as Divisions or Groups. Depending on the size of the organization, mid-level management can extend down to responsibility for work units such as records management, branch libraries or computing services.

Mid-level managers acknowledge the vision, global perspective, and broad overall strategies and policies set by the executive and translate these into specific action programmes that can be implemented by teams or line management. They analyse issues such as the emerging global trends in technology and their impacts on opportunities for innovation in service delivery and future customer requirements, and, summarize these in reports for the executive. Mid-level managers perform a coordinating role between the various parts of the organization which require excellent interpersonal and relationship building skills. High-level communication, knowledge-enabling and collaboration skills are also important in assisting to build the intelligent and learning organization. They have good analytical and technical skills which they use to develop an in-depth knowledge of their area, and how this interacts with other sections or divisions within the changing organizational environment.

Mid-level managers have less need for skills in managing the external political agenda, but will use these skills in managing internal politics and getting things done in the corporate environment. Through their actions they also demonstrate their commitment to excellence and quality and ethics and integrity.

LINE MANAGEMENT AND TEAM LEADERS

Line managers or team leaders are directly responsible for the quality of service delivery within their work units and the administration of resources to meet the parent organization's short-term objectives. They possess strong technical skills and, increasingly, knowledge-enabling skills. Theirs is primarily a supervisory and grievance handling role that requires strong interpersonal and relationship building skills. The grievances can come from staff regarding rosters and other work-related issues or from their customers on service delivery issues. They spend little time with the executive or managers from other organizations; dealing mainly with their staff and customers. Their jobs are hectic with continued interruptions. They often communicate on a one-to-one basis to solve problems and maintain quality standards.

On a one-to-one basis they instil passion for work and service delivery, enable creativity and strive for excellence and quality. They also have an oversight role in ensuring compliance to ethical and best practice, integrity in actions of team members, and that good corporate governance is maintained at the operational and service delivery level.

Conclusion

Sophisticated customer expectations and a rapidly changing environment are requiring significant changes in skills, approaches and mindsets in managing libraries and information services. New roles and activities are developing and levels of management disappearing in response. Activities are now much more proactive in the attempt to create and shape the future, rather than have the organization succumb to an unwanted future or be passed by.

References

Parker, Kevin R. et al. (2005), 'Libraries as knowledge management centres', *Library Management*, vol. 26, no. 4/5, pp. 176–89.
Troll, D.A. (2002), 'How and why libraries are changing: What we know and what we need to know', *Libraries and the Academy*, vol. 2, no. 1, pp. 97–121.

Further reading

Buckingham, Marcus (2005), 'What great managers do', *Harvard Business Review*, March, pp. 70–79.
Corsini, Skip (2005), 'The nine traits of a great manager', *Training and Development*, Sept. pp. 16–17.
Drucker, Peter F. (2004), 'What makes an effective executive', *Harvard Business Review*, June, pp. 58–63.
Morden, Tony (2004), *Principles of management*, 2nd edn, Aldershot, UK: Ashgate.

2 *Strategic Influences*

The context of environments

Consideration of the driving forces and strategic influences on information services over the next decade requires an analysis of the factors that will most likely create the need for change or impact upon people and organizations during this period. Such a consideration is necessary in order to determine the likely management scenarios for the future business direction, to ensure that the delivery of services meet future needs, and ultimately, the information service's and its parent organization's survival. Whilst it is difficult to predict the future accurately, the likelihood of being able to forecast certain scenarios can be increased by analysing trends and strategic influences, and, applying 'what if' scenarios to potential change factors.

Information services operate in the context of two environments – internal and external. Both of these affect the way in which information services are planned and managed. Unless management and staff have a clear understanding of these environments and how they impact upon their operations, they will be working in a vacuum.

The external environment comprises the surrounding conditions in which the information service and its parent organization operate. Today's complex and changing environments continuously create new challenges that must be managed to ensure survival and success. The most consistent feature being that once one set of challenges have been mastered, another new set will take their place.

Maintaining an overview or understanding of the internal environment of an organization requires an equal amount of management attention. The internal environment relates to the internal factors that shape the organization and its operating environment. These include knowledge enabling, innovative capacity, leadership style, culture and values, communication, structure, and the use of technology. Internal environment factors are influenced by the external environment.

A key management task is to assess continually how the information service is performing and adapting to changes in the internal and external environments. This can be achieved through a number of processes. Information on the external and internal environments must be gathered, assimilated and evaluated for use in the strategic planning processes that are discussed in more detail in the next chapter.

Future proofing for tomorrow

The most successful organizations are those that are able to rethink the future so that even the most inconceivable event is possible. An example of this is 9/11 and the impact that this act of terrorism had on threat assessment, global politics and all businesses. Instilling this open frame of mind into the organization is both a risk and an opportunity management strategy. It means that the organization is better placed to manage a catastrophic event if it occurs, than those that are ill-prepared. This mindset is also required for positioning the organization in its preferred future space by capitalizing on ideas about the future through opportunity and innovation. Opportunities come from the external environment, and capitalization occurs through internal responses that recognize gaps and fill these with creative solutions. Innovation is the ability to predict or achieve the inconceivable: i.e. to invent something that no one else has thought of or done before.

POSSIBILITIES AND PROBABILITIES

Possibilities and probabilities arise from consideration of different scenarios for the future, ensuring that the organization is as prepared as possible to meet events as they occur. Predicting the inconceivable is one small part of future proofing the organization. A considerable amount of energy is also spent on identifying the conceivable futures, the possible future and also the probable as part of scenario planning. This is with opportunistic outcomes in mind. By identifying what could conceivably happen, for example in technological advances or lifestyle changes; what is possible given the known changes; and the most probable scenarios, leaders can position their organizations to take advantage of future opportunities successfully.

The third dimension is about positioning and having an impact on the future. This is the consideration of the desirable and the preferable, and is linked to the organization's vision. By establishing the desired and preferred future state for the organization and painting this picture as a vision, leaders are taking the first step in enabling the organization's future.

The vision provides a future reference point that sends a single message to which everyone can aspire. It charts the end goal and gives context to all that the organization does and wishes to achieve.

SHARING THE VISION

Employees are more comfortable with change if they have confidence that strategies are in place to manage the future. One way of doing this is for managers to share a vision of the future as to what the organization will look like in five years' time, the services or information products it will provide, and the types of markets that it will operate in. A shared vision will enable all employees to work together to achieve the same goal. The shared vision can be supplemented by the manager leading by example with regard to the organizational values that support the vision.

The drivers of change and transformation

There are a number of factors that are driving change and transformation in organizations. The following outline some of these drivers that can lead to strategic surprises and have a consequential impact on people and organizations today.

SPEED AND COMPLEXITY OF CHANGE

Change has been a consistent feature of the environment for many years. However, it is both the speed and the complexity of change that most strategically influences the management of organizations and the information services that support their business needs. The successful organizations of the future will be those which are able to create the future, by being in front of their competitors and by being the catalyst for change. They will need to move fast and change fast to keep this position. Even bureaucracies, which traditionally consist of unchangeable procedures, have become more flexible and adaptable in recognition of this factor.

The effect of rapid change in the business environment, be it public or private sector, is that management must now seize opportunities quickly, rapidly redesigning information products and services to meet changing customer needs and finding new ways of doing things cost effectively. Speed is a deciding factor and nothing is exempt from change. Whilst being proactive in identifying new end uses for services, resolving problems that enhance quality of output and reduce waste, and in undertaking organizational change, managers will also need to respond continually to turbulent environments.

THE NEED FOR INTELLIGENT ORGANIZATIONS

In addition to being able to manage change, successful organizations need to be intelligent ones. Information and communications technology (ICT) makes it much easier to access, diffuse and communicate large quantities of information and knowledge, which dramatically increases the usefulness and accessibility of information and increases the overall stock of knowledge and information. However, intelligent organizations are not reliant on ICT alone. Intelligent organizations utilize knowledge, information and its supporting technologies for continuous innovation, productivity improvement and education and skills formation. They recognize that research and innovation are contributing factors in creating new ideas and turning these into dollars and new business advantages. Intelligent organizations value individual intelligence and knowledge and understand that this will lead to a redistribution of power from those who hoard knowledge and information to those who share this with others. Individuals are therefore equipped with new information and new skills in knowledge enabling and life-long learning. Intelligent organizations also put processes in place to increase the receptivity and supply of knowledge throughout the organization.

IMPACT OF THE GLOBAL ECONOMY

Organizations now operate in a global environment in which national interests compete within a global economy and society. Web-based services enable access to information and services from an increasing diverse and international source. Markets are now domestic and international, and trade protection has to be rethought in a borderless world. Research and innovation are both dependent upon and products of global cooperation and collaboration. The large proportion of information sources that are in electronic form and available worldwide has implications for sovereignty and the longer-term ability to sustain uniqueness in national cultures.

Supporting technologies are economic and business necessities that overcome distance and different time zones, allowing all employees immediate access to corporate information. The virtual organization is the reality rather than the exception.

SUSTAINABILITY

Lowered tax bases brought about by large numbers of Baby Boomers ceasing full-time employment and the economic necessities of financial stringency lead to the need to reconsider the economic sustainability of services. The most successful organizations will be those that apply innovation and creativity to the use of information and information technologies, delivering information in new and different cost effective ways.

TECHNOLOGY CHANGES THAT ENABLE CUSTOMER CENTRIC SERVICE DELIVERY

Changes and convergence in information and communications technologies lie at the very heart of the global changes taking place. Information and its supporting communications technologies are both the driver and enabler of transformational change. They can create the need for change whilst assisting the organization through the change processes. For example, an organization that has immediate access to speedy, reliable and up-to-date information about their competitors' strategies, clients' and other stakeholders' needs, and current performance levels is in a much better decision making position about the future than one that does not. As a catalyst, information technologies and telecommunications can be used to strategic advantage by providing customers with specialized services tailored to suit their individual needs.

Mobile commerce and other connectivity solutions are redefining service delivery by providing customized services to a variety of hand-held devices, any time, any place. They also enable public and private sector organizations to provide a single point of contact that makes back-end technical and organizational processes transparent to the customer. The technologies that are driving these opportunities include robust customer relationship management tools, new web-enabling technologies and wireless-based telephony.

To keep in tune with technology advances, content will also need to be tailored to meet clearly defined and individual customer needs, no matter whether it is in the context of operating in a multinational organization, or in delivering public library services in a small community. Information will be customized in format and timing as it is packaged and delivered any time, any place.

In particular the age waves of the Baby Boomers, Generation X, Generation Y and Generation Z have yielded specific needs linked to the level of choice and lifestyle. Each generation or age wave has preferred modes of service delivery. For example whilst Baby Boomers are embracing web services, Generation X, Y and Z look to the mobile device as the preferred mode of service delivery. For the Silent Generation, those born between World War I and World War II, personal service over the counter remains the preferred choice.

The single point of contact philosophy will also drive changes of thinking in the management and location of major cultural institutions. Traditionally institutions such as libraries, archives, telecentres and museums have existed as stovepipes, governed by the materials they housed rather than people's use. Information within organizations, e.g. journals, art pieces, relics, books, specimens, records and databases have been managed according to format rather than content. Indeed whole professions have been created around materials and format. This results in customers having to visit many venues to see the whole picture. The single point of contact philosophy will see libraries along with other information, education, cultural and recreation services converging and transforming into new shapes and forms to deliver seamless service delivery across multiple formats. They will morph into centres for living, learning, growing and connecting people.

QUALITY DRIVERS

Information and knowledge are also the tools that drive quality and improved performance. Whilst aligned to customer service, quality is not just concerned with product or service outputs; quality procedures eliminate costly time, energy and waste in the production cycle. Appropriate information enables management and employees to make decisions in order to provide an environment in which quality is embraced and valued in products and services. This type of information underlines the basis upon which performance is measured and strategies for improvement are decided. Further information about quality improvement and the value chain is included in a later chapter in the book.

DRIVE FOR FLEXIBILITY IN THE WORKPLACE

In order to respond to change, employing organizations require flexibility in the types of services offered and, consequently, the skills and competency profiles and numbers of employees. Contract employment and outsourcing of services are two methods by which organizations can achieve flexibility in the type and skills of employees. The impact on the individual is that they have a series of part-time jobs or contracts, rather than working long-term for a single employer.

Changing work attitudes and lack of job security mean that people will need to be motivated so that excellence in customer service and quality products can be achieved in a changing corporate environment where long-term employment may not be guaranteed. This will require the ability to balance the seemingly incongruent goals of encouraging a sense of belonging, self-control over quality, energy and enthusiasm in organizational environments where change and rapid downsizing may occur.

The need for flexibility and the desire to provide services to customers will require considerable autonomy within organizations. This will be reflected by loose autonomous organizational structures and autonomous individuals working together cooperatively. Leadership styles that support collaborative individualism will be favoured.

Flexibility in the workplace is increasingly leading to a mobile workforce such that people regularly work from home or another location. This is occurring for several reasons:

- the competitive global business environment demands that employees are available to customers and business partners;
- individuals are wanting to balance their work and family responsibilities better;
- environmental considerations and sustainability practices are seeking ways of reducing unnecessary travel; and,
- advanced information and communications technologies are making the virtual workplace of any time, anywhere possible.

However providing for mobility does not just consist of offering a laptop computer and a remote connection. Organizations that are successful in having mobile workforces purposely design their business processes, operational procedures and reward systems around their people to minimize any sense of detachment, encourage work group interaction, and to ensure that the work/home boundaries do not become blurred.

RETHINKING FUNDING AND STRUCTURES

With greater emphasis being placed in rethinking the delivery of all services, some hard decisions may be required about the funding methods, structuring and information service programmes. External funding and sponsorship may need to be attracted for some services. This may require lobbying, negotiation and marketing skills in order to ensure that the integrity and impartiality of services are not compromised.

In an effort to curtail expenditure it may not be easy to abandon services or levy charges. There may be enormous exit barriers to some services both socially and economically. There is also a risk of being locked into certain services that are not sustainable and which in the long term consume more resources than can be realistically afforded. A low coverage of too large a client market is inferior to a good quality service for a focused market. The duplication of services offered by other entities should be avoided.

NEW SKILLS

Whilst a considerable proportion of people have physical access to electronic information through their home, workplace, libraries and other outlets, this will not be enough. Skills in information retrieval, navigation and the ability to synthesize and validate the information provided through the global information networks will be necessary. Such skills may be learnt by the individuals, or they may obtain the services of information specialists to obtain the information for them. With this in mind, the skills of librarians and information workers in describing, linking and organizing multiple media formats may be the path to the future in service delivery.

CROSS-CULTURAL ISSUES

The global information market and the growing diversity in the cultural makeup of the community increase the exposure of information services to cross-cultural issues. Information content can be obtained and disseminated instantly to most parts of the globe, necessitating the management of issues such as national sovereignty and transborder data flows. Secondly, greater cultural diversity will be represented in both employees and customers of the information service. Changing religious and racial compositions in the community have implications for management style and service delivery. Cross-cultural issues will also have an increasing influence on organizational behaviour. The differing cultural values and attitudes of individuals to their own individuality, ambition, job satisfaction, authority and time orientation will need to be recognized and respected.

Strategic influences in the external environment

The need to understand the external environment in which information services operate is fundamental to positioning the services to take advantage of technological change, in determining future paths, and to deliver appropriate services to customers. The external environment needs to be constantly scanned to identify new realities, challenges and uncertainties.

The assessment of the external environment is one of the first inputs into the strategic audit stage of the strategic planning process. It allows managers to identify changes, trends, issues, opportunities and threats, and it provides an information base for the conduct of other assessments such as the capability profile.

COMPLEXITY OF THE ENVIRONMENT

The complexity and stability of the external environment dictates the level of responsiveness and therefore impacts upon the required structure, management style and corporate culture of the internal environment. The complexity of the environment relates to the number of domains that impact or influence the organization. A simple environment is one where only four or five domains impact upon the organization. A complex environment exists when over ten domains readily impact the organization. The stability factor is related to the degree and frequency of change within the domains. If domains continually change in the intensity of their impact and, as a result services change moderately or continually, the environment may be considered to be unstable. Turbulence does not always strike organizations in the same way or at the same time and differs in levels of intensity and predictability.

ENVIRONMENTAL DOMAINS

In addition to the drivers of change that act as critical catalysts for transformation and advancement, there are other environmental domains that require consideration. These include economic conditions, availability of financial resources, geographical situation, degree of technological integration and innovation, the historical development and parentage of the information centre and its parent organization, clientele and markets, demographic patterns, labour market and industrial relations, availability of resources, industry strata, cultural-social conditions and the political climate.

Economic conditions

Economic conditions reflect the general economic health of the country and sector in which information services operate. Economic conditions can influence both demand and customer usage of services, and the supply and demand of resources. For example in times of high unemployment or a rapidly retiring population, the demand for free information services such as those operating out of public libraries increases. High unemployment may also lead to a much larger labour market from which staff may be selected. The information service's purchasing power may be affected by changes in international exchange rates, inflation rates or shortages of supplies in equipment.

The demand for services may have an inverse relationship to the ability to supply services. For example, constrained budgets (appropriations) and declining purchasing power have lessened the available capital for purchases over the past years, whilst customers have demanded more sophisticated services.

The changing characteristics of the economy in terms of inflation, purchasing power, employment, money market and exchange rates should be monitored. Information relating to economic conditions can most readily be obtained from the business and financial pages on the Internet or in newspapers, and by scanning other literature for information on economic conditions in the major publishing countries and their effects on information services.

Availability of financial resources

The trend is towards productivity gains and internal efficiencies, with an emphasis on core services to reduce financial dependencies, Additional costs in service provision are now passed directly to the consumer.

As a result, organizations need to be more accountable, market oriented and entrepreneurial in their use of funds. Entrepreneurial and marketing activities require information about different sources of income and the clients' maximum thresholds in their willingness to pay for services. Alternative sources of income to fund discrete services may also be explored. Likely sources are employment-generating schemes, grants or sponsorships, or the provision of certain value-added services that can subsidize other services.

Geographical situation

The geographical environment involves both the level of reach in servicing customers as well as the geographical spread of operations of the parent organization. Both of these elements can either facilitate or hinder service levels.

Physical proximity to customers becomes less of an issue where services are delivered electronically. Access to broadband telecommunications is far more important. As information is now rich and bandwidth hungry in its presentation, access to broadband (+2 gigabyte) telecommunications is required.

Special libraries or information centres serving employees may still need a physical proximity to an area of heavy use in which to house the specialized journal and printed material collection, whilst also being able to deliver electronic information services direct to the mobile PDA device or desktop.

Barriers such as highways or territorial boundaries such as political borders or campus sites may also determine the extent of service provision to customers. For public service delivery where physical access is required, the preferred option is a single location, merging or co-locating art galleries, museums, visitors' centres, telecentres, libraries and other public access centres near shopping centres within easy reach of car parks and public transport stops.

Degree of technological innovation and integration

The complexity of the technology influences the skills and competences required by the information services' employees and customers. It may also enhance or inhibit the services' ability to adapt to change quickly.

Competitive advantage can be obtained in either being the first to market or having the ability to maintain the leading edge in a unique application of technology to deliver specialized information services to customers. The information service can also provide other services that can strategically position the parent organization in the competitive market place. However, if the complexity of the technology is so great that it inhibits flexibility then the inability to respond to change will itself become a burden for the organization.

Changes in technology occur in such quantum leaps that what is new technology today is old technology tomorrow. The focus should not just be on keeping up to date with new developments in technology, but also in discovering new business applications for existing technology or new combinations of technologies in order to deliver more appropriate services or increased productivity.

The historical development and parentage of the organization

The present and the future are always shaped by the past. In order to predict the future, it is necessary to consider trends of the past. Whilst the future is never certain, the likelihood of recurrent trends of the past being repeated when the same conditions apply tends to make the exercise of predicting the future more successful.

We are all the product of the past. The historical development, the founding corporate philosophy, past and current policies of the parent organization, amalgamations and takeovers will all impact upon the corporate styles and culture, the allocation of resources, and the way in which services can be delivered.

Customers and markets

Awareness of the market is necessary in order to deliver effective services. This includes present and potential customers. The type and level of service provision is also influenced by market expectations and demands; these should be continually analysed in order to gauge the most appropriate service levels.

The needs of potential customers should also be considered, as the information service may not be reaching its full market potential. This may mean that some less used services may have to be reduced or deleted in order to diversify into an area of increased demand. Market changes can occur from either a changed market base or changing needs of an existing market.

Market research may be carried out by using surveys and questionnaires, group interviews and discussions with customers and non-users, and by analysing information about the makeup of existing customers. More in-depth information on marketing is included in a later chapter.

Demographic patterns

Market research can be further assisted by analysing the demographic makeup of the customer and potential customer base. Language, culture, income and purchasing power, age of the population and population distribution and mobility are some of the demographic factors that influence the provision of information services. Employee and organizational profiles that provide details of areas of expertise, positions and nature of responsibilities can be useful planning and market research tools.

Labour market and industrial relations

Industrial relations and award conditions may affect the ability of the information service to attract key people as employees. These conditions will also impact upon budgets, rosters, the makeup and classification of staff, as well as conditions of employment. Government legislation, such as equal opportunity or affirmative action, may influence human resource selection procedures.

Information services, like all organizations are reliant upon a knowledgeable workforce. Without an adequate supply of appropriately trained and skilled personnel, the ability to provide quality information services may be inhibited. The quality and quantity of the supply of labour is reliant upon the level and number of courses in universities and training institutions. Input should be given to the designers of university and training courses so that changes in the market place can be reflected in the requirements of the course outcomes.

Availability of resources

Information services are reliant upon the suppliers of goods and services in order to perform their own tasks. Changes affecting the suppliers' abilities to deliver the goods and services on time may also affect the delivery of information services. Examples of changes may be in industrial disputes, cutbacks in production levels, increased labour costs or discontinuities in products or services.

The information market is itself dynamic, influenced by international takeover bids of information suppliers and service providers. Globalized ownership of the major electronic and traditional media giants and publishing houses, telecommunications service providers and software suppliers will also have a significant impact on competition, supply and prices.

Industry strata

The industry may be defined as those competitors or potential competitors that are in the same type of business. Industries may be further grouped according to the characteristics of ownership, services or markets. Within each industry there are leaders and followers. To ensure a common bond and some measure of quality control within various types of information services, minimum standards have often been developed. Standards may applicable at the international, national or organizational level. International standards often set internationally recognized best practice or cover situations where information needs to be transported and shared across countries, an example being standards or protocols for telephony or facsimile transmission. National standards may be set for meta data, that is data that describes the qualities of data so that it may be used and shared between organizations. Increasingly meta data standards are becoming more universal in description. Organizational standards may relate to the use of a standard operating environment or versions of software for office automation across the organization.

Cultural-social conditions

The social climate and culture of the environment in which the information service operates will affect its services. Social values will need to be reflected in the content, services and employees attitudes to work.

Political climate

The political climate has a major influence upon the management of information services, particularly in terms of the organizational environment, how employees and customers are valued, and the types of services delivered. For example, political philosophies that espouse market testing or contracting out can result in considerable change to the role and focus of management, the change being from that of a service provider to one of contract management and purchaser of services.

Stakeholders may also exercise a major influence upon the making of strategic decisions. Stakeholders do not normally become politically active in 'day-to-day' routines, but can have a considerable influence upon new or strategic initiatives in services.

Strategic influences in the internal environment

The success of an organization in a highly competitive environment is heavily dependent upon the contribution of its people. This is influenced by their perceptions and feelings of well-being towards the organization. People have needs and expectations that are either enhanced or frustrated by aspects of the organization. The interaction of people and structures influence the behavioural processes such as leadership style, planning, communications, conflict management, decision-making processes, problem solving and other interpersonal behaviours. These behaviour processes influence the work output and level of commitment to the organization.

CHARACTERISTICS OF SUCCESSFUL ORGANIZATIONS

The following provides a description of the characteristics most likely to be found in organizations that are successfully undergoing transformation to meet the needs of the knowledge age. These characteristics can be used as a benchmark upon which to assess or judge the capabilities and capacities of existing organizations.

Knowledge enabling

Highly successful organizations acknowledge that strategic gain comes from releasing the creative know-how, intellectual capacity and experience of people and in enabling knowledge and organizational learning. They have strategies in place to add to and build upon existing corporate intelligence, tacit knowledge and individual insight as a means to position the organization in the future.

An empowered workforce or community is one that shares knowledge and information. An important task for the information service is to ensure that knowledge and information is made available when and where it is required in order to make decisions related to work, to allocate resources and to provide better services to customers. As an enabler of knowledge, the information service has a responsibility for ensuring that the corporate memory is complete and that everyone is able to develop high-level skills and proficiencies in knowledge sharing, management and use.

In organizations that have reached advanced stages in knowledge enablement, knowledge management is considered a core competency. Performance appraisals include an assessment of each individual's knowledge-sharing expertise and knowledge-creation abilities. Motivation and reward mechanisms are also in place to encourage and support knowledge sharing and organizational learning. Everyone is responsible for the acquisition, collaboration, documentation and distribution of knowledge and information. A knowledge architecture defines the different components of the organization's knowledge resources, including a description of its value, its attributes, where it is located, who manages and has responsibility for it, and how to access it.

Innovative capability

In advanced organizations with an innovative capability there is a significant shift from an emphasis on the strategic management of material goods to the identification and management of intellectual property, corporate branding and the know-how, talents, skills and expertise of people.

Creativity and innovation are acknowledged for their role in exploiting change and for providing the organization with the means to deal with the unstructured problems arising out of changing environments. People's capacities to solve problems in new ways, to conceive bright ideas and to use entrepreneurial thinking become much more important to the organization. The challenge is to generate an environment in which change is perceived as an opportunity rather than a threat. This enables people to put forward suggestions without ridicule or judgment; and, for risks to be willingly assessed and taken, allowing mistakes to be made as part of the learning process. Systems and processes are in place so that everyone reports regularly on their activities and contributions to the innovative capability of the organization.

Leadership style

In highly successful knowledge age organizations, the leaders are proactive, visionary, entrepreneurial and risk taking. They use these skills to maintain their organization's competitiveness. They share their vision with others and create a collaborative and supportive environment. They also anticipate what could happen, visualizing their preferred future and putting steps in place to ensure a readiness for this. Resistance to change is smoothed by open communication and a participative style where people become used to providing input. Decision making is pushed down to those in the service area through delegation.

Culture and values

Highly successful organizations create a sense of excitement, belonging and commitment. They have strong corporate cultures that are built from the top, with executive management communicating the values personally, by walking the talk. There is mutual respect for people, who are assumed to be interdependent and mature. Individuals are valued and rewarded on performance and innovation rather than on staff functions or length of service. There is public acknowledgment that everyone, regardless of level or position, is capable of providing creative solutions through imaginative thinking. Opportunities for self-development are frequently provided. Importance is attached to expertise, affiliations and ability to network outside the organization. Trust and ethical behaviours are strongly held values.

People management

Like other capital resources, people can only grow if they are valued and there is renewal and investment provided through training and support, personal development, encouragement and opportunity. In highly performing organizations, time is spent on increasing expertise, coaching and developing people, and expanding their capabilities. The emphasis is on the provision of advice and relevant information, rather than instructions and decisions. Communication is open and free flowing, vertically and horizontally. Individuals have access to the appropriate information that they require for decision making. Information is readily shared in a trusting environment within the organization and with stakeholders.

Structure

The complexity and rapid rate of change in the external environment influences the internal organizational structure. Organizational structures become much flatter, with fewer management tiers in order to be more responsive to changing environments. The trend is also to smaller organizations with more flexible structures. This allows the organization to adapt more quickly to change. The global environment means that people will not only work in many cross-functional teams, but traditional organizational boundaries begin to disappear as people work collaboratively with strategic partners at an international level.

Use of technology

Technology is viewed as a transformational tool to assist commercial repositioning and increased communication within the organization and with stakeholders.

Applications are developed as inter-organizational and intra-organizational systems with an emphasis on encouraging customer loyalty through the ability to offer benefits and specific services that others cannot match, customer relationship management, enabling internal efficiencies through integrated systems, and extending the human-to-machine interface to make life more exciting, convenient and enjoyable.

Conclusion

Today's environment means that organizational readiness to manage continuous and discontinuous change is a required capability. Strategic and scenario planning are two tools through which this capability is acquired. By continually analysing the drivers of change and transformation and being aware of the areas of strategic influence in the external environment, the element of surprise and its associated damage can be lessened. Whilst sudden and unprecedented events will still occur, the organization will have less exposure to the shock element and be more prepared to manage the consequential fallout. Having an understanding of the strengths and limitations of the internal capabilities of the organization also assists in readying the organization to succeed and survive. Areas that do not meet expected levels of capability in the industry can be improved and areas of strength maintained at the forefront of industry best practice.

Further reading

Chen, Leida and Nath, Ravi (2005), 'Nomadic culture: Cultural support for working anytime, anywhere', *Information Systems Management*, vol. 22, no. 4, pp. 56–65.

Handy, Charles (1995), *The empty raincoat: Making sense of the future*, Sydney, Aus: Random House.

Pascale, Richard T. et al. (2000), *Surfing the edge of chaos: The laws of nature and the new laws of business*, New York, NY: Crown Business.

Schwartz, Peter et al. (2000), *The long boom: A future history of the world 1980–2020*, London, UK: Orion.

Winston, Mark D. and Quinn, Susan (2005), 'Library leadership in times of crisis and change', *New Library World*, vol. 105, no. 1216/1217, pp. 395–415.

Planning and Managing for Transformation

The theme of Part II is planning. The planning process is the first stage of managing the dynamic environment by adopting a systematic approach to influencing, managing, positioning and transforming the organization to achieve their desired outcomes successfully. Whilst the activities of strategic planning, human, information, technology and financial resource planning are described in separate chapters for convenience, an integrated approach is advocated. Strategic planning sets the overall direction for the organization, within which human, financial, information and technology resources are planned, managed and respond to dynamic environments.

Chapter 3 addresses roles and responsibilities in strategic planning. The reader is taken through several logical steps in the strategic planning process, from defining the mission, conducting the situation audit and needs analysis to developing objectives and programmes. A short discussion on the benefits of scenario planning is also included.

Chapters 4 to 7 deal with planning and management in human, information, technology and financial resources. Chapter 4 considers the strategic approach to human resource management. It also covers how requirements for staff are determined, skills inventories, and the development of the job description and job specification through the job analysis. The various mechanisms for recruitment are discussed, as are processes for selection and induction. Finally, performance management, staff turnover and separation are addressed.

Chapter 5 covers knowledge and information management from the perspective that they are considered a strategic corporate resource. Information is the 'content' of the technology systems. The chapter explains how knowledge and information is used for decision making and advocates a strong consultation process in planning and managing information. Senior management must also action and champion the strategic planning process that includes an environmental analysis, the development of a knowledge and information architecture and a gap analysis. The chapter also incorporates strategies for the management and maintenance of information as a shared corporate resource. These include mechanisms for data classification, information standards, information definitions and information directories.

Technology management is covered in Chapter 6 along with techniques for managing other strategic assets. As information-related technology is susceptible to radical change, the chapter has not provided detailed descriptions of various technologies. Instead emphasis is placed on obtaining business rather than technology solutions. The chapter identifies how the technology presents opportunities for the organization to compete in the market place successfully. The technology planning process is described; role and responsibilities for the planning process are defined and the components of the technology architecture are summarized. The management issues associated with developing the technology to support the business strategy and with implementing the technology strategy are discussed.

Chapter 7 considers financial planning and management. It describes the budget process, the relationships between the budget cycle and the strategic planning cycle, the activities associated with preparing and controlling the budget, and different budgeting techniques. Different costing mechanisms and capital costs are covered. The chapter also distinguishes between cost accounting and activity-based costing, and explains mechanisms for costing such as fixed and variable costs, unit costs, productivity curves, the law of diminishing returns, variable and total costs per unit.

CREATING THE RIGHT CORPORATE ENVIRONMENT

TRANSFORMING THE CORPORATE ENVIRONMENT

MANAGING YOURSELF AND OTHERS

MANAGING IN A DYNAMIC ENVIRONMENT

EPILOGUE

POSITIONING TO EXCEL IN SERVICE DELIVERY

PLANNING AND MANAGING FOR TRANSFORMATION

PART II – PLANNING AND MANAGING FOR TRANSFORMATION

3. **Strategic planning**
Management oversight – roles and responsibilities; The strategic plan; The strategic planning process; Scenario planning

4. **Human resource management**
Management oversight – roles and responsibilities; Planning; Determining requirements; Recruitment; Selection processes; Induction; Personal development and training; Performance management; Staff turnover; Separation

5. **Knowledge and information management**
Management oversight – roles and responsibilities; Managing knowledge and information as a corporate good; Managing knowledge and information as a social and economic good; Information life cycle; Planning; Acquisition; Maintenance; Exploitation; Evaluation and review; Retirement

6. **Technology and strategic asset management**
Management oversight – roles and responsibilities; The value of information and communications technology; Information and communications technology management life cycle; Planning; Acquisition; Maintenance; Exploitation; Evaluation and review;

GOVERNANCE AND ACCOUNTABILITY

Figure PII.1 Planning and managing for transformation

3 *Strategic Planning*

A constant challenge in the knowledge age is the ability for organizations to be able to deal with an uncertain future. One way of doing this is, as far as possible, to predict and prepare for uncertainty. For example, some trends will remain the same, and in these instances contingency plans can be used to respond to situations that are predictable. Some uncertainties can be eliminated through a variety of means including political lobbying, acquisitions, mergers, divesting and transferring risk to others. A third area for concentration is to build the organization's capacity to respond flexibly and adapt to changes arising from the social, technological, economic, environmental or political environment.

Planning techniques can reduce uncertainty and assist in positioning the organization to take advantage of the global knowledge economy and society. Strategic planning is a continuous and proactive technique that can be used where a systematic approach is appropriate. It can be defined as the art or skill of careful planning toward an advantage or desired end. It takes into account the drivers of change and enables organizations to adapt to meet the challenges of the future and to plan a direction or course of action in a proactive manner. The outcome of which is that the organization is much more proactive and better able to influence external forces in accordance with its chosen strategies. It is also more able to initiate new activities conducive to market needs; rather than adjust or respond to those imposed upon it.

Whilst the strategic planning process introduces a systematic approach to managing dynamic environments and enables the information service to respond effectively to new situations, it can blinker or limit the vision to what is known and a single outcome. Scenario planning enables organizations to deal better with uncertainty as it considers a number of possible futures. It identifies patterns and clusters of information from a number of possibilities.

This chapter considers the various stages of the strategic planning process and the roles and responsibilities for strategic planning within the information service and its parent organization. The hierarchy of objectives is also explored in terms of timescale, management responsibility and relationships to the organizational structure. Finally, it briefly describes the value and process of scenario planning.

Management oversight – roles and responsibilities

Whilst creating and articulating the vision and future position of the organization is a key leadership role for the Chief Executive, all stakeholders who have the potential to be affected should be involved in strategic planning at various stages. For example, customers and suppliers may be asked to provide their thoughts on future services to meet emerging needs, whilst members of the governing body and funding allocators may provide input into future funding strategies. The planning process should be inclusive.

To be effective, strategic planning requires the commitment and involvement of executive management. Strategic planning is about the strategic positioning of the organization. There has to be a clear understanding throughout the organization of its purpose and the value of the process. The strategic planning process will fail if inadequate time or resources are spent on it, or if there is a lack of commitment to the process. There should also be good communication channels about the process and outcomes throughout the organization.

Whilst executive management will not produce the plan alone, their personal knowledge, commitment and involvement are crucial to its long-term effectiveness. Their leadership roles include initiating the process, encouraging support and an involvement in overseeing the process. An important responsibility of executive management is to create the necessary environment to dispel fears that will inevitably arise out of the potential for change, and to encourage the enthusiasm of others in the strategic planning process.

MANAGING THE PLANNING PROCESS

Planning must not only be valued and wanted, it should be seen to be valued and wanted. As a vehicle for change it is sometimes associated with negative feelings and connotations. Some consider it to be a mechanism for organizational reorganization with the capacity to engender a loss of power or position. Others may view it as a waste of time and resources. The enthusiasm for strategic planning can be enhanced by discussing what could happen without the process being in place, and by explaining how other information services have benefited from strategic planning. Good strategic planning also benefits the communications and decision-making processes within organizations.

The handling of the management issues arising from the planning process will greatly influence the employees' perceptions and their long-term enthusiasm for its implementation. The process may introduce changes to structure, projects and jobs. It may challenge the comfort zones of individuals or require attitude changes amongst the staff. People's reason for existence, control or power over information may be threatened. Careful handling of the process may pay dividends at the time when the planning process is implemented. If people can participate in the planning process from its inception, especially with reference to their areas of responsibility, they will more readily understand the purpose and objectives of the strategic plan and actively support its implementation.

The strategic planning process for the information service should be integrated with the planning for the parent organization and linked to the planning and management of all of the corporate resources. For example, the manager of the information service should be involved in setting the direction for the parent organization. The strategic plan for the parent organization should also set the strategic direction for the information service.

In order to allocate the necessary priority to the strategic planning process a formalized system should be used that allocates time and resources to the task. All levels of management are responsible for championing the value and importance of the strategic planning process within their teams and throughout the organization, and also to use the process to strengthen their delivery of services to the total community. This will inevitably compete with time to manage the other issues of the day. To reinforce its importance, everyone's contributions to the strategic planning process should be assessed as part of their individual performance appraisal.

The strategic plan

The strategic planning process recognizes that organizations cannot achieve everything they would like to do. Instead, it allows for the allocation of resources and planning of strategies on a priority basis best to achieve the organization's vision and mission within the resource constraints and dynamics of the external environment. The documented outcome of the strategic planning process is 'the strategic plan'. This is the written record of the organization's vision, mission statement, its objectives and the mechanisms to achieve them.

The strategic plan should be objectives driven as it is primarily concerned with outcomes within a two- to three-year timeframe. It should be a simple document and present a clear rationale for the specific objectives; give a clear impression of the relative priorities; and be used as the justification for all projects, activities and resources.

The objectives should be developed at two levels: strategic and operational. The strategic objectives should be geared to the desired future state; identifying opportunities whilst increasing the organization's flexibility and ability to adjust to change, and capacity for creativity. They should lead to the definition of corporate or organizational objectives, policies and standards that may be articulated in other documents.

The strategic objectives are then operationalized into operational plans and objectives. These provide the details of the services to be delivered to meet the strategic objectives. A set of results and outcomes, qualified by performance measures and a timetable for their achievement should be provided for each service or project. The operational plan should also identify how the human, financial, information and technical resources are to be acquired and used to achieve the strategic objectives.

The plan should be flexible, enabling smooth and quick adjustments to meet sudden changes in the environment. However, it should not need extensive modification and should be abandoned if this is the case. When the plan has outlived its usefulness, it should be replaced by another as part of a continuous planning cycle. The replacement plan should not be an extrapolation of the old. It requires the rethinking of the future in the light of the existing environment and prospective changes. The plans should simple and straightforward as complex plans are difficult to understand, implement and monitor.

The strategic planning process

ARTICULATE THE VISION AND DEFINE THE MISSION

The first task of the strategic planning process is to articulate the vision and define the mission. The vision is the desired future state for the organization. A shared vision across the organization becomes its underlying driving force. The mission statement simply articulates how the vision will be achieved.

The mission statement serves as the focal point for individuals to identify with the organization's vision, purpose and direction. It provides information about the future direction of the organization and its client base. In order to be readily understood and remembered by all stakeholders, the wording should be simple and explicit. It should be written in such a manner that avoids:

- a narrow perspective of the organization's role;
- the assumption that the organization will be the sole deliverer of specific services;
- locking the organization into outdated technology or service provision; and
- consideration of options in service delivery.

If a separate mission statement is to be developed for the information service, it should reflect the mission statement of the parent organization. It should clearly identify the core business and purpose of the information service in contributing to the wider organizational mission statement. The mission statement also identifies those critical factors that distinguish the service from its competitors. It may be a declaration of attitude or value that establishes the organizational climate, or a quality statement about customer service delivery.

SITUATION AUDIT

The situation audit enables an understanding of the internal and external environments in which the information service operates and is a necessary precursor to any strategic planning exercise. The following tools can be used in the situation audit:

- a strategic audit;
- an analysis of critical success factors;
- a SWOT analysis;
- a capability profile;
- a needs analysis;
- an outline of the present levels of resources and organizational capability;
- statements of policy and managerial philosophies;
- the formal and informal mandates imposed on the information service;
- a statement of the desired future in terms of major results and outcomes; and
- a statement of organization-wide objectives that represent the philosophical basis for the information service's operations and articulate the desired future conditions to be achieved.

In addition different scenarios can be painted that incorporate the conceivable, possibilities (likely) and probabilities (most likely) events.

Strategic audit

The strategic audit considers the strategic issues from the internal and external environments that have been identified in the previous chapter and which may impact upon the information service and its parent organization. It provides the information services manager with important background information that can be used in the strategic planning process. After scanning and carrying out an analysis of the external and internal environments in which the information service and its parent organization operate, the manager should be able to determine the future role of the information service in its environment, its influence and image, and the appropriateness of the services that it provides.

The strategic audit should also yield information on existing and potential clients, stakeholders, competitors and other important influencing factors. Knowledge of these factors should make the information services manager more aware of the opportunities and threats facing the information service and increase their ability to manage these. If this knowledge is extensive, covering all the relevant domains of the internal and external environments the element of surprise is reduced. This in turn allows the risk to be managed at the appropriate level. The planning task is also more effective as more of the variables are known. Accident and chance will still play their part in a dynamic environment, bringing with them the need for

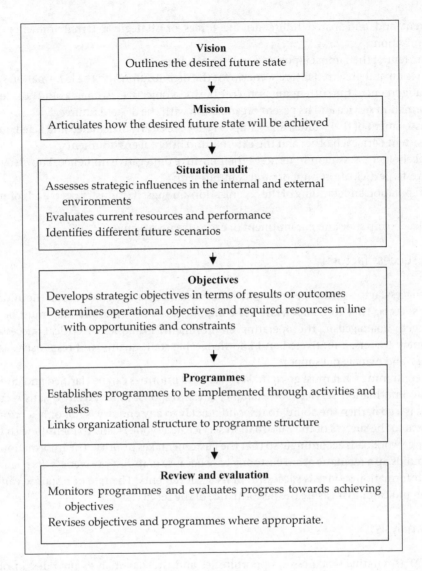

Figure 3.1   The strategic planning process

sudden or unexpected change. However, it is the manager's role to lessen the element of surprise and to respond and adapt to the change as it occurs. Issues to be assessed in the strategic audit include:

- the possible and probable future direction of the information service in the global knowledge economy and society;
- the future direction of the industry sector or business environment in which the information service operates;
- future events likely to impact on the information service or its parent organization;
- trends and patterns that could impact on the organization either positively or negatively;

- current and anticipated future driving forces or strategic external influences on the organization;
- the extent of their impact (positive and negative);
- the vision and preferred future scenario for the organization and the information service;
- the alignment of the current mission, core business objectives, strategies and policies for the information service and its parent organization with the desired future;
- an assessment of their status, for example if they are clearly articulated and acted upon, and consistent with each other and the external and internal environments;
- a stakeholder assessment in terms of their positive or negative influence, knowledge, skills, interests, participation, support and commitment;
- the reputation and standing of the organization amongst its industry peers and competitors; and
- the leadership style and commitment of executive management.

Critical success factors

Critical success factors can be used to identify the most important ingredients for the information service's success. They focus upon the key components or determinants that must be present and correctly managed in the operating environment. Examples of critical success factors are visionary leaders, a motivated and knowledgeable staff, quality and responsive service to customers, and managerial support.

By determining what must go right, key goals and priorities can be clarified and understood across the information service. For example, if the response time taken to satisfy customer enquiries is a goal, then the ability to respond quickly to any enquiry is not only a priority, it is also critical to the success of the information service. Everyone is able to identify with the goal and arrange workloads accordingly so that the customer takes priority. The information service quickly builds up a reputation and customer base because of its responsiveness. Its goals are met and the information service is successful in its achievements. The rate of response can also be used as an indicator to measure the performance of the service.

SWOT analysis

The SWOT (strengths, weaknesses, opportunities and threats) analysis provides an objective assessment as to whether the information service is able to respond to and manage the environmental impacts. The more competent the information service is in dealing with these, the more successful it is likely to be. Strengths and weaknesses deal with factors internal to the organization, whilst opportunities and threats are concerned with its external environment.

A strength is a resource or capability that an organization has to achieve its objectives effectively. In an information service, a strength may be its innovative use of technology, or depth and coverage in content. It may also be a particularly helpful and creative member of staff who consistently applies innovative ways to tackle problems.

A weakness is a limitation, fault or defect in the organization that keeps it from achieving its objectives. Limited technology capacity may prevent an information service from meeting all of its customer needs.

It is often difficult to carry out an objective internal assessment upon the information service's strengths and weaknesses. For this reason it is useful to have an external person undertake the assessment as they can remove themselves from the emotional and personal issues involved.

Information for the assessment can be gathered through interviews with members of staff, stakeholders, customers and non-users, external evaluations, questionnaires and observations.

An opportunity is any favourable situation in the information service's external environment. It may be a trend or a change that supports the development of an enhanced service, or one that has not previously been identified or filled. An opportunity usually allows the information service to enhance its position, and may be brought about by a technical change. The use of the Internet, hand-held personal devices and mobile technologies embracing instant messaging are examples of technology applications that create opportunities to deliver new customer services direct to the individual, regardless of time or location.

A threat is an unfavourable situation in the information service's external environment that is potentially damaging to it or its competitive position. It may be a barrier or a constraint, or anything that may inflict problems on the information service.

The SWOT analysis allows strategies to be planned that can realize the strengths and opportunities and overcome the threats and weaknesses. It is also used extensively in marketing.

Capability profile

The capability profile is the means of assessing the information service's strengths and weaknesses in dealing with the opportunities and threats in the external environment. For example, its capability in the fields of leadership, marketing, technology and finance helps to identify the strengths and weaknesses in dealing with variables in the internal and external environments.

Leadership capability can be gauged by considering how forward thinking the organization is in repositioning itself in the global knowledge economy and society. It also includes assessing the organization's reputation and image as a trend setter, its speed of response to changing conditions, the prevailing corporate culture and communication capacity, and its ability to attract and retain highly creative people.

Marketing capability can be demonstrated by its status amongst its competitors, the level of branding, customer loyalty and satisfaction, the percentage of customers versus potential customers, quality of service and ability to maintain growth.

The presence of expertise and advanced technical skills, the level of sophistication in the application of technology, the utilization of resources and personnel to achieve economies of scale, the level of coordination and compatibility, and the integration and effectiveness of service are some of the factors that may determine the information service's technical capability. Financial capability is determined by access to capital, financial strength and the ability to sustain the required financial position.

To complete the capability profile, a bar chart is prepared detailing the degree of strength or weakness in each category. After completing the chart the relativity of the strengths and weaknesses to each other can be determined. Whilst the capability profile is highly subjective, it is still useful. It provides the means for examining the current strategic position of the information service and highlights areas needing attention.

Needs assessment

The needs assessment provides additional environmental information for the development of the plan. It enables the information service to:

- identify the gap between the current provision and desired level of service;
- forecast future needs;
- plan provision to meet such needs in good time; and
- ensure that the operational policies are effective in meeting real needs.

The needs assessment should not just relate to existing customers of the information service. All stakeholders, including potential customers, should be considered. Many sources of information can be used to provide input to the needs assessment; for example, customer surveys, community analysis, census figures and organizational reports.

The needs analysis should include input in addition to professional judgment or indicators such as (lack of) volume of complaints, comments or suggestions by customers and other stakeholders. To rely just on this information may result in a bias that could lead to an inaccurate assessment of service needs. Underestimation and overestimation are two other pitfalls. Underestimation may arise when the needs of non-vocal sectors of the community have not been brought to attention, or are overlooked. Overestimation of needs can occur by overlooking the fact that a large sector of the customer base is satisfied with the existing provision of service.

The preliminary stage of clarifying what is meant by a need in a particular programme area can be useful in that it forces the examination of real objectives and definition of needs. The concept of need implies a normative judgment: a particular level of need is arbitrary and depends upon attitude. Ideas of what constitutes need can change over time and circumstances in the same way that motivational needs change. 'Wants' and 'needs' should be distinguished; for example, you may want to drive a Mercedes or Porsche to work, yet you may only need a push-bike.

Surveys of both customers and potential customers can be important mechanisms for the collection of information about customer needs. However, they can be comparatively expensive to conduct and require careful planning to provide valid and meaningful results. If such surveys are not properly planned, incorrect information may be obtained that could result in the implementation of a programme totally unsuited to the real needs of the customer base. This could eventually be more costly to the information service in financial, political and social terms than the original costs in conducting the survey.

Implemented correctly, surveys can be a valuable planning tool. However, they should not be relied upon as a 'proven management technique' at the expense of other methods. The gut feeling that arises from a close involvement and working knowledge of the situation should also be considered.

Outline of present levels of resources and organizational capability

The following information can be used in determining the health of the organization and the status of internal resources and organizational capability:

- how closely the information service and its parent organization is aligned to industry standards and profiles of other competing firms in the market place;
- the alignment of information and communication technologies to the strategic objectives and business needs of the organization;
- the consistency between stated or desired corporate culture and the actual prevailing culture;

- the alignment and consistency between the organization's policies and actual practices in the information service;
- the organizational approach to managing and developing expertise;
- the use of power to enhance or detract from organizational success;
- the alignment and fit of decision-making processes and styles to the external and internal environments;
- the rate of turnover of staff in comparison with industry standards;
- the additional skills, competencies and attributes that are needed to transform the organization and enable it to achieve its desired future position;
- the appropriateness of standards and techniques used to evaluate and improve corporate performance;
- the appropriateness, identification and management of risk-mitigation strategies;
- the organizational approach to quality control; and
- the capability of systems to monitor and provide feedback on corporate performance.

Having conducted the situation audit, and made an assessment of the current and desired future state, the objectives can be developed.

OBJECTIVES

Hierarchy of objectives

Objectives may be distinguished according to their level in the hierarchy (see Figure 3.2). There is a relationship between level, scope and impact upon the organization and time frame for implementation. The highest level objectives, the strategic objectives, relate to the organization in its entirety and are usually long term. The objectives become more specific at the lower levels in terms of application within the organization. They are also shorter in time frame.

The hierarchy continues in terms of programmes, projects or activities, and tasks. Activities and tasks are directly related to subsets of the objectives and programmes. They are usually short term or repetitive, easily measurable and relate to groups or individuals.

The hierarchy is generally shaped like a pyramid. The broader and more future-oriented objectives are fewer in number and appear at the pinnacle of the pyramid. The immediate or short-term objectives are to be found in greater numbers. They are more precise in definition and quantification.

Developing objectives

The strategic objectives should be long term in nature and allow for improvement and coordination of corporate operations. Operational objectives are mid- and short-term focused and are translated in turn into programmes and activities. These are framed with inputs, outputs and constraints in mind. Resources for these are allocated through established functions such as the budget process.

Objectives should be developed within the context of the situation audit and the needs assessment. Opportunities for better service delivery or internal productivity gains should be considered as well as the impact of any known constraints on resources. The parent organization's management philosophies or political ideologies may also shape the development of objectives for the information service.

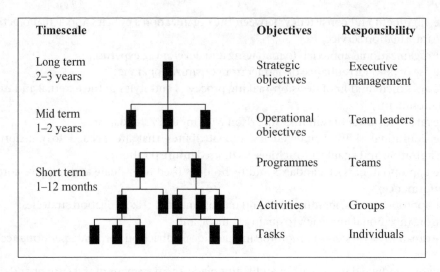

Timescale		Objectives	Responsibility
Long term 2–3 years		Strategic objectives	Executive management
Mid term 1–2 years		Operational objectives	Team leaders
		Programmes	Teams
Short term 1–12 months			
		Activities	Groups
		Tasks	Individuals

Figure 3.2   The hierarchy of objectives

Effectively formulated objectives should result in concrete outcomes desired by the organization. The formulation of meaningful objectives takes careful thought and analysis. The intention of the objective should be clear and its focus well understood. It should stimulate the action as well as specify it. The objectives must be challenging yet capable of achievement. They should be written so that they can be analysed and reviewed.

Objectives should be defined in terms of results or conditions to be achieved rather than in terms of the activities to be performed, as it is against the objectives that performance will be measured. They should be stated in positive terms, that is, in terms of what is to be achieved rather than avoided. Above all, the objectives should be quantifiable, since the more concrete the information, the more likely will be the achievement of real meaning. An example of a hierarchy of objectives within an information service is shown in Figure 3.3.

The quality of results is just as important as the type or kind of results. Time limits or delays in service provision, percentages, workload volumes and frequency rates are measurable points that can be incorporated into information service objectives. Quantifiable objectives and outcomes define and clarify the expectations and results better than verbal descriptions. They provide a built-in measure of effectiveness.

PROGRAMMES

The development of programmes takes place after consideration of the alternative scenarios and strategies whereby the objectives can be achieved. It should be a creative and innovative process, with only the best possible alternatives selected. The selected programmes should represent the best possible use of resources when considered against all other possible uses. They should lead to improved organizational performance or service delivery and derive the greatest possible benefit for the least cost. The evaluation of programme alternatives should assess not only the financial and economic costs and benefits, but also the social and political costs and benefits. Outcomes (quality and quantity) should be measured against inputs.

Programmes are implemented by organizing activities and allocating tasks. Implementation of the plan at this level is often a difficult task as it invariably means organization and personal change. The programmes are often linked to the organizational structure. Consequently any

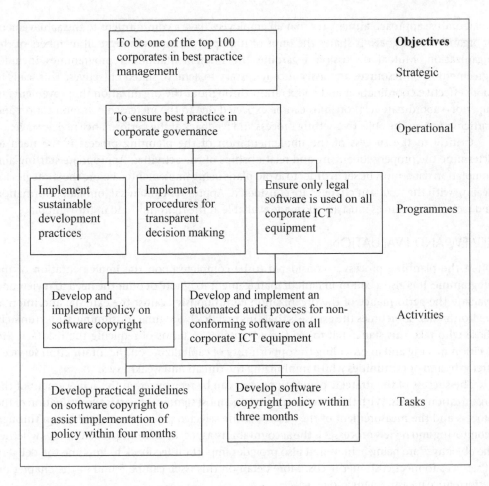

Figure 3.3   A hierarchy of objectives in an information service

major change in programme structure may involve an internal reorganization. Strategies for dealing with the required change should be considered prior to the introduction of the new programmes. Responsibilities should be assigned, and monitoring and control processes devised to measure progress towards the attainment of goals.

In addition to linking organizational structure into programme structure, successful planning processes tie implementation strategies into action plans. For example, personnel should be recruited with skills and outlooks that reinforce the strategies. Personnel performance review systems should be also linked into the achievement of programmes and activities.

In implementing programmes, the emphasis should be on the outcomes of the decisions rather than the techniques by which the decisions are made. Successful implementations are those that improve the quality of service delivery through employee motivation and an increased commitment to the organization's goals. Positive results should be highlighted and reinforced. Short-term improvements can be made permanent through positive reinforcement, monitoring and review.

Information sharing is paramount. All staff are entitled to be fully informed. The need for people to contribute and be involved in operational decision making is important. This collaborative approach anticipates that all employees have a commitment to the achievement of organizational goals. It shares the onus of high performance amongst all members of the organization. Mutual discussion regarding the implementation of programmes includes agreement upon resources and assistance necessary to achieve stated objectives. This leads to more effective coordination and cooperation throughout the organization. Improvements in superior–subordinate relationships can be expected due to the increased communication and participation on the objective-setting process and feedback at the performance review stage.

Critical to the success of the implementation of the planning process is the need to determine the proper sequencing and relationships of the activities. Appropriate starting and completion dates must be set in order to avoid plans being implemented before the strategies for dealing with the resultant changes are considered. Appropriate financial, human, information and technical resources must also be made available at the right time and in the right place.

REVIEW AND EVALUATION

Often the planning process is considered to be complete upon the implementation of the programme. It is also a common fault of management to ignore or omit the need to review and evaluate the performance of the organization continuously against the external and internal environments. Sometimes the excuse is that this practice is too time consuming. Unfortunately those who take this stance fail to see the advantages in terms of reducing the risk factor in decision making and in providing the opportunity of capitalizing on the information service's strengths and opportunities whilst minimizing the threats and weaknesses.

The success of the strategic planning process can be recognized in the achievement of the organization's goals. With this in mind, the last and most significant part is the evaluation of the process and the measurement of the success of the selected programmes. Evaluation through monitoring and review processes is the accountability aspect of planning. It determines whether the objectives are being achieved. It also provides important feedback to finetune the delivery of services to meet customer needs. More detail on this issue can be found in the chapter on performance measurement and review.

Scenario planning

As the business environments in which organizations operate become more complex, organizations have had to shift from forecasting to developing scenarios for the future in order to improve the organization's fit to its environment. Scenario planning enables organizations to determine what is of strategic importance and concern to the organization and to explain this in terms of the impact they have on the organization. Participants in the process are required to look at concerns and uncertainties, future directions, pivotal events, decisions both for the short and long terms, constraints and what people would like to be remembered for, and develop a series of possible scenarios or stories of the future. The scenarios are constructed in a workshop environment and are each given a name that can be instantly recognized, based on the story line or data in the scenario.

Capturing multiple images of the future that together encompass the critical uncertainties facing the organization is one of the two key goals of scenario developers. The other goal is to convince managers at all levels of the organization to consider seriously the strategic and tactical implications of each scenario, (Ringland, 2003, p. 22).

The scenarios are not used to predict the future, but highlight options based on what is known and unknown. The advantage is that scenario planning assists organizations to think outside of the box by challenging and stretching conventional thinking in order to map out the future. Scenario planning can be used in developing the organization's strategic plan particularly:

- in a business environment of high uncertainty;
- for generating new opportunities;
- for developing a common language throughout the organization; and
- where there are strong differences of opinion.

The development of a number of scenarios about possible or probable futures enables people better to construct a reality view of the future. Culturally and psychologically they can:

- promote wider thinking by providing insights into complex situations;
- challenge and free up peoples' mindsets;
- overcome availability bias where people undervalue what is difficult to imagine or conceptualize; and
- shift people's thinking that is embedded in the past.

Other advantages of using scenario planning techniques include:

- the ability to detect early warning signals that a particular future is unfolding;
- an increased capacity to evaluate risk and return options; and
- being able to generate better strategic options in both favourable and unfavourable futures.

However, Ringland (2003, p. 23) found that professional scenario developers are seldom totally successful in connecting with line managers, who see their roile as ensuring day-to-day delivery of a product or service, and who are convinced that scenarios are irrelevant to this task. This can be shortsighted as Ringland explains:

- many early warning signs of new scenarios emerging are first seen as peripheral issues in the market place, for example, in the concerns of stakeholders who are not customers, but who can influence them; and
- good scenarios are insurance that line managers' default assumptions will be identified and modified to fit changing conditions.

Ringland believes that after a scenarion exercise, if managers have fully participated and have been sensitized to recognize early warning signs and report them, the initial signals of critical change are less likely to be ignored. She goes on to say that making scenarios accessible to line managers requires four stages of preparation before introducing them:

- creating scenarios clearly grounded in today's events and trends;
- identifying business options under each scenario;
- having a clear process for making choices based on the scenarios; and
- developing a clear set of events that would be early indicators for each scenario.

A typical scenario presentation for each scenario would cover:

- what is happening now that makes the scenario credible;
- a description of the world at the end of the scenario; and
- early indicators of each scenario, and specific events to watch for.

Most of the strategic management and marketing tools used in information services such as the strength, weakness, opportunity and threat (SWOT) analysis and the Boston Consulting Group matrix analysis can be used very effectively with scenarios. Generally between four and six scenarios are developed, incorporating the major cause and effect issues identified in the planning process. These are then used as the basis for further research and organizational review from which action plans are developed as part of the strategic planning process.

Conclusion

The activities associated with setting and sharing the vision, collectively planning for the future, articulating the organization's objectives and creating an understanding of its purpose and values are useful leadership activities in their own right. They can generate a greater knowledge and understanding of the organization and, ultimately, increase the level of commitment, communication and cohesiveness across the organization. This in turn leads to individual feelings of empowerment and strengthens the common goal of all.

References

Ringland, Gill (2003), 'Scenario planning: Persuading operating managers to take ownership', *Strategy and Leadership*, vol. 31, no. 6, pp. 22–8.

Further reading

Learning from the future: Competitive foresight scenarios (1998). New York, NY: John Wiley.

Lindgren, Mats and Bandhold, Hans (2003), *Scenario planning: The link between future and strategy*, Basingstoke, UK: Palgrave Macmillan.

Mintzberg, Henry et al. (1998), *Strategy safari: A guided tour throough the wilds of strategic management*, Hemel Hempstead, UK: Prentice Hall.

Ringland, Gill (1998), *Scenario planning: Managing for the future*, Chichester, UK: John Wiley.

Van der Heijden, Kees (1996), *Scenarios: The art of strategic conversation*, Chichester, UK: John Wiley.

Van der Heijden, Kees et al. (2002), *The sixth sense: Accelerating organizational learning with scenarios*, Chichester, UK: John Wiley.

4 Human Resource Management

People are an organization's most valuable resource, both in terms of contribution and cost. The rich combination of the people's talents, experiences, know-how, skill sets, imaginations, thoughts, philosophies and capabilities is what sets the organization apart and distinguishes it from its competitors. People's knowledge and innovation capabilities are two of the most important ingredients for transformation and change in organizations today. Their attitudes and perspectives can also reinforce the corporate outcomes and organizational values. Development and learning opportunities add to these abilities and knowledge, increasing the employee's contribution to the organization.

From a cost perspective, salaries and associated overheads such as superannuation are often the most expensive component of a budget. Managed appropriately, an organization's workforce is its life breath. Managed inappropriately, the workforce becomes an expensive commitment that leads to few rewards but many problems.

Effective human resource management is planned and executed at a strategic and operational level. The strategic component of human resource management includes planning and forecasting competencies, attitudes and requirements to meet the mission and organizational objectives, as well as the organization's future directions. They link to the organization's strategic plans for its future (e.g. projections for growth or diversification). Operational human resource management activities relate to the personnel processes of recruiting and selecting the right individuals, and managing performance. The emphasis is on the need to 'marry' the job, the person, the organization and the situation. Employees' skills, knowledge, outlook and experience ought to support and add value to the organization's objectives and programmes. Motivation, training and personal development build on these by further improving personal performance and efficiency. More information on these management topics can be found in later chapters in the book.

Like all planning, human resource planning should be a continuous and proactive process. It should take into account external and internal environmental influences. Personnel programmes and activities should be related to organizational objectives. There should also be mechanisms for review and feedback. As part of the integrated planning approach, the human resource planning process for the information service will be influenced by the parent organization's strategic planning strategies and its human resource policies.

Industrial relations, legislation awards and workplace agreements will govern conditions of employment. Economic conditions, changes in academic requirements and the organization's ability to attract and keep appropriately skilled people will also influence recruitment outcomes.

Internally, the size, structure, culture and type of organization affect human resource planning, whilst the degree of specialization, personnel configurations, professionalism, levels of technology adoption and financial capacities will influence the capacity to attract people.

Management oversight – roles and responsibilities

In keeping with the philosophy that people are an organization's most valuable resource, commitment to equitable employment and selection practices and their continued well-being and personal development is part of the leadership role for the Chief Executive. The day-to-day operational management of people is a line management responsibility. Adequate time or resources should be spent on identifying future skills and knowledge requirements, developing and managing people, performance management and giving regular feedback, whilst ensuring that the workplace is safe and attractive to work in.

Planning

ENVIRONMENTAL ANALYSIS

The first stage of strategic human resource planning is in determining the requirements based upon the environmental analysis. It looks at what the organization is trying to achieve, its preferred future position and how well structured it is to do the job. It also takes into account the productivity, growth, developmental stage of the information service and its parent organization, together with any other influencing factors and trends.

Determining requirements

GAP ANALYSIS

Having taken into account the future projection of the skills, knowledge and expertise required for the future (needs), a gap analysis is undertaken. This compares the projected requirements with the current status of the existing inventory (availability) and expresses these as a match, excess or deficit of personnel and skills. These may relate to specific skills, occupations or levels of staff and may not be consistent across the organization. Programmes may differ in their types of activities and require different skills and numbers of staff.

Alternative actions are considered in order to overcome anticipated gaps. These may involve recruitment, redeployment and/or termination of personnel, changing the technology, the redesign of jobs or reorganization of work processes to improve productivity, changing the skill and competency requirements for prospective employees, or developing skill-training programmes.

Proper human resource planning encourages organizations to plan for their future skills, expertise and staffing structures and to take into account changes in services and technology. Exercised properly, and on a continuing basis, it should eliminate problems of oversupply or undersupply of particular skills and expertise within the information service. It also aids in the determining of training needs in relation to required skills.

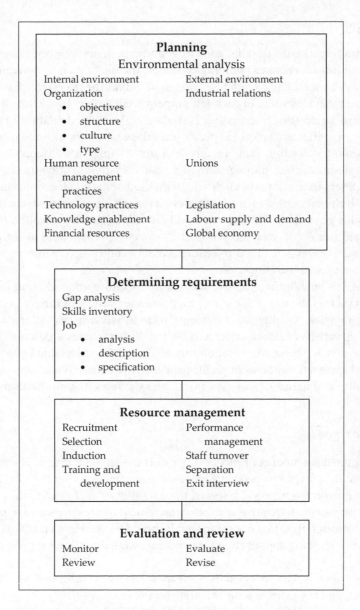

Figure 4.1   An integrated approach to human resource planning

SKILLS INVENTORY

A skills inventory is a management information system that describes the organization's workforce. Skills inventories may be designed for several purposes. They may be used to strategically monitor workforce capabilities and performance, or to assist in the identification of employees for promotion, transfer and/or training. The usefulness of any skills inventory depends upon the appropriateness, accessibility and current validity of the data. A simple file system may be adequate for a small, relatively stable organization, whilst a computerized data system, updated daily, may be required for a large, more dynamic organization.

JOB ANALYSIS

Once the required organizational skills, knowledge and experience have been identified through the strategic and human resource planning processes, the next task is to determine how these requirements can be met. The job analysis process identifies the necessary characteristics and skills to fulfil the responsibilities of each job properly as described by the job description and job specification. To do this, information is studied and collected relating to the purposes, responsibilities, activities and tasks of a specific job – the what, who, why and when.

The process of collecting data usually consists of interviews (individual or group), observation, questionnaires, filming activities, daily diaries or timesheets, and written descriptions. Observation is a particularly useful method of data collection if the job is simple and repetitive. If this is coupled with an interview, it may result in the provision of information that is not readily observable. The interview will also allow verbal verification of information already obtained from observing job practices. A sincere, attentive and assuring attitude on behalf of the interviewer is required to ensure accurate and complete information, since job analysts are often viewed with suspicion.

The job analysis provides quantitative and qualitative information. Quantitative statements include details such as the size of the work group and the number of times a task is performed per hour, day or week. Qualitative statements refer to working conditions and personnel requirements. A variety of information is collected. This includes a description of the job, attitudes, competencies, behaviours, conditions, levels of skill, ability and knowledge, types of equipment and expected standards of performance. The job analysis also collects information on accountability and nature of supervision, such as the reporting mechanisms and levels of responsibility.

JOB DESCRIPTION

The first and immediate product of the job analysis is the job description. The job description is as much a guide to assist prospective applicants determine whether the job is of interest to them, as it is to provide the means of assessing the suitability of applicants to the position. It sets the scene and provides a descriptive and factual statement of the duties and responsibilities of a specific job. However, this does not mean that it should be boring. A creative description can attract innovative thinking applicants, whilst encompassing the following information:

* Job identification – Provides details such as a creatively described job title, group or department, and any other specific identifier for the job.
* Organizational relationships – Identifies the level of influence within the organizational structure. It can describe the immediate reporting arrangements, and other positions where collaboration takes place or where influence is extended in achieving outcomes.
* Job summary – Gives meaning to the job and its key responsibilities. It provides a description of the job in terms of how it contributes to the organizational mission and objectives.
* Duties performed – This describes the what, how and why of the position. For example, the development of IT systems that assist business units achieve their objectives. Visual guides such as pie charts add contextual meaning to the description of duties as they provide an immediate impact and graphically illustrate the important components and relationships of the job, rather than providing just a list of responsibilities and percentages. An estimation of the approximate percentage of time devoted to each major duty is helpful, as is the degree of supervision received.

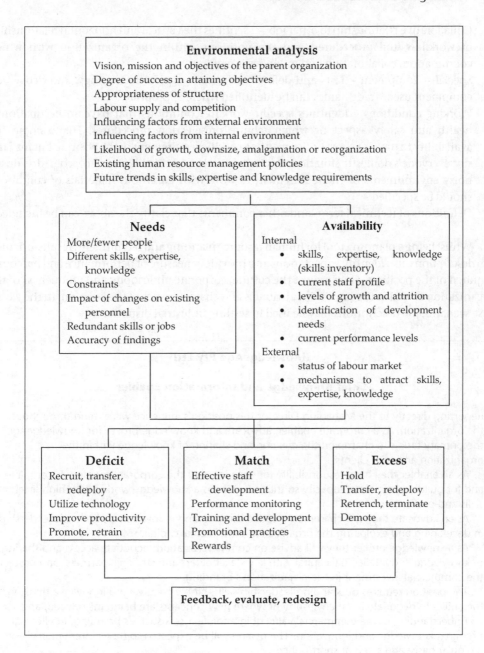

Figure 4.2   Determining requirements

- Achievable results – Sets the benchmark by which measures of performance can be judged. It describes what the position is to achieve and the minimal acceptable employee performance of the specified duties.
- Reporting-supervising functions – Identifies the immediate reporting requirements and positions of influence. It can also provide information about the degree of supervision received and given.

- Collaborative relationship to other jobs – Identifies the vertical and horizontal relationships of workflow and procedures, and the positions within the organization with which coordination, collaboration and influence is required.
- Specialist equipment – Lists and defines each major type of technology, knowledge and equipment used. Trade names can be identified where appropriate.
- Working conditions – Identifies specific working conditions that have an occupational, health and safety aspect or which require preselection procedures. For example the availability to travel at short notice may be a specific requirement of the position but may not suit everyone's domestic situation. Environmental conditions such as hot, cold, dry, dusty, noisy environments or the requirement to work with hazardous materials or conditions should be specified.
- Definitions of technical terms and other comments that clarify the above can be included.

Whilst being a planning tool for human resource planning and recruitment, results-oriented job descriptions also identify expectations and provide a measure of performance and outcomes required of the position. They project the culture, corporate philosophy and uniqueness of the organization as well as the important attributes and characteristics of the position. In the worst-case scenario, job descriptions may be used in settling industrial disputes.

KnowledgeAge Pty Ltd

Chief Knowledge and Information Enabler

Reporting directly to the Managing Director this position's influence will extend throughout the organization. As a corporate enabler, advocate and knowledge broker for KnowledgeAge the primary task is to champion the creation and sharing of knowledge within the organization and with clients.

As an enabler they have responsibility for ensuring that the corporate memory is complete, and for building corporate capacity so that everyone is a knowledge worker with high-level skills and proficiencies.

As an advocate they will champion creative thinking and innovation and provide leadership in developing and exploiting the organization's intellectual capital.

As a knowledge broker they will advise on commercialization, negotiate access and sharing of knowledge and intellectual capital with key stakeholders and strategic partners, and protect the commercial investment in the organization's branding.

The position requires outstanding leadership skills, highly creative and innovative thinking, the ability to negotiate in an environment where new concepts are being introduced, and an understanding of the commercial value of intangible assets such as branding, intellectual property, knowledge and innovation. The person will be expected to travel internationally on a regular basis, and often at short notice.

Motivation and reward mechanisms include attractive salary packaging including a share of profits and a family-friendly working environment.

Figure 4.3   A sample job description

Job descriptions need to be continuously updated if they are to be effective. Otherwise they become irrelevant and ignored. Unfortunately it is often the case that a job description is only updated when a position becomes vacant and a new staff member is to be appointed. An ideal opportunity to update the job description is at the time of the annual performance appraisal interview. This is especially important as information service positions often involve rapidly changing technology; environmental changes in such technologies make the updating of job descriptions a regular and important task.

Job descriptions need to leave some scope for initiative and innovation input on the part of the incumbent in the position. If they are too generic, specific or detailed, practices could be continued without regard for initiative and creativity, or continued improvements in productivity or service delivery.

JOB SPECIFICATION

Whereas the job description describes the job, the job specification describes the desired skills, natural talents, attributes, knowledge and qualifications of the person doing the job. It is a statement of the competencies and qualities required to perform a job properly. Such requirements are usually established for individual jobs on the basis of judgments (such as those of the job analyst), but in some instances they are based upon statistical validation procedures.

Examples of skills and abilities that may be described in the job specification include:

- Leadership skills – Setting direction, leading, gaining the commitment of others and motivating staff.
- Communications skills – Capabilities in transferring knowledge, being articulate and having good written and verbal communication skills, responding to adult learning needs, being able to write concisely, ability to communicate with people at all levels, or, having good listening skills.
- Information inputs to the position – Interpretations of perceptions, verbal or auditory interpretation, environmental awareness, and visual input from materials – for example, visual appraisal of condition of stock in a library.
- Mental processes – Decision making and ability to make sound judgments, information processing, problem-solving skills, use of job-related knowledge, analytical and conceptual abilities, abilities to relate and compare data, or identify customer requirements.
- Interpersonal skills – Ability to relate to others, dealing with sensitive, confidential or cross-cultural matters, negotiation skills.
- Education – The level of education and specific qualifications.
- Physical output – Skills and technical abilities, the use of equipment or technology ability.
- Supervisory skills – Supervising of staff activities, public contact, communicating instructions, directions or other related job information.
- Job context – Potentially stressful/unpleasant environment, potentially hazardous job situations, personally demanding situations.
- Stakeholder relationships skills – Dealing with stakeholders in a helpful and positive manner, meeting stakeholder requirements, acting professionally, efficiently and effectively.
- Planning and organizing skills – The ability to work under pressure, meeting deadlines, prioritizing, planning and monitoring workloads, being able to work with minimum supervision, scheduling work to meet a range of deadlines.
- Work experience may also be included.

The job specification is a guideline to the knowledge, skills and competencies required to perform a specific job and can form the base upon which applications are screened and interviews conducted. However, it should not control the recruitment process to the extent that, all other

Defining requirements

Analysis

Skills inventory

Job analysis – Qualitative and quantitative information on:
- tasks and nature of work activities
- working conditions
- personnel requirements
- key competencies
- nature and degree of supervision

Job Description – Factual statement of duties and responsibilities:
- job summary
- organizational relationships
- duties performed
- achievable results
- levels of influence and relationships to other jobs
- specialized equipment and working conditions

Job Specification – Desired attributes and competencies:
- qualifications
- experience, skills, knowledge
- specific abilities or personal attributes
- key competencies

Recruitment

Internal recruitment
- promotion
- internal transfer
- redeployment

External recruitment
- advertising
- specialist employment/recruiting agencies
- recommendation
- universities or colleges
- unsolicited applications

Selection process
- interviewing
- personality and other aptitude tests
- reference checks

Induction

Training and development

Performance management

Staff turnover and separation

Figure 4.4   Human resource management

things being equal, an applicant who is qualified and capable but deficient in some aspect fails to be appointed.

The job specification can be condensed and form part of the original advertisement and is given to prospective applicants along with the job description so that they are fully informed of the position for which they are applying.

Recruitment

INTERNAL RECRUITMENT

Once the position requirements have been adequately described the position can be filled. This may be through identifying existing staff that have the required expertise, recruiting new people with the required skills and expertise, or developing and retraining existing staff.

Filling a position internally has the advantage of increasing the general level of morale by providing an example of career path development within the organization and stimulating others to greater achievement. The process of recruiting internally can be more predictable in its outcome as the applicant's history and work performance within the organization will be known. Whilst there is a risk these may involve some subjective observations, the internal knowledge can be more reliable than curriculum vitae or external references furnished by external applicants.

Internal promotion is not always in the organization's best interest. External sources may provide differently skilled people than existing staff, or the organization may need some new ideas injected into it.

EXTERNAL RECRUITMENT

A number of external sources for recruiting information service personnel are available. These include recruitment advertising, employment agencies, recommendations by present employees, educational institutions, unsolicited or casual applicants or networking.

Advertisements

Advertisements may be placed on electronic job boards, in the local or national press, trade journals or professional media. The choice of media will depend upon the level of the position to be advertised. Information relating to the organization, job description and specification should be included in the advertisement to assist in self-screening. The advertisement should include details of the organization, the name of a contact person, telephone number or email address for further details, closing date, email address to which applications should be sent, and the details required.

The advertisement layout, design and copy will send a message about the information service and the type of staff it wishes to recruit. It is a valuable opportunity to project the organization's image. A high-quality design can boost the immediate response as well as the image.

Employment agencies

Employment agencies can be used for executive searches and to screen potential applicants. Employment agencies want to keep their clients happy by effectively working toward the client's goal, and they do this by effective placement of staff. Sometimes concerns are expressed about the amount of commission fees that employment agencies charge, without recognition for the time spent internally reading through applications, in selecting and notifying candidates and in conducting interviews.

Recommendations

Current employees may suggest prospective candidates for job vacancies. Here it is presumed that the employee knows both the organization and the acquaintance, and would therefore want to please both. The hiring of relatives is an inevitable component of recruitment programmes. Some organizations have policies that discourage this practice.

Education institutions

As in the above alternative, staff in education institutions are often in positions to advise on outstanding candidates or suitable newly qualified professionals. Some institutions maintain a job register or have bulletin boards where advertisements can be displayed.

Unsolicited applications

Unsolicited applications, either in person or by email, provide a source of recruitment. Policies differ between organizations as to how such applications are handled. Some keep all applications for future reference, whilst others note only outstanding ones. Some may refuse to take such applications, advising applicants to apply again when formal advertisements appear in the media.

Selection processes

There are a number of means through which selection can take place, including interviewing, skills tests, presentations, job trials, psychological and personality testing.

INTERVIEWING

The interview is the most widely used method of selecting individuals for jobs. The aim of the interview is threefold; to collect information about the applicant; to give information to the applicant; and to begin the induction process for the successful applicant. Interviews are useful in assessing an applicant's intelligence, level of motivation, and interpersonal skills.

Ideally the interview or selection committee should have between two and four people who collectively bring knowledge of the job and the organization, diversity of thinking and an independent view. It is also preferable that the selection committee has a gender balance and includes the immediate supervisor. The selection committee's role is to make an objective judgment about which applicant best fits the job and the future direction of the organization by:

- acquiring and interpreting information that is relevant to the job;
- evaluating and correctly interpreting what the candidate is saying; and

* drawing conclusions and making objective judgments at the end of the interview.

The following qualities are needed: good interpersonal and listening skills; a warm and engaging manner and an ability to establish rapport quickly; sensitivity to social situations, vocal intonation and hesitation; quickness in perceiving implications in the remarks of others; and an analytical and open mind. Interviewers should also possess a mature personality with sound practical judgment and freedom from bias.

The interview questions should be directly related to the duties of the position and the skills, expertise and knowledge requirements that are critical to the performance within the job. It is important to ensure that subjectivity does not occur. This may be through a lack of knowledge in the person(s) conducting the interview; or, the 'halo effect' which causes the interviewer(s) to read into discussions an intent that was not intended.

Equity and equality are important in the process. All procedures should be consistently followed so that each applicant has exactly the same chance. The committee should determine in advance a set of questions that can be consistently asked to each applicant, in the same order and by the same member of the committee. Incomplete answers or problem areas should be probed whilst avoiding leading questions, yet maintaining an atmosphere of trust. If sample answers to questions have been determined in advance by the committee, interviewee responses can be rated on an explicitly defined scale. Answers to questions should be documented for future reference and in case of legal challenge. Basic information questions given on the application forms should not be repeated.

Interviews are a two-way process. The interviewer is able to deliver appropriate and accurate information about the information service and its parent organization to the interviewee. The prospective applicant also evaluates the organization and makes decisions as to its suitability as an employing body. The interview is often the first contact with the information service and provides the first impression of its culture and dynamics.

Correct interviewing procedures set realistic job expectations, where applicants can determine whether the position meets their own needs for personal and professional development. If there is a fit between their personal expectations for the position and the employer's description of the job, their needs will match the job. There will be high job survival, high levels of motivation and job satisfaction.

If an incorrect decision is taken on the strength of the interview the results can be expensive, not just from a financial view. If too high or too low a level of expectation has been set for either the applicant or the job, the work experience could fail to match the new employee's expectations. This may result in dissatisfaction and a realization that the job does not suit, lowering morale and productivity for both the employee and their co-workers. If the ultimate outcome results in resignation it will be unsettling for other members of staff and leave a vacancy to be filled.

OTHER SELECTION PROCESSES

Other selection tests can provide a more objective approach to personnel selection. Written and skills tests as well as case studies can be used to test intelligence, aptitude, ability and interest. Performance job simulations such as work sampling create a miniature replica of a job. These, and on-the-job trials provide practical scenarios where applicants are able to demonstrate the degree to which they can do the job. Likewise, the preparation and delivery of a presentation and the provision of portfolios of work also provide tangible evidence in presentation and analytical abilities. Formal assessments such as psychological tests, personality and aptitude tests can also be administered by trained professionals. Referees can also be used to screen or clarify a candidate's suitability to the position.

Induction

The induction programme is the first stage of a number of activities that enhance the development and performance of both the person and the job. It is a very important facet of management as it establishes what is required of the new employee. Induction orientates and introduces the new employee to the organization. It allows the employee to become conversant with the job and how this relates to the information service's programmes and activities. If the employee is new to the organization, the induction process can provide them with insight into the organization's culture.

The induction process should provide background information to the organization; employee benefits; salary schedules; safety; probationary period; time recording and absences; leave conditions; grievance procedures; hours of work; lunch and coffee breaks; and use of facilities. This can also include information visits to other departments within the organization, introductions to all senior officers and a complete overview of special programmes or facilities within the organization. As the new employee begins to be aware of the corporate culture and subcultures they may need some explanation as to why certain things occur and the values that are most prevalent within the organization.

A typical induction programme involves:

First day

- Greet and review employee's work experience, education and training. Discuss their background and interests. They are likely to feel nervous or uneasy at first, so make them feel that the job genuinely needs them and enquire if they have any problems.
- Explain the work to be done – Break it up into tasks and have their job description available for discussion. Explain when, where and how they will be paid and other specific conditions of the position. Introduce them to their co-workers and explain who they report to, and who reports to them.
- Show them the physical layout – This includes the restroom facilities, canteen, locker room, car park. Have their desk or office and supplies organized. Indicate safety hazards and alert them to job standards.
- Explain their role and contribution – Explain the work, goals and objectives of the department, its relationship to the total organization and other departments. Clarify their position in the department, their role and contribution to the bigger picture.
- Arrange guidance and maintain contact – Identify the people to approach to solve work problems. Provide a policy and procedures manual and make sure they are not left alone to fend for themselves.

Second day

- Maintain contact – Check over things from the first day. Encourage them to talk about problems they have encountered. Answer their questions readily, explaining in more detail how their work fits into overall activities. Provide information on things that affect them personally.

Within the first week

- Review and give feedback and further information – Help them to develop a sense of belonging and show interest in their progress. Help them with problems they have met, but avoid criticizing them. Be alert for personal problems that could affect their work performance. Clear up any misunderstanding.

Second week

- Explain rules, norms and values – Discuss the values of the information service and how these affect employees. Listen for dissatisfaction. Counsel them and discuss how emerging issues could be resolved.

End of first month

- Maintain regular contact – Regular contact during the first month should help prevent grievances setting in. Check progress. Correct errors by arranging further instruction, not by pointing up the failures. If they have done a job well, tell them so. Let them know that their efforts are appreciated.

Within first three months

- Review progress regularly – If they have trouble settling down, a transfer to other work might be discussed. If their performance improves, let them know.

Personal development and training

Successful organizations in the knowledge age invest in organizational and individual learning as a means of maintaining and renewing knowledge and keeping ahead of their competitors. They consider training and personal development to be a strategic and ongoing investment; balancing the individual's personal training and development needs that have been identified as part of a performance appraisal system, and those that support the organization's and work group's programmes and activities.

Training and personal development may take the form of on-the-job training, attendance at conferences and seminars, management placement programmes, targeted management and professional courses or further study. Opportunities for internal promotion should also be developed and a reward system put in place to encourage productivity and innovation. These opportunities are also important in creating a highly motivated staff and maintaining morale levels.

Performance management

Performance management is an important part of developing highly motivated individuals and a corporate environment that is creative, productive and happy. It is a day-to-day management task where continuous monitoring, counselling and feedback on performance take place in a positive environment where the bottom line is success for all.

Supplementing this ongoing exercise, the performance interview is an opportunity where parties take time to discuss how to improve the organization, and for the employee to map out how their future work programme and personal development desires will contribute to the organization's success.

The words 'appraisal' and 'performance review' infer some judgment on an individual's performance. Managed constructively, performance monitoring and appraisal systems can lead to discussions on:

- how the supervisor can make the person's job easier (360 degree feedback);
- what needs to change in the organization to make the job easier (productivity);
- what new ideas the organization could implement to make it more successful (innovation);
- how to make the organization a better place to work (motivation); and
- opportunities that can enhance skills, behaviours, physical and emotional well-being of all employees (corporate development).

The interview should also focus on the personal career ambitions and future personal and professional development needs of the individual concerned. This is because improvements in performance cannot take place without adequate skills and knowledge development. They can also be used to develop an inventory of human resources that forms the basis for career planning and skills inventory from an organizational point of view. Counselling when negative activities are identified should be balanced with rewards and recognition that reinforce positive ideas and output.

Staff turnover

Staff turnover can be beneficial and detrimental to the information service, depending on the consequences. On the positive side it allows the opportunity to recruit people with new skills and outlook and can increase the level of flexibility in the type and numbers of employees. This is particularly important in circumstances where the technology, external environments and customer expectations rapidly change. There is often some financial gain in a controlled turnover of employees as this can contain the level of incremental salary creep.

The negatives are associated with the expense in terms of loss of corporate knowledge, finance, time and employee moral. Financial costs are incurred in severance pay, advertising and the recruitment of new personnel, as well as in their orientation and training. There is often an associated downtime in the use of equipment and lost output and productivity until the new person gains the knowledge and skills of the previous incumbent.

Different jobs will experience different turnover rates and the economic climate will also influence the turnover rate. Notwithstanding this, there is an optimum turnover rate. This is the point between having insufficient turnover and having too much. Too slow a turnover rate will result in a staid organization; too high a turnover rate is unsettling and disruptive for those remaining. It is often a symptom that there is a problem within the organization.

At a personal level there are many reasons why people leave organizations. Some of these are voluntary; such as to relocate, to undertake a different career path, to experience a change in a work environment, or to retire. There are also occasions where the person leaves on an involuntary basis. For example, individuals may also be transferred out of an area to meet operational needs, but may still remain employed in another part of the organization. Redundancy and dismissal, both of which need to be managed sensitively, are other reasons for separation.

Separation

REDUNDANCY

This occurs when employees are released from employment because the organization no longer has a need for their services. Redundancy may be voluntary or involuntary. Redundancy may mean that the individual is placed elsewhere in the workforce, or, it may mean total severance. Redundancy can arise through the introduction of new technologies, through business reengineering, a takeover, or downsizing the organization's operations. Depending upon the reason for the redundancy and the individual's abilities, opportunities for retraining or reskilling may be few.

DISMISSAL

This is probably the most distressing method of separation for both the manager and the individual as it may be the culmination of a difficult or emotional situation in terms of behaviour, performance or attitude.

Dismissal should only occur after all attempts to improve or correct the offending aspects have failed. It should be recognized that at some stage, the individual concerned was recruited by the organization for their skills and attributes. Having employed the individual the organization has an obligation to develop the person according to its needs and values. There is also a responsibility for ensuring that every opportunity is provided for an individual to succeed. This includes the provision of adequate communication, counselling, training and supervision. Managers also have a legal and ethical obligation to ensure that the person's case has been heard objectively and fairly before they are dismissed.

Information services should have formalized grievance procedures that are made known and accessible to management and staff. No employee should be dismissed for a first breach of discipline, and no disciplinary action should be taken unless the case has been carefully investigated.

THE EXIT INTERVIEW

Many managers overlook the exit interview as an opportunity to obtain feedback about their management style and the organization from an employee's viewpoint. Progressive organizations use the technique of holding an interview with employees when they leave. This allows them actively to seek out suggestions that will enable them to be a better employer.

Whilst there should be mechanisms in place to provide for continuous feedback, the exit interview is sometimes more effective. Employees who are about to leave may feel more at liberty to make comments in the knowledge that their job is not threatened or that retaliative measures cannot be taken. Open communications should allow employees to bring their concerns to the attention of management at all times. However, some employees may only feel able to discuss matters that have been of concern to themselves or others when the bond between the employee, the manager and the organization is broken. The highlighting of both the positive and negative aspects of the organization should, if taken notice of, make the organization a better place to work. For example the exit interview might highlight inappropriate policies or procedures or ineffective communication channels that were previously unknown to management.

Conclusion

Effective human resource management involves more than developing procedures for annual review or supporting equal opportunity. It is a continuous yet rewarding process. Human resource management focuses on having the best people who can achieve personally and corporately; ensuring that they are given the opportunity to develop their personal and professional competencies to maximize their contribution to their own and the organization's success.

Further reading

Branham, Leigh (2005), *The 7 hidden reasons employees leave: How to recognise the subtle signs and act before it is too late*, New York, NY: Amacom.

Conger, Jay A. and Fulmer, Robert M. (2003), 'Developing your leadership pipeline', *Harvard Business Review*, Dec., pp. 76–84.

Crawford, Tom (2005), *Employer branding*, Aldershot, UK: Ashgate.

Munro, Andrew (2005), *Practical succession management: How to future-proof your organisation*, Aldershot, UK: Ashgate.

5 Knowledge and Information Management

Knowledge and information are important corporate assets that need to be managed strategically for competitive advantage and business outcomes. They are often referred to as intangible assets, assets that are not physical or touchable. However, this is not to imply that they are insubstantial. Knowledge and information concern content rather than the technology itself. They comprise the tacit knowledge in people's heads and the content that is held or transported in storage and communication devices. In the global knowledge economy and society, a lot of this content now resides in systems that can be across companies, governments, national and sectoral boundaries.

The increased availability of information and knowledge, largely brought about through the proliferation of information and communications technology (ICT), has driven economic productivity, structural change and the emergence of more open societies. In this environment, libraries and information services have the dual responsibilities of planning and managing their own corporate intelligence and knowledge and information, as well as facilitating access and disseminating knowledge and information to assist people and organizations in predicting the future, facilitating decision making, for life-long learning and personal development.

Knowledge management will become increasingly critical for blending business processes and social networks to enhance individual capabilities, maximize productivity and drive competitive advantage. Managers in libraries and information centres can play a significant role in creating and building intelligent organizations and communities in this environment. Their abilities to blend processes and networks, unlock corporate or community knowledge, expertise and innovation, and manage these as valuable intangible assets form important components of their role.

This chapter predominantly focuses on managing intelligence, knowledge and information from a corporate perspective rather than from managing stock in a provisioning role. With this in mind the management focus is on maximizing the use of information and knowledge through sharing and enabling corporate and individual knowledge and information, as well as reuse and collaborative techniques.

The essential objectives of the knowledge and information management are to ensure that:

- knowledge and information are recognized and managed as valued and valuable strategic business or community assets that enable good decision making and advantageous outcomes;
- an appropriate range of knowledge and information is provided to meet the core business strategy and objectives of the organization;
- critical knowledge and information is identified, documented, shared and secured;

- knowledge and information is managed, maintained and available in an integrated manner regardless of its source and format; and
- information content, knowledge and information flows and delivery mechanisms are compatible with the business and decision-making processes.

Supporting these are operational processes that result in the information being consistent, relevant, accessible, concise and accurate.

Management oversight – roles and responsibilities

The rapid evolution of the intensely connected global knowledge economy and society means that developing knowledge capabilities is a business and social imperative. In a world where competitive advantage has shifted from machinery and finance to knowledge about customers, dissemination of in-house knowledge and skills, and the ability to make sense of a flood of external information, successful knowledge and information management is dependent on executive management being committed and championing the process. They also need an understanding of the issues and opportunities that knowledge enabling and information sharing present for the organization. In particular how knowledge and information can add business value; whether this is for better decision making, in building social capital and customer relationships, supporting research and development, or for more time-critical risk management. Their role is essential in:

- assisting the organization anticipate its future knowledge and information requirements;
- ensuring that the process is given the required impetus, status and commitment within the organization; and
- guaranteeing that others contribute their time and resources to ensure its success.

This is especially true in the initial stages. Ongoing patronage and oversight of the information planning and management strategies may later be delegated to the information services manager or another senior manager. However, it is imperative that executive management continues to be seen to be supportive and involved in the process. It is also important for the person who later takes over the process to have sufficient authority to override differences and resolve conflicting requirements that may arise from different parts of the organization.

In often being the primary sponsor, the information service manager plays an intrinsic part in the knowledge and information management process. They need to be able to talk the talk of executive management in selling the importance of knowledge and information to the organization; helping them understand the issues and opportunities by using examples that they can relate to and using terminology and language that they can understand.

Consultation regarding the information planning and management processes should be organization-wide and include other stakeholders who may either contribute to, or need, information. The processes should emphasize the importance of existing and potential intra- and inter-organizational interactions, as well as the touch points where value can be added. Cross-functional collaboration and sharing of knowledge and information should be encouraged in the planning process as well as in the outcome.

As communication, knowledge enabling and information sharing are very personal issues, individuals are the bastion of the knowledge and information space. Basic information skills and ICT skill proficiencies are increasingly being recognized as an essential third set of skills alongside literacy and numeracy for everyone. Knowledge management workers also need special skills to identify and share their knowledge sources as well as unlock the key to ensure that knowledge and information is shared amongst others. This is no mean feat and Skyrme (1998) has identified the knowledge and skills required of knowledge management workers as follows:

- technical skills – information (resources) management, information technology skills;
- business knowledge – industry, markets, customers, competitors, and general business context;
- interpersonal skills – networking, listening, interpreting, challenging, teamwork, communication;
- management skills – motivating, coaching, facilitating, influencing;
- company/organization knowledge – knowledge of procedures and culture; and
- personnel characteristics – integrity, confidence, openness, trust, supportive, honesty, willingness to learn.

Managing knowledge and information as a corporate good

THE CORPORATE VALUE OF KNOWLEDGE AND INFORMATION

As ICT makes it easier to access, diffuse, communicate and manipulate large quantities of information and knowledge, it dramatically increases the usefulness and accessibility of information and knowledge as corporate goods, as well as the overall stock. The real corporate value of knowledge and information is found in the contribution and abilities to:

- plan strategically;
- facilitate consistent and rapid decision making;
- support and improve policy making;
- enable effective and efficient utilization of resources;
- identify and manage risk;
- encourage and capitalize on research and development;
- utilize resources better and identify waste or inappropriate use;
- monitor quality and performance;
- meet legislative and regulatory requirements;
- know what competitors are doing;
- understand the mix of products and services their customers need;
- protect the interests of the organization and the rights of employees and customers;
- provide evidence of business transactions and activities in the case of litigation; and
- evaluate and deliver increased productivity.

These are some of the touch points where value can be added through the astute and efficient use of knowledge and information.

Parker et al. (2005) summarize other benefits that can be attributed to well-planned knowledge management (KM) that include:

- KM encourages the free flow of ideas, which fosters insight and innovation and creates new value through new products or services;
- KM improves customer service and efficiency by streamlining response time;
- KM enhances employee retention rates by recognizing the value of employees' knowledge and rewarding them for it;
- KM streamlines operations and reduces costs by eliminating redundant or unnecessary processes and promoting reuse;
- KM facilitates better, more informed decisions by reducing uncertainty;
- KM contributes to the intellectual capital of the organization;
- KM boosts revenues and enhances the current value of existing products by getting products and services to market faster; and
- KM leads to greater productivity by increasing speed of response.

MANAGEMENT PRINCIPLES

As competitive tools in the knowledge age, knowledge and information are a corporate rather than an individual or work unit good or resource. The corporate good philosophy lessens duplication, empowers individuals, opens up the flow of knowledge and information and ensures that decisions are based on the same knowledge and information. Quality information is available in real time throughout the organization. It is not a privilege of any group or individual.

Using the corporate good philosophy, information and its supporting technologies should be designed and managed so that:

- relevant knowledge and information can be easily identified and retrieved by those who need it, when they need it, whilst preserving privacy and commercial confidentiality;
- appropriate security measures are in place;
- the diverse knowledge and information resources and systems within the organization are accessible in a seamless and consistent way; and
- being mindful of the changing environment, the knowledge and information architecture is flexible to withstand organizational restructures and changes to business direction.

KNOWLEDGE AND INFORMATION FOR DECISION-MAKING ACTIVITIES

The knowledge and information required to make decisions differs in the degree of detail and comprehensiveness at different levels in the organization.

Executive management

Executive management focus on issues related to positioning the organization within the external environment. Most of their knowledge and information comes from external sources such as information about new markets, competitors, business trends, new technologies, or new or impending changes to legislation that may affect the business strategy.

Whilst some management information relates to internal performance and strategic planning and is sourced internally; a large proportion of knowledge and information is obtained verbally from external sources, either in meetings, presentations or during conversations with their peers. Other information is summarized in reports, electronic mail messages and executive information systems. Due to constraints on their time, executive management is only interested in a highly summarized view, frequently presented on a single sheet of paper. They often employ research or executive assistants to provide these summaries for them.

Management levels	Information requirements	Organizational decision making
Executive management	External knowledge and information to position the organization strategically, competitive analysis, external factors	Strategic business direction
	Information to assist planning, internal coordination, resource management, budget control, strategic problem solving	Organizational-wide operational objectives
Mid-level management	Information for planning, implementing, managing and evaluating resources and programmes, service performance, and project scheduling.	Programme management
	Information for routine decision making, scheduling activities and problem solving within groups	Activity management
Line management and team leaders	Information for decision making in service delivery and individual projects	Task management

Figure 5.1 Information needs and decision-making activities of various levels of management

Mid-level management

Mid-level management need information from both external and internal sources. They require knowledge and information for decision making on organizational-wide resource utilisation and budget control, as well as the coordination of service delivery programmes and work unit outputs.

Mid-level managers are usually interested in evaluating the performance of the work units and assessing the progress of major projects. Data is gathered from in-house sources relating to the allocation of human, financial and technological resources, budgeting and performance measures. It is combined with other knowledge and information from external sources. This is used for evaluative and comparative purposes to measure performance, to solve problems and to prepare reports for executive management. This information may be used to influence strategic planning and policy-setting processes at the executive level.

At this level of management, external information is significantly different in source and character from internal information or that received by executive management. It often comprises telephone conversations, hearsay and overheard snatches of conversations; the reliability and relevance of which should be determined before using it for important decisions.

Line management

Line managers and team leaders require knowledge and information for routine decisions relating to the scheduling of activities, accounting for the use of resources, as well as for problem solving.

They obtain nearly all of their information in-house. They receive instructions from mid-level management and gather data relating to individual and group or team activities at a transactional level. They have to make operational decisions related to day-to-day matters or specific activities such as rostering of staff based upon policies and operational requirements.

Service delivery teams

People working at the front counter or in the field require information for decision making in service delivery. This includes knowledge and information about the customers, the customers' history and their specific service requirements. They also need access to knowledge and information about the parent organization, the services and products that it offers, customer service policies and procedures. This is so that they can inform customers of the products or services offered by the organization, answer the customers' questions quickly and provide a better customer service.

Customers

The information needs of the parent organization's employees (the internal customers) should be distinguished from the information needs of the parent organization's clients. For example, the information services of a police service will need to support the police officers and civilian staff (the internal customers) in their operational roles in tracking and minimizing crime, maintaining security and presenting evidence relating to alleged offenders. The information needs of the clients of the police service itself (e.g. victims of crime, alleged offenders, and other members of the community) will be very different. Their information needs will relate more to their rights and responsibilities. The police service may also have other clients such as insurance companies, universities or crime research bureaus who may want to purchase or have access to statistical information relating to incidences such as break-ins or robbery in the form of information products.

Customers need information to help them make a decision about their choice of service or product. They may already have knowledge and information about the competitors' products and services and require information to allow for comparisons in making their choice. Customers and other stakeholders will also have legal access to any personal information that is held by the organization under privacy or data protection and freedom of information legislation.

Other stakeholders

Stakeholders such as suppliers have information requirements for ordering and logistical purposes. Some may utilize electronic commerce for the ordering, supply and payment of goods and services. Finance and insurance companies also require information returns. There are also legislative and regulatory requirements for information to be lodged with government agencies. These include industrial relations agencies, corporate and securities commissions, revenue collection and taxation agencies. Increasingly, this information is provided or lodged electronically.

Managing knowledge and information as a social and economic good

In a wider context, knowledge and information enable communities and societies to develop better economic relationships through productivity improvements, trade, investment and the exchange of information, knowledge and skills. Content itself is an emerging business opportunity, especially where it is delivered for information and entertainment to mobile devices. Innovation through knowledge is also a key driver of wealth creation.

From a societal viewpoint, individual access to information, skills and knowledge is an important component of life-long learning, day-to-day living and democracy. The public collections of cultural and heritage materials can lead to a more enriched life and an understanding of the past, the present and the future. Community learning and information services also play an important role in increasing knowledge and skills, greater community cohesiveness and enhanced community development.

Information life cycle

Information resources have a life cycle similar to that of other resources. The life cycle comprises six phases: planning, acquisition, maintenance, exploitation, evaluation and review, and retirement. The information service has a responsibility for ensuring that all information, regardless of source or format, is subject to a managed life cycle.

Information is planned, acquired, maintained and exploited through many outlets and resources. Library holdings, office automation systems, electronic and paper records and files, inter- and intra-organizational information systems and databases need to be considered in the management and planning processes. These processes are also applicable to all formats, e.g. sound, image (graphic, pictorial, moving), text, data, or multimedia.

Knowledge and information are supported by ICT applications which capture, store, organize, secure, process, track, retrieve, present, transmit or distribute information. Whilst the processes to be outlined will concentrate on the knowledge and information as content, they should not take place in isolation from these ICT applications and infrastructures.

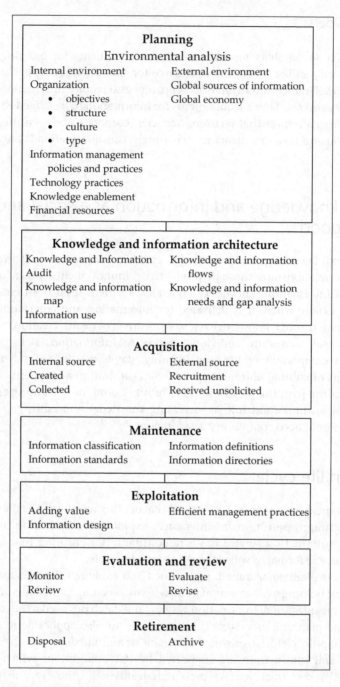

Figure 5.2   The information life cycle

Planning

Knowledge and information planning is used to:

- guide the acquisition and redundancy of information;
- support the knowledge and information flows;
- facilitate the integration and sharing of knowledge and information; and
- provide a proactive basis for the meeting of the organization's business and information needs as well as those of its clients and other stakeholders.

ENVIRONMENTAL ANALYSIS

The first step is the environmental analysis that identifies drivers in the external environment as well as the organization's business needs, corporate culture and future direction. The culture has a potent influence on how knowledge and information is used and valued within organizations. For example, the level and abundance of knowledge and information flows and the extent of knowledge and information sharing influences and is influenced by the effectiveness of team work, and the levels of trust and confidence between team members.

KNOWLEDGE AND INFORMATION ARCHITECTURE

The knowledge and information architecture and its supporting technology architecture, classification scheme, language control and index should be designed to be used across work units and be flexible enough to withstand organizational restructures and changes to business direction. For accountability purposes, it should also be capable of tracking ownership of business decisions and records over time. The knowledge and information architecture is the vehicle for determining organizational knowledge and information needs. It shows how the activities and the knowledge and information that the activities require can be grouped and sequenced, allowing the information service to plan the knowledge and information and its supporting technology architecture around the business objectives of the parent organization.

In supporting the mission and objectives of the organization, and underlying knowledge and information needed for the organization to carry out its business, the knowledge and information architecture:

- models how knowledge and information is acquired, managed and stored within the organization (knowledge and information audit);
- graphically displays the relationships between sources, suppliers and users of the knowledge and information (knowledge and information map);
- analyses how knowledge and information is used internally by the employees of the parent organization, its clients and other stakeholders (knowledge and information use);
- looks at communications, interrelationships and movement of knowledge and information throughout the organization, and, with clients and other stakeholders (knowledge and information flows); and
- brings these together with the needs of the organization, customers and other stakeholders to analyse shortfalls in the knowledge and information architecture (knowledge and information needs and gap analysis).

Knowledge and information audit

The first stage of the knowledge and information audit is to identify all the current knowledge and information resources and how these are acquired or created. This includes the formal and informal records of the organization; information in databases and inter-organizational systems such as electronic commerce and electronic mail systems; the printed and electronic holdings in the library, divisional and individual collections; information that can be accessed through external databases; multimedia and information in other formats, information held in office automation systems; and, finally, knowledge critical to the business of the organization that is stored in the minds of individuals.

The next stage identifies those people or systems that store, manage or add value to the information, as well as:

- the cost of the management overheads (including maintenance and storage);
- the knowledge and information's value and use within the organization;
- the appropriateness of the format and storage devices;
- the technical and other means of accessing the information;
- the availability of knowledge and information throughout the organization, to clients and to other external parties who may wish to access and make use of the knowledge and information;
- whether the management of the technology is appropriate and linked to the management of the knowledge and information;
- statements of policy or objectives for acquiring, using and discarding information; and
- the appropriateness of procedural manuals or instructions for processing or distributing information.

Knowledge and information map

The knowledge and information map identifies those who use the knowledge and information, mapping the users against those who manage, input, process and store it.

The knowledge and information map is scalable. That is, it can be applied or developed:

- with details of just the major customer groups; or
- by identifying individuals as customers.

It can be used to map different levels of knowledge and information use with key personnel (the internal customers), clients and other external stakeholders. The level of detail should be chosen according to the organization's objectives and business needs.

Knowledge and information use

The next stage is to analyse how knowledge and information is used within the organization, by its clients and the other external stakeholders within the boundary chosen. It should consider what and how knowledge and information is used, for example:

- customer profiles to enhance service delivery or sell new products or services to existing customers;

- financial records to monitor the level of financial expenditure;
- scientific or technical knowledge and information for research and product development;
- existing information held in libraries or in databases that is combined or made available in a different format to create a value-added information product; or
- statistics and other management information to measure productivity or efficiency.

Knowledge and information flows

The knowledge and information flow analysis traces the flow of knowledge and information between people and groups within the organization (the internal customers), and, between the organization, its clients and other external stakeholders. The objective is to determine that the correct knowledge and information is flowing to the right areas and that those who need access to knowledge and information are able to receive it. The knowledge and information flow analysis may also highlight opportunities for improved knowledge and information performance. For example it can expose:

- systems that do not add value to the business strategy;
- activities that are not linked with others in electronic information chains necessitating the rekeying of information;
- activities that create information that is not useful;
- knowledge and information that could also be used elsewhere for better decision making or to support others' activities within the organization;
- undocumented decision processes; or
- ill-defined or inconsistent business processes.

Knowledge and information gap analysis

This exercise identifies the shortfalls between the available knowledge and information and the critical knowledge and information that are required. The critical knowledge and information needs of the internal customers, the organization's clients and other external stakeholders should also be matched against knowledge and information availability. The knowledge and information gap analysis should consider both current and future needs.

Business systems planning can be used for the knowledge and information gap analysis. This is a two-phase process, the first phase requiring the identification of the business processes, defining information classes, the analysis of systems and getting the executive's, employees', clients' and external stakeholders' perspective. It should be focused on business processes and customer needs. The second phase involves setting priorities for the organization in terms of its future development and identifying the knowledge and information requirements that will arise from this.

A second methodology that can be used to identify shortfalls in knowledge and information is critical success factors. This methodology identifies the critical things within an organization that must be done and the knowledge and information required to do them. These can be defined through a series of interviews within the organization and with stakeholders.

Once this has been determined, the findings should also be related to how the knowledge and information can be used to achieve the organization's objectives, customers' and stakeholders' needs, together with the knowledge and information needed to monitor performance in the critical areas.

Acquisition

The acquisition phase involves strategies to capture, collect or purchase knowledge and information. There are many mechanisms through which knowledge and information are acquired; for example:

- created internally;
- captured from an external source such as in electronic messaging services;
- acquired by recruiting a person with specific knowledge;
- received unsolicited such as external correspondence; or
- collected as part of case management such as medical records.

In some government departments and libraries, electronic data and information and printed materials are obtained through a legal requirement to deposit certain material. Information is also purchased in the form of databases, subscriptions to journals and electronic information services, and the commissioning of reports. Information may be acquired in a variety of formats such as electronic mail, published and unpublished reports, spatial information in geographic information systems, video and satellite imagery.

To ensure its accuracy and reliability, information needs to be captured as close as possible to the original source of the information. The capture and use of some information types and formats of information may need specialized technology. For example, moving imagery and large volumes of spatial information require high broadband capacity to manage the transfer and use of the information.

For accountability purposes, the information may need to be registered on receipt or creation. Examples of formal registration processes are:

- entering details of the item in an asset or acquisition register;
- registering a file or document upon its creation or receipt; or
- logging the transaction in a system.

Copyright and sometimes moral rights may also need to be cleared for the use and reproduction of the information. The information service may have to identify the copyright owner and obtain their permission for a specific use of the information. In some cases, payment to the copyright holder may be required in return for the right to use the information or copyright work.

Maintenance

To be totally effective, knowledge and information should be managed, maintained and secured as a shared corporate resource for the benefit of the entire organization. Consistency and connectivity are important; the underlying principle is that it can be cost-effectively shared and used by others for a variety of purposes.

The artificial boundaries that occur by reason of media or format, location or work unit ownership should be removed. They should still be managed and made accessible in a consistent way, with standard forms of identification and retrieval procedures.

Vital or valuable information that is to be retained within the organization not only needs to be secured, it also needs to be preserved. In the case of electronic information, this includes additional responsibility for managing different electronic versions of the same information, for example, by managing the version control of information contained in reports, and, by ensuring that all information is kept in a form that can be read by the software and hardware in current use. As new technology or versions of software are introduced, the information on disks must be upgraded so that the information can be used at a later date. This particularly applies to significant documents or reports that have been produced on word processing or desktop publishing systems and that require continuous use.

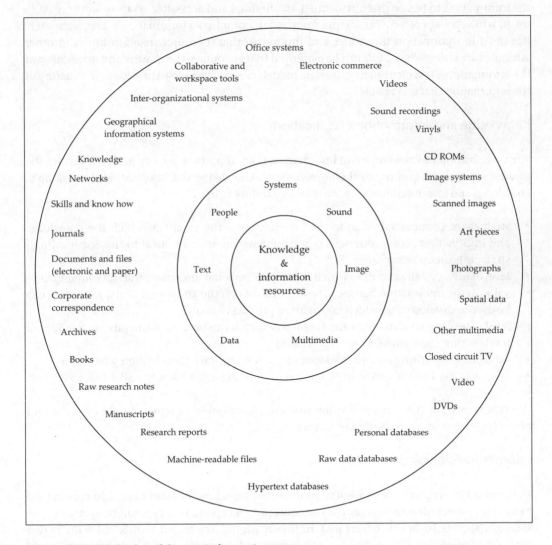

Figure 5.3 Examples of diverse information resources

Storage requirements in electronic and physical forms may be assessed according to the:

- physical characteristics of the information;
- business objectives and client needs of the parent organization;
- source and level of risk; and
- required level of security.

Security classifications may need to be assigned to different types of information or its content in order to ensure that only authorized persons have access.

The use of classification schemes, standards, definitions and directories assist in enabling the information to be consistently defined, maintained and accessible by those authorized to use it, whilst being protected from unauthorized use or misuse. Information can be accurately described in information directories and indexes so that its source, relationships and other attributes are known. Standards can be employed that encourage the sharing and integration of the information. Data dictionaries and data models can also be used to provide a clear picture of the information that is available.

Knowledge and information classification

The classification of knowledge and information is an important activity in that it defines the parameters of access and use of the organization's knowledge and information. For example, knowledge and information may be classified according to its:

- strategic or commercial value to the organization – the extent to which the knowledge and information is of a commercial-in-confidence nature or critical to the organization's strategic business advantage;
- level of privacy – the extent to which it contains personal information about individuals;
- value in the information market – the extent to which the knowledge and information can be used to develop value added information products for sale;
- level of security type and use – the extent to which it can be used in the various activities or levels within the organization or externally;
- subject area – existing records management index or library classification scheme; or
- format or source – the extent to which it is sourced externally or internally, and, its format.

Where possible, knowledge and information classification schemes should be consistent across the organization, regardless of format.

Information standards

To maintain its accuracy and currency, information should be collected once, and then reused to meet all information requirements. The collection or capture point should be as close to the source as possible. In order to ensure that the information can be reused, transferred or integrated with other knowledge and information, the capture and management of the information should be according to predetermined standards.

The standards should be set by the organization. The choice of standard should be based on a business case and will depend upon:

- the extent to which the information is to be integrated with external information or used by external stakeholders; and
- efficiency and effectiveness.

The use of standards must be cost effective. Information should not be maintained at a higher level standard that is necessary. However, future needs and environments must also be considered when deciding on standards. Standards should be chosen to add value to the use and management of information rather than create an unnecessary level of workload or bureaucracy. Information should not be over processed for the sake of conforming to national or international standards if this is not warranted by the business case or customers' needs. The purpose of adopting information standards is to maintain the degree of consistency and connectivity that enables information to be shared. For example:

- information used externally by clients or external stakeholders will need to be captured, maintained and transferred according to a national or international standard;
- information used internally across the organization should be captured, maintained and transferred according to an agreed standard within the organization; and
- specific information that is captured and maintained to support a single programme or activity should also conform to organizational standards.

Globalization and the increase in inter-organizational sharing of information means that national or international standards will increasingly be used; what is more likely to vary is the level of adoption of the standards.

Information definitions

Information definitions provide information, or meta data, about the information itself. Their purpose is to increase the understanding about the information and its relevance to a particular use. They may provide information about the quality, rules of use, source, accuracy, currency, projection type or scale, format, coverage in terms of geographical area or timescale etc. Information definitions may be created as part of a data dictionary in a database administration system.

Knowledge and information directories

Knowledge and information directories identify what knowledge and information exists and where it may be found. Library catalogues and other tools that identify sources of information are examples of information directories. As a location tool, they contain information about source, access and use constraints, purpose, availability, point of contact for further information, cross-references and other appropriate information found in the information definition.

Data definitions make up a large proportion of an entry in an information directory. Initially, the knowledge and information directory can be produced through the knowledge and information audit and mapping processes as these identify what knowledge and information is available and its source. To be of long-term use the meta data must be continually updated.

To assist users, the knowledge and information directory should be designed so that it is searchable on a number of fields. It should be easy to use, convenient to access and available in an appropriate format.

Exploitation

The exploitation phase provides the return on investment for the information service and the corporate knowledge and information resource. Unless the information service exploits its information to its fullest extent, the rest of the efforts in planning, acquisition and maintenance will be under utilized.

ADDING VALUE

The exploitation phase involves being proactive about doing more with the organization's knowledge and information resource, particularly at the touch points where value can be added. It entails looking at strategies and activities for designing and adding value to the original knowledge and information to meet new market needs or in identifying new uses for the existing information. This may include the combining or overlaying of information in a system, considering different delivery media mechanisms and formats, or in presenting the information in a different way.

The exploitation phase also requires consideration of the means of use of the knowledge and information as well as accessibility, dissemination, distribution and delivery mechanisms. Customer requirements to access information ought to be met whilst protecting copyright, privacy and confidentiality. The background, skills, knowledge and perspective of the customers will influence their ability to use the information. The customer may also have a particular preference for information in a certain format or language, or, may wish to use a particular distribution method such as facsimile or electronic mail. Further information on channel management and customer needs can also be found in later chapters such as Chapter 31, Ensuring Service Quality.

The physical environment in which the information is to be used can influence the method and format in which the information is distributed. For example, information may be required to be updated continuously or in batch mode at a remote site; or individuals may work in all weathers and climates and require information in a format that is durable in inclement weather.

Information and its supporting technologies should be designed so that relevant information can be identified, retrieved, manipulated and made available to appropriate individuals when and where they require it. This is where value can be added and the strategic business advantage lies. As Bertrot et al. (2004) identifies: 'network-based services and resources offered by libraries today, including digital references, digital collections, online databases, e-journals, and e-books, enable libraries to operate in an anytime/anywhere mode, allowing patrons with internet access to access content, services, and resources 365 days a year, 24 hours a day.'

Information should be well defined. There should be a standard or corporate classification scheme, language control and index. These should be chosen to fit the business needs of the organization. They should also be devised by the information service in consultation with users, and maintained to reflect changing business needs. Information services staff and other employees within the parent organization should be educated about the use of the corporate classification scheme, language control and index. Everyone should be able to base their decision making on the same knowledge and information and employees should only need to check one source. The intention is to increase customer satisfaction; as information can be obtained more readily and faster, the requirement for analysis time is shortened and so the decision can be made more quickly.

INFORMATION DESIGN

Information and its supporting technologies should be designed to complement communication flows and information needs. In most traditional organizations, information flows upwards and commands are passed downwards. The information is prone to distortion and manipulation. Decentralized, highly integrated informal organizations require technology architectures that enhance information flows and extend across work group boundaries visibly and simultaneously.

Teams and groups require networks, tools, electronic mail and messaging facilities in order that they all receive the same information at the same time. They also make greater use of collaborative processing and shared work space applications that support more flexible work patterns and teamwork. Not only is hard information required, teams and groups rely upon more qualitative information in both external information and internal information such as members' knowledge experiences, views, successes and problems. Knowledge repositories, expertise access tools, discussion technologies, knowledge representation, expert systems, e-learning applications, synchronous interaction tools, and data warehouse and data mining tools are quoted by Parker et al. (2005, p. 181) as being sources of qualitative information for decision making.

Information and its supporting technologies can also be designed to overcome distance and time barriers. People from diverse geographic locations and those whose personal situations require them to work from home or during non-traditional hours can work together in the same team to create a boundary-less organization with the use of the right technology and human resource management policies.

Information and its supporting technologies should be designed to be:

- accessible – information should be able to be accessed easily and quickly at the right time and in the right place by the appropriate people. Access should be seamless, regardless of source or format, with a choice of delivery channels. It should take into consideration any necessary security and privacy considerations;
- comprehensive – information should be useful, related to need and appropriate to the level of the decision-maker. There is a difference between providing information that is comprehensive enough to satisfy information needs and information overload. Too much information can be as problematic as too little information;
- accurate – information should be accurate, complete, reliable and current;
- appropriate – information content, information flows and delivery mechanisms should be appropriate to the business processes, decision making and information needs of management, employees, customers and other stakeholders. Irrelevant information is costly in terms of capture, storage and use. Information should also be presented in a manner that is meaningful and best fits the skills and competencies of the user;
- timely – the information should be continually kept up to date; although in some cases, historical data is required;
- clear – information should be free from ambiguity. The source and purpose for use should be immediately obvious to the individual so that they can make informed choices as to the usefulness of the information;
- flexible – the systems and information content should be designed to be flexible to allow for growth and change within the parent organizations and tailored to suit different service delivery channels. It should also allow a variety of users to navigate through the system(s) to locate the required information;

- verifiable – the information content should be capable of being verified in terms of source, accuracy and authenticity;
- free from bias – the information content should not be entered, modified or displayed in such a way as to influence the user's course of action;
- consistent – data definitions and terminology should be consistent across the organization regardless of format, storage device or location; and
- compliant – where international or national information or technology standards are used to support the parent organization's objectives and business strategy, all information and its supporting technologies within the organization should be according to the chosen standard.

MANAGEMENT PRACTICES

Inefficient information management practices should be avoided as they can be costly in terms of time, money and lost business opportunities. Inefficient practices include:

- collecting and storing information when it is no longer used;
- disseminating information too widely (information overload);
- not making information accessible to potential users; or
- duplicating information across the organization.

Evaluation and review

The desired outcomes in managing knowledge and information are that:

- appropriate knowledge and information is available to meet the business needs of the organization and the information needs of clients and stakeholders;
- information flows and delivery mechanisms ensure that knowledge and information is made available when and where users need it;
- the knowledge and information needs are understood, with the result that information is available to users in a relevant and meaningful form;
- information is appropriately secured in terms of accessibility, integrity and confidentiality;
- information is consistently defined across the organization;
- information is accurate and complete, including there being a complete, reliable and accurate documentation of the organization's business activities and transactions (including accounting and finance);
- all legal, evidential and accountability requirements are met; and
- information is constantly reviewed to avoid redundancy and to evaluate its appropriateness to the organization's business needs.

Efficiency and effectiveness measures should be developed to measure the above and ensure that the planning and management processes are meeting the organization's objectives and the information needs of the internal customers, the organization's clients and stakeholders.

Retirement

The retirement phase involves decisions about information that has been identified as redundant. Information becomes redundant when it is superfluous to requirements, outdated or inactive. Not all information reaches a redundant stage. A significant proportion of information that exists in live information systems is continually updated, although the information systems can become redundant if they no longer fit the purpose, objectives or business needs of the organization.

The retirement phase requires consideration of if, how and when the information may be disposed. Information should not be kept beyond its useful life as this leads to unnecessary and inefficient use of storage space, equipment, staff and resources. Not all information can be destroyed. Legislative and regulatory considerations require certain corporate information to be kept for a minimum period of time. Some information may also be of archival value. Vital or valuable information may be identified and be made subject to corporate retention and disposal schedules.

Information should be retained, removed or destroyed in accordance with authorized processes. If the information is to be removed off site or off line, such as to an archive facility, the security and ease of retrievability should be considered. Information should be deleted from hard and floppy disks before either the computer or disk is disposed of. Disks should also be physically destroyed to avoid information being retrieved. If printed information is to be destroyed, it should be burnt, pulped or shredded. It ought to not be disposed of through normal refuse disposal facilities.

Conclusion

Knowledge and information management is now gaining the prominence and awareness that it deserves. Organizations are recognizing the true corporate value of knowledge and information as a resource critical to survival and success in the global knowledge economy and society. Whilst the life cycle of knowledge and information is akin to the planning and management processes of other resources, each has quite distinct phases that require different techniques. By systematically managing each stage of the life cycle in a manner that enables knowledge and information to be shared, valuable and essential knowledge and information will be available when and where required.

References

Bertrot, J.C. et al. (2004), 'Capture usage with e-metrics', *Library Journal*, available at www.libraryjournal.com/article/CA411564?display=FeaturesNews&industry.

Parker, Kevin R. et al. (2005), 'Libraries as knowledge management centres', *Library Management*, vol. 26, no. 4/5, pp. 176–189.

Skyrme, D. (1998), *Knowledge management – A fad or a ticket to ride*, www.skyrme.com

Further reading

Broadbent, Marianne and Kitzis, Ellen S. (2005), *The new CIO leader: Setting the agenda and delivering results*, Boston, MA: Harvard Business School.

Brown, David F. et al. (1998), 'Measuring intellectual capital: A knowledge enhancement strategy', *Accountability and Performance*, vol. 4, no. 2, pp. 79–89.

Davenport, Thomas H. (2005), *Thinking for living: How to get better performance and results from knowledge workers*, Boston, MA: Harvard Business School.

Leveraging corporate knowledge, (2004), ed. Edward Truch, Aldershot, UK: Ashgate.

Megill, Kenneth A. (1997), *Corporate memory: Information management in the electronic age*, East Grinstead, UK: Bowker-Saur.

Nair, Keshavan (1998), 'Leading knowledge-based businesses', *Executive Excellence*, vol. 15, no. 9, Sept., pp. 6–7.

Orna, Elizabeth (2004), *Information strategy in practice*, Aldershot, UK: Gower.

Orna, Elizabeth (2005), *Making knowledge visible: Communicating knowledge through information products*, Aldershot, UK: Gower.

Senge, P.M. (1990), *The fifth discipline: The art and practice of the learning organization*, New York, NY: Century Business.

Sveiby, K.E. (1998), *The new organizational wealth*, San Francisco, CA: Berrett-Koehler.

Vincere, Albert A. (2000), 'Ten observations on e-learning and leadership development', *Human Resource Planning*, vol. 23, no. 4, pp. 34–46.

Wiggins, Bob (2000), *Effective document management: Unlocking corporate knowledge*, Aldershot, UK: Ashgate.

6 Technology and Strategic Asset Management

Strategic assets comprise tangible belongings such as plant, machinery and equipment, including information and communications technology (ICT) infrastructure, software and equipment, real estate and buildings, motor vehicles and cultural assets, as well as intangible assets such as branding, intellectual property and know-how, knowledge and information. This chapter concentrates on planning and managing ICT with consideration for the other tangible assets described above. As ICT is subject to rapid change the operational management of specific technologies has not been addressed.

ICT business applications in a corporate world support business growth, lower costs and increase the quality and personalization of customer quality services. ICT applications in a consumer world enable the customer to receive their choice of information in a combination of formats, voice, image and data through the multiple delivery channels and access channels.

ICT infrastructure enables the transport of knowledge, data and information in many different formats and media to support strategic corporate intelligence capability and the sharing of knowledge, intelligence and information between internal and external systems and stakeholders. It includes mobile and wireless technologies, networks, e-commerce systems, artificial intelligence, intranets, extranets, the Internet, web services, portals, back-end, office, client and supplier systems and their subsequent replacement infrastructure.

ICT equipment includes desktop, portable devices as well as servers and other program and storage devices and is the end device for the delivery of ICT applications. Supporting the ICT infrastructure and equipment are security features to ensure accessibility, confidentiality and integrity, and methods, protocols and standards that enable rather than enforce the business strategy.

The planning and management of strategic assets, including ICT should be undertaken with the view to:

- maximize the return on investment for the asset;
- utilize the asset as a business tool to create the advantageous edge;
- enhance competitiveness and improve customer relationships and service delivery;
- deliver positive, tangible results and outcomes;
- provide a point of differentiation in the market place; and
- reduce future resource requirements by prolonging the asset's life or strengthening its disposal value.

Management oversight – roles and responsibilities

As with knowledge and information planning, information services have the dual responsibility of adding value to business policy and strategy, planning and managing all corporate ICT, providing an efficient and flexible infrastructure, and finding competitive opportunities for technical innovation for the whole organization on an enterprise-wide basis, as well as for their own internal operations.

ICT is a critical business asset, the application of which offers both considerable opportunities and immense challenges in further developing business capacity and capability. The importance of its application is such that it is a driving force in which senior and executive management need to take a leadership role and be actively engaged; determining and championing the strategic technology direction and management of all ICT assets. This does not require a strong technical background; rather assuming a strategic direction-setting role and business-focused understanding, ownership, responsibility and accountability for the technology-based assets and outcomes that can be delivered: outcomes that will result in business value and transformation; delivering quality customer services, global competitiveness and enterprise-wide connectiveness in internal operations.

As a leader of business strategy and fusion, the information services manager must chart the way forward for ICT applications, infrastructure and equipment in a manner that delivers value to all, enhances the business capability and capacity, and customer service proposition to a degree that puts the organization's credibility and competitive position ahead of others. They have the responsibility for clearly understanding and promoting ways in which ICT as a strategic business asset can add agility and business value to the whole enterprise; lowering costs, integrating the business value chain, assisting the delivery of quality information and services, refining processes, ensuring security and finding opportunities for new ICT applications that can differentiate the organization's business from others. They should be able to canvass and explain technology alternatives in understandable terms to others; as well as advise on sourcing strategies.

Whilst the information services manager has a focus on the business application of technology, they also need strong people management skills for their immediate operations and for future positioning. New technologies will bring the requirement for new skills and know-how in their own staff and users. In having a holistic view of the organization, the information services manager is in the unique position of blending the skills, knowledge, processes, capabilities and relationships of people in their use and application of ICT across the whole organization. They should also continually evaluate the capabilities and use of ICT by their own staff as well as users, in terms of meeting the business requirements including business intelligence applications and process integration, as well as training requirements and supporting customer relationships.

The information services manager will also need to build alliances with ICT vendors to take advantage of new developments in products and applications. With this in mind they will spend increased time on building relationships with people outside of the organization in order to influence wider stakeholder relationships and organizational effectiveness in its external environment.

Effective planning requires both users and information services managers having a clear vision and objectives of when and what is to be achieved. Many projects fail because of unrealistic expectations or inadequately scoped requirements and specifications. Users should look for integrated service offerings that have an holistic approach to business needs, and also be objective in determining the need for additional training and business process reengineering to take full advantage of the technology implementation. There should be a clear and concise statement of requirements that is mutually agreed by all parties and strongly aligned to the business requirements and outcomes of the strategic plan.

The value of information and communications technology

Information and communications technology is intricately linked to core business processes and outcomes. Up to 50% of organizational capital spend can be on ICT. By themselves ICT and other assets do not provide a competitive advantage; they have a value that is in accordance with what the last bidder is prepared to pay. Technology today is cheaper, more accessible and ubiquitous, but this should not lead to complacency. It is the way that they are planned, managed and put to use that creates the real value and gain for the organization. They can either be smart investments or expensive headaches. Properly planned and designed ICT enables knowledge and innovation to be central to the organization's capacities to model future scenarios, add value, discover new opportunities and act quickly on intelligence from internal and external systems.

ICT often requires a substantial financial investment with a short pay-back period before the next business-led application is needed. There is an art to keeping the ICT investment finally balanced between seeking business opportunities at the leading edge of technology where the risk may be high, and, maintaining cost-effective solutions without being technology led.

The choice of the ICT platform can commit the organization to a technology direction that will be built upon over a number of years. The information services manager and senior management must have sufficient confidence in the chosen strategy that it will not only bring competitive advantage through the delivery of information, but that it is flexible enough to cope with changes in the environment, mergers and acquisitions, and to sustain the competitive advantage in the long term.

Managed in a clever way, ICT can reduce inventory levels and make other resources more efficient, free up capital for use on other activities, provide real-time visibility and control, and improve internal operational efficiencies. ICT can also be a source of accomplishment and innovation; offering differentiation and improvements in customer relationships and service, meeting individual client needs, reducing time to market and increasing the return on investment.

Information and communications technology management life cycle

As with knowledge and information, ICT and other strategic assets have a life cycle that includes planning, acquisition, maintenance, exploitation, evaluation and review and retirement. To assist in the management of ICT through these life cycles, best-practice methodologies have been developed. Two of the most common are the IT Infrastructure Library (ITIL)[1] which identifies best practice in regards to managing IT service levels, the how you do it, and, the Control Objectives for Information and related Technology (COBIT)[2] that covers what to do.

---

1   ITIL was developed by the Central Computer and Telecommunications Agency of the UK Government (CCTA), in accordance with the British Standard BS15000 for IT Services Management.
2   COBIT is issued by IT Governance Institute.

In focusing on identifying best practice, ITIL focuses on planning to implement service management, service support, service delivery, security management, application management, ICT infrastructure management and the business perspective. In comparison, COBIT is strong on controls and metrics; breaking ICT down into a set of thirty-four processes in four domains; planning and organization, acquisition and implementation, delivery and support, and monitoring.

Planning

To gain maximum benefit from the investment decisions, planning for strategic assets, including ICT entails:

- aligning and integrating with the business strategy and business processes that are being supported to ensure a value focus and connectedness with the business enterprise;
- knowing the assets' usable lives, performance, capacities and applications;
- employing the most cost-effective use of the asset;
- considering future trends in the industry, technology and application;
- determining sourcing strategies and relationships; and
- incorporating an element of innovation or surprise in the application to distinguish the organization from others.

Strategic asset and ICT planning also involves:

- identifying the extent of the long-term contribution of the asset to the organizational direction;
- identifying the business opportunities presented by new directions in the market place, and the threats that may come from any competitor's use of similar assets;
- prioritizing areas where ICT and other assets can add the most value to success of the organization;
- identifying where the processes and business practices within the organization require reengineering to maximize the total benefit; and
- measuring and evaluating the potential value and contribution of the asset to organizational success.

Without these considerations, the exercise can be extremely costly with ill-fitting and over-priced solutions that will deliver little or no business advantage. The historical path of ICT is littered with examples where new technology has failed to reap the benefits because existing and out-of-date processes have been automated with the result that inefficient or bad processes just run faster.

ENVIRONMENTAL ANALYSIS

The environmental analysis is the first step in the planning process. In addition to the usual organizational issues, the internal analysis considers the existing asset and ICT management policies, the degree of technology integration and innovation, business processes and financial resources as well as the enterprise-wide upgrade policies and requirements.

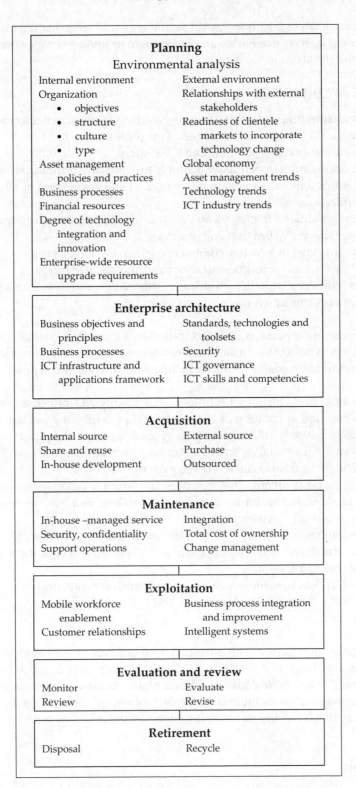

Planning

Environmental analysis

Internal environment	External environment
Organization	Relationships with external
• objectives	stakeholders
• structure	Readiness of clientele
• culture	markets to incorporate
• type	technology change
Asset management	Global economy
policies and practices	Asset management trends
Business processes	Technology trends
Financial resources	ICT industry trends
Degree of technology	
integration and	
innovation	
Enterprise-wide resource	
upgrade requirements	

Enterprise architecture

Business objectives and	Standards, technologies and
principles	toolsets
Business processes	Security
ICT infrastructure and	ICT governance
applications framework	ICT skills and competencies

Acquisition

Internal source	External source
Share and reuse	Purchase
In-house development	Outsourced

Maintenance

In-house –managed service	Integration
Security, confidentiality	Total cost of ownership
Support operations	Change management

Exploitation

Mobile workforce	Business process integration
enablement	and improvement
Customer relationships	Intelligent systems

Evaluation and review

Monitor	Evaluate
Review	Revise

Retirement

Disposal	Recycle

Figure 6.1   The strategic asset and ICT life cycle

The external analysis identifies global technology and asset management trends, the readiness of client markets to embrace and incorporate technology change, trends in the ICT industry and the global economic state.

ENTERPRISE ARCHITECTURE

The enterprise architecture underpins the business drivers of the organization and enables ICT to be used strategically to support the business of the organization. It:

- integrates business strategy planning and ICT strategy;
- moves the organization from reactive planning to a proactive planning focus;
- takes an holistic approach to planning, managing and governance of all ICT across the whole organization;
- provides the governance framework and context for aligning and integrating ICT with the organization's mission, objectives and processes;
- defines the principles by which decisions are made and ICT managed;
- guides ICT investment, acquisition, development and maintenance; and
- maximizes efficiency through ensuring collaboration and the inter-operability and portability of systems, applications and networks.

The enterprise architecture is designed to be flexible to reflect changing business needs and opportunities. It takes into consideration environmental trends, business strategy and the current architecture to determine the future architecture. It typically comprises:

- High-level objectives, high-level business requirements and principles that define and govern the use and application of ICT. High-level principles may include systems being designed to be business driven, protection of confidentiality and privacy in information, use of proven standards and technologies, and consideration for total cost of ownership;
- a restatement of the business drivers that govern the use of ICT;
- a business process taxonomy that describes key business processes and their objectives to assist in determining business proposals, funding and procurement, application development and improvement, evaluation and review;
- a framework for the ICT application, systems and network architectures;
- governance structures for the overall goals, directions, investments, use and outcomes of ICT within the organization;
- security architecture to ensure accessibility, confidentiality and integrity;
- standards, technologies and toolsets in use; and
- services available.

The enterprise architecture is an enabler not an enforcer of the organization's business strategies. Whilst it can be used as a driver for change in business and process reengineering, it should not overtake the business strategy. The enterprise architecture is strongly linked to the knowledge and information architecture. It is the business information needs, objectives and business strategy that determine its future direction, not the other way round.

Acquisition

After satisfying the planning requirements, new ICT projects can be acquired through:

- sharing and reusing an existing system (either internally or externally owned);
- in-house development;
- purchasing an off the shelf or shrink wrap product; or
- commissioning an external agent to create the ICT project.

The manner in which the ICT project is acquired will require consideration as to whether it is to be managed in-house or outsourced to a third party. Outsourcing is often used to acquire services where there is a desire to reduce overhead costs, improve service levels, gain access to know-how, or to take advantage of new technology directions. Further consideration of this follows under the maintenance section.

Whilst the provision of services can be outsourced, accountability for the service levels and strategic decisions relating to service provisions cannot. The fundamental responsibility and accountability for the outcomes and quality of the end product and service still resides with management.

DETERMINING THE TOTAL COSTS

ICT acquisition should take into account not just the cost of the hardware, software, peripherals and associated infrastructure, but also the costs of implementation and reengineering. This includes the full costs of integration, maintenance and support, as well as data capture and conversion. Intangible assets, data capture and conversion are often overlooked, yet they form a significant proportion of the full acquisition costs. Likewise the costs of business and process reengineering and retraining also need to be considered in order to provide a total cost of both the capital investment and implementation expenditure.

In selecting the most appropriate asset to fit the business purpose it is often useful to employ a total cost of ownership approach. This means that all financial costs are considered, not just the capital acquisition costs. What might initially be considered a cheaper option may over the course of its life cycle cost considerably more than its alternative. For example a motor vehicle may initially have an attractive purchase price, but prove to have higher fuel consumption, maintenance overheads and insurance costs than its competitor over time. Significant ICT projects may also attract variances in the time to deploy and manage, employee and end-user productivity, and effort required to customize or enhance application usage.

Total cost of ownership considers the ongoing operational and development costs, the retirement costs and the initial capital investment cost to provide a true whole-of-life cost. This can be used to compare properly the long-term investment and expenditure on the asset at the point of selection, as well as understand the true cost of owning and operating the asset.

PLANNING FOR CHANGE

In commencing any technology project, the impact of change upon individuals will need to be taken into consideration as the people factor can make or break the introduction of new technology. Introduced with thought, ICT can deliver major benefits to individuals in their ability to access and use information, and, to the organization in terms of increased productivity, broadening the business base and improving the delivery of products and services. However, it should be properly planned to take into account the information and business needs, the corporate culture, the need to change or reengineer business processes, education of users and technical staff, and the financial and resource capacity of the organization. Those with the potential to be adversely affected should be kept informed of any changes and given training and retraining opportunities.

Maintenance

One of the decisions to be made for managing, maintaining and securing assets is whether to undertake this in-house or to outsource in the form of a managed service. This decision frequently focuses on:

- whether the organization wishes to concentrate solely on its core business;
- organizational size;
- availability of expertise;
- overhead costs; and
- financial capacity to fund asset investment.

Common areas where managed services are employed include ICT maintenance, management and support services, transportation services and corporate services such as financial accounting, human resource recruitment and office support services. In the case of ICT and transportation this obviates the need to invest in ICT and specialized vehicle assets.

Managing and maintaining ICT includes ensuring:

- the most cost-effective solution and use of ICT resources in meeting business needs;
- ICT services support agreed customer requirements and expectations at all times;
- the efficient operation of ICT services without loss of utilization and functionality for 99% of the time;
- the health and safety of users;
- security, confidentiality and legal obligations are met;
- ICT services add measurable value to the business processes at every stage; and
- ICT services are aligned with and support the corporate culture.

Exploitation

Extending business reach in a global market, the need for workforce flexibility, growing inter-organizational research and development and pressures to reduce travel all influence how the ICT infrastructure is structured so that it may exploited for organizational gain. To maintain competitive advantage, the ICT infrastructure must enable and support virtual teamwork and collaboration irrespective of geographical or organizational boundaries, using both fixed and mobile devices. This scenario is also reflected by Cleyle (2002, p. 291) who urges libraries to 'walk away from the paper paradigm' and realize that they are no longer managing assets, but providing a portal to the world.

Increasingly sophisticated client needs, and the push for process improvement, increased user productivity and reduced costs also influence how technology and assets are managed for profit and business gain. The bottom line for managing the ICT infrastructure is to increase the speed, quality and flexibility of services to users and clients at lower costs, and to provide an aspect of uniqueness that makes it difficult for competitors to replicate the exact nature of the business services.

Supporting this is a full integration of mobile commerce, electronic commerce, back-end, client and supplier systems that enable seamless workflows, shorten product cycles and increase value chain based production. Radio-frequency identification (RFID), electronic document image processing, intranets and electronic commerce enable information to be captured at its source and used throughout the value chain. This reduces input errors, overcomes the need for duplicate data, provides better access to decision-making information and reduces processing time. Protocols and standards ensure the capacity to share knowledge and information across a range of access devices and media programs.

Evaluation and review

The desired outcomes in managing ICT and other assets are to ensure:

- they are deployed in the most cost-effective and advantageous way to maximize the return on investment;
- customer requirements and expectations are met at all times;
- ICT services operate without loss of utilization and functionality for 99% of the time;
- the health and safety of users;
- security, confidentiality and legal obligations are met;
- ICT services add measurable value to the business processes at every stage; and
- ICT services are aligned with and support the corporate culture.

Efficiency and effectiveness measures should be developed to assess and evaluate these outcomes.

Retirement

In the retirement phase, obsolete, under-performing assets or specific elements of assets that are under-performing are identified with a view to considering their viability. Obsolescence can occur where:

- a change in business strategy requires the use of new types of assets or new technology applications;
- significant changes in clients' or suppliers' technology architectures occur to the extent that inter-organizational systems are no longer compatible; and
- the maintenance of the technology is no longer supported in the market place.

The effective management of an asset during its life cycle should result in the asset's life being prolonged and its disposal value being at the optimal level. When disposing of assets, especially those where there may be residual toxic matter, it is important to ensure that they are disposed in an environmentally friendly manner. Recycling is one way of ensuring that old equipment does not unnecessarily add to landfill.

Conclusion

Developing the right planning and business processes for the management and utilization of ICT and other assets is critical to the organization's use of knowledge and information, service delivery, productivity, customer retention and return on investment.

Assets, including ICT are expensive to acquire and maintain in monetary terms. The correct choice of strategy aligned to the business drivers will deliver considerable return on this investment. An incorrect choice of strategy or no strategy will make the business risks and impact even more expensive.

References

Cleyle, S. (2002), 'E-books: Should we be afraid', *Serials Librarian*, vol. 41, no. 3/4, pp. 281–92.
COBIT: http:/www.isaca.org/cobit.
ITIL: http://www.itil.co.uk.

Further reading

Chen, Leida and Nath, Ravi (2005), 'Nomadic culture: Cultural support for working anytime, anywhere', *Information Systems Management*, vol. 22, no. 4, pp. 56–65.
Christensen, C.M. (1997), *The innovator's dream: When new technologies cause great firms to fail*, Cambridge, MA: Harvard Business School Press.
Geroski, P.A. (1999), 'Early warning of new rivals', *Sloan Management Review*, vol. 40, no. 3, pp. 107–16.
Lafferty, Susan (2004), 'Disruptive technologies: What future universities and their libraries?' *Library Management*, vol. 25, no. 6/7, pp. 252–64.

CHAPTER 7

Financial Management

Financial planning and management involves the process of identifying, costing and allocating income and expenditure to resources and activities that achieve the objectives of the information service. It also ensures that there is optimum use of these resources.

This chapter introduces the concept of an integrated approach to financial planning and the relationship between the budget cycle and the strategic planning cycle, the preparation of budgets and methods of calculating expenditure. Different budget techniques are explored, as are mechanisms for financing and costing information services and activities.

Management oversight – roles and responsibilities

The preparation and coordination of the budget are often the responsibility of the financial services manager, who is also entrusted with administering the allocation of funds within the organization's overall programmes and activities. Accountability for the overall financial position of the organization rests with the Chief Executive Officer, who delegates responsibility, and to some extent, accountability to mid-level operational managers.

Mid-level managers may prepare their own budgets and submit these to the senior management. However, mid-level management is rarely the final arbitrator on the amount of funds to be allocated. This decision is usually made at the executive or ownership level of the parent organization. Therefore it is most important that managers keep the senior management and stakeholders of the parent organization fully informed of their progress and achievements throughout the year.

Whilst discussions about the value of items on the budget will be part of the budget preparation process, justification should not just be limited to this time period. The review and questioning about the appropriateness of services and levels of funds should be a continuous exercise. The senior management of the parent organization and other relevant stakeholders such as board members should have their views sought on policy directions and matters for the forthcoming budget well before the presentation of the information service's budget. Proposals for new services should be introduced in regular or special reports, not in the budget documentation, as budget committees do not usually view too kindly strange budget proposals for items that have not previously been discussed.

Whilst it is important that the proposed budget is fully supported with documentation justifying the proposals and linking these with approved plans and business outcomes, it is not enough. The information services manager should take the time and effort to understand the politics of the budget process within the parent organization. They need to win the budget arguments, not just be part of them. Where possible they should be involved in the budget deliberations so that they may learn the rationale behind their bids being accepted or rejected. Networks may be formed with key stakeholders in the treasury or finance department in order to put the information service's point of view forward and gain support for certain proposals.

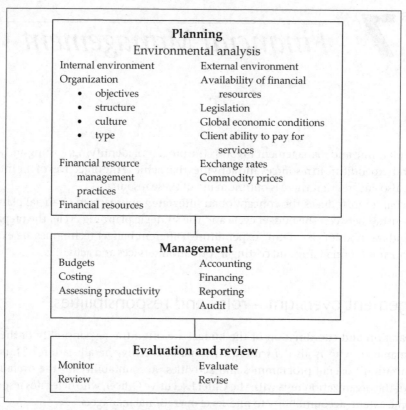

Figure 7.1   An integrated approach to financial planning

The lack of a personal opportunity to participate in the final budget deliberations should not prevent the information services manager from obtaining their required budget allocation. Credibility of the budget details and a recognized value of the information service are what matters most. The justification for the information service's budget will already have been made if the arguments for the services have been well presented in detailed and timely reports throughout the year. If the information services manager's personal network has been effective, key members of the budget committee will be supportive of the activities and associated budget.

Planning

The planning for financial resources should be integrated into the planning of the other corporate resources in both timing and content. The activities of the budget process should fit the ongoing activities of the strategic planning process.

Budgets

The budget is the financial statement that identifies how all income and expenditure should be allocated and managed for specific period. Usually it is prepared to cover a financial or calendar

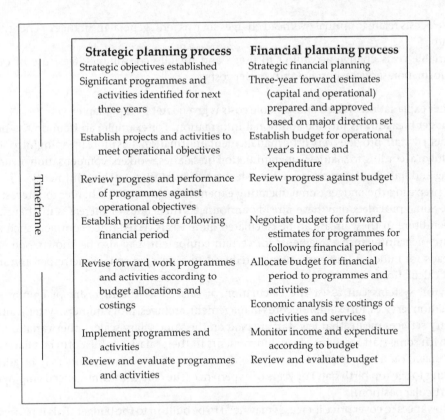

Strategic planning process	Financial planning process
Strategic objectives established	Strategic financial planning
Significant programmes and activities identified for next three years	Three-year forward estimates (capital and operational) prepared and approved based on major direction set
Establish projects and activities to meet operational objectives	Establish budget for operational year's income and expenditure
Review progress and performance of programmes against operational objectives	Review progress against budget
Establish priorities for following financial period	Negotiate budget for forward estimates for programmes for following financial period
Revise forward work programmes and activities according to budget allocations and costings	Allocate budget for financial period to programmes and activities
	Economic analysis re costings of activities and services
Implement programmes and activities	Monitor income and expenditure according to budget
Review and evaluate programmes and activities	Review and evaluate budget

Timeframe (vertical label on left side)

Figure 7.2   Relationship between the activities of the strategic planning process and the financial planning process

year, but can cover a longer period of time – for example, a triennium. Occasionally, a half-yearly budget is planned.

As it is prepared in advance the budget serves as the means of control as to how monies are spent and a check on what monies should have been received. It earmarks the amounts of expenditure and anticipated income for items and services delivered by the information service.

Budgets are often broken down by either programmes or activities across an organization. These may be further related to cost centres such as branch libraries, records management office or the geographic information services section. Cost centres may be further broken down to cover specific services.

CALCULATION OF INCOME AND EXPENDITURE

The preparation of a budget necessitates the calculation of income or revenue and capital and operational expenditure. Capital expenditures are one-off items of significant expenditure such as a new library building or major information technology system.

Operating expenditures are current, ongoing costs associated with the day-to-day operations of the information service. These may be divided further into fixed and variable costs:

- fixed costs relate to annual overhead charges such as rent, general insurance or energy costs; and
- variable costs change according to usage and include consultancy fees, use of on-line information services, postage and courier costs.

A further explanation of fixed and variable costs is given later in this chapter.

Budget breakdowns provide additional information. For example, an item on the budget just labelled 'staff' provides very little management information. It is more meaningful to show a breakdown according to salaries, superannuation on salaries, workers' compensation insurance, training and staff development, conference fees, and advertising staff appointments.

In preparing the budget, some operating expenditure costs will be harder to forecast than others. Some providers may have already announced their rates or increases in charges and so expenditure in these areas can be calculated quite easily. Fixed-price contracts such as for cleaning or maintenance agreements for certain equipment may also be known. Sometimes overheads for buildings are conveniently reduced to a rate per square metre per annum for budget calculations.

Payroll systems can assist the calculation of salaries as the diversity of employees in information services, for example records management, archives, programmers, systems analysis or library services means that few staff are paid on the same salary scale. Other variations may occur with some staff receiving annual increments in their salaries, whilst others' salaries may be calculated on a ratio associated with profit increases. Annual increments may be adjusted according to age (on birth date) or years of experience (the date they commenced employment in a particular position).

Allowances to cover price increases may need to be built-in to the budget. This is particularly the case with capital expenditure items such as new buildings that are costed in preparation for the budget far in advance of when they are contracted out. Inflation rates and international currency exchange rates will contribute to variations. These changes must also be taken into account when preparing the budget. Assistance in forecasting changes to these rates can often be found in finance areas.

It is important to anticipate correctly revenue patterns and levels. Any income revenue in excess of expenditure at any given time is often invested in the short-term money market to provide additional funds for the organization. Variances in income revenue will disrupt the ability to plan investments wisely. Although some changes in income levels may be unavoidable, any anticipated changes in policies which could affect the income revenue levels should be accounted for in the budget. Examples would be the anticipated increase from the introduction of a new user-pays service or additional income from an increase in the use of a fee service such as a photocopying or scanning machine.

BUDGETING TECHNIQUES

Line-item budgets

This is the most traditional approach to budgeting. It divides expenditures into broad categories such as general administrative expenses, motor vehicles, operating expenses, employment expenses and occupancy costs. There are further subdivisions within these categories. Most line budgets are prepared by projecting current expenditures to next year, taking likely cost increases into account.

Whilst they are easy to prepare, very few organizations use line-item budgets today. This is because it is difficult to relate the line-item budget to the organization's objectives, or to the benefits or outcomes that arise from the allocated monies. Line-item budgets provide few incentives for management to question programmes or activities or look for alternative solutions.

Zero-based budgeting

Zero-based budgeting or ZBB combines strategic planning and decision making with the budget process. Zero-based budgeting encourages the manager to question priorities and consider alternative methods of service delivery. Activities and programmes are assessed across the whole organization in accordance with the:

- anticipated benefits from the programme;
- desired results;
- advantages of retaining the programme's current activities;
- consequences of not having the programme;
- overall efficiency of the programme; and
- evaluation of the alternative methods of providing the programme.

Budget allocation is based on the priority of the programme in meeting the organization's objectives rather than across the board appropriations. The required resources and associated costs for the programme are calculated. The programmes are grouped and ranked by management according to a hierarchy based on their cost-benefit and ability to achieve the organization's objectives.

The programmes are progressively funded within the priority hierarchy until the budget is exhausted. At some point in the hierarchy there is a cut-off point where some programmes are to be funded and others not. The cut-off point corresponds to the organization's total budget allocation. Those programmes ranked in priority above the funding line are funded; those below it are left unfunded.

Zero-based budgeting does not allow for incremental growth in budgets. It considers efficiency and the relevancy of programmes to organizational objectives. It exposes all information service activities to the same scrutiny as others within the parent organization, preventing programmes from being approved solely on the basis of tradition. More efficient ways of achieving the corporate objectives are sought by examining different methods of service delivery or activities.

To be effective, zero-based budgeting requires decision makers to have a thorough knowledge of the organization as it can lead to trade-offs among the programmes and objectives. The executive management team decides the level of funding that they are prepared to commit and the programmes and objectives that they are prepared to forgo. Managers and their teams need to know why they want to spend money, where and what to spend it on and the outcomes that can be achieved if funding is available. To do this effectively they must be aware of their service's characteristics and objectives, and major customer groups. Activities and programmes must be well conceived and strengths and weaknesses be known.

There are some disadvantages to zero-based budgeting. It requires commitment of time and effort; it involves a great deal of preparation, planning and organization; and it relies upon all participants being aware of priorities.

Programme budgeting

Programme budgeting is based upon the provision of programmes rather than individual items or expenditures. It allocates monies to activities or programmes; having previously explored different means to providing services that have been identified as needed by the customers. Each programme has certain funds allocated for staff, operating expenses, materials and publicity. There are no direct budget allocations to the cost centres, only to the individual programmes. Programmes may run across a number of cost centres, for example a programme that facilitates the provision of information networks to lecturers within a university may cover a number of cost centres at the faculty level.

Performance budgeting

Performance budgeting bases its expenditure on the performance of activities and services. It is similar to programme budgeting in format but is concerned with efficiency. It uses cost-benefit analysis techniques to measure performance and requires large amounts of data. Performance budgeting has been criticized as it emphasises economics rather than quality of service.

Planning-programming budgeting systems (PPBS)

PPBS combines the best of programme budgeting and performance budgeting. It combines the functions of planning, programming and budgeting into one. The information service's objectives are established and short-term objectives are stated in a quantifiable manner. Alternative means (activities) of achieving the objectives are considered and selected on the basis of cost-benefit. These activities are grouped into programmes and funded.

Once the programmes are established they are controlled by comparing them with the stated objectives to see if these are being achieved. The results are evaluated so that corrective actions can be taken. PPBS allows costs to be assigned to programmes so that the benefits can be measured in relation to cost.

Whilst the approach appears to be simple, it is complex in practice and can be time consuming. It does not provide an operating tool for line managers or provide the mechanism to evaluate the impact of various funding levels on each programme. Finally, it does not force the continued evaluation of existing programmes and activities.

BUDGET CONTROLS

The budget control process is a continuing one. Generally, expenditures and income must be made within the framework of the amount allocated against each item. This is part of an accountability process.

Income and expenditure are usually documented in either weekly or monthly budget reports. These reports show the total income and expenditure amounts budgeted at the beginning of the financial year, the actual expenditure or income received to date, and, the committed expenditure to date. Actual expenditure refers to the amounts already paid (expended) for goods or services received. Committed expenditure refers to the outstanding expenditures for goods or services which have been ordered but not yet paid for. The goods or services may or may not have been received by the cost centres in the information service. In calculating total expenditure costs to date, both the actual and committed expenditure amounts should be added together.

Statements of committed and expended funds should be regularly monitored and reviewed in order to control the budget and meet accountability requirements. Appropriate budget adjustment mechanisms should be available to allow for unexpected events or changes in priorities that could not be foreseen when the budget was framed. Any anticipated increase in expenditure above that provided by the budget must often be offset by either an increase in income to offset the expenditure, or a decrease in expenditure in another activity in that area. Unexpected expenditures such as costly emergency repairs to buildings may incur a reallocation of funds from elsewhere. These readjustments of funds need to be authorized by senior management and endorsed by a board if it exists.

Costing

COST ACCOUNTING

Cost accounting measures what it costs to complete an activity. It is a tool that can be used to determine the anticipated value of certain activities, to calculate a minimum charge for a product or service, and for comparative purposes to measure efficiency. Cost accounting is the simple process of breaking down resources to the activity being carried out and then collating the monetary cost to show the cost of the activity. An example of this follows under the section relating to unit costs.

Special costing exercises can provide a comparison of costs of current operations with the estimated costs of alternative methods. These can then be used along with benefits realization models to determine the best possible outcomes.

CAPITAL AND OPERATING COSTS

Capital costs represent long-term investments. They are associated with the up-front development and acquisition expenditures associated with an asset. These include the acquisition of real property or equipment, construction costs, furniture and fittings as well as intangible assets. As capital costs often incur large sums of money, their payback is usually funded over a number of years (see financing options later in this chapter). Capital expenditures can recur over time, but they are not ongoing costs.

Operating costs or expenses are associated with recurring or ongoing activities, such as salaries, electricity, telecommunications and training and are funded through the annual budget provision.

FIXED AND VARIABLE COSTS

Fixed costs are those that do not vary with output. Costs which vary with output are called variable costs. Knowledge of both fixed and variable costs is necessary in order to budget effectively.

Staffing costs are variable costs as an increase or decrease in the number of staff employed will result in a corresponding increase or decrease in the budget for salary, superannuation, training and work-cover insurance.

Energy costs for lighting and air conditioning are examples of fixed costs as they remain unchanged unless the number of staff increases considerably. Energy costs will only increase if longer opening hours are required or additional physical space is necessary that requires lighting, increasing the energy consumption.

DIRECT AND INDIRECT COSTS

Direct costs are those that can be attributed directly to an output or activity. These are usually easy to determine, for example printing, office equipment and salaries, superannuation and workers' compensation insurance costs of those members of the team associated with the activity.

Indirect costs can be harder to quantify and calculate. These are overheads and other costs that are not directly attributed to a definite activity or output, but which contribute the cost of the service or product. An example of an indirect cost might be rent on a building from which a number of activities or outputs operate. Indirect costs are usually apportioned to individual activities or outputs on:

- a usage or benefit approach; or
- a pro rata approach.

UNIT COSTS

Unit costs are used to measure output. As it is not always easy to compare the rising curve of total costs, economists convert the total cost figures into unit costs. They do this by dividing the total cost of the activity by the number of units, for example, the number of incoming and outgoing pieces of correspondence that are processed by the records management office. This results in a figure for the average cost per unit of output. Unit costs can also be used in time terms. They may be used to measure performance by comparing inputs to outputs.

Unit costs concepts may also be used to allocate a cost to an information product or service, to determine a minimum selling price or to compare costs between different information products or services. They can also be used to develop a standard cost for a job in either time or cost terms. The following example outlines how unit costing can be used to determine the price to be charged for four services: a helpdesk call out to a remote user desktop, a premium research service, an information brochure, and a CD-ROM of data.

The first stage in the exercise is to calculate the total fixed and variable costs (operating expenses) of the information service of the year (see Figure 7.3). In the case of the example these are $4,280,500 per annum. Next the variable costs that are associated with the specific product or service are calculated on a unit basis. In the example given in Figure 7.4 for the CD-ROM, these costs total $33.00:

Once the total fixed and variable costs (operating expenses) and the variable cost per unit are known, a percentage of the operating expenses has to be allocated to the unit as a fixed cost per unit. This is calculated by:

- determining the percentage contribution of the product or service to the overall business operations of the information service; and
- the likely number of units to be sold per annum for the product or service.

In the case of the CD-ROM, it is deemed that it contributes 1% of the overall business operations expense ($4,280,500) and that 3,000 CD-ROMs are likely to be sold in the calendar year. Therefore the proportion of the operating expense that can be attributed to each CD-ROM as a fixed cost is calculated as:

Operating expenses	
General and administrative expenses	
Accounting	10,000
Advertising	25,000
Bank charges	1,000
Borrowing fees	1,000
Consultants	930,000
Courier	4,000
Depreciation	40,000
Donations	5,000
Fines and penalties	1,000
Hire – plant and equipment	6,000
Licences and registration fees	10,000
Lease – equipment	60,000
Legal fees	70,000
Insurance	26,000
Postage	2,500
Repairs and maintenance	15,000
Stationery/office supplies	70,000
Freight paid	2,000
Subscriptions	90,000
Travel and accommodation	122,000
Motor vehicles	
MV – fuel	23,000
MV – repairs and maintenance	15,000
MV – registration	9,000
MV – parking	500
MV – taxi	3,000
Operating expenses	
Cleaning	15,000
Employment expenses	
Employment tax	20,000
Staff amenities	10,000
Staff training and development	40,000
Wages and salaries	3,500,000
Workers compensation insurance	80,000
Superannuation payable	350,000
Medical expenses	5,000
Uniforms	40,000
Occupancy costs	
Electricity	55,000
Gas	6,000
Property insurance	3,000
Rates	12,000
Rent	80,000
Water rates and consumption	12,000
Waste removal	2,000
TOTAL	4,280,500

Figure 7.3 Table of expenses for input into costing model

Variable costs	Helpdesk call-out	Research service	Brochure	CD-ROM of data	Annotation
			Identifying variable cost per unit		
Product raw materials	0.00	0.00	3.00	2.00	Unit cost of any raw materials eg CD-Rom
Product value add presentation post sale	0.00	5.00	5.00	1.00	Unit cost of packaging or presentation for sale
Product development pre sale	0.00	0.00	4.00	4.00	Unit cost of any research and development to assist in product
Printing	0.00	5.00	5.00	5.00	Unit cost of printing
Mastering	0.00	0.00	0.00	1.00	Unit cost of production
Telephone calls	5.00	20.00	3.00	1.00	Average cost of telephone charges associated with product/service
Casual wages	0.00	0.00	5.00	5.00	Average cost of casual wages per unit – assistance in supply, after sales etc.
Marketing attached to volume	1.00	1.00	1.00	1.00	Cost of marketing of product/service per unit
Commission	5.00	5.00	5.00	5.00	Commission costs set per unit
Travel	75.00	0.00	0.00	0.00	Travel costs associated with delivery of product/service
Consultancy	0.00	0.00	10.00	0.00	Unit cost of special consultancy/advice associated with product
IT	1.00	1.00	1.00	1.00	Unit costs associated with provision of specialised IT services
Distribution	0.00	0.00	5.00	5.00	Unit cost of distributing the product/service
Postage	0.00	0.00	2.00	2.00	Unit cost for postage
Total variable cost per unit	**87.00**	**37.00**	**49.00**	**33.00**	Total variable cost per unit of the specialized service/product
			Identifying selling price per unit		
% Fixed costs	10/100/15000	2/100/250	1/100/1000	1/100/3000	Percentage of overall budget expenses allocated to product or service/total/average number of units
Fixed Costs % of $4280500 operating expense	28.54	342.44	42.81	14.27	Unit cost based on percentage contribution to the overall budget expense as per above(see expense table showing total expenses as$4,280,500.00
Profit	2.85	34.24	4.28	1.42	Profit required per unit product/service (based on 10% of fixed costs per unit
Fixed + Profit	**31.39**	**376.68**	**47.09**	**15.69**	Total of percentage of fixed costs and profit
Total variable cost per units	87.00	37.00	49.00	33.00	Total variable cost per unit of the specialised service/product
Total variable cost plus fixed and profit	**118.39**	**413.68**	**96.09**	**48.69**	Total cost per unit (variable cost + percentage of fixed cost +profit)
Minimum selling price rounded up/down	120.00	415.00	96.00	48.70	Minimum selling price rounded up or down

Figure 7.4   Identifying variable costs and selling costs per unit

$$\frac{1\% \text{ of } 4,280,500}{3,000} = \$14.27$$

As in the example, a profit margin of 10% has been included, the total unit cost of the CD-ROM (the variable cost + fixed costs of the unit + 10% profit) is:

$$\$33.00 + \$14.27 + \$1.42 = \$48.69$$

Rounded up, the minimum selling price for the CR-ROM would be calculated as $48.70.

Changing the contribution percentage of the business operating expense, or the number of services or products being sold will·change the final unit cost figure. For example, if it is anticipated that the information service will only sell 1,000 CD-ROMS, then the fixed cost associated with the annual operating expenses will be allocated across fewer units ($42.80) and so the final unit cost figure will be higher ($33.00 + $42.80 + $4.28 = $80.08). In decreasing the number of sales for the CD-ROMS, the information service must make a minimum charge of $80.08 to break even; an additional amount of $31.39 to the cost where 3,000 CD-ROMS are sold.

Generally fixed costs per unit decline as outputs rise, and rise as outputs fall.

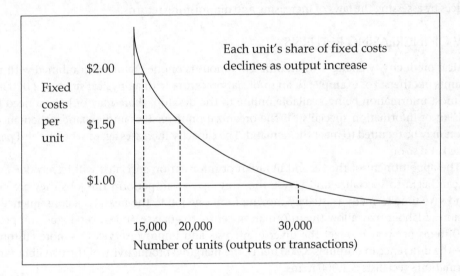

Figure 7.5 Profile of fixed costs per unit

Where variable costs per unit are involved the situation is more complex. It depends upon marginal productivity and the productivity curve (law of variable proportions).

In the example above, the term minimum price is used as pricing does not always relate directly to cost. Pricing is associated with the amount someone is willing to pay for a product or service. Some products and service will attract a premium price; for example where services are fast tracked ahead of others, where there might be a more frequent update or delivered in real time, or the product or service is new or has an element of innovation.

ACTIVITY-BASED COSTING

Activity-based costing costs the whole process, including those indirect costs involved in supply, process, installation and service delivery. It links all costs to the activity or output and gives a better picture of the total cost of the service. For example, it also takes account of the costs associated with lost opportunities, namely:

- downtime of equipment, such as when the equipment is sitting idle out of hours or is inoperable whilst waiting for a spare part;
- the cost of goods sitting in a warehouse; or
- the cost of reworking a piece of programming.

Activity-based costing can be used in competitive markets to highlight those activities that are unexpectedly unproductive and those that are yielding the greatest return on investment.

Assessing productivity

Productivity curves can be used to determine the optimum levels of efficiency in information services by assessing the laws of increasing and diminishing returns.

LAW OF INCREASING RETURNS

Physical productivity changes when different amounts of one factor are combined with fixed amounts of others. For example, in an information centre with a physical stock of 2,000 items and most information being available online to the desktop, there may only be a need for a librarian or information specialist. If the organization diversifies and expands, then another person may be required to meet the demand. The capacity increases again when a third person is hired and so on.

The appointment of the second librarian or information specialist will have value as the two can begin to specialize and divide the work. Each will perform the jobs they are better at and save time formerly wasted by moving from one job to the next. As a consequence this division of labour may allow the information centre to analyse, index, catalogue and process 5,000 items per year to meet the diverse interests and improve services to more customers. Since the difference in output is 3,000 items, the marginal productivity of the two librarians or information specialists is 3,000 items.

The marginal productivity of labour is not be spoken of in terms of the second person as, by themselves, their efforts are no more productive than those of the first staff member. If the first staff member left, the second person would still analyse, index, catalogue and process only 2,000 items. What makes the difference is the jump in the combined production of the two librarians once specialization can be introduced. It is regarded as the changing marginal productivity of labour, not the individual.

Increased specialization takes place with the third, fourth, fifth librarian or information specialist so that the addition of another unit of labour as an input in each case brings about an output larger than was realized by the average of all the previous librarians. This does not necessarily mean that each successive person is more efficient and productive. It means that, as units of one factor [librarians or information specialists] are added, the total mix of these units plus the fixed amounts of the other factors form an increasingly efficient technical combination.

The range of factor inputs, over which average productivity rises, is called a range of increasing average returns.

Every time a factor is added efficiency rises. The rate of increased efficiency will not be the same, for the initial large marginal leaps in productivity will give way to smaller ones. However, the overall trend whether measured by looking at total output or at average output per person will still be increased. This continues until a point of maximum technical efficiency is reached.

LAW OF DIMINISHING RETURNS

The law of diminishing returns is used to detect the point of maximum efficiency. Using the previous example, there is a certain point where the marginal output no longer rises when another person is added to the staff. This is the point of maximum technical efficiency. Total output will still be increasing, but the last person to be employed will have added less output than their colleagues. Labour is now beginning to 'crowd' equipment or the premises. Opportunities for further specialization have become non-existent.

This condition of falling marginal performance is called a condition of decreasing or diminishing returns. The information centre is getting back less and less not only from the 'marginal' librarian or information specialist but from the combined labour of all the staff members.

If labour goes on being added, a point will be reached at which the contribution of the 'marginal' librarian or information specialist will be so small that the average output per person will also fall. Eventually, if even more librarians or information specialists were added, the factor mix would be so disrupted that the total output would actually fall resulting in a condition of negative gains.

In the example of Figure 7.6, the marginal productivity begins to diminish with the fourth librarian or information specialist who will analyse, index, catalogue and process only 3,300 items rather than the 3,500 processed by the third person. Average productivity continues to rise until the addition of the sixth person, because the fifth librarian or information specialist, although producing less than the fourth, is still more productive than the average output of all four colleagues. Therefore marginal productivity can be falling while average productivity is still rising.

Number of librarians or information specialists	Total output (items analysed, indexed, catalogued, processed)	Marginal productivity (change in output)		Average productivity (total output – number of librarians/information specialists)	
1	2,000	2,000	Increasing marginal productivity	2,000	Increasing average productivity
2	5,000	3,000		2,500	
3	8,500	3,500		2,853	
4	11,800	3,300	Decreasing marginal productivity	2,950	
5	14,800	3,000		2,960	
6	17,300	2,500		2,883	Decreasing average productivity
7	19,500	2,200		2,785	

Figure 7.6 Law of diminishing returns

In summary, as successive units of one factor are added to fixed amounts of others, the marginal output of the units of the variable factor will at first rise and then decline. This is called the law of variable proportions or the law of diminishing returns or, the physical productivity curve (see Figure 7.7)

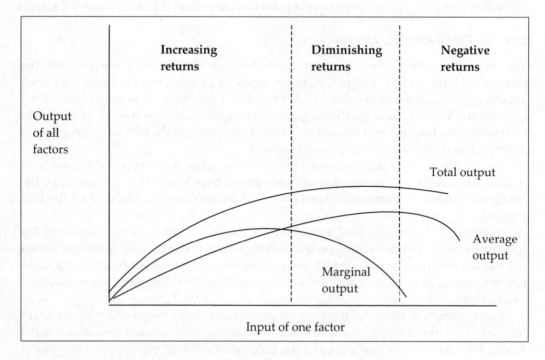

Figure 7.7 Law of variable proportions

VARIABLE COSTS PER UNIT

Variable costs per unit can be used to cost increased efficiency in information services. As in the case of the previous example of librarians or information specialists analysing, processing, indexing and cataloguing the items, the total number of items processed (units produced) will rise at first rapidly, then more slowly with the addition of more librarians. To convert the schedule of physical productivity into a unit cost figure, the total variable cost for each level of output should be calculated. This should then be divided by the number of units to obtain an average variable cost per unit of output.

In the example, the average variable cost per unit (items analysed, indexed, catalogued and processed) declines at first and then rises. This is because the variable cost increases by a set amount ($60,000 per librarian or information specialist). Output, however obeys the law of diminishing returns. The variable cost per unit of output will therefore fall as long as output is growing faster than costs. It will begin to rise as soon as additions to output start to get smaller.

Number of librarians/ information specialist	Total variable costs at $60,000 per librarian/ information specialist	Total output (units)	Average variable cost per unit or output (cost-output)
1	$60,000	2,000	$30.00
2	$120,000	5,000	$24.00
3	$180,000	8,500	$21.17
4	$240,000	11,800	$20.33
5	$300,000	14,800	$20.27
6	$360,000	17,300	$20.80
7	$430,000	19,500	$22.05

Figure 7. 8 Calculating the average variable cost per unit output

Accrual accounting

In accrual accounting all expenses and income are recognized that relate to the budget period. This 'total cost' approach includes provision for depreciation on tangible and intangible assets, interest and loan repayments.

DEPRECIATION COSTS

Asset depreciation allows the cost of an asset to be written off over a period of time. Two common methods of determining the depreciation costs are:

* the prime cost or straight line method; and
* the diminishing value method.

The prime cost method allocates the cost of an asset over the number of years of useful life. For example, personal computers are generally written off over a period of three years. The difference between the personal computer's original cost and the expected proceeds from the sale of the asset at the end of the three years is calculated, and then spread uniformly over each of the three years of its useful life. The diminishing value method allocates a higher proportion of the cost of the asset to the earlier years of its life. For example, a motor vehicle may be written off at a higher rate in the first year, and then at a lower rate in the following two years.

OPPORTUNITY COST OF CAPITAL

The opportunity cost of capital recognizes that funds invested in assets could have alternative uses and that an allowance should be made for a rate of return on the asset.

Financing

Once a programme has been proven to deliver a combination of financial, economic and social benefits, the financing alternatives need to be considered. Options include sharing risks and innovation with another party.

LEASING

Leasing offers a number of benefits including the transfer of risk to the financing party, a competitive pricing arrangement, taxation incentives and improved budget management. Leasing can also facilitate a significant investment such as new premises or equipment without the need for a major up-front capital outlay, or free up capital that may be used in the purchase of the property or equipment for other purposes.

Leasing is a viable alternative where there might be uncertainty about the timeframe over which the asset may be used, or where the asset is only required for a short period of time in relation to its economic life. An example may be the leasing of specialized or additional equipment to support a special project that has a limited timeframe. Quantity discounts might also apply to lessors above those available to the information service, which may make it an attractive proposition if the purchase price is significant.

Under the leasing arrangements the asset user (the lessee) has the right to possess and use the asset in return for lease payments to the financier (the lessor) who is the legal owner of the leased asset.

The most common lease arrangements are:

- operating leases – such as rental agreements for equipment. In this instance the lessor is responsible for all insurance, repairs, maintenance and taxes associated with the equipment. Operating leases can generally be cancelled at little or no cost;
- financial leases – a non-cancellable lease in which the benefits and risks are transferred to the lessee; and
- sale and lease-back – where an asset owner sells the asset to another party for the market value and leases the asset back. The title to the property is relinquished and the lessee then makes lease payments. This type of arrangement is often used to provide cash flow to leverage further investment.

PUBLIC PRIVATE PARTNERSHIPS

Public private partnerships involve the procurement of public infrastructure and ancillary services through a joint arrangement of public and private sector organizations.

Reporting

INTERNATIONAL FINANCIAL REPORTING STANDARDS (IFRS)

Global financial and investment markets have led to expectations of consistency and transparency in accounting standards and their interpretations regardless of the country of origin. The IFRS have been developed by the International Accounting Standards Board to meet this need. They have been designed to provide a single high-quality, understandable and enforceable international accounting standard for use by participants in global capital markets.

The IFRS offer many more benefits than traditional financial reporting mechanisms. They provide better financial information for shareholders and regulators, enhanced comparability, improved transparency of results, and increased capacity to secure cross-border listings and funding.

Audit

The audit is one means of safeguarding the integrity in financial reporting. This is a process by which the accounts and finances are independently verified. Usually these are carried out annually at the end of the financial year where the accounts and financial statements are analysed to ensure conformance and integrity. Specific projects may also be subject to an audit; this is often the case where grant funding is used. Finally, spot audits may be carried out as a risk management measure as part of the accountability and governance process.

Audit practices allow the independent review and judgment of internal compliance and control systems, performance and objectivity, significant decisions, records and reporting, risk management and finances. Independence in auditing is important; the parties should be impartial and unconnected with any activity being audited. They should also be provided with the necessary resources, power, access to management and information to meet their needs.

Hamilton (1998, pp. 227–9) provides examples where audits can identify problem areas where decisions need to be made:

- gaps in existing provision;
- duplication in existing provision;
- under-use of resources;
- incompatibility of IT systems;
- use of outdated, slow and cumbersome systems;
- 'jams' in information flow;
- need for extra staff;
- need for extra resources; and
- training needs.

Conclusion

Financial planning and management is integral to the strategic planning and management process. It ensures that resources are managed effectively and efficiently. Budgeting assists the library services manager to do the right thing in terms of making decisions about the most cost effective services, whilst the costing exercise enables the information services manager to do things right, the act of doing things in the most cost efficient manner.

References

Hamilton, Feona (1998), 'Information auditing', *Handbook of library and information management*, ed. Ray Prytherch, Aldershot, UK: Gower.

Further reading

Rowley, J. (1997), 'Principles of price and pricing policy for the information marketplace', *Library Review*, vol. 46, no. 3/4, pp. 179–89.

Snyder, H. and Davenport, E. (1997), *Costing and pricing in the digital age: A practical guide for information services*, London, UK: Library Association Publishing.

Woodsworth, A. and Williams, J.F. (1993), *Managing the economics of owning, leasing and contracting out information services*, Aldershot, UK: Gower.

PART III

Creating the Right Corporate Environment

The theme for Part III is ensuring that the corporate context is able to sustain flexibility, innovation and transformational change. It considers the political and cultural issues that determine whether an organizational environment is creative, innovative and intuitive. It provides some psycho-social guidance to the people interactions within organizations.

Chapter 8 considers the values, beliefs, norms and behaviours that create an organization's culture. It explains how corporate cultures develop and evolve and how there can be more than one culture within an organization. This chapter also describes the activities that take place within organizations as corporate rituals. It provides advice on developing and maintaining a corporate culture within the information service, and addresses the question of ethics and values in information services.

Chapter 9 covers the nature of politics and political behaviour from both an individual and organizational perspective. Not all organizations are equally political, and likewise differ in individuals and their political gamesmanship. Politics is a natural phenomenon arising out of differentiation, competition, and the use of power and influence. The chapter describes a number of political tactics that are commonly used in organizations, and it characterizes these as ethical and unethical. Advice is given on the presentation of political arguments on paper and the use of lobby groups.

Policy making is addressed in Chapter 10. This chapter provides strategies for developing policy and identifies the type of issues for which policies are appropriate. It emphasizes the need to identify and consult with stakeholders whilst developing the policy. The chapter discusses the policy framework and provides examples of general and specific policy issues that can be found in information services.

Chapter 11 considers innovation and creativity. The chapter provides strategies to create an innovative environment. It identifies the different roles and functions within organizations that foster a creative environment through which a continuous business advantage over others can be achieved.

PLANNING AND MANAGING FOR TRANSFORMATION

CREATING THE
RIGHT
CORPORATE
ENVIRONMENT

MANAGING IN
A DYNAMIC
ENVIRONMENT

TRANSFORMING
THE CORPORATE
ENVIRONMENT

MANAGING
YOURSELF
AND OTHERS

PART III – CREATING THE RIGHT CORPORATE ENVIRONMENT

8. **Corporate culture**
    Development of corporate cultures; Strong and weak corporate cultures; Organizational subcultures; Corporate culture types; Values; Beliefs, norms, shared meanings and behaviours; Corporate rituals; Communicating corporate values

9. **Politics**
    The political roles of managers; Politics in organizations; Political tactics; Presenting political arguments; Lobbying and lobby groups

10. **Policy making**
    Use of policies; Policy development; Policy framework

11. **Innovation and creativity**
    Management oversight – roles and responsibilities; Creating the innovative environment

EPILOGUE

POSITIONING
TO EXCEL IN
SERVICE
DELIVERY

GOVERNANCE AND ACCOUNTABILITY

Figure PIII.1   Creating the right corporate environment

8 *Corporate Culture*

All organizations have a corporate culture. Some are more noticeable or stronger than others. A corporate culture is the system of values, beliefs, norms and behaviours that create a certain organizational climate. Tangible factors such as the external environment, technologies, organization size and structure, corporate environment and leadership and management styles also influence the corporate culture.

Corporate culture is the product or outcome of behaviour patterns and standards that have been built up by individuals and groups over a number of years. Successful organizations have strong corporate cultures that guide beliefs and values upon which all policies and actions take place. Effective corporate cultures translate cultural values at the organizational level into behaviours at the individual level.

Information services can have many different corporate culture types. There can also be subcultures. Subcultures arise out of the functional differences between traditional work units such as software development, libraries and records management. They are natural, healthy phenomena unless they interfere with or detract from the overall corporate culture.

Development of corporate cultures

Effective corporate cultures are developed and communicated by senior executives and managers in their activities and behaviours. Their desire for organizational clarity and attitude towards their staff and customers shape the corporate culture. They determine whether the culture is progressive, outward looking and service oriented, or, traditional and inward looking. In information services where traditions and values are deeply rooted, certain behaviours and customs become deeply ingrained. New employees quickly have to learn how the organization operates in order to 'fit in'. Many of these behaviours are tangible issues, such as whether appointments have to be made to meet with senior executives, or whether employees are encouraged to make suggestions to better the organization. Others are more intangible, such as an acceptable topic of conversation in the lunchroom (there may be taboos on certain subjects), who goes to lunch first or whether superiors are addressed formally by title, or informally by first name.

The person who establishes the service creates the initial, and usually the strongest, corporate culture. This is achieved through both conscious and unconscious acts. For example, their values and beliefs will be translated into policies and procedures. They will recruit staff who share the same ideas and values. These values will then be unconsciously manifested into norms and behaviours over a period of time. If the culture is strong and effective, it will remain long after the founding person has left the service.

The managers' styles and behaviours must be congruent with the organization's values and behaviours. Employees will look to their managers to shape shared meanings, define and create values and demonstrate corporate beliefs. They can act as agents for change and minimize the conflict between inner and outer directed beliefs. Inner and outer directed beliefs often surface in the conflicts that exist between organizational and professional beliefs. The information services manager should assist their staff to come to terms with any conflicting beliefs or values.

Where information services have been formed through the bringing together of different work units there may either be a single strong culture or a number of subcultures. In the case of the former, the strong culture will either reflect the person who brought the units together, or it will be representative of the dominant work unit. If there are a number of subcultures these will relate to the cultures of the individual work units. The information services manager will need to promote a single unifying culture and merge the subcultures over time.

Strong and weak corporate cultures

Successful information services have strong corporate cultures. Strong cultures provide meaning and direction to members' efforts. Everyone knows the information service's objectives; people feel better about what they do and, as a consequence, are likely to work harder. The organization's networks carry the beliefs and values.

Strong cultures come from within and are built by the founders and by individual leaders, not consultants. These are people who care about their employees. No matter how distant the work units are from the organization's head office, all sites are treated equally. This is important in information services, where work unit sites may be geographically dispersed over wide areas.

Strong cultures are created, sustained, transmitted and changed through social interaction. This can be through modelling and imitation, instruction, correction, negotiation, storytelling, gossip and observation. They are communicated and reinforced by organization-wide action. High-performing information services ensure that they have well-conceived human resource programmes that reinforce the culture.

Strong cultural values are important to information services as they provide employees with a sense of what they ought to be doing, and knowledge of how they should behave consistent with organizational objectives. Strong cultures represent an emotional feeling of being part of the information service and its parent organization, and lead to greater employee commitment and motivation.

Poorly performing information services may still have a strong culture; although this may not necessarily be an effective or healthy one. In these cases the pervading culture is often dysfunctional; focusing upon internal politics rather than external commitments such as clients' needs.

Organizational subcultures

Organizational subcultures arise out of the functional differences between departments in information services. These include the use of different technologies; the identification of different values and interests; the use of different terminologies or languages; the employment of different approaches to problem-solving techniques; and the different aspects of the interactive external environment. Poor organizational performance is sometimes blamed upon the presence of subcultures.

Subcultures can also be based on gender, occupation, status, task, tenure, or ethnic origin of the work group. Socio-economic and educational backgrounds can also lead to subcultures being formed. In strong cultures subcultures do not cause problems as the overall values and beliefs are clear. However, in weak cultural environments they can be very destructive as they may obscure overriding values and result in cultural drifts.

Corporate culture types

Information services can have many different corporate culture types. In small operations there should only be one culture. This should reflect the corporate culture of the parent organization. In larger information services, where extensive differentiation occurs, more than one culture may exist.

Organizational influences	Traditional organizations	Knowledge age organizations
Vision	In the present, bettering the status quo	Universal, futuristic
Leadership	Enhancing current performance	Entrepreneurial, anticipating and positioning for the future
Corporate values	Technical perfection and efficiency	Creativity, innovation, risk taking, global thinking
Corporate culture	Bureaucratic	Fast moving, innovative, intuitive
Relationships	Competitive	Collaborative
Change	Viewed as a threat	Viewed as an opportunity
Heroes	Champions are those with technical knowledge	Champions are those with new thoughts and ideas
Behaviours	Self-preservation, anxiety, confusion, blaming	Belonging, openness, learning, trust, pride, respect for others' ideas and mutual support
Attitude to mistakes	Not tolerated	Considered part of the learning experience and innovation process

Figure 8.1 Corporate culture differences between traditional organizations and knowledge age organizations.

Source: KnowledgeAge Pty Ltd 2005 – Reprinted with permission all rights reserved.

Differences in corporate culture types arise out of organizational influences such as organization structure, the amount of risk associated with decision making and feedback received from the environment. It is important to understand the culture type in order to work effectively within and with it. There is no universally correct culture. The culture of the organization should be appropriate for the circumstances and the people involved.

Figure 8.1 illustrates the corporate culture differences between traditional organizations and those that have embraced new thinking to be effective in the knowledge age.

Values

Values are core to the organizational culture and the basis of human activities. Values comprise those matters most important to an individual, group or organization. They have a moral dimension and influence the beliefs and attitudes of individuals and groups. Examples of such values are honesty, openness and loyalty. Values contribute to the corporate climate by reflecting desired behaviours or states of affairs and influencing people's perceptions of situations and problems, choices, preferences and decisions. Consequently the corporate values should be shared between management and their people.

Corporate values espouse clear, explicit philosophies about the information service's or its parent organization's objectives. Information services and their parent organizations may not necessarily share common values. Different work areas may place different emphases on work processes, behaviours and priorities. As a result, different values emerge. These need to be acknowledged and understood.

As a service organization in an innovative environment, the information service's values are likely to be manifested in innovation, good customer service, professional standards and a commitment to quality and productivity improvement, increased employee pride and loyalty, equal opportunity and respect for individuals and their privacy, openness and accountability. Values can be reinforced through the values statement, see Figure 8.2.

Information service
Values statement

As an organization we are committed to the sharing and enabling of knowledge and information through:

- Excellence – quality products and solutions
- Respect – for ideas, opinions and the environment
- Innovation – creativity and inspiration
- Ethics –integrity and openness
- Achieving – performance and results
- Consideration – privacy and confidentiality
- Responsive – receptive to ideas and promptness in service
- Equity – in service and workplace

Figure 8.2 Values statement

Corporate values also provide the opportunity to develop an ethical philosophy within the information service. Appropriate and workable ethical principles, values and behaviours can be developed and reinforced through the corporate culture. Johannsen (2004) emphasizes personal integrity, professional drive, social skills, new thinking and ethical conscience as the most desirable characteristics of staff. Personal integrity is reflected in empowerment, pride, recognition and self-respect. Professional drive, or 'new thinking' is related to change and quality management oriented values such as care, creativity, entrepreneurship, flexibility, innovation and quality consciousness. Social skills are emphasized through values of recognition and team spirit.

Beliefs, norms, shared meanings and behaviours

BELIEFS

Beliefs are the acceptance or convictions about values. They are to a great extent shaped by the consistencies or inconsistencies between values statements and actions or behaviours of senior executives within the information service or parent organization. If there is consistency then their actions will influence the beliefs that would be expected to evolve from the stated values. Inconsistencies between values statements and actions will result in different beliefs and weaken the organizational culture.

To be successful, corporate beliefs should be visible, known and acted upon by all members of the organization. This can only be the case if they are communicated throughout the organization and reinforced through human resource management processes, recognition and rewards. They then become permanently infused and accepted as the norms by which the organization exists.

Rites and ceremonies are efficient and effective methods of communicating and instilling beliefs into an organization. In performing these, people make use of language, gestures, ritualized behaviours, artefacts and settings that heighten the expression of beliefs and shared meanings appropriate to the occasion. Logos also represent organizational symbols with which people identify.

NORMS

Norms are standards or patterns of meaningful behaviour that are passed on to others through modelling, instruction, correction and a desire to comply with others. When people interact they exchange words, tones and pitches and non-verbal behaviours such as gestures, appearances, postures and special relationships. This interaction forms patterns that, after repeated use, become accepted as the rules and systems that determine everyday behaviours and are transmitted unconsciously within organizations.

SHARED MEANINGS AND BEHAVIOURS

Shared meanings are different to social norms as they focus upon message exchange, interpretation and interaction sequencing. Shared meaning assumes that people have similar attitudes, values, views of the world and feelings about situations. Most positive actions take place on the basis of shared meaning or on an assumption that people in the same situation share common experiences and viewpoints. Shared meaning is consequently the system that allows actions, events, behaviours and emotions to take place.

Shared behaviours guide work practices, decision making and dealings with customers, clients, and people in the workplace. They set the standard of interaction and service that builds the image of the information service. Examples of shared behaviours that may be emphasized by the information service include listening to and having a mutual respect for customers and other people, solving problems as they occur, or, behaving in an ethical manner.

Corporate rituals

Many activities in organizations are expressions of corporate rituals, the consequences of which go beyond the technical details. Examples include induction, training, organizational development activities, high-profile sackings, and end-of-year celebrations or other festive occasions. Trice and Beyer (1984, pp. 653–69) have identified some organizational rites or activities that have social consequences in organizations and these are described below.

RITES OF PASSAGE

Rites of passage begin with the induction and basic training processes. These allow employees to part with their past identities and status and take on new roles. They minimize the changes that occur in the transition from old to new and re-establish the equilibrium in ongoing social relations. The induction interview with the Chief Executive Officer or the refurbishment of an office for a new manager is part of the incorporation rite. Retirement ceremonies and farewell parties are part of the rites of passage when employees retire or resign.

RITES OF DEGRADATION

Rites of degradation take place when the Chief Executive or person of high authority is fired and replaced, dissolving his or her social identity and power. Such an action may be interpreted as the organization's public acknowledgment that problems exist. As a consequence, group boundaries may be redefined around the previous close supporters of the executive. These supporters may or may not be incorporated into the newly formed groups. The social importance and value of the role are reaffirmed if the executive is replaced. If the position is not filled, it is an indication that it had no importance in the organization.

RITES OF ENHANCEMENT

Enhanced personal status and the social identification of individuals who have been successful within the corporate or professional environment are provided for by 'rites of enhancement'. Examples of such are the granting of membership to an elite group, or the granting of a fellowship or life membership to a member of a professional association. Such a membership is usually jealously guarded by those who have attained such status. Rites of enhancement spread good news about the organization and by association enable others to share some of the credit for these accomplishments.

RITES OF RENEWAL

Rites of renewal are provided in organizational development activities such as strategic-planning processes, job redesign and team-building programmes. These are rites that are intended to refurbish or strengthen the existing social structure and improve its functioning. The latent consequences of rites of renewal are that members are reassured that something is being done to correct organizational problems. However, they can be used to focus attention away from one problem to another.

CONFLICT REDUCTION RITES

Conflict reduction rites involve collective bargaining or feigned fights of negotiation where parties may become hostile, threaten to boycott or walk out of the negotiating process whilst the other parties speak of compromise, point to areas of cooperation and attempt to overcome the anger in a ritualistic way. These actions may deflect attention away from solving problems.

Other forms of conflict reduction rites are the formation of committees, advisory groups or task forces. Most of these groups serve to re-establish equilibrium in disturbed social relations. Confidence is often renewed when it is known that a committee or advisory group has been formed to investigate or advise on an issue.

RITES OF INTEGRATION

Rites of integration encourage and revive common feelings that bind members together and commit them to a social system. Such rites are found in the corporate end-of-year functions. They permit emotions to be vented and allow the temporary loosening of various norms.

Communicating corporate values

Communication is both a consequence and an enabler of the corporate culture. A corporate culture is learnt and maintained through the interaction of the people in the organization. It is also expressed through language, symbols, myths, stories and rituals. Specialized terminology, corporate logos, myths and stories of heroes and their successes, receptions for important visitors and ceremonies to launch new services are examples of these. They are symbolic devices that serve to identify and reinforce the guiding beliefs and values upon which all policies and actions take place.

Cultural values are communicated and reinforced through the various human resource management processes. The selection interview, induction process, training and development practices, performance appraisal, career development and reward systems all provide opportunities for the cultural values to be communicated.

The induction process provides the ideal situation to communicate the information service's philosophies and values and the associated management practices. Here the reasons why certain norms and behaviours are acceptable and others are not can be explained. Training and development programmes can reinforce the foundation values and philosophies.

The performance appraisal interview provides the opportunity for discussion, feedback and reinforcement of the required values and philosophies. Underlying subcultures may be detected and corrected if they contradict the overall culture. Incentives and rewards can be used to reinforce the important values and to initiate behaviours leading to good organizational performance.

Corporate stories, legends, slogans, anecdotes, myths and fairytales are also important as they convey the information service's shared values. Anecdotes and stories provide the opportunity for people to share their experiences. The significant stories are those told by many people. These are the ones that are active in the cultural network and provide evidence of the corporate culture. Newsletters and memoranda are other examples where the corporate culture is communicated.

Stories of 'heroes and villains' provide an insight into corporate values and the personal qualities of employees who are likely to be successful or unsuccessful. The attributes of those heroes who are in high esteem emulate those qualities likely to be found in successful employees. 'Villains and outlaws' are those whose values or attributes were opposed to those of the organization. They provide the corporate guidance of 'what not to do'. Villains are remembered long after they have left the organization for their 'sins'. They are the outlaws.

The rules of communication are themselves part of the corporate culture. These are tacit understandings about appropriate ways to interact with others in given roles and situations. They are generally unwritten and unspoken. As prescriptions for behaviour, they function to coordinate, interpret and justify interactive behaviour and act as self-monitoring devices. They provide guidelines as to what is acceptable interactive behaviour within the organization.

Conclusion

The corporate culture is one of the most significant influences on an organization and the behaviours of the people who work there. In fact an information service's culture may be more influential on employee behaviour than the organization structure because of its subtlety and pervasiveness.

They can be reinforced by the selection interview, induction process, training and development processes, performance appraisal interview and reward systems. Cultures are sustained and transmitted through the communication processes of languages, storytelling about the heroes and villains of the past, and through rituals and ceremonies.

Successful organizations in the knowledge age have strong innovative cultures that tolerate mistakes as part of the learning experience and which champion new ideas. The values statement is an important tool through which the organization can communicate its expectations regarding the behaviours of individuals towards each other. Values such as honesty, respect, fairness, integrity and openness should be reinforced and made part of the corporate culture through management actions, practices and procedures.

References

Johannsen, Carl Gustav (2004), 'Managing fee-based public library services: Values and practices', *Library Management*, vol. 25, no. 6/7, pp. 307–15.
Trice, H.M. and Beyer, J.M. (1984), 'Studying organizational cultures through rites and ceremonials', *Academy of Management Review*, vol. 9, Oct., pp. 653–9.

Further reading

Chen, Leida and Nath, Ravi (2005), 'Nomadic culture: Cultural support for working anytime, anywhere', *Information Systems Management*, vol. 22, no. 4, pp. 56–65.
Semler, Ricardo (1993), *Maverick: The success story behind the world's most unusual workplace*, London, UK: Century.
Semler, Ricardo (2003), *The seven-day weekend: A better way to work in the 21st century*, London, UK: Century.

9 *Politics*

Political behaviour is a natural process within organizations. It is both an individual and organizational phenomenon, linked to power, influence and competition and different values and interests. Even if everyone's interests are catered for, there can be a perception that some individuals, groups or organizational units have been treated more favourably than others. The basis for this is often politics and the personal interpretation of facts. It is inevitable in a competitive environment that people will personally interpret the facts to support their own, or their organizational unit's needs and objectives.

The activity of organizational politics is evident in the competitive behaviour between groups or individuals. Usually this is to ensure that they achieve a higher level of recognition, resource allocation, power or persuasion than their counterparts. To be effective in competitive organizational environments, it is vital that information services managers and their staff identify the political behaviours of others and manage their own. They need also to be aware that, even if their actions are not personally politically motivated, others may assume so.

Most politics and competition are beneficial to organizations as they increase the motivation and output of the various programme units or work groups. Influencing or attempting to influence the distribution of advantages and disadvantages within the organization for the benefit of the information service is part of the role of the manager. However, if unchecked politics or political behaviour are used to further an individual's needs at the expense of others it can be detrimental to all concerned. In considering whether the tactics should be condoned, the deciding feature should be the ethical impact upon the organization and individuals.

The political roles of managers

Generally, the higher the individual is in the organization, the more political their position will be. This is because senior managers need to extend their influence beyond and across organizational boundaries to achieve successful outcomes. At this level, the organizational environment is often turbulent and very competitive, with the decisions made at senior management level sometimes being politically influenced.

The political role of the information services manager is to make things happen. This requires them to create a vision and convey this to others meaningfully. For information services managers this is likely to be creating a vision and understanding in the minds of executive management of the benefits and critical importance that information sharing and knowledge management have to the success of the organization. To move the vision forward, they must know how to get things done within the parent organization and use their power constructively to drive the change. This requires them to interpret the political environment correctly, to 'open doors', to identify supporters and sponsors, and, to build networks quickly, gaining commitment and support. Noting the importance of political behaviour, Pors and Johannsen (2003, p. 57) included political actions as part of a study on library leadership:

- the director has to make the library visible in the political system;
- the director's political legitimacy will be very important;
- the director must create political contacts and networks.

Information services managers who are politically astute know what is going on within the parent organization and have control over the rules of the political game. They manage the boundaries of the information service so that it is viewed in a favourable light by those in positions of authority. Skilled political managers understand what the parent organization wants and position their services to provide creative solutions to the important problems facing the organization. They stay focused and do not let distractions or operational tasks sidetrack them.

In their political role, information services managers must speak the language that is understood and valued by the senior decision makers. They regard everyone within the parent organization as a customer and pay attention to how they project their personal image and that of the information service.

Politics in organizations

Political gamesmanship will occur when resources are scarce, when those in control feel threatened, or where there are competing views, values or agendas. Not all organizations (or groups) are as conspicuous in their political behaviour as others. In some organizations politics are overt and rampant, whilst in others politics are virtually non-existent. Furthermore, some organizations refuse to admit that political behaviour exists, preferring to believe that all is well. Usually this is because they are ill equipped to manage the conflict that is often associated with political behaviour.

The extent and type of political behaviour in organizations is influenced by the internal and external environment. Organizations that operate under pressure, have a role ambiguity and a low level of trust amongst employees are more likely to witness an overt and Machiavellian style of political behaviour than those that have clear and objective performance measures, an open and trusting environment and plenty of resources.

In bureaucratic organizations the politics will emphasize standards of control, rules, policies and procedures. The power of particular individuals to control and enforce adherence to these will lead to internal politics. In open environments characteristic of knowledge age enabled organizations there will be less emphasis on these aspects. Here the politics will operate within units, work teams or groups, and stress trust and cooperation.

In diverse organizations where there are different objectives, processes and service delivery mechanisms within units or groups, politics and conflict will often arise through misunderstanding and a lack of knowledge of others' tasks and responsibilities. The diverse structures within information services may create an environment where conflict and political rivalry may occur. For example, helpdesk people or reader services librarians who are used to dealing with diverse and immediate demands of customers may view technical service personnel as inflexible, bureaucratic or bogged down with unnecessary rules. Technical service personnel may likewise view customer services personnel with suspicion.

In changing and competitive organizational environments, the competition and uncertainty leads to differences of opinions and values, and conflicts over priorities and goals. This is true regardless of the size of the organizational unit. Whilst there will be no internal competition in a cost centre run by one person, the person would still need to compete for resources. Their power, influence and political persuasion must still be used on an organization-wide basis. Competition also leads to the formation of pressure groups, lobbying, cliques and cabals, rivalry, personality clashes and alliances. All of which are evidence of organization politics.

Politics and competition are beneficial to all organizations as they usually result in increased output between the competing groups or individuals. However, unchecked politics can result in the organization losing its sense of direction, or in its spending too much time resolving the problems at the expense of pursuing its corporate objectives.

Political behaviour that is used to further an individual's own needs may be damaging to others or the organization. An example would be an individual who influences management's perception of a co-worker to the extent that the co-worker was viewed unfavourably for promotion. This is the negative side of political behaviour and should be neutralized.

Political tactics

Politics is unavoidable and a necessary part of life. People have in the past and will continue in the future to engage in political behaviour to further their own ends, to protect themselves from others, to further goals which they believe to be in the organization's best interests, or to acquire and exercise power. Even if an individual perceives politics to be unethical, they cannot help but be occasionally involved in political battles and political networks.

Individuals who regularly engage in political behaviour often exhibit certain traits that characterize their political style. Those who are highly competitive and have excessively high self-actualization and power needs are more likely to be involved in a Machiavellian political behaviour. They look for career shortcuts and quick fixes. Other traits include the willingness to manipulate people or situations, a high need for control and the ability to exploit situations for their own self-interest.

A second type of political behaviour is the collaborative style; more attune to knowledge age environments. These people get things done through others based on knowledge, rapport and respect. They build networks of important people by serving on and contributing to strategic committees. They keep people informed and build their power based upon knowledge and doing favours for others.

Whilst organization politics may be viewed ambivalently, most people will regard any political tactics that are used by individuals for their personal gain at the expense of others as being unhealthy and unfair. Political tactics can also be genuine, ethical practices that can be beneficial to the organization.

The information services manager should readily be able to identify and use intra-organizational politics for their own benefit and that of the information service. Becoming a 'political animal' takes considerable skill, and necessitates the exercise of caution because, if the tactics are used inappropriately, the exercise will almost certainly backfire. In particular they should need to be skilful at identifying and taking action against political tactics that are adversely affecting them or their service.

There are several effective political tactics which are commonly used in organizations. Some of these are ethical, others are not (see Figure 9.1).

Clean tactics (ethical)	Dirty tactics (unethical)
Establishing an alliance with others who are willing to support the preferred position or action These may include peers, subordinates and superiors – but it is important that the right allies are chosen. These should be people who have something to contribute and who can be relied upon. Arising out of such an alliance can be the formation of a power coalition	**Attacking or blaming others** Creating a scapegoat by falsely attributing blame for negative outcomes to others is both unethical and unprofessional. A test of leadership is accepting responsibility for: • taking charge in adverse situations; and • all outcomes – good and bad
Choosing a powerful mentor Having an influential mentor can be beneficial to one's career. Such a relationship can be an effective tactic to acquiring power as others view associates of powerful people as being powerful themselves – part of the aura is passed on. Powerful mentors can assist in the reaching of important goals by 'opening doors' or establishing networks. They can also provide protection and guidance when necessary, a valuable asset in the tough times	**Deliberately misleading others** Creating perceptions or holding others responsible for events they did not produce
Developing a base of support for one's ideas In effect it enhances the individual's personal power base through the use of reverent power. Once a base of support for one's idea is gained, the supporters will want to identify with the individual and their idea	**Use of hidden agendas** Announcing one agenda for meetings and then following a totally different 'hidden' one. Preventing opponents from being adequately prepared
Creating obligations and a basis for reciprocity IOUs can be scattered by doing favours for others, assisting them with problems or supporting them against their opponents. All these actions will place them in debt. Effective users of these strategies will always get more than they give. The value of a favour may be worth more to the receiver than to the doer, the doers usually find the favours smaller and easy to perform	

Figure 9.1 Ethical and unethical political tactics used in organization

In deciding which tactics are ethical or unethical, the impact of the political behaviour upon the rights of others should be addressed. If basic human rights are violated, the political tactics are unethical. The principles of equity and fair play should also be considered, both in terms of individuals and the organization. Often political behaviour is judged according to a utilitarian approach, being the greatest good for the greatest number. Where behaviours are viewed as unethical or illegitimate they should be made to cease immediately.

Several steps can be used by the manager or supervisor to minimize the political behaviour of subordinates where it can be seen to be detrimental to their position or that of the information service. These include bringing dispute or disagreements into the open where they can be solved, and providing challenging situations and feedback to all.

Presenting political arguments

Not all dealings with people can be face to face where there is the ability to respond to verbal and non-verbal messages to reinforce the political argument. Similarly, the information services manager may not always be present at meetings to respond to questions, reinforce arguments or apply political persuasion. Therefore skills in presenting political arguments in reports are needed.

In presenting arguments, it is important that each item is properly researched and simply portrayed with the appropriate level of detail and content. Often the audience will have little time to read and consider the report. The more explicit and lucid the comment, the more favourably the report is likely to be received.

The contents of the report should anticipate and answer likely questions and be self-explanatory. The argument being presented should be able to stand on its own accord. Reports should include an executive summary that covers the important issues, benefits and recommendations for action. In some situations the executive summary can be the only part of the report that is read, so it should articulate the main points that will lead the decision makers to a favourable outcome.

The full body of the report should be clearly signposted. It should be broken down into headings and subheadings to make it easy to read and find relevant information. It should include an introductory heading, an introduction, current information on the subject of the report, viable alternative courses of action, and a recommendation(s). The opening paragraph of the main body of the report should summarize any previous history or background and indicate why the report is necessary. The current situation should be described providing up-to-date, relevant information in as precise and brief a form as possible. The alternative courses of action should be identified. These should discuss the relevant advantages, disadvantages, costings and outcomes. A preferred option should be recommended with reasons where applicable.

Lobbying and lobby groups

Lobbying is an attempt to influence decisions at the ownership level through persuasion and the provision of information. Occasionally the information services manager may lobby as a political strategy when there are important issues for the information service at stake.

Good communication channels between all levels of the organization will enhance the spread of information. At times, it may be necessary to supply additional information which will further the information service's cause. Lobbying occurs when this is provided to higher levels, either verbally or in writing, in an attempt to influence the decisions. Lobbying is a legitimate practice if used positively and with care and thought.

The information services manager may also be the subject of lobbying from lobby groups or industry. Lobby groups are a form of political group that attempt to impose their view or influence others. They may try to influence the information service on some issues, or see it as a vehicle through which their cause may be further supported. Managers will also be involved in lobbying in the course of their duties. For example, they may lobby senior management or other stakeholders before important decisions relating to the information service are made.

Lobby groups that result from organized interest groups are features of modern democratic societies. The information services manager should balance the lobby group's concerns with the overall needs of the customers, the community and industry's desires with the requirement for probity. This should be to ensure that no one sector of the community or industry influences the services to the detriment of others.

Lobby groups often regard government as a pervasive and powerful source, influencing every facet of an individual's life. Most information services are also seen to be influential as information is perceived to be power. Lobby groups may attempt to make the information service an avenue through which their point of view is promulgated to the detriment of the opposing point of view.

Lobby or interest groups can constitute the principal potential avenue of influence outside official government interaction. They need to be considered but not allowed to impose their requirements upon the organization. If possible, their energies should be channelled in a direction that can help the information service and its parent organization.

Conclusion

Politics is a natural process within organizations, as individuals and work units compete for recognition and scarce resources. Politics is also about the distribution of advantages and disadvantages and how individuals use their power and influence in this distribution process. Whilst those who lose may perceive politics to be unfair, many are quite ethical. However, unchecked or unethical politics are unfair. They have the capacity to harm the organization as well as its people and should not be tolerated within the organizational culture.

To be successful in a competitive environment it is important that the information services manager is politically astute and able to engage with key decision makers in a way that they can understand the issues and opportunities that the information service can present, as well as manage the organizational politics for the benefit of the information service.

References

Pors, Niels Ole and Johannsen, Carl Gustav (2003), 'Library directors under cross-pressure between new public management and value-based management', *Library Management*, vol. 24, no. 1/2, pp. 51–60.

Further Reading

Bacharach, Samuel B. (2005), 'Successful leaders are politically competent', *Leadership Excellence*, June, pp. 6–7.
Kakabadse, Andrew et al. (2004), *Working in organisations*, Aldershot, UK: Ashgate.

10 *Policy Making*

Organizations are made up of individuals and groups of people with different values and interests. Policy making is one mechanism to ensure that these individual interests are managed for the greater good, and to ensure that individuals within the organization are moving forward in the same direction. Policy making is also necessary to safeguard individual rights such as in the case of policies on the protection of privacy and commercial confidentiality.

Policy development is an ongoing process that evolves through continuous consultation with internal and external stakeholders. The information service and its parent organization can also be subject to policies and standards that have been established by external parties, such as government bodies or international standard setting organizations.

Use of policies

Policy making incorporates the development of policies, standards and guidelines that ensure decisions are in keeping with the organization's philosophies. They can be used to enhance the image of the parent organization as a good corporate citizen. Policies, standards and guidelines are used within organizations to:

- solve a recurrent problem at the organizational level;
- provide guidance for individuals in decision making;
- ensure consistency in approach across the organization;
- declare an intention or enable a stance to be taken on a contemporary issue;
- clarify organizational values and intentions;
- make a commitment; and
- grant rights or entitlements.

Policies are guides to the decision-making process. Like objectives, policies can either be general or specific. General policies are used throughout the organization, and are usually broad and comprehensive. They affect all work units and levels of staff. General policies address issues such as the use of desktop equipment for home or personal use; or security and risk covering access to systems and the need to protect personal information. Some general policies will be influenced by legislation or policies and standards that have been established by external parties. For example, general policies on the protection and use of software may be influenced by copyright legislation or the parent organization's licence conditions with the software vendor.

Specific policies often relate to operational issues. They have significance for a particular department or work unit and are more relevant to day-to-day issues or specific activities. Only those individuals who are directly concerned with the activity or work unit will be affected by the policy. A policy that relates to the selection process in a children's collection in a public library is an example of a specific policy.

Effective information service policies solve problems or channel decisions towards achieving the objectives of the service and its parent organization. Once overall policies or standards have been established, they can be effective tools for moving decision making to the point of service delivery. With an effective policy framework, individuals and groups can take initiatives in making decisions, knowing that the outcomes will still be in line with the ultimate achievement of the organization's objectives.

Examples of information service policies include those that determine the type of material eligible to be archived or how information services and products will be charged to clients. Examples of standards include naming standards for records or data capture and transfer standards.

Policy development

Policy making is a complex activity that requires lots of consultation with individuals and groups from within the information service and parent organization and with other external stakeholders. This is because policies are usually performed by people other than those who design them. Good policies are developed with this in mind, for if they cannot be implemented effectively they will fail.

The policy-making process, including the development of standards and guidelines, should be well planned and thought out in terms of strategic timing, costs, issues at stake, and the values and attitudes of the internal and external stakeholders. The implementation of a policy often implies some form of change, whether at the strategic or operational level. As a result, conflict may arise through the change processes that may in turn jeopardize the policy.

Policy making is an ongoing process. It does not start or stop in the form of discrete events. Effective policy making involves continuous modification and adjustment. This continuous improvement processes should reflect amendments to the corporate objectives or repositioning of the organization within the changing competitive environment.

STEPS TO POLICY DEVELOPMENT

Policy development should be undertaken through a series of steps (see Figure 10.1). The first step is to ensure that all environmental factors that could impact upon the policy are taken into consideration. Those developing the policy should be cognizant of the financial, social and political context of the parent organization and how these could shape the available options and strategies. For example, the financial situation of the parent organization may limit the choice of outcome or scale of the policy or call for a gradual implementation of the policy.

The policy development process should take into account known values of all stakeholders. The likely future scenarios for the organization and the environment in which the policy will operate should be identified so that the policy can be designed with the future state in mind. Timing is an important consideration in policy development, particularly when the policy may have some political impact for the organization.

The next step is to identify the issue and to determine whether this can be solved through a policy or an alternative mechanism. Not all issues can be solved through policies. Likewise, policies should not be created for aggrandizement or self-importance. Policies are useful to resolve common sources of disagreement or provide guidance on an emerging issue that has been identified through the environmental scanning process.

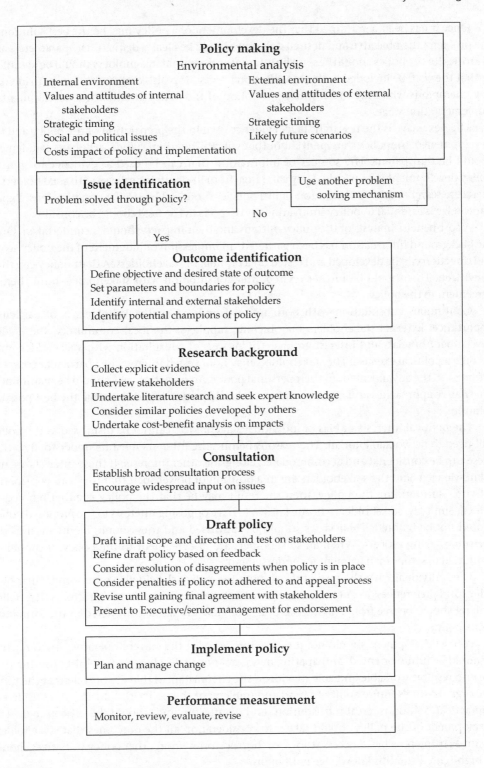

Figure 10.1 The policy development process

Once it has been determined that the development of a policy may be the best solution to the problem, the objective and desired outcome should be clearly defined. The parameters and priorities for the policy should be set. The internal and external stakeholders should be identified so that they can be included in the consultation process. It is also useful at this stage to identify any champions who may assist in the promotion of the policy at either the development or implementation stage.

The next stage is the research stage. Evidence used in the preparation of the policy and the development of the policy statement should be explicit. The criteria used for the basis of judgment should be transparent. The sources of information that can be used as evidence to support policy development vary widely. They can range from in-depth interviews with stakeholders to literature searches and consideration of like policies produced by similar organizations. Expert knowledge is essential to policy innovation and experts in the field should be consulted.

A cost-benefit analysis of the policy options and their impacts should be undertaken. Once the background information has been gathered, an impression or judgment of the policy scope and direction can be developed and tested on a number of stakeholders. A draft policy can then be written. This should be further revised after consultation with stakeholders until there is agreement to the policy.

Continuous consultation with both internal and external stakeholders is of particular importance. External stakeholders may include suppliers, the local community, the media, government officials and interest groups. The process of consultation with stakeholders may become a political exercise. The stakeholders may hold vested interests in a particular course of action or in the advancement of their personal power. An objective view should be maintained. Alternative approaches and counter-scenarios should be developed to enable the best possible solution.

The political interests or bias of individual stakeholders cannot be dismissed as the policy will need to be workable for all. The reasons behind the interests must be understood so that these can be considered and accommodated alongside other interests. If these interests are not acknowledged, and the stakeholders are in a position of power such that they can control the activities surrounding the policy, then the result may be that the policy is either ignored or vetoed. Similarly, stakeholders who are known to have opposing interests to the proposed policy should not be ignored. Their views should be canvassed and they should be involved in the decision-making process. When all stakeholders are in agreement to the policy, it should be submitted to senior management for endorsement.

The individual with the task of developing the policy should also ensure that their own values and preferences do not influence the subject matter. The underlying factor is that policy making should be free from bias and all points of view should be considered in the formation of the policy.

Policy development should not just take into account the current operative environment. It should be future oriented, anticipating new demands or developments, whilst ensuring that the end result is workable and able to address the circumstances that are prevalent at the time. The organization's future ability to fund and implement the policy should also be considered. Impractical solutions create frustration and confusion and should be discounted. The development of the policy should take into consideration all the outcomes that stakeholders regard as being possible. 'Success stories' or 'horror stories' from other policy initiatives should be highlighted and this knowledge built upon.

The policy development process should take into account how issues may be resolved where there is disagreement about the contents of the policy once it is in place. Where appropriate, a disciplinary process and penalties for failing to act within the policy should be developed. Any disciplinary process should be matched by an appeal process.

The development of the policy is the first part of the policy process. Once developed, the policy needs to be implemented and its performance monitored. It may need to be refined to take into account changing circumstances.

INHIBITORS TO EFFECTIVE POLICY DEVELOPMENT

Very few policy development processes are fully resourced or provided with sufficient time to investigate and present different options. Often the need for a quick decision limits the level of consultation. There is also the danger that policy development is 'fitted in' to existing workloads and priorities. In these situations, policy solutions can be limited in input, relevant expertise, innovation and strategy.

Policy framework

The policy framework of an information service comprises policies, standards and guidelines. Standards differ from policies in that they are usually technical in nature. They define levels of conformity and input, and establish performance outputs. Guidelines supplement policies and standards, providing further background information. They are often used to provide advice regarding the implementation of the policy and standards.

POLICY STATEMENT

The policy statement describes the policy. It is usually brief. The policy statement may be supplemented by statements about:

- the policy objective and scope;
- responsibility for implementation, review and audit;
- background issues; and
- implementation strategies.

STANDARDS

Standards provide for consistency in the use of resources. In information services, standards provide rules about the choice and management of information and its supporting technologies. Standards may be set at the international, national and organizational level. They include protocols, data capture and transfer standards, bibliographic descriptions and standards for record keeping. Standards may also determine accommodation requirements and service levels. These will be particularly important in identifying customer service levels or in instances where services are contracted out to third parties.

GUIDELINES

Guidelines provide a more in-depth description about the policies and standards. They are often very practical and address the implementation and operational issues that are associated with the policies and standards.

Policies, standards and guidelines are usually promulgated on the organization's intranet as this is a convenient way of ensuring that everyone has access. Many organizations may also have a set of unwritten rules or policies. Putting policies on the intranet avoids duplication of effort and eliminates the possibility of out-of-date policy material being used in decision making. Making new members of staff aware of the policies and their existence on the intranet is an important part of the induction process.

Conclusion

Policies are mechanisms for ensuring that individuals are treated fairly and equitably and that individual interests are managed for the greater good. They are guides to decision making. Accordingly they should be developed through a consultative process with all stakeholders to ensure that different values and interests are considered in decisions.

11 *Innovation and Creativity*

Innovation is the ability to turn knowledge and bright ideas into an opportunity or to use these ideas to solve a problem. Creativity occurs when people are inspired to show ingenuity, have originality in thought and are willing and able to demonstrate inventiveness.

Today, senior executives are under constant pressure to find new sources of growth in an increasingly demanding and competitive business environment. Innovation and creativity are the new business enablers and sources of growth. They are necessary ingredients to future proof organizations by providing:

- imaginative insight and out of the box thinking when identifying possible risks and opportunities and in forewarning of major changes in the environment;
- the means to deal with the unstructured problems arising out of competitive and rapidly changing environments; and
- vision, imagination and inventiveness to create new product and service offerings ahead of competitors.

Organizations that are advanced in their thinking in the knowledge age recognize that there is a shift from the strategic management of material goods to the strategic management of intellectual property and branding. In attaching more importance to intangible assets than material goods, systems are put in place to identify and properly manage all the intellectual property.

Supporting this shift in thinking is the recognition that productivity alone is no longer as significant a contributor to success as it was in the past. People's capacities to solve problems in unique ways, to conceive bright ideas, and use entrepreneurial thinking have equal importance. Their know-how, talents, skills and expertise need to be recognized as an important corporate asset and their further development encouraged. To meet this challenge, Leavy (2005) says that 'CEOs must learn to inspire their organizations to new levels of inventiveness in everything that they do, not just in marketing or new product development'.

The creative environment is one that taps into the creative potential of all employees and allows champions of change to set standards, promote ideas, to build support and to implement new ideas. It requires a corporate culture that values flexibility and adaptability; one that is risk taking and supportive of open communication as well as being open to new ideas. A creative environment is fostered through leadership and management practices, as well as making itself attractive to more diverse and unconventional talent. Rewards systems and performance reviews that support and actively encourage ideas generation and divergent thoughts in problem solving also assist in maintaining and reinforcing the creative culture.

Supporting these ideas, Leavy (2005) identifies four climate-setting factors that help create an innovative culture:

- placing of people and ideas at the heart of the management philosophy;

- giving people room to grow, to try things and learn from their mistakes;
- building a strong sense of openness, trust and community across the organization; and
- facilitating the internal mobility of talent.

Management oversight – roles and responsibilities

Innovation and creativity have need for a balanced mix of leaders, ideas generation, champions, intraprenuers, upholders, gate keepers and coaches. These key functions call for people with specific skills and personal attributes.

In traditional thinking organizations, leaders often viewed themselves as having sole responsibility for the new ideas that contributed to the success of the organization. Leaders who are in tune with knowledge age thinking acknowledge that they do not necessarily need to be the idea generators. Everyone in the organization contributes these ideas in different ways. Their most significant role is in providing strong leadership that is open to challenge and fostering a creative corporate environment where there is:

- interaction between individuals to bounce ideas off each other;
- a substantial body of knowledge and a learning environment from which new ideas can be drawn;
- a customary thought process that enables new combinations of ideas; and
- time allocated where people are encouraged to participate in new thinking.

The idea generators are those with expertise in the field and who enjoy conceptualization. They are also good at problem solving and seeing new and different ways of doing things. Idea generators need sponsors who are sufficiently high up in the organization to marshal the required resources to support the proposed activity. Executive management has a sponsorship role in ensuring organizational commitment and that the necessary resources in people, knowledge, time and money are available.

Another set of people who perform critical functions are champions. Champions are energetic and determined, they demonstrate a commitment and push ahead with the idea no matter what the roadblocks. Champions take risks in getting things done, sometimes at a personal cost. Whilst they might not have a strong knowledge of the discipline, they are visionary in that they can see how the idea can be applied and sell the idea and its application to others.

Intrapreneurs are the entrepreneurs who champion creativity and change within an organization. They have the cross-specialized talents of entrepreneurship, risk taking, idea generation and gate keeping and the attributes to lead and manage natural love–hate relationships, confrontation and conflict.

Their work is often managing the interdepartmental rivalries and conflicts that need to be resolved with care to ensure that creativity is not stifled, that ineffective compromises are not made and that interdepartmental communication and cooperation are not adversely affected during the period of change.

Every innovative idea will need an upholder. Upholders plan, support and organize the innovation as it moves from being an idea into a project or production mode. Upholders focus on the administrative tasks of finance, marketing and coordinating, and know how to progress things within the organization. They also ensure that the legal requirements are met, which might include registration of a trademark, design or complying with copyright. In successfully moving the project forward, they also know and acknowledge where there may be sensitivities in coordinating groups and people involved in the project.

Gatekeepers span the boundary of the organization and the discipline. They possess a high level of technical competence and keep themselves informed of future trends and developments in their field of expertise, which they readily share with others in the organization. They have strong networks and are seen as an authoritative and credible source of knowledge in a particular subject. Gatekeepers are good communicators and are often aware of competitor moves through their connections. They are usually approachable and enjoy the contact with others.

Coaches help develop others' talents and provide encouragement and a sounding board for new ideas. As a source of objectivity, they provide legitimacy and organizational confidence in the innovative project. They also have credibility and can play both a protective role by buffering the project from unnecessary constraints as well as a linking role to other significant stakeholders.

Creating the innovative environment

MANAGING CHANGE

Creativity produces change that further creates conflict. Creativity can also be used to manage resistance to change and conflict. The conversion of conventional work practices and values into ones that are entrepreneurial and risk taking takes considerable skill and foresight. A culture needs to be created that not only values knowledge sharing, ideas generation, open communication and entrepreneurial thinking, but also sustains that commitment year after year. This means a major shift in the values for some people, not just a slight increase in awareness of entrepreneurship or the establishment of one or two new programmes or activities for the year. The people leading the change will have to champion their cause, motivate and prepare others to readily accept change.

People must be receptive to innovation and willing to perceive change as an opportunity rather than a threat. Most people are creatures of habit and resist change, seeing it as threatening their existence. It takes leadership skills to create an environment in which change is encouraged and accepted as the norm.

WILLINGNESS TO TAKE RISKS

Creating an innovative and creative corporate environment as described above requires a culture that supports risk taking without penalty when mistakes occur. Management must be willing to take risks and allow their people to make mistakes as part of the learning process. If failure means the loss of a job or not being given the opportunity to try something new again either on a group or individual basis, creativity and innovation will be discouraged. Furthermore, the corporate culture will hold the belief that if you value your job, it is not worthwhile to attempt anything difficult or challenging.

Risk taking is a balancing act. It does not mean proceeding with an action prior to considering all its possible consequences, and it is important not to create an impression that only winners get promoted. It is about creating an environment where everyone is valued for bringing their bright ideas to work rather than leaving them at home, where there is a culture of asking 'how' rather than 'why', and people are comfortable with offering ideas that have been thought through.

OPEN COMMUNICATION

Creativity and innovation are dependent upon open communication channels to share knowledge and new ideas. Unnecessary bureaucratic procedures and lines of authority can stifle the exchange of ideas and experiences between people. Whilst everyone should be encouraged to be creative; divergent thinkers should be particularly motivated and encouraged to share their ideas with others. Individuals with talent should be recognized and persuaded to champion their ideas.

ORGANIZATIONAL STRUCTURE

Successful organizations are designed to encourage creativity and change. Organizations that consist of small teams or groups are more likely to foster creativity as new ideas and fast action can flourish without bureaucratic overheads. Strong lines of authority often prevent initiative and creativity. Organizational structures also influence the behaviours, communication and interactions of people. A structure that facilitates the sharing and testing of ideas is a prerequisite for creativity and innovation.

ENCOURAGING PEOPLE TO THINK CREATIVELY

An innovative climate is reinforced through policies and practices that encourage opportunistic practices. Whilst some people will be more creative than others, everyone has the capacity to contribute new knowledge and use their ingenuity regardless of their background and experience. Even the most unusual idea should be given consideration by management. People should be given the freedom to try new ways of performing tasks and their successes celebrated. Challenging, yet realistic, goals should be set and immediate and timely feedback on performance given. Participative decision making and problem solving should be encouraged. Responsibility should be delegated to allow staff to be self-guiding in their work.

Personal development strategies allow for creative pastimes. The balance of right and left brain activities is necessary to assist personal growth and achievement. Creativity can also play a part in making personal career decisions in times of contracting employment opportunities. Individuals who are creative in setting their career goals and who proactively seek opportunities to achieve these will be more likely to succeed than those who do not.

PRIDE AND COMMITMENT

Innovative organizations generally have a culture where acceptance of responsibility and a commitment to the organization goes beyond the individual's functional role. The organization exhibits pride and there is positive reinforcement of it being an employer of choice and a role model for others. Success breeds on success and this in turn reinforces the commitment and dedication to the organization.

RECRUIT AND MOTIVATE CREATIVE TALENT

Innovative organizations go out of their way to recruit and keep talent. Leavy (2005) says that innovative companies thrive on a diversity of talent and outlook. Accordingly, they put much thought and effort into the recruitment process and Leavy identifies three ways of recruiting creative talent:

- hire individuals with a range of abilities and interests;
- hire people with a variety of backgrounds and personalities; and
- involve peers heavily in the selection process.

Conclusion

Innovation and creativity are critical to organizational success in the knowledge age. Innovation requires a strong corporate culture that is flexible and open. Innovative organizations are highly skilled in measuring, managing and improving their intellectual capital, knowledge and know-how. People are inspired to show ingenuity and creativity by senior management and are judged on their contribution, which can come from many roles. The corporate culture encourages originality and resourcefulness, celebrates success and views mistakes as a learning process. These beliefs are communicated formally and informally. Although conflict is inevitable during the change that innovative processes bring, successfully innovative organizations manage this to ensure that creativity is not stifled.

References

Leavy, Brian (2005), 'A leader's guide to creating an innovation culture', *Strategy and Leadership*, vol. 33, no. 4, pp. 38–46.

Further reading

Brown, J.S. and Duguid, P. (2001), 'Creativity versus structure: A useful tension', *Sloan Management Review*, vol. 42, no. 4, pp. 93–4.

Davenport, T.H. et al. (2003), 'Who's bringing you hot ideas and how are you responding?', *Harvard Business Review*, vol. 81, no. 2, pp. 58–64.

Drucker, Peter F. (2002), 'The discipline of innovation', *Harvard Business Review*, vol. 80, no. 8, Aug., pp. 95–8, 100, 102–3.

Dundon, Elaine and Pattakos, Alex (2002), 'Cultivating innovation', *Executive Excellence*, vol. 19, no. 11, Nov., pp. 6–17.

Hamel, Gary (1998), 'Strategy innovation', *Executive Excellence*, vol. 15, no. 8, Aug., pp. 7–8.

Higdon, Leo I. Jnr. (2000), 'Leading innovation', *Executive Excellence*, vol. 17, no. 8, Aug., pp. 15–16.

Kanter, Rosabeth Moss (2000), 'A culture of innovation', *Executive Excellence*, vol. 17, no. 8, Aug., pp. 10–11.

PART **IV**

Transforming the Corporate Environment

The theme for Part IV is how to transform traditional thinking organizations into those that embrace an organizational philosophy and culture in keeping with the knowledge age environment. It focuses on the leadership, interpersonal and people management roles needed to effect change and reposition the information service in the global knowledge economy and society, as well as manage the impact of sudden and strategic changes that emanate from the external environment.

Chapter 12 addresses the issue of leadership. It describes the roles, skills and attributes of transformational leaders and provides tangible mechanisms for measuring the effectiveness of a leader.

Chapter 13 introduces the concept of change and how it can be initiated and managed in a positive manner. New technologies, increased competition and complex external environments mean that information services have to change rapidly and radically for their survival. In fact information and communications technology (ICT) is often used as a critical tool for effecting transformational change in organizations. Change can be planned, arising from organizational life cycles and other proactive forces, or it can be sudden and discontinuous. The strategies for managing change differ according to whether the change is continuous or discontinuous. This chapter includes strategies for managing both continuous and discontinuous change. It considers resistance to change at both the organizational and individual levels. The chapter also introduces the concepts of business and process re-engineering that are being used by organizations to rethink their mechanisms of operating in complex and competitive environments.

Chapter 14 provides an understanding of group and team dynamics at the organizational and individual levels. Most organizational structures comprise groups and teams as these are a more effective means of handling diversity and continually changing environments. A manager's understanding of group or team behaviour is as important as understanding individual behaviour. This is because people act differently when they are in a group. In order to achieve outcomes, managers have to recognize and manage different group roles and stages of group development.

Both informal and formal groups can be found in organizations. The presence and leadership of informal groups will often provide an insight into the power, politics and authority within the information service and its parent organization. As groups develop they assume certain characteristics that are associated with group norms, member roles and group cohesiveness. As members of groups, individuals play different roles. These roles can change the way in which people behave in certain situations; they can also create a situation of personal conflict. Chapter 14 explains this and why conflict occurs at the personal level, between members of the group during the development stage and between groups.

A further aspect of group development is team building. The major difference between a group and a team is that groups generally have one leader. In a team, all the members are leaders. Chapter 14 explores mechanisms to build high-performing teams. Team building involves all the leadership and facilitation skills that are required to accomplish individual performance, and applies these to a team environment. The chapter also considers a model that can be used to maximze the performance of a self-managing team by enacting different leadership roles at different stages in the development of the team.

Motivation is a key driver in getting other people to do things to achieve the corporate objectives. Not everyone is motivated by the same thing. Chapter 15 considers strategies to motivate individuals at both the organizational and individual levels. At the organizational level, workforce flexibility, performance-based compensation, job enrichment and job enlargement can be used to motivate people. At the individual level, individual needs must be taken into account.

In changing and transforming environments conflict is inevitable and is a healthy sign of organizational growth and competition. It can also be destructive and inhibit things being done within the information service. Chapter 16 looks at sources of conflict at both the organizational and individual levels. The advantages of conflict are identified. The chapter includes sections on managing and resolving conflict, interpersonal styles for managing conflict and methods for detecting conflict in information services.

Negotiation is a key mechanism for effective transformational change. Chapter 17 is about negotiating to achieve desired outcomes. It includes sections on effective negotiation, the process of negotiation, problems in negotiations and factors for successful negotiations.

PLANNING AND MANAGING FOR TRANSFORMATION

CREATING THE RIGHT CORPORATE ENVIRONMENT

TRANSFORMING THE CORPORATE ENVIRONMENT

MANAGING YOURSELF AND OTHERS

MANAGING IN A DYNAMIC ENVIRONMENT

EPILOGUE

POSITIONING TO EXCEL IN SERVICE DELIVERY

PART IV – TRANSFORMING THE CORPORATE ENVIRONMENT

12. **Leadership**
Transformational leadership – roles and responsibilities; Transformational leadership skills and attributes; Traditional leadership styles; Measuring leadership effectiveness

13. **Engaging in change**
Sources of organizational change; Creating and engaging change; Overcoming resistance to change; Reengineering and change

14. **Group dynamics and team building**
Types of groups; Stages of group development; Group cohesiveness; Group roles; Group norms; Effective team building; Self-managing work teams; Managing inter-team conflict

15. **Motivation**
Organizational strategies; Individual strategies; Traditional motivation theories; Satisfiers and dissatisfiers in information services

16. **Conflict management**
The place for conflict in organizations; Sources of organizational conflict; Identifying personal conflict; Resolving conflict; Conflict management styles; Detecting conflict in information services

17. **Negotiation**
Effective negotiation; The process of negotiation; Issues affecting negotiation; Strategies for effective negotiations; Bargaining

GOVERNANCE AND ACCOUNTABILITY

Figure PIV.1   Transforming the corporate environment

12 *Leadership*

Leadership was once considered to be an influencing role that used motivation techniques to persuade others to undertake certain tasks to achieve an outcome. In the knowledge age the expectation of a leader is much larger and more complex. The connected and intelligent world requires a far-sighted and transformational approach that creates a sense of passion, energy and excitement about the future, but is ready to make quick and effective decisions in a time of crisis. Leadership in the knowledge age is of a transformational nature.

Transformational leadership entails proactive, visionary, entrepreneurial and risk-taking people. These are individuals who look to the future for opportunities in an age of high uncertainty and fast-changing environments, yet provide a clear understanding of what their organization is trying to achieve and why. In adverse scenarios, transformational leaders are those who find the exit strategy or the way out when others consider that the situation is lost.

Transformational leadership – roles and responsibilities

Transformational leaders have a different perception on their role and outlook as identified in Figure 12.1. They have a wider perspective on issues, seeing the whole and making connections. Managing, enabling and empowering people to share knowledge and information are considered key roles in creating and innovative environment.

The principal role of transformational leaders is to be the creator of the future and of corporate environments and capacities. These leaders visualize their preferred future for the organization and then make it happen. They share their vision with others, so that they can join with them in creating this future. They instil a sense of excitement and passion about future challenges, opportunities and possibilities. Being entrepreneurial, they are concerned with ensuring that the organization is well positioned for the future, that it keeps inventing new business advantages by which it can remain out in front of its competitors.

Transformational leaders work across geographic and organizational boundaries. They have a global view and anticipate and manage the driving forces that will shape the external environment. They also concentrate on what the organization needs to have in place to outperform others in a globally competitive environment. They do this by creating a corporate capacity to exploit knowledge and innovation in preparing for the future, to think globally, plan for the unthinkable and outwit the competitors. They involve everyone in this process, maximizing the input of ideas and knowledge.

Transformational leaders must also exhibit a grounded approach when needed. In problem solving they take a strategic view. They also have a strong and analytical focus on planning. By nature of their position, they must have a whole picture perspective and a thorough understanding of the interdependence of various parts of the organization when making decisions for the future.

Roles and responsibilities	Traditional leadership	Transformational leadership for the knowledge age
Principal role	Enhance current performance	Entrepreneurial, anticipate and position for the future
Boundary spanning	Creates and relies on boundaries	Creates opportunities, ignores boundaries
Horizon	Internal and immediate	Global, universal
Decision making	Rules and regulations based. Quantitative analysis	Looks beyond rules and regulations. Intuitive, uses critical thinking, making the connections thinking
Knowledge enablement	Information considered source of power – closely held	Enabling knowledge and information sharing considered a critical role in creating an innovative environment
Outlook	Preserve status quo. Considers why things can't be done. Anticipates and looks for roadblocks	Continually pushes comfort zones and boundaries. Views adversity as a challenge. Looks for the way around roadblocks
Perspective	Components	Whole picture
Problem solving	Cause and effect of static individual local issues	Sense making, interconnectivity and relationships in dynamic global environment
Rationale	Questions why?	Questions why not?
Relationships	Coordinating individual components	Coaching to understand rapidly changing environment
Reputation	Efficiency	Visionary, creating preferred future, passion, vitality, nerve, risk taking

Figure 12.1 Leadership roles and responsibilities in traditional and knowledge age environments.

Source: Knowledge Age Pty Ltd 2005 – Reprinted with permission all rights reserved.

Transformational leaders both create and make sense of change. To keep the organization ahead of its competitors they must create a changing environment. They must also make sense of the environment that is changing around them, making connections and applying intuition. They also help other people to do this and to see the imperative for change. In facilitating internal change, they initiate coping strategies that enable people to let go of the old ideas and practices in order to instil new ways and thinking.

Transformational leaders strive for excellence and deliver on results. However, they recognize that there will also be hard times and catastrophic occurrences, when they have to share bad news and show courage. Transformational leaders ready the organization to deal with these occurrences by identifying and planning actions to overcome potential adverse scenarios, and in building organizational responsiveness and trust in its capability to do this.

Transformational leaders create an achieving atmosphere in which others are encouraged to exceed their expectations of themselves. They have passion, commitment and a willingness to make a personal investment in people, the organization and its outcomes. They recognize that they do not have a monopoly on all the ideas, that people are the most precious commodity, who need to be inspired and motivated. They foster an open culture and open communication, where there is respect for differing opinions and cultural backgrounds.

To do this, good leaders build relationships and personal connections with people in the organization, with those around them and with key stakeholders. In growing the skills and competencies of their people, they demonstrate high expectations for others and drive people to do their best. They give people important activities and sufficient autonomy to exercise their own judgment in undertaking the tasks. They monitor their results and provide continuous feedback on how they perceive their performance and if they have met their needs and expectations.

In their enabling role, transformational leaders align structures, systems and cultures to support the future business direction of the organization. They also ensure that individual and team roles are aligned with corporate goals and that everyone knows and understands how they contribute to the overall success and direction of the organization.

Transformational leaders set high expectations of themselves as well as others, especially in the area of ethical behaviours. As the moral guardians of corporate ethics, integrity and professional conduct, their role is to set and lead by example in their behaviours and in communicating these core values. Synonymous with this, trust is also important. These leaders create a high-trust and highly cooperative environment where there is consistency in messages and a confidence in people acting with integrity.

Transformational leaders are risk takers. They are willing to take measured risks and consider new and untested approaches themselves. They also help people overcome their fear of risk taking by creating a corporate environment in which it is acknowledged that mistakes are part of the path to innovation.

Transformational leadership skills and attributes

Transformational leadership is about who you are, which then influences what you do. The leadership role of surviving, thriving, innovating and excelling in a dynamic environment calls for qualities of resilience in adversity and passion to energize and enthuse others and for the cause. These leadership qualities are based on skills and natural gifts and strengths, most of which can be learnt. Transformational leadership skills are best developed in a corporate climate that fosters encouragement, cooperation, admiration, trust and loyalty and where there are role models to provide examples of effective leadership.

Transformational leaders display the following personal merits and traits. Whilst these personal traits may not naturally occur, they can be practised so that they become normal conduct and behaviour:

- strong commitment and eagerness to enable the organization to survive and excel, often to the point of being a zealot;
- passion to inspire, energize and excite others;
- energy, drive and capacity to engage and keep others enthusiastic, even in difficult circumstances; and
- strong personal commitment to ethics, truth and integrity.

Transformational leaders are good communicators. They also have strong intuitive and critical thinking skills. They are able to deal with complexity and view roadblocks and adversity as a challenge.

Traditional leadership styles

Traditional leadership behaviours are still exhibited in organizations. Generally they can be classified into four groups: the bureaucrat, the democrat, the visionary and the politician.

THE BUREAUCRAT

The bureaucrat is generally pleasant and mild mannered. They are slow and cautious in approach, relying upon structure and well-developed management systems. They use working parties to advise and decide upon issues; this slows down decision making. They focus upon facts, rules and rationale for past decisions. They operate through formal channels of communication. The bureaucrat has a high need for legitimate power and control. They can be authoritarian, their authority being based upon position.

THE DEMOCRAT

The democrat operates within the organization as though it is a family. They focus on the people issues, sometimes to the detriment of the strategic issues. They use strong consultation mechanisms that inhibit quick decision making. They communicate their feelings and seek to understand others' feelings, needs and thoughts. The democrat relies upon their personal characteristics to get things done. Their power is based upon referent power.

THE VISIONARY

Visionary leaders inspire others through symbols and personal charisma. They are often very energetic, enthusiastic and creative. They have well-developed interpersonal skills but can lack attention to detail. They act as a facilitator and catalyst by focusing on the vision and values. The visionary influences through persuasion.

THE POLITICIAN

The politician regards the organizational environment as a jungle. They spend much of their time negotiating, focusing on conflict and building coalitions and networks with stakeholders. They will occasionally make contact with the staff, asking how they are getting on, but provide little guidance and feedback. Strategic initiatives by staff are well supported, particularly if they are in line with their own objectives. Non-performers are either quickly dispensed with or generally ignored. The politician is an innovator, using a mix of coercive and reward power to achieve outcomes.

Measuring leadership effectiveness in information services

Leadership effectiveness can be judged by how well the organization is positioned for the future as effective leaders create and share a vision for the future and instil a sense of excitement about the challenges, opportunities and possibilities faced by the information service. However, the end game is not to be judged on always being the 'best of all breeds' in showcasing the latest and best in technology at the expense of other things. Rather, it is on focusing on being 'best of breed' on the components that the service identifies as being critical to its success. For example, a reputation for high-quality service delivery, being an employer of choice, and professional recognition of the organization's preparedness to be innovative are worthy indicators of effective leadership.

Effective leaders display a passion for their own work and instil a sense of excitement and enthusiasm that leads to a highly motivate staff within the information service. Where there is strong leadership, and an alignment of structure, roles, systems and corporate culture with the business direction of the organization, motivation will be higher. In contrast, an inappropriate leadership style and a lack of clarity in goals will lead to individual dissatisfaction and lowered morale. Effective leadership is demonstrated when people:

- have a clear understanding of what the information service is trying to achieve and why;
- have a clear understanding of how their tasks fit with their team's and the information service's goals;
- look for opportunities and engage in change from within; and
- come to work enthusiastic about their work and organization.

Individuals rely upon the leadership skills of their managers to allow them to achieve their need for motivation, rewards and ability to perform their allocated tasks. Consequently, the leader's ability to reduce the roadblocks and increase the opportunities for personal satisfaction can be tested through satisfaction levels with the work that people have accomplished at the end of the day. According to Pors and Johannsen (2003, p. 58) the least important leadership roles are as a controller, rule maker, professional expert and administrator. They believe the leadership roles that are expected to have the greatest importance in the future are:

- strategic leaders and vision shaper;
- creator of results;
- value creator and carrier of culture; and
- network builder.

Trust and ethical behaviour in the corporate environment are important indicators of leadership effectiveness in information services. These can be measured by considering:

- the extent to which people trust the organization they work for;
- the level of high-trust, highly cooperative working relationships between teams; and
- the extent to which people perceive the information service to be a high-trust environment.

The high uncertainty and fast-changing environment that typifies the knowledge age can be confusing for many. The extent to which leaders change people's awareness of issues and help them to look at issues in new ways are also measures of effectiveness in this environment.

Conclusion

Leadership in the knowledge age environment is an enabling act of transforming people and organizations so that they are better prepared to capitalize on opportunities and minimize threats. It involves setting a vision and providing clarity of direction, ensuring commitment and creating synergies in a trusted environment where values of ethics, integrity and honesty are honoured. Transformational leaders foster open communication that is respectful of differing opinions whilst leading to innovation and new solutions to problems.

Transformational leaders create excellence and deliver results that capitalize on opportunities. Whilst they are optimistic about the future they understand that undesirable events happen and ready the organization to overcome adverse scenarios and find solutions to negative situations.

Transformational leaders excite people through their passion and build loyalty and respect for themselves and the organization. They demonstrate courage and persistence and transform people by tapping into their dreams and ideals.

References

Pors, Niels Ole and Johannsen, Carl Gustav (2003), 'Library directors under cross-pressure between new public management and value-based management', *Library Management*, vol. 24, no. 1/2, pp. 51–60.

Further reading

Broadbent, Marianne and Kitzis, Ellen S. (2005), *The new CIO leader: Setting the agenda and delivering results*, Boston, MA: Harvard Business School.

Byham, William C. (2002), '14 leadership traps', Training and Development, vol. 56, no. 3, March, pp. 56–63.

Chernin, Peter (2002), 'Creative leadership', *Executive Excellence*, vol. 19, no. 5, May, pp. 3–4.

Covey, Stephen R. (2004), *The 8th habit: From effectiveness to greatness*, New York, NY: Free Press.

Forster, Nick (2005), *Maximum performance: A practical guide to leading and managing people at work*, Cheltenham, UK: Edward Elgar.

Hernez-Broome, Gina and Hughes, Richard L. (2004), 'Leadership development', *Human Resource Planning*, vol. 27, no. 1, pp. 24–32.

Kakabadse, Andrew et al. (2004), *Working in organisations*, Aldershot, UK: Ashgate.

Mant, Alistair (1997), *Intelligent leadership*, London, UK: Allen and Unwin.

Priestland, Andreas and Hanig, Robert (2005), 'Developing first level leaders', *Harvard Business Review*, June, pp. 112–20.

Quinn, Robert E. (2005), 'Moments of greatness', *Harvard Business Review*, July–Aug., pp. 74–83.

Rooke, David and Torbet, William R. (2005), 'Transformations of leadership', *Harvard Business Review*, April, pp. 67–76.

Sorcher, Melvin and Brant, James (2002), 'Are you picking the right leaders?', *Harvard Business Review*, vol. 80, no. 2, Feb., pp. 78–85.

Vicere, Albert A. (2002), 'Leadership and the networked economy', *Human Resource Planning*, vol. 25, no. 2, pp. 26–33.

13 *Engaging in Change*

Engaging in change is a leadership issue that has both proactive and reactive components. Engaging in proactive change requires leadership skills in building and shaping an organizational capacity to think differently, to be innovative, to create and embrace change, and in developing ownership and commitment to action throughout the organization. In these situations, change is energized from within.

The reactive component occurs when sudden strategic shocks are encountered through the external environment. Leadership qualities come to the forefront in these situations in both a proactive and reactive capacity. Those organizations best able to survive these situations are ones that have already been proactively readied to withstand unprecedented circumstances and have a resilience and capacity to think innovatively, act and adapt quickly, and find the single survival path to the future. The reactive capacity occurs at the moment of shock or crisis in that strong and directive leadership skills are needed to assess and take charge of the situation, make quick decisions and provide direction.

Change can be defined as an alteration in relationships or the environment. By their nature, information services can be catalysts for change as information and communications technology (ICT) is in itself an agent of disruptive change as well as often being used as a tool for innovation and transforming organizations. Transformational change is also necessary in changing traditional bureaucratic organizations to be agile, flexible and engaged knowledge-based organizations.

People and organizations will often be resistant to change. Resistance by individuals is usually caused by feelings of loss and uncertainty which in turn lead to insecurity. The most effective way of overcoming resistance to change is to encourage those involved to be part of the planning and decision-making process. Training, open communication and evidence of clear, tangible benefits as an outcome of change also facilitate the change process.

Business and process reengineering are two approaches that are being used to rethink organizational activities in order to manage in a competitive and changing environment. These approaches take advantage of the potential for change that is offered through the introduction of new technologies.

Sources of organizational change

Organizational change occurs in response to changes in the external environment that impact upon the organization or are energized through internal forces. It can be in two forms; incremental or continuous change that occurs from within, or radical or disruptive change that occurs as a result of sudden strategic shocks that arrive unannounced and unanticipated.

Incremental change occurs as a result of an organization adapting naturally to growth and maturity, as well as responding to the need for innovation and revitalizing itself as it expands and develops in a changing environment. It is a necessary part of organizational life; it occurs naturally as part of the organizational life cycle and is an essential means for survival. The Japanese notion of 'kaizen' is predicated on ongoing mutation based on quality in service delivery. Incremental change is usually planned, allowing some control over outcomes and providing time for thought. It can occur through exposure to different ideas, new ways of doing things and fresh thinking, as well as desires for business growth, seeking new business advantages, lowering costs and increased quality of service in a controlled environment.

Radical or discontinuous change occurs in response to an abrupt event in the environment. It can be described as a strategic shock that transforms everyday life, alters cultures and values, or disrupts institutions. Examples are a corporate takeover that changes the entire corporate culture and environment, a biological or technical discovery that renders previous achievements obsolete, or a global phenomenon such as a tidal wave or terrorist attack. Both continuous and radical change result in transformed organizations.

External forces that are causing information services to rethink their processes and operations in the knowledge age are:

- new ICTs that are changing expectations and attitudes to the speed and quality of service delivery;
- recognition that innovation, knowledge and information are valuable intangible assets that have a value and require protection, often through complex intellectual property rights;
- a new emphasis on managing client, intellectual and social capital in addition to the traditional forms of capital found in financial, human, built and natural environmental resources;
- changes in the outlook and behaviour of organizations as a result of globalization and global markets;
- a renewed interest in governance and accountability, community engagement in decision making, sustainability and diversity in lifestyle, the economy, the environment and in cultures; and
- changing cultural and social conditions that reinforce individual rights and probity.

Internal forces are most likely to come from a desire to transform or reinvigorate all or part of the organization and can result from:

- strategically rethinking the information service's programmes to create a knowledge-enabled and learning organization;
- a greater strategic focus on agility and the modification of processes to achieve operational excellence, new levels of cost performance and quality customer services;
- shifts in employees' socio cultural values; or
- changes in work practices and attitudes such as work being organized for life, rather than life being organized for work.

ORGANIZATION LIFE CYCLES AND CHANGE

Another internal force for change is growth within an organization. For example, as an information service and its parent organization grow, they progress through an organization life cycle. Changes in managerial structure, processes and style occur. The fundamental reason for this is found in systems theory. As systems grow they move in the direction of differentiation and elaboration with greater specialization of function. As differentiation proceeds, it is countered by processes that bring the systems together for unified functioning.

When an information service is first established it has a youthful and energetic presence. The emphasis is on creativity. Services and information products are created and introduced in order to prove its worth. The founding person devotes his or her energies to establishing and marketing the services. As there are generally few staff, the organization and management style are flexible, informal and non-bureaucratic. There is often less differentiation and people perform a variety of tasks. Long hours may be experienced. There is often not enough time for proper procedures to be documented; most decisions are based upon professional knowledge.

As the service grows, more staff are added. People are promoted from within. It is an exciting place to work. However, the increased numbers of people compound the complexity, nature and number of relationships, ideas and ways of doing things. Without formal policies and procedures confusion and duplication of effort can occur. The founding person may not be interested in the operational details of management, more in his or her area of expertise. Strong leadership and direction are needed to guide the information service through this stage.

If the leadership is strong, clear goals and direction are provided. Differentiation occurs, specialization takes place, teams are established to perform different tasks, and authority is created. This marks the beginning of the division of labour. New positions and levels within the information service may be created. Whilst it may be pleasing for members of the information service to fill these new positions, this may not always be possible or desirable. New people bring new perspectives, fresh insights and ideas that are in themselves sources for change. Those individuals who are unsuccessful in terms of promotion may need to be given other opportunities for personal development.

The need for formal governance processes becomes apparent. Management systems are introduced for accounting budgets, inventory and acquiring items. Communication becomes more formal, and elements of bureaucracy may become apparent. The challenge at this stage is to ensure that formalized processes do not stifle creative thinking, energy and enthusiasm.

As growth continues, restrictive practices can begin to impede the service and this should be resisted. Senior managers begin to delegate responsibility to others, concentrating more on strategic direction setting, coordination and managing the external interface. The internal control systems formalize communication. The challenge is to ensure that communication does not become less frequent or restricted to a few individuals. New specialists and services are added as continuous renewal takes place. Consultants are often hired to review policies and procedures. As a result, taskforces, project and matrix groups are formed to improve coordination. The solution to this stage is in collaboration and cooperation, ensuring that new thinking and ideas are continually considered and that energy and momentum are sustained. Managers develop skills for confronting problems and resolving interpersonal differences. Formal systems are simplified. The organization transforms into a more open and reactive environment.

The developments in the organization life cycle produce significant changes and challenges from one stage to the next. For example, the first stage requires boundless energy and creativity in terms of establishing services, thinking of new ways of doing things, and letting people know about the information services and products offered.

The challenge of the second stage is to keep the creativity and energy going whilst establishing systems that assist rather than hinder service delivery. In the latter stages, there is a need to keep momentum, ensuring that energy and vitality continue, and that new service delivery opportunities and business advantages are sought to avoid the organization becoming stale or obsolete.

Growth needs to be managed in the context of the strategic direction of the parent organization. It is important for managers to recognize the stage at which their information service is in the organization life cycle in order to manage the change, prepare for the future and avoid the pitfalls.

Creating and engaging change

The magnitude and type of the change alters the way in which the change process should be sold and managed. If there are only one or two dimensions to be considered then it is easier to predict what is probable or possible. As the number of dimensions for change increase, then the number of relationships and uncertainties as to how they could be affected increases. There is less certainty about the impact of change and the extent of the alteration to the environment. Each additional dimension adds another level of complexity and another set of relationships to the other dimensions to be considered within a set period of time.

STRATEGIES FOR ENGAGING CHANGE

Like all organizations, libraries and information services now operate in continuously changing environments such that the need for innovation and building individual and organizational energy and engagement in change is an everyday requirement. True engagement in change is demonstrated where people themselves identify and suggest where change is necessary in order to enhance the quality of services or do things more productively.

Building an agile and flexible organization with the capacity and commitment to embrace and engage in change is an important leadership function. A spirit of support, cooperation, collaboration and enthusiasm needs to be created, in which people feel comfortable with the status quo being uncertainty. People need to see and understand the big picture; a total view of the environment where turbulence is the norm and transformational change is necessary either in anticipation of, or in response to, sudden strategic shocks.

The right people need to be engaged, especially those who have access to important information, those who can either make an impact or will be significantly impacted, those who have an authority to effect change and make critical decisions in the area of change, those with responsibility for the areas affected, and those who may oppose the change. Richard Axelrod (2002, p. 41) has identified several questions for the leader of change to ask when engaging the right people in change. He comments that it is not the leader's role to provide all the answers to the questions, but to ensure that the answers are developed:

- what needs to change and why?
- what needs to be different in the organization?
- what are the boundary conditions?
- whose voice needs to be heard?
- who else needs to be here?
- how do we build the necessary connection between people and ideas?
- how will we create a community of people who are ready and willing to act? and
- how will we embrace democracy throughout the process?

A sense of urgency should be created to overcome indifference, apathy and the sentiment 'that things aren't really going to be any different'. A free flow of information incorporating both the good and bad news is a fundamental requisite so that people can discuss and make sense of change.

Different views of the world need to be canvassed in order for everyone to gain a complete view of the environment in which the change is or will take place. These include perspectives of the environment by:

- stakeholders, especially on how the change may impact on their own environment and relationships with the organization;
- executives, particularly on their view of the external environment issues and impacts; and
- teams, particularly on their view on the internal operational environment issues that might be affected.

The involvement and contribution of ideas and concepts, emotions and values, knowledge and experience by people from all parts of the system or value chain is necessary in order that the different parts of the organization or processes are connected, and the whole system and impact is visible to those involved. It is also a necessary process in building shared meaning and engaging participants in discussion so that better and more coordinated outcomes can be developed.

In building a common purpose and shared meaning, the reason for the change and its implications should be clarified to all stakeholders in order to develop a universal understanding and commitment to the new environment. This should include exploring what needs to go right and what needs to be done differently in the new environment by both the organization as the collective entity and each individual. Past and present achievements and successes also need to be recognized and honoured, as these will form the basis upon which the future is built. People also need to be reassured that their efforts in the past have not been wasted.

In explaining the implications of the change, some of the anticipated concerns of individuals should be addressed. Change sparks powerful emotions in people, yet at the same time people are required to make changes in their behaviours. The changes in behaviour cannot be learnt if individuals are distracted by fear, anger or uncertainty. These feelings need to be openly acknowledged and dealt with as a natural course of events arising out of the change. The need to empower individuals to manage their emotional response is as important as providing them with the necessary skills and training for the new situation. People also need to be given opportunities in which it is seen that their voice counts.

Building a critical mass of engaged and committed individuals at all levels throughout the organization is vital in setting the example, for relationship building and in creating the impetus and momentum to champion the change. The faster the momentum for change can occur, whilst allowing for consultation and involvement, the more successful it is likely to be. Urgency and energy in the change processes avoid people holding on to old ways and operating in a destructive twilight zone where confusion and the part implementation of new processes serve no one well. Obstacles that prevent people from operating and thinking in new ways should be identified and removed or overcome.

Collaboration, relationship building, information sharing are all critical functions in developing a will and willingness to work together to effect change and for engaging people in change. Change agents fulfil a critical role in communicating and sharing information, ideas and feelings when empowering others to embrace the change. Instilling self-confidence and liberating people from old ways and old thinking are powerful mechanisms for enabling people to start making their own decisions in the new environment. Visible proof that the new environment is working by having people take action and embrace new thinking or having some 'quick wins' will provide credibility, energy and impetus for the change process.

The timing and frequency of the planned change need to be considered. Ideally, changes should be implemented at a time when the information service is least pressured and has been made ready for the change. However, this is not always possible, particularly in the case of reactive change.

The turning point in change, which occurs between the second or resistance stage and the third or exploring stage, is the most critical. This is the stage where emotions are high, push back occurs from those who are resisting the change and some find ways to undermine the change process. Energy, persistence, drive and self-confidence are required to continue the momentum with those who have already embraced the change, to build on the quick wins and consolidate the new change culture.

STRATEGIES FOR MANAGING STRATEGIC SHOCKS

Despite having built an organizational capacity to engage readily in change, organizations will still be subject to unprecedented and sudden significant strategic shocks that result in fundamental shifts in the organization's circumstances. 9/11 is an example of an unprecedented sudden and strategic shock. It not only had an immediate global impact; it disrupted the entire airline industry and for the institutions housed in the Twin Towers, it meant that many of their people and organizations did not survive. Other organizational examples may be where a rapid downsize occurs as the result of a merger between two organizations, or where a totally different political philosophy is introduced overnight as a result of a change of government.

The difficulty in managing in these environments is that, as the often radical decisions are made to counter the situation, the shock waves travel through the organization. The hard task is to identify where the shock wave will be felt most and what the impact will be. Crisis conditions frequently prevail. The resulting chaos and time factors may not allow measured consideration of the impact of all decisions.

The uncertainty brought about by the magnitude and suddenness of the change needs to be managed through strong and direct leadership. Trust, consistency, the ability to make connections and make the right decision quickly and in an unwavering manner are all leadership qualities required in this reactive situation.

New roles, tasks and interim structures should be quickly put in place for the transition period. Strategic areas that are working well should be quickly identified and if possible quarantined in order to preserve and build upon their success. Areas within the information service that do not support the new direction should be dealt with immediately.

COMMUNICATING ABOUT CHANGE

Communication and actions are central to effecting successful change, as people interpret the messages about the change according to what they hear and how they see others being treated. Even where individuals are not immediately affected by the change, they will watch with interest and interpret its effect on others. People will view the changes through their own eyes, not those of the leaders of change. So the way in which managers treat any one individual will send signals to the rest of the people in the organization. These signals can be very powerful in determining the people's expectations as to how they may be treated, valued, rewarded or penalized by the organization in the future.

The messages that people hear of changes through the grapevine and through what they are officially told by their managers may not always be consistent or correctly interpreted. It is therefore important to ensure that any actions or signals send the correctly framed message. If the message is distorted because of other political agendas, or if mixed messages are received, people will quickly become despondent and confused. The message should be simple and clearly identify what needs to be achieved by the information service through the change process. Strong internal communications and access to counselling may help individuals deal with their personal anxieties about their own and the organization's future.

MANAGING THE CHANGE CYCLE

As change occurs, individuals and groups progress through four stages: denial, resistance, exploring and commitment. Each of the four stages has quite distinct behavioural reactions and needs to be managed in different ways. As change occurs, it is unlikely that all individuals will progress through the four stages at the same time. Figure 13.1 illustrates the four stages of change.

Stage one (denial) is characterized by individuals ignoring any signals of change or being frozen in traditional ways. They may be silent observers who neither oppose the change nor actively support it. Others may experience shock if they could not see that change was required, or relief that the inevitable had actually happened. Individuals in this stage of change require information about what the change will mean to them and to the organization, a sense of urgency and pressure to move forwards with the change, and mechanisms to unfreeze their thinking and traditional ways of doing things.

The second stage of change (resistance) is characterized by fear, apprehension, negativity and self-doubt. This is often expressed in terms of sabotage, absenteeism, anger, anxiety, suspicion and cynicism. During this stage, the information services manager will need to deal with illogical arguments and hostility. The important management process at this stage is to listen with empathy and understanding, rather than to reason or argue. Active listening will help to build trust in people.

The manager may also need strong conviction for the vision and change outcome as they may be subject to personal attacks from those who are feeling vulnerable. They should empathize with staff whilst trying to reconnect them to reality and giving them a sense of direction. Staff will feel a sense of loss and require support whilst still keeping the pressure to move forward.

The third stage (exploring) is the most critical stage as it is the point of transformation. Some people have begun to buy into the change, becoming active participants and exhibiting new behaviours. The change process at this stage relies upon people being given tangible things to do and decisions to make that reinforce their new roles and new thinking. Staff should be encouraged to acknowledge what has happened, reinforcing the positive things of the past whilst exploring the future. Individuals will still feel insecure but their hostility will be diminished.

This stage marks the formation of the new team; with new behaviours, new trusted relationships, new shared experiences and new freedoms. The information services manager should provide information and support through discussion and problem solving. People should be involved in all discussions and provided with opportunities to succeed in the new environment. To mark the transition there should be a launch of something new that signifies a change within the corporate culture. This may be a new logo, new stationery or refurbishing the existing premises.

The final stage is commitment. New behaviours are in place, diluting the power of traditional ones. Those that remain in old thinking are in the minority and have little influence. The information services manager should have a watching brief at this point, being available for consultation and concentrating where needed on making the change complete in the new changed culture. Staff should be allowed to get on with their work and own it.

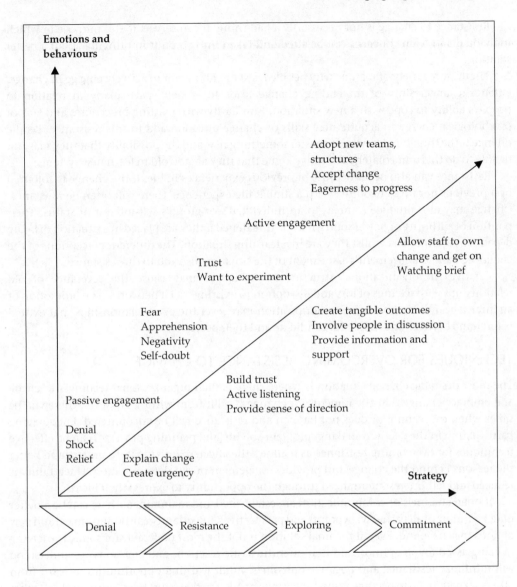

Figure 13.1 The four stages of change

Overcoming resistance to change

Resistance to change is a natural process and will occur at both the organizational and individual levels. Organizations have inbuilt mechanisms that produce stability and resist change. The selection process and culture of the organization create a persona that is difficult to change. Group norms may also act as a constraint to change. Individuals will react to change in one of three ways:

- accept and support the change (active engagement);
- comply with the change in action but not in spirit (passive engagement); or
- actively resist the change (anti engagement).

Resistance to change is not necessarily a bad thing. It can serve a useful purpose in which individual and team concerns can be aired and taken into account in bringing about a better solution.

There are a variety of reasons why people resist or choose not to actively engage in change. Often the uncertainty of impending change leads to anxiety, particularly in relation to people's ability to cope with a new situation. Familiarity with existing procedures and lack of psychological energy to acquire new skills or change direction add to this resistance. People often fear the thought of having to master something new and the possibility that they may not be able to do this immediately. They may argue that they are too old to learn new systems.

Resistance can also occur because of previous experiences in life. If the change is coloured by a previous negative encounter with a similar life experience, there will often be resistance. Change may also produce a threat to an individual's or group's self-interest or status. Their position of authority or power source may be threatened if they are placed in a situation of being dependent upon others whilst they are in a learning situation. The different perceptions of the employee's and management's assessment of the situation also add to the resistance.

Changes in organizational structure or workplace may cause the severance of old relationships with feelings of loss and disruption to existing social networks. The promotion of an internal candidate to a more senior position may sever the close relationships that existed beforehand between the successful candidate and their peers.

TECHNIQUES FOR OVERCOMING RESISTANCE TO CHANGE

The most desirable change situation is where there is such organizational readiness to create and embrace change that the impetus for change is built from within. However, there will be times when this cannot or does not happen and resistance will be encountered. Encouraging participation in the decision-making, problem-solving and planning processes can be effective techniques for overcoming resistance as it allows the affected individuals to understand better the reasons behind the change and provides an element of self-determination. Uncertainty is reduced and self-interest neutralized through the opportunity to express their ideas.

If open channels of communication are established and maintained, there can be a better understanding of all parties' viewpoints and perspectives, uncertainty can be minimized and new options may be found. Even if the final solution is not the most preferable for some, the feeling of being asked for an opinion and that unenthusiastic reactions and emotions are understood will minimize resistance and negative outcomes. Adult learning opportunities to learn from others' experiences, to become skilled at the new work practices, and to know more about what needs to be done differently and the anticipated results will also help reduce resistance.

It is important that the change quickly results in a positive and relative advantage, the benefits of which should be clearly apparent to the individuals being asked to change. The sooner the benefits can be identified, the more likely people are to accept and continue the newly introduced practices. The changes being advocated must be compatible with the existing values and experiences of the individuals otherwise they will be discarded as threatening or inappropriate. Change agents can also be used to facilitate and support individuals through the change.

If resistance to change continues it may be the symptom of one of two causes. Either the correct 'fit' between the change situation, change agent and persons involved has not been found, or, the proposed change is a poor strategy and is not in the organization's best interest.

SYMPTOMS OF UNSUCCESSFUL CHANGE

Unsuccessful change can be recognized by the absence of feedback, even though a feedback mechanism is available; or, by strong feedback in the form of protests or complaints. A drop in productivity below that anticipated by the learning curve also indicates a problem. Likewise, withdrawal symptoms characterized by lack of cooperation, absenteeism, resignations or transfers indicate that something is wrong. When any one of these symptoms appears, it should be immediately investigated in order to isolate and correct the problem.

Reengineering and change

The need for transformational change in the competitive environment and opportunities offered through the introduction of new technologies require organizations consciously to manage their most significant business processes in a holistic manner. It requires them explicitly to rethink, redesign and stream line their business and business processes with an end-to-end view, rather than through a series of ad hoc incremental approaches.

Business reengineering is the ability to rethink fundamentally the mindset or way in which organizations deliver their products and services in line with their business strategy. Process reengineering is a narrower set of business reengineering. It concentrates upon rethinking and streamlining the processes within an organization to achieve better outcomes either in terms of higher levels of efficiency or productivity or to deliver something of value to the customer. Instead of concentrating on functions, process reengineering looks holistically at all the steps that contribute to the process of creating the outcomes as a single value chain.

BUSINESS REENGINEERING

Michael Hammer (1990, pp. 104–12) identified the notion of discontinuous thinking. He argued that organizations should use the power of ICT to redesign business processes radically in order to achieve dramatic improvements in their performance. Organizations could not achieve major breakthroughs in their performance just by trimming the fat or automating existing processes. Organizations needed to recognize and break away from outdated rules and fundamental assumptions that underlie operations in order to avoid simply speeding up inappropriate processes.

His basic principles of reengineering were:

- organize around outcomes not tasks; design a person's job around all the steps in the process instead of a single task;
- have those who use the output of the process perform the process; use the technology so that the individuals who need the result of the process can do it themselves. When the people closest to the process perform it, there is little need for the overhead associated with managing it;
- subsume information-processing work into the real work that produces the information; move the work of processing the information to the area that processes it. For example, let the section that receives the goods or services also process the payment of the account;
- treat geographically dispersed resources as though they were centralized; use ICT and standardized processing systems to get the benefits of scale and coordination while maintaining the benefits of flexibility and service;

- link parallel activities instead of integrating their results; use ICT to forge links between parallel functions and coordinate them whilst the activities are in process rather than after they were created;
- put the decision point where the work is performed, and build control into the process; let the people who do the work make the decisions. Build controls into the process through expert systems and the way in which ICT is designed; and
- capture information once and at the source; overcome the delays, input errors and costly overheads of duplicated data in 'silo type' systems by capturing information at the source and using this throughout the information chain. Use ICT to provide better access and reduce processing time in the provision of better services to customers.

Today business reengineering takes a more radical approach, completely rethinking and transforming processes and service delivery to enable productivity rather than cost cutting, and significant first to market competitive initiatives that rewrite the rule books in product and service offerings. It is business strategy and opportunity driven and requires commitment and drive from executive management.

A significant proportion of business reengineering strategies are information related. As such, business reengineering creates a major change process for any information service. The traditional functional and organizational boundaries are ignored in the global business environment. Cross-functional and cross-organizational processes are emphasized. This necessitates the reshaping of job designs, information flows, organizational structures and management systems. The focus is on managing the cultural dimension of the organization as well as the people, technology and structure.

The impact is also found at the interface with the external environment. Customer relationships and needs become a major driver. The relationships with stakeholders such as suppliers and clients change as they become part of the information chain. Negotiations will be required between them and the organization about the redesigning or elimination of processes and the choice and compatibility of equipment that interfaces between them.

PROCESS REENGINEERING

Process reengineering brings together and streamlines multiple functions such as customer needs identification, budgeting, purchasing of materials and delivery of customer services to form a value-added process that delivers a specific outcome in a timely manner. The emphasis is on response time and the outcome of the process rather than the success of the individual functions.

The traditional approach of managing functions within an organization created situations where differing priorities and time horizons between functions led to delays in customer service. Those people performing the functions halfway through the value chain had little idea of the impact of any delay for the client at the service delivery end. For example, a payments section could be very efficient about paying their accounts by the end of the month, but if urgently required software or library materials were held until the account was paid or delayed through the asset management process, the service delivery to the client would be impaired. Electronic transactions, instant messaging in an always on environment and seamless service delivery changes this, requiring instantaneous service and response, and immediate feedback. Instead of streamlining individual functions, process reengineering now manages the total value chain, seeing it as a whole and making transformational or step change improvements across all functions. More importantly, it also redesigns processes to enable an instant response to ICT that pervades a worldwide environment. The objective is to lead competitiveness in the global market space through the ability to increase the response speed, quality and flexibility of services to customers whilst seeking significant productivity improvements.

The transition from the functional state to the process reengineering state requires analysis and planning so that value chains are created. Every process should be reviewed in order to determine the value and improvement gap that it adds to the business strategy and customer needs. Workflows should be analysed for bottlenecks and inefficiencies. The aim is to avoid doing things just because they have always been done.

Conclusion

The only constant in the world today is that it is an era of continuous change. In this environment, change management strategies are important in order to smooth the transition of change, and importantly, to initiate and manage the change itself for the strategic advantage of the information service and its parent organization.

The most desirable situation is for change to be energized from within. This requires leadership skills in building and shaping the organization to think differently, embrace change, and to develop a commitment to action throughout the organization.

Change that has the potential to affect the whole organization should be sold and managed quite differently to minor changes affecting one or two people. Radical disruptive change requires strong leadership capable of making quick and far-reaching decisions. Open channels of communication are very important in any change scenario, so that there is a free flow of information in order to build the vision, to discuss concerns of individuals openly, understand the impacts of the change and be committed to the change. In all instances credibility and relationship management needs to be maintained.

In addition to good initial planning, the abilities to demonstrate 'quick wins' and maintain momentum through people acting and making decisions in the new environment are critical to implementing successful continuous change.

References

Axelrod, Richard H. (2002), *Terms of engagement: Changing the way we change organizations*, San Francisco, CA: Berrett-Koehler.
Hammer, Michael (1990), 'Reengineering work: Don't automate, obliterate', *Harvard Business Review*, July–Aug., pp. 104–12.

Further reading

Black, J. Stewart et al. (2002), *Leading strategic change: Breaking through the brain barrier*, Upper Saddle River, NJ: Financial Times Prentice Hall.
Covington, John (2001), 'Leading successful, sustainable change', *Executive Excellence*, vol. 18, no. 11, Dec., pp. 15–16.
Galbraith, Jay Downey et al. (2002), *Designing dynamic organizations: A hands-on guide for leaders at all levels*, New York, NY: AMACOM.
Klein, Janice A. (2004), *True change: How outsiders on the inside get things done in organizations*, San Francisco, CA: Jossey-Bass.

Smith, Ian (2005), 'Achieving readiness for organisational change', *Library Management*, vol. 26, no. 6/7, pp. 408–13.

Smith, Ian (2005), 'Managing the people side of organisational change', *Library Management*, vol. 26, no. 3, pp. 152–6.

Smith, Ian (2005), 'Resistance to change – recognition and response', *Library Management*, vol. 26, no. 8/9, pp. 519–23.

The essentials of managing change and transition, (2005), Boston, MA: Harvard Business School.

14 *Group Dynamics and Team Building*

Increasingly, fixed and hierarchical organizational structures are being replaced with groups of individuals who work together in teams. This provides greater flexibility in managing changing environments and also assists in transforming processes and thinking. Groups can be formal or informal. Formal groups or teams are defined through the organization's hierarchy or centre on a particular task. Informal groups are based upon individual psychological need, activities and interests.

The role of the team builder is not to manage people as individuals, but to facilitate the group's management of its members. The objective is to obtain a higher level outcome than would be provided by the same number of people working individually. This requires an understanding of group behaviour because people act differently when they are members of a team or group. Their behaviours will change according to their role in the team or group.

Groups develop through a four-stage process of forming, storming, norming and performing. As groups develop, they assume certain characteristics of group cohesiveness, group norms and member roles. Interteam conflict can increase competition and group productivity. However, like all forms of conflict it may have an adverse effect upon the performance of individuals and the information service. In such a case, steps should be taken to minimize or remove it.

Types of groups

A group is a collection of people who regularly interact with each other to pursue a common purpose. There are four basic components of a group:

- it needs at least two people to exist;
- the individuals must interact regularly in order to maintain the group;
- all group members must have a common goal or purpose; and
- there should be a stable structure.

FORMAL GROUPS

Formal groups or teams are created to accomplish a number of tasks within an indefinite or definite timescale. They often relate to the organizational structure. Formal groups are created through formal authority for a purpose, as in Figure 14.1.

Management team

In most organizations there will be a management team consisting of senior managers. It may be called the executive management team. This team will meet to consider the strategic issues confronting the parent organization.

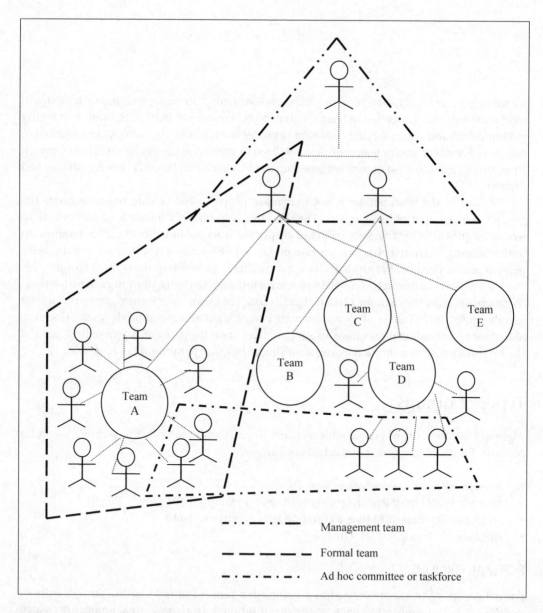

Figure 14.1 The organization as an interlocking network of formal groups

Other activities undertaken by the management team are the endorsement of the strategic plan, the ratification of policy and the approval of the overall organizational budget. The information services manager may be a member of this team. As they may also be a member of the various work teams reflecting the work units within the information service, they will form the link between the management team and the work teams.

Managers will be involved in groups in different capacities: as ordinary members or as leaders of a team or number of teams. As leaders they may have the role of a supervisor or a chairperson. They will also be part of an informal group network.

Work teams

Work teams are the most recognized form of formal groups. They are the functional teams established to achieve corporate objectives and business outcomes. These formal teams usually remain in existence until there is some change in the organizational structure. They have clearly distinguishable line management relationships and are often identified in the formal organization chart as a work team, department or division. The size and level of the work team is scalable according to the size of the parent organization.

In some organizations the information service may be regarded as a work team. In others the research centre, branch libraries, records management section and the ICT services unit will be regarded as individual work teams, with the senior research officer, branch librarian, records manager or information technology manager being formally designated as the leader of the permanent team or work team. Work teams may also reflect the organization's clients or markets.

Taskforce

Taskforces are project teams that are created for a particular purpose; usually to accomplish a relatively narrow task within a stated or implied timescale. They are temporary formal teams with a 'sunset clause'. Ad hoc committees also belong in this category.

The team membership is usually specified by management, but may also comprise volunteers. They often have a designated chairperson or a formal leader who is accountable for the results. Like the work team manager, the task or project team leader should review progress at regular intervals and provide performance feedback to members of the team. They must have the appropriate interpersonal skills and be prepared to accept responsibility and accountability.

Taskforces are often used in a matrix style of management. The individuals forming the team have two managers; the work team manager and the taskforce manager. A dual chain of command is established.

INFORMAL GROUPS

Informal groups exist for purposes that may or may not be relevant to the organization. They emerge within organizations without being formally designated by someone in authority for a specific purpose. Each member chooses to participate without being told to do so. As they are formed through a common interest, the activities of the group may or may not match those of the organization.

Informal groups can be a powerful organizational force. The identification of the leaders of the informal groups may provide insight into the politics, power and authority within the information service and its parent organization. Informal groups can coexist with formal groups in an attempt to overcome bureaucratic tendencies or to foster networks of interpersonal

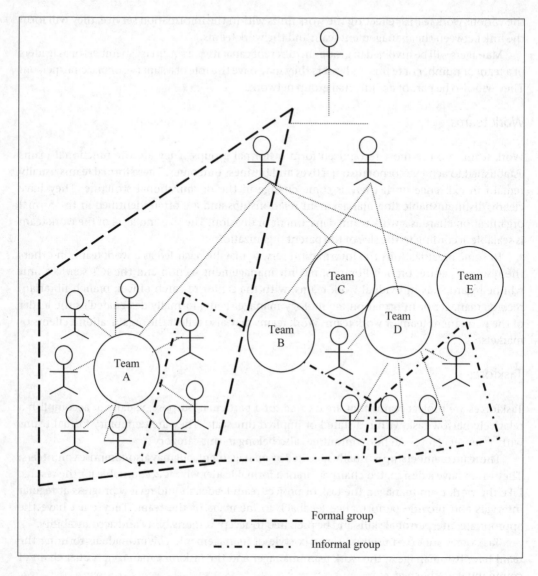

Figure 14.2 Formal and informal groups as they exist in organizations

relationships that aid workflows in ways that formal lines of authority fail to provide as in Figure 14.2.

The formation of an informal group is often a healthy sign of comradeship and is not necessarily an indication that there is anything wrong within the organization. Social or friendship groups are often formed within organizations across formal work team boundaries for the purpose of sharing a common interest. Informal groups help individuals satisfy shared needs or may be used to provide alternative support to the formal team affiliations within the organization. The choice of informal group may be based on interpersonal attraction, an interest in the group's activities such as sport or chess, or an interest in the group's goals such as environmental sustainability.

Stages of group development

After a group has been created, either formally by the organization or by group members, it will spend time developing. Group development occurs in four stages: forming, storming, norming and performing. These stages do not occur as discrete steps but are usually quite discernible because of their distinct activities and need for different management techniques as in Figure 14.3. The passage of time between the stages of group development will differ according to the timescale set for the outcome.

THE FORMING STAGE

The forming stage occurs as individual members of the group become acquainted with each other and begin to test which interpersonal behaviours are acceptable and which are not. Group boundaries and group rules are defined. The real task of the group is clarified.

The forming stage usually takes place at the first meeting of the group. Typically, the different members of a group describe their background and personal interests in the group's goals. This serves to define a common purpose and shared values. The members of the group could be drawn from many different work units within the information service, the parent organization or from other organizations. As such, they are often not aware of the role and potential of the other members and where their expertise and values can be shared. Members may act aloof until they become aware of some shared meanings and each other's needs. As they become aware of each other, they achieve higher levels of interaction and mutual identification in pursuit of the common purpose.

The management roles are to clarify tasks and direction for the group, the reasons for its formation and outcomes envisaged, whilst creating a sense of urgency. Communication should be encouraged as members explore the roles, responsibilities, norms and values of different members in the group.

THE STORMING STAGE

The second stage (storming) is usually highly emotional, involving tension among members and periods of hostility and infighting. Each member wishes to retain their individuality and may resist the structure that is emerging. Interpersonal styles are clarified and negotiations take place in an effort to find ways of accomplishing group goals whilst satisfying individual needs. Gradually a group leader emerges. Attention is paid to items that prevent the group's goals from being met. In practice, the storming stage is the stage where problems are confronted, criticism is made and discussion becomes more open.

The management role in this stage is as a facilitator, enabling members to confront, work through and overcome the problems associated change, with the proposed structure and individual roles. In assisting individuals to cope with change and to encourage new ideas, discussion and exploration of new solutions should be encouraged. Purpose and direction should be further clarified to minimize uncertainty and to share the vision or bigger picture.

THE NORMING STAGE

The third stage (norming) begins the integration process. Each person begins to recognize and accept his or her role and those of others. The group becomes more cohesive, adopting group norms that serve to regulate individual behaviour in order to achieve the group's goals. The group begins to be coordinated and teamwork emerges. Harmony is emphasized and minority viewpoints are discouraged.

As group harmony and teamwork develop, the role of the manager is to encourage collective engagement, cooperation and collaboration. Confidence in the group's and individual contributions may need to be reinforced and direction fine-tuned.

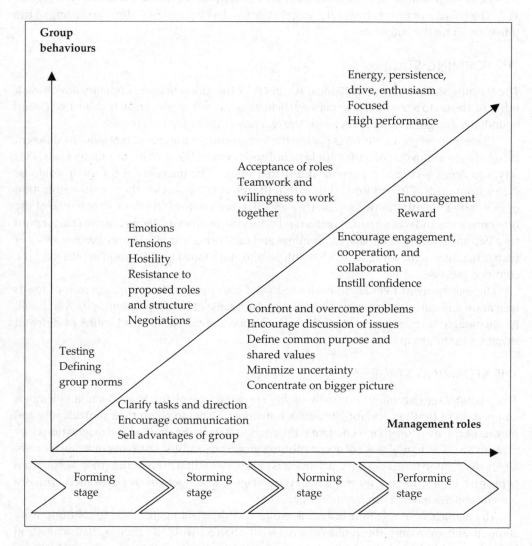

Figure 14.3 Stages of group development

THE PERFORMING STAGE

Performing is the final stage of group development. The group is totally integrated and is able to focus on the situation at hand. It functions well and can deal with complex tasks through the interaction that occurs. The structure is stable and members work as one unit.

In this stage, the group should be left to perform, with encouragement, support and rewards being openly given.

Group cohesiveness

Group cohesiveness is the extent to which members of the group are attracted to each other and to the team as a whole. Highly cohesive teams occur where members are attracted to each other, accept the team's goals and help work toward meeting them. Cohesion is likely to be higher in teams where members share similar attitudes and needs. Teams based on a particular expertise are usually cohesive because they share common professional values and attitudes. Not all cohesive groups are productive for the organization. Some groups can inflict considerable harm if their goals and values are contrary to those of the parent organization.

Group cohesiveness can be increased through intergroup competition, having supportive management, through personal attraction amongst those of the team, by rewarding the team rather than the individuals, by frequent interaction and by agreement on the team's goals. Group cohesiveness can be decreased by competition within the team, by the domination of one party, by disagreement on the team's goals and by team size.

As the size of the team increases, the number of possible relationships between its members increases. This leads to the need for increased communication and coordinator amongst the team members. It also leads to the development of subgroups that may be damaging to the overall team's cohesiveness and its associated productivity. Smaller teams enable members to interact more frequently and increase their cohesiveness. The optimum number for a team is between five and seven people.

Group member roles

A role is a typical behaviour that characterizes a person in a social context. As members of a group, people play different roles. Their behaviours will change according to their role in the social structure of the group. One of the communication tasks in life is to understand the role that a person is playing when they exhibit certain behaviours.

There are several terms that are used to describe the various roles. The expected role is that which the other members of the group expect from an individual. The perceived role is what the individual perceives the role to mean. The enacted role is what the individual actually does in the role. This then further influences the expected role. By rights, these three roles should be congruent. However, this may not always be the case.

ROLE DILEMMAS

Role dilemmas are a normal part of life. However there are limits to which people can cope with role dilemmas. If these limits are reached and left unchecked, they can become sources of internal tension or frustration. They may also result in job disenchantment or dissatisfaction, poor performance and a high staff turnover. The following provide examples where role dilemmas cause individuals to act or exhibit behaviours that are inconsistent with their normal behaviour.

Role ambiguity

Role ambiguity results when there is some uncertainty in the minds of either an individual or members of a group as to precisely what their role is at any given time. If an individual's conception of their role is unclear this can lead to role ambiguity even if it is clear to others. The use of job descriptions can help to overcome role ambiguity in an organizational sense.

Role conflict

Role conflict occurs when the appropriate behaviours for enacting a role may be inconsistent with the appropriate behaviours for enacting either another role or other requirements of the same role. The expectations of each role may be quite clear and the expectations compatible for each role, but the roles themselves may be in conflict.

Role conflict is generally categorized into two types, inter-role and intra-role conflict. Inter-role conflict is found where there are incompatible demands of two or more different roles being played by the same person. The need for the information services manager to act as service provider and policy maker may cause an inter-role conflict. In intra-role conflict contradictory demands within a single role are perceived by an individual. This might occur where the information services manager may have to cancel the annual leave of a staff member whilst recognizing that they have been overloaded with work and need a break.

Individual-role conflict occurs where a person is asked to fulfil a requirement that is against their own values, attitudes or needs. Such an example may be where the librarian must avoid acting as a censor and so is forced to stock material that is in conflict with some very strong personal beliefs.

Role conflicts may sometimes be eased by reducing the importance of one of the roles, or by compartmentalizing the two roles so that they do not overlap. It is important to take steps to reduce the conflict as role conflict is recognized as a source of stress and poor performance.

Role overload

Role overload occurs when expectations for the role exceed the individual's capabilities. Individuals are required to perform more roles than they originally envisaged or have the capacity for. An example may be where a person is required to be a decision maker in a complex and changing environment, but they have a low tolerance for uncertainty. Role overload should not be confused with work overload.

Role underload

Role underload occurs when an individual feels that they have the capacity to handle a bigger role or greater set of roles than is assigned to them. Role underload may be overcome by assigning additional roles or by delegating tasks and responsibilities.

Both role overload and role underload can be the outcome of a position being filled by someone who was incorrectly advised about the job at the interview. An unrealistic assessment of a position during the interview situation may lead to role overload or role underload and a person's subsequent dissatisfaction with the job.

Group norms

Group norms are standards of behaviour that the group adopts for its members. These are informal rules that enhance the group's structure and reinforce a certain degree of conformity among group members. Norms differ from organizational rules in that they are not written. They are subtle standards that exist and regulate group behaviour.

Group norms are established during the third stage of group development. They are created through a series of actions by individual members and the others' responses as a group. The ways in which the responses are made provide the basis for the norm. The norms that survive are those that produce the most successful outcomes. The norms are reinforced through their success in positive problem solving and in integration. Gradually it is assumed that if a norm is followed, success will result. As a result, norms are followed unconsciously.

Norms help groups avoid chaos and influence behaviours. They can be:

- performance related, such as identifying levels of daily work output or appropriate channels of communication;
- social related, such as how to address senior management in public, or acceptable levels of course language;
- behaviour related, such as setting standards of integrity, quality of service and professionalism; and
- appearance related, such as setting standards of dress.

As norms can have either a positive or negative influence on both the group's and the organization's productivity, it is important that positive norms are supported. Positive norms can be supported by rewarding desired behaviours and by monitoring performance and providing feedback regarding the desired and undesired behaviours.

Effective team building

Team building involves all of the leadership and facilitation skills that are required in extending individual performance and applies these to the team. This includes the development of interpersonal relationships within a team so that members share information and collectively set goals and outcomes to be achieved. The team builder will also need to facilitate mechanisms for managing expertise for the collective good and identifying the roles that each team member will play.

Whilst this sounds straightforward, it may not be easy. Most people value their individuality and independence, taking responsibility for their choice of assignment and their own outcomes within the organizational context. They may be content to work in a group but usually expect to be assessed and rewarded on their individual performance. Teamwork changes this as work and results are shared. The team is assessed on its collective outcome. It can even be promoted in this way. Team members jointly decide upon the choice of assignment, how the task will be accomplished, and their goals and rewards within the context of the overall environment.

In the early stage of building teams, the builder has to balance the need to address concerns about individual loss of independence and control whilst building support for team decision making. Multi-skilling and changes to differentiation between professional and non-professional staff are some of the issues to be considered in building teams in information services.

Teamwork builds upon the principles of process reengineering in that the whole of the activity associated with the provision of the service is managed within the team. Consequently, the team builder has to improve the coordination between team members and have the members of the team work together to deliver outcomes.

In information services, teams can be established to provide specialized services to specific client groups, where all team members are involved in planning, customer relationship management and supplier liaison. Training is essential to equip all team members with the necessary skills to carry out their cross-functional tasks. Training may also be required in interpersonal skills and conflict management.

The success of teams rests on there being very high levels of trust and openness between the team members. Team members should be encouraged to discuss their perception of the situation and what is required of them as a team and in their individual roles.

The team builder needs to be competent at recognizing and resolving conflict. Negativity should not be allowed to grow to the extent where it can weaken the team's cohesiveness. Individual negativity can grow if attention is paid to it, so a judgment call needs to be made as to the reason and whether it is initially best ignored. In this instance, attention should be focused upon the positive energies of the team. If the negativity continues to the extent that it has the potential to be destructive, then the source of the negativity should be openly discussed and dealt with.

Teams also develop a culture of self-discipline. They develop group norms and values and work within these to exercise control over individuals without harming their egos. High performing team members care about the success and growth of others. In this way, teams can be a very supportive mechanism during times of stress and crisis.

In enhancing performance and quality, team communications and team building should encourage employees to review one another's work and suggest alternative ways of doing things. Working properly, teams can be highly creative and innovative in their provision of service and identification of solutions to issues.

Self-managing work teams

Self-managing work teams consist of highly motivated specialists who do not have a formal hierarchy. They bring a variety of skills that they collectively use to deliver end products and services. They value the ability to operate independent of managers, being given a high degree of self-determination in the management of their work.

Instead of having one leader, the leadership responsibilities are shared by all team members at different times. Individuals assume leadership in their particular areas of expertise. This distributed form of leadership occurs over a period of time as people assume, through their actions, responsibility for different leadership functions. Their flexible work structure allows the participants to work efficiently and effectively. The team sets its own controls and quality audits, and collectively determines how the team will go about its work to achieve its goals.

David Barry (1991) has created a distributed leadership model for three generic classes of self-managed teams. These are project teams, problem-solving teams and policy-making teams. All of these classes can be present in information services.

Barry argues that the performance of a self-managed team is optimized when certain basic leadership roles and behaviours are differentially enacted at specific times during the team's life. The self-managed team's performance is maximized by having the right role presented at

Element	Traditional approach	Team approach
Channels of communication	Highly structured controlled information flow	Open. Free flow of information across teams
Decision making	Taken within formal line management position	Taken by empowering individuals with relevant expertise within the team
Work emphasis	Formal procedures handed down	Teams devise own effective processes
Adaptability	Slow and reluctant even when business circumstances warrant change	Changes occur in line with continuous improvement
Operations	Uniform and restricted	High degree of cooperation, methods and tasks vary between teams to suit needs
Control	Tight through strict, formal systems	Teams devise own measures in line with fulfilling process role
Behaviour	Contained by need to follow job description	Role and responsibilities evolved to meet needs of team and process
Management role	Commands and controls	Empowers, enables and motivates

Figure 14.4   Differences in traditional approach and team approach to work

the right time. The leadership roles and behaviours fall into four broad clusters: envisioning, organizing, spanning and social.

Envisioning involves the facilitation of idea generation and innovation, defining and championing goals, as well as finding conceptual links between systems. Envisioning leaders often have trouble functioning in a group, preferring to invent and create independently. Sometimes they continue to provide new ideas after the group has committed itself to specific actions. The true role of the envisioning leader is to help others to see the vision in order to foster group ownership of the ideas.

The organizing role brings together the disparate elements that exist within the team and its tasks. This person focuses on details, deadlines, time, efficiency and structure. They often work within a few well-chosen solutions. Whilst it is a necessary role in keeping the group from straying off the task, it can be counter productive when a completely new and innovative direction is needed.

The spanning role includes networking, presentation management, developing and maintaining a strong image with outsiders, intelligence gathering, locating and securing critical resources, bargaining, being sensitive to power distributions and being politically astute. Their natural tendency is to circulate outside the group environment. They can also be self-centred. To compensate for this, the spanning leader should provide the group with a constant source of reality checks, ensuring that the outputs of the team are well received with others in the organization.

The social role focuses on developing and maintaining the team from a social-psychological position. They show concern for individuals and ensure that everyone has their views heard. They are sensitive to the team's energy levels and emotional state. They provide encouragement and reinforcement and are able to mediate conflicts.

Managing interteam conflict

Interteam conflict occurs when members of a group or team perceive that they are being prevented from achieving their team goals by the actions of another group or team. Most interteam conflict in organizations occurs between work units or departments. This may be linked to differentiation in expertise or cultures. For example, technical support staff may feel that they are prevented from giving a good service to clients because of requirements by the finance or treasury department that all costs and work charge outs are documented in a time-consuming fashion.

Conflict may also occur between hierarchical levels over issues of power, authority and control. Proposed takeovers or mergers of teams or departments will lead to conflict on a hierarchical basis and on a horizontal basis for power and control.

Due to the differences in the technologies, values, work tasks and individuals' attributes in teams within large information services, some interteam conflict or rivalry will be ongoing. Such conflict will be productive by increasing team cohesiveness and output. It is a necessary part of subcultures within organizations. However, when conflicts emerge above the subculture level and become destructive or damaging to performance, managerial action should be taken.

In a major conflict situation, the cohesiveness of each team or department will increase, whilst communication between the conflicting departments will tend to decrease. The group that loses the conflict will find that it will also lose its cohesiveness. It is advantageous with any major conflict involving teams or departments that the issues are resolved quickly and in such a way that each party gains. A win-win situation can be achieved by skilful negotiation and setting a superordinate goal. That is, one that has to be achieved by the cooperation of both groups.

Conclusion

Groups perform a number of functions. Formal teams are established to achieve corporate objectives and business outcomes, whilst specialist project teams, ad hoc committees and taskforces perform a specific task. Individuals will also join informal groups that serve a personal interest and comprise like-minded people.

There is an increased focus on teamwork within organizations to manage complexity and transformation. Many organizations favour a project team approach when dealing with complex issues that affect a number of work units. Consequently, managers need to be aware of the issues that are associated with team activities in order to maximize the performance of the team.

References

Barry, David (1991), 'Managing the bossless team: Lessons in distributed leadership', *Organisational Dynamics*, Summer, pp. 31–47.

Further reading

Druskat, Vanessa and Wheeler, Jane V. (2004), 'How to lead a self-managing team', *MIT Sloan Management Review*, Summer, pp. 65–71.

Edwards, Abigail and Wilson, John R. (2004), *Implementing virtual teams: A guide to organizational and human factors*, Aldershot, UK: Ashgate.

Ghais, Suzanne (2005), *Extreme facilitation: Guiding groups through controversy and complexity*, San Francisco, CA: Jossey-Bass.

Kakabadse, Andrew et al. (2004), *Working in organisations*, Aldershot, UK: Ashgate.

Katzenbach, Jon R. and Smith, Douglas K. (2005), 'The discipline of teams', *Harvard Business Review*, July–Aug., pp. 162, 164–71.

15 *Motivation*

Understanding the nature of human motivation and using this knowledge to motivate people to excel beyond their expectations is a critical role in transforming organizations to meet the challenges of the knowledge age. Not everyone is motivated by the same thing. The key to effective transformational management is to understand what motivates each individual and to be flexible enough to satisfy these diverse needs. The extent to which they motivate others can be used as a measure of a manager's performance as an effective leader.

Motivation is linked to management flexibility. Technology change and flexible working hours as well as other conveniences allow individuals to pursue differing lifestyles whilst increasing their commitment and contribution to the organization.

Motivation will also increase if the job becomes more meaningful through an increased level of responsibility and decision making, as well as giving individual freedom, independence and discretion in scheduling and determining how their work will be carried out. Knowing how certain tasks contribute to the end results and outcomes will also increase individual performance and satisfaction.

Organizational strategies

WORKFORCE FLEXIBILITY

Today's workforce is diverse and no longer fits a stereotype. Flexible benefits and work arrangements recognize individual differences and circumstances. They allow individuals to pick and choose from a variety of options that meet the needs of both the organization and the individual. The reward factor is that individuals can choose the benefits and work arrangements that best suit their personal needs.

Flexible work arrangements lead to greater output. Arrangements such as flexitime and job sharing can lessen the level of absenteeism and often utilize the individual at the time of their peak of productivity. Flexible work arrangements can increase individual enthusiasm and make it easier for the information service to recruit new people.

The concept that work is a thing we do, rather than a place we go to is relevant here. Increasingly the point of service delivery will be to a remote device such as wireless-enabled portable device rather than within a fixed service point. This change in location for the end point in service delivery opens up the opportunity for rethinking the point of service execution. In a number of instances people may not always need to travel to a single place of work to do their job.

PERFORMANCE-BASED COMPENSATION

Individuals were traditionally compensated for the time that they spent on the job. Additional compensation was provided where they spent more time on the job, for example in overtime payments or after-hours meal allowance. Traditional compensation methods penalized those who were more efficient and productive and failed to take into account innovation, personal contribution or effectiveness. Individuals also received increased compensation linked to years of service rather than to the success or failure of the information service or parent organization.

Performance-based compensation provides incentives for individual or group effort to work smarter not harder by rewarding innovation and performance. Performance based compensation can be linked to specific performance measures or outcomes. It provides additional reward mechanisms for innovative thinking and when certain project milestones or productivity outcomes are reached. Compensation can be in the form of one-off payments, pay loadings, or the sharing of productivity gains. Not all compensation needs to be in the form of a monetary payment. Other mechanisms can be considered; such as the attendance at a conference in addition to that normally considered part of training and personal development.

JOB ENRICHMENT AND JOB ENLARGEMENT

Skill variety and job challenge can increase job satisfaction and act as a motivating force. Job enrichment and job enlargement are two different methods to achieve this. Job enlargement occurs when additional responsibilities of a horizontal nature are given to employees. If the additional responsibilities are of a vertical nature, encompassing self-control, the process is called job enrichment.

Whilst still respecting those individuals who have a professional standing for their knowledge and expertise, managers may seek to improve the job satisfaction of those undertaking the more operational tasks through providing skill variety and work that challenges people's abilities. Variety can be produced by adding functions through job enlargement under business and process reengineering. There is psychological value in enabling the individual to see the completed process within which they work. The identification and performance of the initial and end tasks and/or processes, together with all of the tasks in between, makes the job more meaningful to the individual and provides a sense of achievement and purpose. However, the type of work assigned needs consideration. There is no point in enlarging a job merely by adding further onerous duties to an existing list of disagreeable tasks. If anything, this will have a negative effect on motivation.

Job enrichment is not the allocation of more tasks, but the allocation of increased autonomy and responsibility for work outcomes. Responsibility and autonomy can be increased by:

- allowing individuals to set their own work schedules;
- providing skill variety and rotating monotonous tasks between individuals on a regular basis;
- allowing experienced personnel to train less-experienced workers;
- enabling individuals to establish direct relationships with the customers and so increase the significance of their tasks and activities; and
- encouraging staff to make their own quality checks.

Job enrichment will only work when the motivating potential of the job is high. The psychological needs are very important in determining who can, and who cannot, be internally motivated at work. Individuals with high growth needs will eagerly accept the added responsibility. Those people whose growth needs are not so strong may respond less eagerly at first, or react negatively at being 'stretched' or 'pushed' too far.

As with job enlargement, the process has to be instituted selectively and with an acute knowledge of the motivational forces of the individuals. In the worst case, job enrichment can have a negative effect on employee morale if people perceive the information service to be increasing duties and responsibilities without the proportionate increases in compensation. The motivational issues will then be lost in a jungle of pay disputes in which the organization will be viewed only as a 'money-saving' entity with no regard for its employees.

Feedback is a necessary part of motivation. This can be measured by the degree to which an individual, in carrying out the work activities required by the job, receives information about the effectiveness of their efforts. Feedback is most powerful when it is received directly from the work itself.

Individual strategies

EXPECTATIONS AND NEEDS

The traditional theories of motivation were aligned to the cause and effect in meeting individual expectations and needs, for example, in meeting the three tiers of existence or lower-order needs such as physiological and safety needs, relatedness needs such as interpersonal relationships and the intrinsic needs for personal development. Whilst these theories are still relevant to some degree, most managers today believe that their employees want to perform well. Letting people know that they are valued and helping to increase confidence in their personal capacities to excel are two ways of motivating people. Individuals who are given personal and professional development opportunities and are allowed to take risks will often have a higher self-esteem and estimation of their abilities than those who have not had their personal comfort zones stretched or been allowed to experiment with their ideas.

Individuals have different values and needs in order to be motivated. Whilst one individual may be motivated by the expectation of a pay rise, another may be motivated primarily by recognition. It is essential for the information services manager to understand the motivating values and needs of each of their staff and to be flexible enough to meet these.

Individual needs are met through two outcomes: the immediate or primary outcomes and secondary outcomes. Immediate positive outcomes are represented by money, promotion, feelings of achievement, recognition by peers or, negatively, by being shunned by fellow employees. Secondary outcomes arise out of the immediate outcomes. They include the new car that is purchased from the pay rise or the self-esteem that arises out of promotion.

Individuals translate their needs into behaviour in different ways. Some may openly express their wants and desires, whilst others' needs may be latent. Likewise, individuals' actions may not always be consistent, nor the needs that motivate them. At various stages of their careers circumstances will differ and people will be motivated by different needs. Finally, individuals may react in different ways when they fail to fulfil their needs. Some may become withdrawn whilst others may become aggressive. Some may even increase their performance levels.

Traditional motivation theories

Two traditional motivation theories can give insight into how the base needs of individuals are met. These theories are Maslow's Hierarchy of Needs and Herzberg's Two-Factor Theory.

MASLOW'S HIERARCHY OF NEEDS

Abraham H. Maslow's (1943) proposed that people have a complex set of needs that are arranged in a hierarchy of importance. There are four basic assumptions in the hierarchy:

- a satisfied need is not a motivator. When a need is satisfied, another need emerges to take its place, so people are always striving to satisfy some need;
- the need network for most people is very complex, with a number of needs affecting the behaviour of each person at any one time;
- in general, lower-level needs must be satisfied before higher-level needs are activated sufficiently to drive behaviour; and
- there are many more ways to satisfy higher-order needs than there are for lower-order needs.

The basic need in all humans is the physiological need for food and safety. In a working situation basic needs relate to basic salaries and safe working conditions. Safety also incorporates the need for security and protection, as well as stability in the physical and interpersonal events of day-to-day life. A further lower-order need is a social need where there is a sense of 'belongingness' with their peers. Social needs are found in compatible work groups, friendships at work and an approachable and relationship-oriented boss.

Esteem is a higher-order need that can be demonstrated by respect, prestige and recognition. The highest order need is that of self-actualization. This is a need to fulfil one and to grow and use personal abilities to the fullest and most creative extent. Maslow argued that self-actualization was not a motivator of priority unless the needs of love, self-esteem, social approval and self-assertion were fairly well satisfied.

HERZBERG'S TWO-FACTOR THEORY

Herzberg and his associates noted that the aspects of jobs that produced satisfaction were different from those that produced dissatisfaction. The satisfied worker was not a person in whom dissatisfaction was always minimal, as satisfaction and dissatisfaction were evoked by different stimulus conditions.

Dissatisfaction was caused by extrinsic factors such as pay, supervision, working conditions and company policies. However, the removal of these unsatisfactory extrinsic factors was not in itself satisfying, or indeed motivating. It merely eliminated dissatisfaction. For instance, whilst low pay or bad supervision could both lead to dissatisfaction, good pay or good supervision may not necessarily lead to satisfaction. This was because satisfaction and motivation came from a different set of factors called 'motivators'. Motivators include recognition, achievement, responsibility, and personal growth.

The two sets of factors identified by Herzberg are called motivation factors and hygiene factors. Motivation factors relate specifically to work content and are the satisfiers. Hygiene factors relate to the work environment and are the causes of dissatisfaction.

The linkages between Maslow's and Herzberg's theories are shown in Figure 15.1.

The combination of these two theories indicates that the higher order needs are those that create higher levels of satisfaction and motivation. These include:

- the recognition of individual efforts;

- the setting of standards for achievement and the provision of mechanisms to enable others to strive to succeed;
- assigning responsibility to individuals for outcomes; and
- enabling personal growth by extending the boundaries or comfort zones of people, or, providing different work experiences.

Maslow's Hierarchy of Needs	Herzberg's Two-Factor Theory	
Needs	**Hygiene factors**	**Motivation factors**
Self-actualisation		Satisfiers:
		Achievement
Esteem		Recognition
		Work itself
Social		Advancement
	Dissatisfiers:	
Security	Interpersonal relations	
	Supervision	
Physiological	Pay	
	Working conditions	

Figure 15.1 Integration of Maslow's Hierarchy of Needs with Herzberg's Two-Factor Theory

Satisfiers and dissatisfiers in information services

Figure 15.2 identifies some satisfiers and dissatisfiers within information services today.

Poor working conditions include inadequate physical working environments such as bad lighting, lack of air conditioning and heating, long hours or lack of physical security. Low pay and lack of benefits in comparison with other services may also act as dissatisfiers. These dissatisfiers increase in situations where there is also lack of job security, such as when an organization is downsizing.

Satisfiers	Dissatisfiers
Flexibility	Poor working conditions
Promotion	Feeling of being overlooked
Satisfaction with pay and benefits	Dissatisfaction with pay and benefits
Sense of achievement	Unrealistic or unattainable targets
Openness and sharing	Poor communication and understanding of corporate goals
Challenge	Unclear standards of required performance
Sense of usefulness	Skills and abilities do not match the job
Sense of belonging	Unproductive rivalry
Respect	Management by threat
Able to take risks	Personal initiative is stifled
Personal growth and continuous learning of new skills	Little or no personal and professional development opportunities

Figure 15.2 Satisfiers and dissatisfiers in information services

Conclusion

Organizational strategies that promote performance-based compensation, job enrichment and job enlargement can also act as motivators. Examples of these are having a family-friendly working environment, tailoring work conditions to meet individual needs, by giving praise and showing confidence in people, by providing personal development opportunities and by enriching the work experience to allow individuals to achieve the desired performance levels.

References

Herzberg, F. (1968), 'One more time: How do you motivate employees?', *Harvard Business Review*, Jan.–Feb., pp. 53–62.
Herzberg, F., Mausner, B. and Snyderman, B. (1959), *The motivation to work*, New York, NY: Wiley.
Maslow, A.H. (1943), 'A theory of human motivation', *Psychological Review*, vol. 50, no. 4, July, pp. 370–96.

Further reading

Davenport, Thomas H. (2005), *Thinking for living: How to get better performance and results from knowledge workers*, Boston, MA: Harvard Business School.
Kakabadse, Andrew et al. (2004), *Working in organisations*, Aldershot, UK: Ashgate.

16 *Conflict Management*

Conflict occurs as the result of a disagreement, threat or opposition between individuals or groups, or within an individual or group. Conflict also serves as a catalyst for change. Whilst it may be destructive if it is not handled correctly, conflict can be a healthy sign of organizational growth and competition. In fact, if conflict within an organization ceased, stagnation could set in.

Individuals and groups have two drives; to maintain psychological equilibrium and harmony and to actualize their potential. Conflict arises when an individual or group perceives either a threat or opposition to one or both of these drives; when two antagonistic drives or needs have to be satisfied simultaneously; or where there is a tendency to simultaneously accept and reject a course of action.

Conflict is a test of power. At the organizational level conflict situations test the strength of management and their employees, or their unions if they are acting on their behalf. On an individual basis, conflict can test a person's willpower.

Conflict has traditionally been viewed as destructive; a state of affairs to be suppressed or eliminated. Managers now realize that there are some positive actions in conflict and that in changing and transforming environments conflict will need to be managed.

Individuals who are faced with personal conflict may react in either of two ways – flight or fight. Whilst the source of the conflict may not be in the organization, its effects will be manifested through the individual's actions. If their actions begin to affect the output of others the conflict will need to be resolved. There are various methods and styles for resolving conflict. Some are more effective than others. In most instances, it depends upon the conflict situation.

The place for conflict in organizations

In many instances conflict is a sign of a healthy organization. Conflict of a competitive nature generally leads to improved organizational performance. Throughout history, potentially damaging encounters with natural and physical sources has led to the adaptation of a species, race or community that has been essential for its growth and survival. In a corporate context these encounters and adaptations can be experienced by individuals, teams or the whole organization. Some of these conflicts will result in changes and solutions that are creative or innovative. For instance, budgetary pressures can lead to new and imaginative methods of delivering customer services.

Conflict is a source of intelligence and feedback to management as it brings issues to the surface. Under stress, individuals are more likely to express their real feelings or problems, which makes it easier to identify and resolve the real issues of concern. Issues can be addressed that otherwise may never have surfaced. It can also act as a safety valve. Minor conflict can prevent pressure from building up to the point where it is destructive. Petty complaints are often examples of tension release.

Conflict can serve as a unifying function within a group. Internal differences are often overcome when a group is faced with an external source of conflict. For example, if a merger is mooted, people will work more closely together to be the dominant force in the new organization.

Sources of organizational conflict

Conflict is inevitable in changing environments. Sources of conflict include the organizational differentiation, uncertainty about change, organizational growth, competition for the use of scare resources, role expectations, communication channels, interpersonal relations and behaviours, personal interests of individuals or groups, physical separations and the dependency of one party on another.

ORGANIZATION DIFFERENTIATION

Individuals working in teams in information services undertake different kinds of work which may require different time horizons, values, goals and management styles. The greater the differentiation between teams or work groups, the greater the likelihood of conflict and the need for mechanisms that will integrate these groups. It is frequently the integration that is a source of conflict. Complex organizations often expect very different groups or work units to integrate their efforts towards accomplishing organizational objectives without having any understanding of their differences.

Likewise the possibilities for misunderstanding and the opportunities for conflict increase when groups of people are physically separated by location or shiftwork. Information services are particularly vulnerable to this type of conflict as employees often work in a number of physically separated locations (e.g. computing centres or branch libraries), and have to work rostered hours in order to support customer services.

UNCERTAINTY ABOUT CHANGE

Uncertainty brought about by change and repositioning will inevitably lead to conflict between individuals or groups as each strives for their continued existence and new order in the changed circumstances. The knowledge that new skills will have to be learnt or alternatively may be acquired through external recruitment, together with a concern for their future will leave some individuals feeling vulnerable.

Where the future is certain, activities are routine and predictable. In a changing environment, the basic rules and regulations may no longer be relevant. As a result, conflicting opinions may arise as new problems have to be solved and new systems and policies are established. Conflict can also arise where the new policies, structures, practices and procedures are not in the main interests of some of the parties. This is particularly so where the new policy or structure removes decision making or responsibility from one of the parties.

ORGANIZATIONAL GROWTH

For similar reasons to uncertainty brought about by change, conflict can also arise through organizational growth. As information services grow to meet new service needs, new systems and policies evolve that govern tasks and behaviour. Communication and reporting channels may change as additional levels, functions or groups are created. Conflict will arise as individuals and work units vie to influence or assume the higher positions in the hierarchy.

COMPETITION FOR RESOURCES

Resources that are scarce and in demand, or determine the interdependence and independence of teams or departments are another source of conflict. Teams or groups that have to share resources such as motor vehicles or photocopiers may require them at conflicting times resulting in conflict over ownership where one party may seek to impose their systems or requirements on others. To overcome this, units may strive for their independence, thereby creating further tensions and conflict as they demand their own. The perception that teams 'own' their vehicles or equipment, rather than seeing it as a corporate resource often exacerbates the reluctance to share with others.

PROFESSIONAL TERMINOLOGY AND ACRONYMS

The use of acronyms and specific terminology associated with an area of expertise can lead to distortion and conflict as they are not always recognized or interpreted by others in the same way. Likewise, technical terminology or acronyms that describe events or objects can also threaten people who do not understand their meaning.

CONFLICT OF INTERESTS

Individuals may experience personal conflicts of interests. For example, there may be a conflict of interests between their professional values and organizational demands. Conflicts of interests also arise in balancing time and priorities to meet the needs of the job, to have a home life and care for dependants, to further a professional career, and to pursue personal interests. All of which are important. The conflict may be identified through feelings of guilt or being pressurized to give more attention to one aspect of life than another.

Role conflict also occurs where the information services manager has to compete vigorously for funds with other managers during budget deliberations, yet needs to cooperate at all other times with these as peers.

Identifying personal conflict

When faced with conflict an individual's natural instinct (which is common to all living things) is to react through either 'fight' or 'flight'. Either method of conduct is an attempt to adjust to the conflict situation. So to assist individuals to adjust to conflict and substitute acceptable and efficient attitudes and responses, there needs to be an understanding of what lies behind their conduct.

If a reliable staff member suddenly begins to act unpredictably, their actions may be a symptom of conflict. The cause or source of conflict may not be within the information service, but its effect will most certainly be felt there. In such a situation, it is the manager's responsibility to try to help resolve the conflict either by providing advice or by referring the individual to an appropriate source of advice. If the source of the conflict lies within the information service's control the manager must help resolve the issue. If the source is beyond the manager's control, they can choose whether or not to be involved. However, their involvement becomes essential when other staff begin to be affected.

Fight or aggression can be identified by negativism, dominance, displaced anger or hostility. A member of staff may be contentious for no apparent reason or rebellious without cause. Some individuals may become uncharacteristically domineering towards their peers or fellow workers; or instances of anger will be levelled at colleagues rather than management. Others may become sarcastic, or make cutting comments or criticise. All of these are symptoms of an underlying conflict that must be resolved.

Flight can be identified by absenteeism, apathy or hypochondria. A staff member who suddenly begins to arrive late for work or absents themselves from others by being aloof or refusing to become involved is using flight as an escape mechanism from a source of conflict. Other examples of flight are daydreaming and absent mindedness, an overindulgence in food, substance abuse or continual tiredness.

Occasionally other adjustments to conflict are made. The individual may establish defence mechanisms or perform attention-getting activities in an effort towards self-deception. Compensation tactics may be used in order to reduce the sense of uselessness. The individual may substitute satisfaction in one kind of achievement for the lack of it in another. For example, the person may put more personal energies into sporting activities than their work.

A less well-adjusted form of compensation is used when an individual will bask in the reflected glory of another. Individuals may also push the blame on to someone or something else, such as the boss or personal computer; or attribute to others the faults that really reside in themselves.

Resolving conflict

The effective resolution of conflict is critical in ensuring that a potentially damaging situation is turned into a positive outcome for all parties. Conflict resolution methods are not only needed in a manager and team member situation; they are required in peer-to-peer negotiations and in negotiating between the organization, customers and other external stakeholders. Conflicts are often resolved in three ways, win-lose, lose-lose, or win-win. The results or outcomes of the first two are not always desirable.

WIN-LOSE METHODS

In win-lose methods one party inevitably wins and the other inevitably loses. Win-lose methods constitute an authoritarian approach to conflict resolution as legitimate or coercive power is often used to bring about compliance. The dominant party will pursue their own outcomes at the expense of others, and the other party will be forced into submission, often by the use of threats. In organizations, majority rule and the failure of the managers or team leaders to respond to requests for change are also considered to be win-lose methods.

Whilst win-lose methods may prove satisfactory to the winner they can result in resentment and have negative effects on future relationships and the performance of individuals and the organization. Win-lose methods can sometimes lead to grudges or retaliatory action that may cause a further breakdown in the relationship and the associated loss of control will affect work output. Respect for the other party will be diminished.

LOSE-LOSE METHODS

Lose-lose methods leave no one entirely happy. One such method is the compromise. This is based on the assumption that half a solution is better than none. Another lose-lose strategy involves side payments. One party agrees to a solution in exchange for a favour from the other party. A third strategy is to submit the issue to a neutral third party. The results of this action may be disappointing as arbitrators frequently resolve issues at some middle ground between the positions held by the disputants. Although each gains something, the outcome is rarely satisfying to either side.

WIN-WIN METHODS

Win-win methods provide a solution that is acceptable to all. Win-win conflict resolution strategies focus upon ends and goals, identifying the sources of conflict and then presenting these as problems to be solved. Superordinate goals (goals that are greater than those of the individual, team or organization) are established. These reflect the objectives or outcomes that all parties must work towards.

The identification of the superordinate goals reminds conflicting parties that even though their particular goals are vitally important, they share a goal that cannot be achieved without cooperation. The win-win approach uses participative management techniques in order to gain consensus and commitment to objectives. The desired solution is one that achieves both individual or work unit goals and the organization's objectives, and which is acceptable to all parties.

Conflict management styles

There are several different styles in managing conflict that can be used. Each has its purpose and, if used appropriately, will be successful. If a style is used to avoid or suppress an issue it will have a negative effect on relationships.

AVOIDANCE STYLE

In the avoidance style, the person attempts to dispose of the problem by denying that it exists or by avoiding the issue. They may try to remain neutral or withdraw from it. Examples of this can be found where managers are unavailable in their office, defer answering a memo, fail to return a telephone call, or refuse to get involved in the conflict. In most instances the conflict will not go away. In fact, it will often escalate to a point where it becomes unmanageable.

Whilst not avoiding the issue, there are circumstances where it is appropriate to not get directly involved. These are:

- where the issue is of minor or passing importance that it is not worth the time or energy to confront it;
- where bringing attention to the issue will fuel its intensity in a detrimental way;
- where the person's power is so low in relation to the other party that there will be little or no positive outcome by being involved; or
- where others can more effectively resolve the conflict between themselves.

SMOOTHING STYLE

The smoothing style refers to the tendency to minimize or suppress the open recognition of real or perceived differences in conflict situations, whilst emphasizing common interests. This style fails to recognize the positive aspects of openly handling the conflict. The manager acts as if the conflict will pass with time and appeals to the need for cooperation. He or she will try to reduce tensions by reassuring and providing support to the parties.

The smoothing style encourages individuals to cover up and avoid expressions of their feelings. It is effective on a short-term basis in three situations:

- when there is a potentially explosive emotional situation that needs to be defused;
- where harmonious relationships need to be preserved or where the avoidance of disruption is important; or
- where the conflicts are of a personal nature between individuals and cannot be dealt with within the organizational context.

FORCING STYLE

The forcing style refers to the tendency of a person to use coercive or reward power to dominate the other party. Differences are suppressed and the other party is forced into adopting the lesser position. This style results in winners and losers. The losers do not usually support the final decision in the way that the winners do and this can create more conflict.

The win-lose forcing style is appropriate when there is an extreme urgency and quick action is needed or where there has been constant deliberation between the parties with no resulting outcome. It can also be used when an unpopular course of action is necessary for the long-term survival of the information service. It is sometimes used as a self-protection when a person is being taken advantage of by another party.

COMPROMISE STYLE

The compromise style is often used when negotiating. There is often a tendency to sacrifice positions when seeking a middle ground for the resolution of conflict. Early use of compromise results in less diagnosis and exploration of the real nature of the conflict. The real issues often surface much later in the negotiating or conflict resolution process.

The compromise style is desirable when both parties recognize that there is a possibility of reaching an agreement that is more advantageous than if no agreement was reached. It is also useful if there is a likelihood that more than one agreement could be reached, or where there are conflicting goals.

COLLABORATIVE STYLE

The collaborative style requires the willingness of the individual to identify underlying causes of conflict, openly share information, and search out alternatives considered to be mutually beneficial. Conflicts are recognized openly and evaluated by all those concerned. Sharing, examining, and assessing the reasons for the conflict leads to a more thorough development of alternatives.

The collaborative style is inappropriate when time limits are imposed to the extent that they inhibit direct confrontation of feelings and issues involved in the conflict, and, when there are no shared meanings (norms, values, feelings) between the parties.

The collaborative style uses win-win methods to resolve conflict. It is used more by people who are relationship oriented than by those who are task oriented. It is found more frequently in open organizations than in bureaucratic ones. The collaborative style is recommended:

- when individuals have common goals;
- when consensus should lead to the best overall solution to the conflict; and
- where there is a need to make high-quality decisions on the basis of knowledge and expertise.

Detecting conflict in information services

GRIEVANCE PROCEDURES

Formal grievance procedures enable dissatisfaction to be communicated to management through official channels. Such procedures assume that the individual has the courage to submit their complaint for discussion, that they wish to make a formal approach in addressing the situation and that the grievance officers are approachable. Grievance procedures are most effective when practices are put in place to ensure appropriate confidentiality, where there are designated grievance officers that are representative of differing levels in the organization hierarchy and when grievance officers are given appropriate training.

OBSERVATION

Interpersonal sensitivity and direct observation can often identify interpersonal or intergroup conflicts. Conflicting motives are usually apparent when clashes between individuals or groups occur or work output deteriorates.

INTRANET GRAPEVINES AND SUGGESTION BOXES

Grapevines and suggestion boxes on corporate intranets may be used as gripe boxes. These can incorporate chat or instant messaging features where issues can be resolved quickly. It is important that these facilities are monitored to ensure that individuals are not unduly targeted or defamed; that sensitive, private or delicate issues are managed; and that objective answers are quickly given to issues as they arise. Avenues should also be provided where employees can make suggestions whilst preserving their anonymity.

An open-door policy is another effective means of creating an open environment where conflict can be identified and resolved.

EXIT INTERVIEW

The exit interview can be one of the most reliable indications of subversive conflicts within information services. Employees may be willing to discuss such matters when they have no further affiliation with the organization. Sometimes conflict may lead to the resignation of an employee and in such cases the employee may not be willing to discuss their dissatisfaction for fear that this may affect some future job reference. The interviewer should be impartial and stress the positive outcomes of the exit interview for resolving future conflicting situations.

Conclusion

Conflict is inevitable in changing environments as people adjust to change. Constructive conflict and competition are healthy within organizations as they will often result in the improved performance of individuals and teams. Conflict can also lead to a better understanding of different individuals' or groups' problems. The discussions that take place may find issues that can be resolved to the advantage of both parties or, identify common goals that were previously unknown or overlooked. Conflict also acts as a safety valve. The sources of conflict and the resulting actions need to be effectively managed to ensure that only positive outcomes arise from conflict.

Further reading

Roberto, Michael A. (2005), *Why great leaders don't take yes for an answer: Managing for conflict and consensus*, Upper Saddle River, NJ: Wharton School.
Tidd, Simon T. et al. (2004), 'The importance of role ambiguity and trust in conflict perception: Unpacking the task conflict to relationship conflict linkage', *International Journal of Conflict*, vol. 15, no. 4, pp. 364-84.

17 *Negotiation*

Negotiation can be defined as a process in which two or more parties try to reach an agreement on matters where there are both common and conflicting goals. Successful negotiating requires that both parties have experience, confidence, and high-level communication skills. The parties deal directly with each other in an effort to persuade or compromise with the view to reaching a desirable conclusion. The availability of time and information are critical factors in successful negotiations.

The ability to negotiate effectively is a critical component of the task of transforming organizations and can occur with varying degrees of formality. Negotiation is commonly used in the resolution of conflict and in the implementation of decisions. It is also used in the preparation and finalizing of budgets, industrial relations, contract management and policy development and implementation. Not all issues can be settled through negotiation, so it is important to identify where outcomes can be better achieved through other solutions.

Effective negotiation

Whilst compromise is the cornerstone to negotiating, effective negotiation uses both compromise and collaboration. Collaboration enables the realization of common interests, whilst finding the middle ground on conflicting interests. Effective negotiating should result in shared meaning between the parties. That is, the convergence of values, views, attitudes, styles, perceptions or beliefs to enable a common view or action.

The role of a negotiator as an agent may range from being an emissary commissioned only to state the position, to a free agent with considerable latitude. This range of responsiveness is likely to affect the negotiation process. For example, the effect of the 'person' variables in the negotiating process will be felt more strongly in instances where the negotiator has more latitude to manoeuvre.

Negotiators have to strike a balance between being steadfast in their desires whilst allowing concessions and being sufficiently cooperative with the other party to allow negotiations to take place. This is particularly true when personal interests are at stake as emotions are prone to be far more volatile in these situations.

Negotiation requires trade-offs between short- and long-term gains to put into effect a workable outcome. This is particularly true when negotiating the implementation of a decision where it is inherent in this exercise that the parties to the decision will need to continue to work with each other after the event. Apparent honesty and openness are important features of the negotiating process. However, complete honesty can sometimes run the risk of being exploited by the other party. To overcome this, the motives of each party must be made clear.

The physical properties of the negotiating room and seating arrangements will affect the negotiating atmosphere. The shape and size of the table will place participants in a position that is either compromising or contending. For example, round tables are less threatening than square or oblong ones. Opposing parties will often want to sit opposite each other. This allows them to pick up their opposite members' non-verbal communication signals and places each party in a competitive position. At times when a compromise is to be achieved, opposing parties may sit next to each other. Sitting side by side neutralizes any feelings of competition or animosity between the parties.

The success of negotiation also depends upon the people who are involved. Outer-directed people, whose values, skills and attitudes are gained from outside themselves, are easier to change attitudinally than inner-directed people. Inner-directed people resist group pressure, do things their way and have a sense of independence; all of which limit their sense of negotiation.

In some situations, negotiators must be willing to give up more than they would like in order to obtain a preferable long-term outcome. The result may be a less than perfect solution for the conceding party, but in the longer term one that has a better outcome than the next-best alternative. Faces may be saved and important working relationships preserved. A positive outcome of any negotiation process is that the parties learn a good deal more about each other than they may previously have known.

SKILLS AND COMPETENCIES

Good negotiators are experienced in the negotiating process. They have high aspirations, are articulate and have great presence and self-confidence. Their self-confidence arises out of their technical knowledge of the field in which they are negotiating and in their past negotiating experience. Effective negotiators are creative, yet determined and disciplined. They need a high frustration or tolerance level to withstand frustrations.

Age can make a difference. In their early years of negotiating, negotiators tend to be very competitive, showing signs of aggression or abrasiveness. In their later years there tends to be a higher tolerance of others, tempered by experience. Ideally, the negotiator should be between these two stages – that is, experienced but still keen to be successful. Above all, the negotiator must enjoy negotiating and have an understanding of how to devise mutually beneficial alternatives.

Negotiation can be very much a personal process, even though the negotiator may be acting on behalf of other people. It is an exercise in predicting the other's position without the negotiator disclosing their own. However, there still needs to be some leeway to tantalize the other party into wanting to know more about what is being offered.

High-level interpersonal skills with sensitivity to the behaviours of others will help the negotiator in their task. Negotiators are better able to anticipate and evaluate others' responses to the offers being made if they are:

- attentive to what is being said;
- able to distinguish between what the other is saying and what they really mean; and,
- able to translate their offers and demands into what is the real situation.

To be effective, the negotiator should be able to identify both their role and that of the opposite number. The negotiator should also take steps to identify the apparent game plan of the opposing team. Each member will have their individual purpose and strategies. The studying of the non-verbal communications of the members of the opposing team will assist the identification process.

The process of negotiation

THE FIRST STAGE

The initial meeting of the parties establishes the climate that prevails during the ensuing negotiations. The atmosphere created in the first few minutes of the meeting and greeting stage is critical. Tensions need to be relaxed so that commonsense prevails, rather than outright confrontation. Non-verbal clues such as eye contact, posture, gestures and patterns of movement will add to the feeling of the meeting.

The first meeting is usually devoted to establishing the bargaining authority possessed by representatives on both sides. If the parties are unknown to each other, a 'pecking' order will be established and personal interactions developed. The negotiating rules and procedures will also be determined. This stage may be omitted where all parties are known to each other as the negotiating rules and procedures will be well established.

THE SECOND STAGE

The second stage is characterized by each side attempting to consider the opponent's position without revealing its own. Each side will try to avoid disclosing the key important factors in their proposal in order to avoid being forced to pay a higher price than is necessary to have the proposal accepted. Negotiators will also attempt to get greater concessions in return for granting those requests that their opponents want most.

The proposals may be discussed in the order of their appearance on the agenda or in some other sequence. The sequence in which they are discussed may also be a subject for negotiation. If the discussion of the most important issues is deferred until last, this can often serve as a leverage for gaining agreement on more minor issues that precede the important ones.

THE SETTLEMENT

A process of haggling, bargaining, and settling then begins. The proposals are resolved at a stage when agreement is reached within the limits that each party is willing to concede. The agreement is then ratified. In settling and ratifying the agreement, all the points and concessions of the agreement should be summarized and all actions accounted for. A record should be produced that accurately reports what was achieved. Finally, responsibility should be allocated to individuals or groups for the implementation of the agreement.

Issues affecting negotiations

STRESS AND TENSION

The environment of negotiators has been likened to a fishbowl, with everyone interested in the negotiating performance. The face-saving techniques that are often used and their associated anxiety enhance the stresses and tensions of those who are involved in the negotiating process.

High levels of stress and tension can have a debilitating effect on negotiations. They may cause greater hostility among negotiators, leading to harder bargaining strategies. This can result in less successful outcomes. Increases in tension beyond a certain point may make members of either party less capable of evaluating information and making the fine discriminations necessary in order to achieve a mutually satisfying solution. It is important that negotiators are aware of their personal stress levels when undertaking any negotiating procedures. They should monitor their tensions, looking for physical symptoms such as aggression or tension headaches.

CONSERVING THE POSITION

The psychological need to impress others and maintain a reputation of strength is poignant in negotiation. Taken too far, it is likely to lead to rigid and contentious demands that may spoil the negotiating process. Skilful negotiators like their concessions to be seen as a willingness to deal from a position of strength rather than a weakness. They also like their concessions to be allowed because of their competency and reputation as a good negotiator.

Some negotiators find it tempting to commit themselves to tough negotiating positions when discussions bog down, in an effort to impose such a considerable cost to the adversary that causes them to yield under pressure. However, it is a mistake to assume that all negotiators can be pressured into arriving at a settlement. The threat of an impasse being reached when time expires may be sufficient in itself for a result to be obtained closer to the time. To adopt an entrenched attitude will result either in the perpetrator having to retreat to their former position, losing credibility in the process, or opening the way to subsequent exploitation by the other.

EMOTIONS

The negotiation process is complicated by the fact that not all people are alike. Not everyone is a self-actualizer and not everyone wants to participate in the decision-making or negotiating process; some even may resist. Negotiators meet a multiplicity of emotions as they try to negotiate. These need to be understood if the negotiating process is to be successful.

COMPLEX SITUATIONS

The complexity of the situation may increase the intricacies in negotiations, with different parties developing different conceptions of the situation or preferring a different structure for handling the negotiations. This situation can also arise if a member of the party is someone who has not previously been involved in the decision-making process, or is not sufficiently knowledgeable or obligated to the issue at stake.

An impasse may result from the inability to resolve the differences, and a mediator may be required to alter perceptions or definitions of purpose on behalf of either party. This could delay or jeopardize the implementation of the negotiations. Therefore different negotiating strategies are necessary to suit different environments and different situations.

Strategies for effective negotiations

TIMEFRAMES

One of the most critical aspects of the negotiating process is time. Time can be either a constriction or an advantage. It is important not to let the opposing side know of any time constraints that the negotiator may have. Time pressures have two effects. First, as the deadline approaches, decisions will be made faster, leading to one party losing their demand power. Second, to declare any time constraint may result in the other party holding their real negotiating process until close to the deadline, in order to place the first party in a more vulnerable or critical position.

The negotiator should be patient, realizing that the other party must have a deadline too. As the deadline of the other party comes close there may be a shift in power back to the first party.

KNOWLEDGE AND INFORMATION

Knowledge and information are critical to the negotiating process. The negotiator should quietly and consistently probe the other party for information. They should listen rather than talk, asking questions rather than answering them. It may be useful to check the other party's credibility by asking questions to which the answer is already known. Attentive listening and observation are critical. Often unintentional clues can be given out. Negotiators should have faith in their own problem-solving abilities.

AGENDAS

Momentum for results can sometimes be encouraged by placing easier items earlier on the negotiation agenda, so that both parties are able to build upon their successes. The opening bid should be put firmly, without reservation or hesitation. For the 'sellers' it should be the highest defensible bid. For the 'buyers' it should be the lowest defensible offer.

USE OF THIRD PARTIES AS MEDIATORS

A mediator may serve as a valuable communications link between the parties, coordinating movement towards a compromise. Trust, too, is important, but it is the absence of distrust that makes negotiating more effective.

BREAKING DEADLOCKS

If a deadlock is threatened there should be a break in the negotiating procedures. This can either be achieved by using a time break such as lunch or morning refreshments, or by talking about some aspect other than that where a deadlock is threatened. A mediator or third party may also be used to help the negotiating process at this stage.

BARGAINING

Bargaining is a key management skill in the resolution of conflict and in the implementation of decisions in the information service. It can also be used in industrial relations such as negotiating an award agreement, contract management, the acquiring of resources, policy development and implementation. Effective bargaining requires experience, confidence and the possession of high-level communication skills.

Conclusion

Effective negotiation can be used in resolving conflict and implementing decisions. It is a skill that can be learnt, building upon experience and utilizing high-level interpersonal and communication skills.

Managing Yourself and Others

The theme for Part V is managing the well-being of the people who work in the information service, which includes managing personal well-being. Managing the well-being of people is important from a duty of care perspective as well as being strongly connected to motivation and productivity factors. In a busy and competitive environment it is sometimes tempting to focus on the demands of the job and overlook personal life needs and those of others.

Chapter 18 considers the human side of communication. It identifies the interpersonal communication skills required of information service managers and their staff. It also describes the communication process and issues associated with interpersonal communication that may affect the communication process. These issues include self-image and attitude to others, listening, stereotyping and the halo effect. Barriers to personal communication are also explored in this chapter.

As part of interpersonal communication, networks allow managers to function successfully. They can be used to seek and provide information, for support and to influence outcomes. Chapter 18 explains the value of networks for getting things done, how a network acts as a group, and provides advice on how to establish networks.

Chapter 19 is concerned with stress management. It explores why some individuals are vulnerable to stress at certain stages in life. It identifies factors in the workplace that can be stressors and different personality types that cause some people to handle certain types of pressure better than others. Finally, the chapter considers personal and workplace strategies for the management of stress.

Chapter 20 is about career planning and personal development. People's personal satisfaction with themselves, their lifestyle and their work, and their sense of self-worth and purpose in their career and life goals can be supported through the activities of career planning and personal development. The chapter looks at the relevant responsibilities for the organization, the information services manager and the individual in career planning. It considers a holistic approach to lifestyle planning using a mind map exercise. The aspect of managing oneself and personal image is also covered.

Chapter 20 also includes the topic of training. It covers the identification of training needs, designing the training programme, maintaining the behaviour learnt in the training programme and evaluating the training programme. Finally, it considers performance reviews and appraisals to provide feedback to individuals on their performance and as a mechanism for identifying training and personal development needs.

The management of expertise is very important in information services as they often comprise groups of people with diverse professional backgrounds. Chapter 21 expands on some of the concepts put forward under group and team dynamics and explains why differentiations occur between people with differing expertise, backgrounds and age groups. People of different generations and whose roles, functions and expertise differ will often place a different emphasis and value on priorities, time horizons and outlook, all of which need to be managed.

PLANNING AND MANAGING FOR TRANSFORMATION

CREATING THE RIGHT CORPORATE ENVIRONMENT

TRANSFORMING THE CORPORATE ENVIRONMENT

MANAGING YOURSELF AND OTHERS

PART V – MANAGING YOURSELF AND OTHERS

18. **Personal communication and networking**
The communication process; Effective interpersonal communication; Effective listening; Using emotional intelligence; Effective networking; Networks as groups; Establishing networks

19. **Stress management**
Stress in the workplace; Stress and personality; Stress management techniques

20. **Career planning and personal development**
Career planning; Lifestyle planning; Self-management; Professional development and training

21. **Managing expertise and generation gaps**
Differentiation through specialization; Why differentiation occurs; Generation gaps; Developing the common good

MANAGING IN A DYNAMIC ENVIRONMENT

EPILOGUE

POSITIONING TO EXCEL IN SERVICE DELIVERY

GOVERNANCE AND ACCOUNTABILITY

Figure PV.1   Managing yourself and others

18 *Personal Communication and Networking*

All human interaction is dependent upon interpersonal communication for the exchange of information and the conveyance of ideas. Influencing and getting things done in the corporate environment requires good interpersonal skills that include networking with people and clearly communicating across organizational boundaries and with all levels of people internal and external to the organization.

The passage of information or ideas between two people does not constitute communication. The message or idea must reach and be meaningfully understood by the other party to be part of the communication process. Communication occurs when the messages flowing between two parties arrive at a stage where the images and ideas that each is trying to pass to the other have the same meaning to the receiver as to the sender.

People employed in information services spend most of their day listening, making judgments, evaluating, reasoning, providing advice, networking, reassuring and appeasing their bosses, peers, customers and stakeholders. These activities all require highly developed verbal and non-verbal communications skills and take place in a variety of ways, for example in formal and informal meetings, face to face, by phone or by email, through formal report writing or casual conversation.

Good interpersonal communication skills are extremely important in information services. For example:

- in understanding client needs;
- in being informed about operational issues within the information service;
- in updating knowledge about new and emerging communication techniques and of the latest developments in service delivery; and
- in being an effective member of a team.

The very nature of the activities in information services requires individuals to have highly developed communication skills as well as the ability to assess, select, manage, process and disseminate vehicles of communication in a variety of formats:

- they have to manage and use information in multiple formats to provide information services to their customers;
- they must be expert in recognizing the most appropriate vehicle to communicate information and deliver interactive services to a large number of people; and increasingly
- they also have responsibilities for the sharing, development and brokering of knowledge across organizations.

The information discipline is particularly strong in its use of technical terms and jargon which can be daunting to those who do not have the same technical background. It is therefore important to be able to communicate technical issues to people without using the technical terminology.

The communication process

Communication is a process that takes place and is interpreted at the individual level. This occurs even if the individual is acting on behalf of others, or interacting with a machine, group or organization. For example, in negotiating, individuals may be representing and communicating the views of others in their messages; however, they will initially perceive incoming messages from their personal viewpoint.

The key elements of the communication process are a source, a message, a receiver, feedback and noise. The source is the person or element that is responsible for encoding an intended meaning into a message. This may be the person who translates their thoughts and ideas (the message) into a language, such as French, English or uses technical terminology in the hope that it can be understood by the other person(s). The receiver decodes the message into a perceived meaning. If both parties speak the same language and share a joint perception of the message then they are communicating. Feedback from the receiver to the source may or may not be given. If it is, it serves either to confirm the message or to show that the message has not been received correctly. In the latter case another message reinforcing the context of the first one is usually sent. 'Noise' is anything present in the perceived signal that is not part of the originally intended message. It may originate from the sender or the receiver, or it may be the preoccupation of either party with some other pressure that may prevent them from fully listening to or understanding the implications of the message. Noise distorts the original message.

Messages may be sent over more than one channel at a time. Whilst it is unusual for two people to continue to speak to each other at the same time, it is usual for non-verbal communication to be concurrently transmitted between people. This is often unconsciously acknowledged and interpreted by the other person, who may change or adapt their next verbal message as a result.

Effective interpersonal communication

The existence of various avenues or media for communicating does not always ensure that communication takes place. The communication process may fail for a number of reasons as no two individuals are alike. Individuals have different perceptions of others and situations that are governed by their past experiences, cultures, values, knowledge, attitudes, expectations and self-image. This can result in an inability to build a two-way communication process because the process is based upon subjective analysis or perception of the other person(s) rather than the objectivity of the message conveyed.

To improve their interpersonal communication, individuals or groups must understand each other better. Strategies for understanding the other person include:

* seeking clarification or more information about the issue;
* exploring mutual ideas;

- emphasizing and sharing an appreciation of feelings; and
- reflecting upon their own and the other party's position and what is being said.

There are also differences in listening abilities that may be coloured by natural tendencies to judge and evaluate both what is being said and the person saying it. These can lead to differences in the interpretation of the message. Problems may be oversimplified in the message or deliberately generalized, distorted, or omitted. Alternatively, the receiver may be insensitive to the problems expressed in the message and so not listen properly to what is being said. There may also be a lack of distinction between information and communication, or a lack of clarity as to who needs the information. Finally, relevant information may not be able to be synthesized due to the overabundance of irrelevant information. Being over informed is as inhibiting as being under informed.

Effective interpersonal communication in these instances can be achieved by focusing upon concrete evidence and issues rather than being vague or abstract. Opinions should be formed upon descriptive actions, not judgmental ones or inferences. The emphasis should be upon developing alternatives and the sharing of ideas and information, rather than the giving of advice.

Managers can enhance their interpersonal communication skills by being accessible and by defining each individual's or team's areas of responsibility. Goals should be kept clearly in mind. In situations where a person requires guidance, their actual behaviour should be focused upon rather than their personality. The manager should develop trust between all concerned and be frank with individuals on plans and problems. Above all, effective listening skills should be developed.

SELF-IMAGE AND ATTITUDES TO OTHERS

It is helpful when communicating with others to appreciate and understand the complexity of interpersonal communication. The interpersonal aspect of communication has been described by Lippitt (1982) and involves the searching and understanding of the self and others' self-image, needs, values, expectations, standards and norms and perceptions.

Self-image involves the perceptions of an individual about themselves or the group or organization to which they belong. The concept of a group can also be extended to include a nationality or religious group. Self-image takes into account ego, pride, culture, traditions and ambitions. Needs reflect requirements that enable psychological or physiological yearnings to be satisfied. They include love, security, recognition and success. Values reflect subjective ideas held dearly. Expectations are anticipated outcomes, desired or otherwise, which are likely to be the consequence of actions or the lack of actions.

Standards are found in fixed norms that reflect cultural background and experience. Perceptions are preconceived ideas that may or may not distort an individual's views. To this may be added a background of stored information, understanding and knowledge based on the past, and an experience, understanding and knowledge of the present. None of these can be mutually exclusive, and all interact to influence the interpersonal communication process at the time.

Lippitt (1982) also describes interpersonal communication as being a circulatory process. The individual has a picture of their self and an understanding of the kind of person they are. This is known as their self-image. Individuals also possess a set of attitudes towards the person(s) with whom they are communicating, which either can be positive or negative. As a result of the self-image and set of attitudes, intentions to behave in a certain way are formed. These intentions are coloured by past experiences in similar situations, and perceptions of the attitudes of the other(s) towards themselves.

Receivers filter the behaviour as it is being received according to whether they like or dislike the senders. The receiver also has some prior expectations as to how the sender should behave. Incoming behaviour is evaluated as to whether it meets these expectations. As a result of the valuation, the receiver responds to the sender. The original sender also filters the incoming behaviour according to their prejudices, attitudes, etc., and the process begins again.

STEREOTYPING AND HALO EFFECT

Stereotyping

Stereotyping involves forming generalized opinions of how certain people appear, think, feel and act. It is an attempt to classify or categorize individuals so that they lose their individuality and are in turn assigned the characteristics of an entire group of people.

Stereotyping affects the interpersonal communication process because it keeps individuals from understanding one another. Stereotyping is 'noise' that prevents one party from hearing the message that the other party is sending. It colours attitudes and creates prejudices.

Halo effect

The halo effect is a tendency to judge an individual favourably, or occasionally unfavourably. In many cases this is on the basis of one strong point on which the other party places a high value. Halo effects can have positive or negative consequences for the other party. It affects the communication process in that anything that they say is consistently interpreted in either a positive or negative fashion.

Effective listening

A good communicator is also an effective listener. Poor listening is one of the most inhibiting features for the communication of ideas. People with effective listening skills often elicit invaluable information from others as they quickly create an atmosphere of understanding and respect. This can lead to higher levels of productivity, increased motivation and a willingness to cooperate.

Effective listening requires the individual to listen to what is being said in terms of what is being meant. Key words, inferences, prejudices, provide meaningful details that explain underlying thoughts. Effective listeners also remember what has been said and the context in which it was said. They try to understand the viewpoint of the other party, even though it may contradict or challenge their own ideas and values. They ask pertinent questions providing a feedback mechanism to the other party and demonstrating that they are listening to what is being conveyed.

Hearing is not listening. Listening involves interpreting non-verbal communication signals such as mood, aggression, nervousness, and incorporating these into the verbal message that is received. Active listening allows the listener to place themselves in the other party's position and look at things from their point of view.

Effective listening skills can be improved through practice, training and concentration. Good listeners do not interrupt or attempt to finish others' sentences. They are patient, allowing the other party plenty of time. They try to put the other party at ease and make an effort to remove or minimize distractions. Finally, good listeners never show anger or criticize the other party.

Using emotional intelligence

Many of the reactions that leaders and managers have to deal with in driving transformational change are based on emotion. Emotions such as fear, anger, surprise, joy, sadness or disgust are manifested in behaviours such as aggression, distrust, optimism and eagerness. By identifying, using, understanding and managing emotions that may have been uncovered through good interpersonal communication and listening skills, the manager can be more effective in their transformational change role.

Caruso and Salovey (2004, p. xv) identify how the emotionally intelligent manager can leverage his skills:

- identifying how all the key participants feel, themselves included;
- using these feelings to guide the thinking and reasoning of the people involved;
- understanding how feelings might change and develop as events unfold; and
- managing to stay open to the data of feelings and integrating them into decisions and actions.

People who are skilful in identifying and managing emotions know what people feel and talk about feelings. They read people accurately and are good at expressing their own feelings. They listen, ask questions and determine how they and the other party are feeling. They examine the causes of the feelings and try to understand what might happen next and the type of emotional encounters that they might encounter; whilst also looking at actions that can be taken to alleviate the emotion.

In looking to understand emotions, Caruso and Salovey (2004, p. 52) have identified that skilful people try to make correct assumptions rather than misunderstand people. They know the right thing to say and have a rich vocabulary, rather than find it hard to explain their feelings. They also understand that a person can feel conflicting emotions towards another or about a situation. In managing emotions, skilful people are open to their feelings and those of others, they connect with people and take steps to manage feelings appropriately by calming people down or encouraging or cheering others up.

Effective networking

Personal networks allow information services managers and their team members to function and communicate effectively. They can be used to seek and impart knowledge and information, for support, and to positively influence outcomes.

Networking is a sharing process where knowledge and information is freely given as well as obtained through formal and informal communication channels. To function effectively, it is important that personal networks are established with relevant people within the organization, various professional bodies that are represented or interact with the information service, and with external stakeholders, such as industry, trade suppliers and politicians. These networks will enable the individual to establish alliances with key stakeholders who are likely to support preferred positions or actions, or supply needed resources or services.

Networks are particularly important for individuals who work in professional isolation. They provide a source of professional knowledge, information and opinions and can be useful in sharing resources. Networks can also comprise a group of trusted people to whom the individual can turn for guidance and personal advice.

Belonging to the right network will 'open doors'. Many legitimate political tactics rely upon networks. In belonging to others' networks valuable information is often obtained that would not otherwise be forthcoming. This will often lead to improved decision making or allow corrective or appropriate action to be taken to avoid undesired outcomes. Networks also provide sponsorship and can influence outcomes. This may be useful at budget time or when major decisions take place about the future role of the information service.

Networks as groups

A network is a natural coalition. That is a group whose joint interests, viewpoint and preferences need to be protected. Within a network support and advice is freely and positively given. Networks are a closed group phenomenon, with those belonging to the network holding sacred certain unchallengeable values and norms. Intra-organizational networks are often identified by common behaviour modes, certain dress codes and modes of thinking. There are four types of networks which are based on a common purpose of power, ideology, people or profession.

PRACTICIAN-ORIENTED NETWORKS

These networks are formed for a common purpose that benefits those who belong. They may be practician oriented and comprise individuals who have similar expertise, training or professional interests. They provide true intellectual and professional stimuli for new ideas and innovations. In support of their ideals, they may attempt to influence other employees or organizations.

POWER NETWORKS

Privilege or power networks comprise people who wield substantial influence or wish to be influential. These culture clubs operate through personal power bases. Introductions to the group are either by invitation or through the 'old school tie network'.

IDEOLOGICAL NETWORKS

Ideological networks comprise different types of people who wish to pursue particular ideas. Pressure groups are an example of ideological networks in that they are formed to pursue particular social objectives.

PEOPLE-ORIENTED NETWORKS

The most common networks in organizations are the people-oriented networks that exist for the sake of their members. These networks are important as they are valuable sources of information and support.

THE GATEKEEPER ROLE

The entrance to the network is facilitated by identifying a gatekeeper, who is an influential member of the group. Personal sponsorship by a gatekeeper is important as this enables the person entering the network to become quickly acquainted with senior network members and enhance his or her channels of communication and success.

In establishing their own networks, individuals may choose to occupy this central position, through which all information is channelled. This allows them to exert influence over others and provides a power base.

Establishing networks

In any new position, individuals should quickly develop their own personal networks inside and outside their organization in order to satisfy their need for information and to establish their power base. This is particularly important in a management role where resources have to be obtained, relationships between organizational units established, and organizational politics managed.

Upon joining any organization, an individual is at first ineffective because they have not established their own internal organizational networks. This situation is often short lived, but until such networks are established communication and decision making that takes into account corporate culture and other differences cannot be totally effective in the new environment. For example, the individual will not truly know who they can trust, who to go to for accurate advice or information, or who their allies or supporters are likely to be. Whilst it is likely that they will have brought established external networks with people or organizations from their previous appointments, they will still need support, information and advice from within their new organization in order to deal with everyday internal matters.

Personal networks should be established with thought. Individuals operating in key areas as the executive, finance and personnel sections and who are likely to provide support should be identified and contact made with them. It is often more favourable for the initial contact to be made on a face-to-face basis. This is more personal and polite and enables the person to explain who they are and exchange some of their work ideas and values on a one-to-one basis. In the process of the exchange it will become clear whether common values are held, whether support may or may not be forthcoming and whether the individual may be regarded as a useful ally and member of a network.

Personal contact also allows non-verbal communication channels such as body language to be assessed. The non-verbal communication processes will provide valuable information as to the actual support that may be given. In areas where vital relationships have to be established, and where initial reactions may not be as favourable as had been hoped, it is useful to continue to interact on a person-to-person basis. The positive side of the work relationship should be emphasized until such times as a firm relationship has been established.

Conclusion

High-level interpersonal, networking and communications skills are an integral part of information work as information services personnel are required to communicate with all levels of staff within the organization as well as assess, select, manage and disseminate knowledge and information to meet customer needs. Networks are also a vital component of information service management in that they can be used as a mechanism of influence to achieve outcomes, as well as providing personal support, information and advice.

References

Caruso, David R. and Salovey, Peter (2004), *The emotionally intelligent manager: How to develop and use the four key emotional skills of leadership*, San Francisco, CA: Jossey-Bass.

Lippitt, G.L. (1982), *Organizational renewal: A holistic approach to organizational development*, 2nd edn, Englewood Cliffs, NJ: Prentice Hall.

Further reading

Eaton, John and Johnson, Roy (2001), *Communicate with emotional intelligence*, Oxford, UK: Communications/How to Books Ltd.

Jay, Joelle (2005), 'On communicating well', *HR Magazine*, Jan., pp. 87–90.

Johnson, W. Brad and Ridley, Charles R. (2004), *The elements of mentoring*, New York, NY: Palgrave Macmillan.

19 *Stress Management*

Stress is a response to an environmental force, either real or imagined, that interacts with an individual's tolerance level. It can have a motivational or stimulatory effect, or it can be damaging to the individual. Stress is the response that the human system makes in adjusting to the demands of activating life events. It is not the event itself. The life event is known as the stressor. All individuals are potentially vulnerable to stress: being constantly exposed to life events that are threatening. However, stress tolerances differ between individuals, some being more able to control or manage their responses to stressors than others.

Stress implies a vulnerability to a stressor. Individual vulnerability to specific stressors varies widely. Vulnerability alters with age and is related to phases involving change and failures in the life cycle. Vulnerability also changes according to day-to-day events, moods and individual experiences, roles of individuals in particular settings, perceptions of expectations held of the individual by others, and the ability to control or alter the situation. Stressors produce symptoms only when the context and vulnerability are ripe. The individual must be particularly vulnerable or be in a generally threatening environment to experience the effect of the stressor. Personality has a particular relationship to stress. Certain characteristics predispose individuals to experience more or less stress than their peers.

Stress is also a physiological state. The conditioned body responses, characterized by arousal to meet situational demands and relaxing when the task is accomplished, are natural characteristics of survival in transitory stress-producing situations. If these responses are allowed to accumulate beyond the adaptive capacity of the body they can result in physiological or psychological illnesses. This is because the build-up of physical energy inside the body is inappropriate to the modern life situation. Man is no longer a primitive animal requiring sudden bursts of energy for survival.

Stress is not necessarily unhealthy. Everyone needs a certain amount of stress in order to function well. It is constant or excess stress that produces unpleasant or harmful side-effects. If the stressor's force exceeds the individual's stress tolerance level it will have a debilitating effect upon the individual.

Occupational or status level bears no relationship to the incidence of stress-related disease. However, each stage of life has its particular vulnerability. It is important that these stages are recognized so that managers can assist themselves and their people to manage their stress levels. The stages are:

- young adult, the stage of transformation from child to adult. This is characterized by growing, maturing and learning;
- the twenties, a stage of establishing a home and career;
- the thirties, this stage provides minor crises of uncertainty concerning career choice;
- thirty-five to fifty-five, the so-called mid-life crisis stage. This is a potentially stressful stage when most people reach their status in life. It is a time associated with reflection, significant

changes in occupation, interpersonal values and commitments, and role conflicts between family and career. The more ambitious a person is, the more they are likely to suffer; and

- the latter work years, this stage may be associated with apprehension of retirement or feelings of competition from younger members of staff.

Stress may be controlled or reduced by management techniques that can be employed at individual or organizational level.

Stress in the workplace

People experience potential stressors in their everyday work situation. Role conflict, role ambiguity, role overload and role underload all have the potential to be stressors depending upon the vulnerability of the individual. However, as Raitano and Kleiner (2004) point out, stress management is as much the responsibility of employees as it is managers. Both must maintain the lines of communication and feedback to determine appropriate means of diagnosis and a suitable mix of primary, secondary and tertiary prevention methods.

In their boundary-spanning role managers will be involved in investigating complaints, troubleshooting and interacting with people and situations, all of which may cause stressful situations. Planning, decision making, negotiating and other management responsibilities can have stress potential. Economic and time pressures, technological change and obsolescence are other environmental factors that are potential stressors.

Potential stressors for any individual in the workplace can be found in job insecurity, lack of work autonomy, unhappy work relationships, group conflict, constant work interruptions, lack of a defined career path, organization demands, promotions and demotions or transfers. Some individuals want to achieve perfectionism in everything that they do and place excessive demands upon themselves. These types of people are their own stressors.

In dynamic environments, people may perceive that changes are imposed solely for the benefit of the organization. Strategies to improve working conditions, increase opportunity, pay or security are interpreted as being intended to meet the goals of management, to increase productivity or reduce costs rather than for the benefit of the individual. This can create a lose-lose situation for management who have often tried very hard to improve the conditions.

The physical work setting, health and safety practices can also be a stress source. Desktop devices, networks, printers and other equipment that continually fail, a lack of natural light and ventilation and poorly designed work areas can inhibit productivity and cause conflict, which in turn become potential stressors for people.

Balancing work and family responsibilities is also a source of stress. People can feel guilty about putting either their work or home responsibilities first; they may worry about the possible impact of promotion or relocation on their family or partner, and they may experience role conflict between their responsibilities for their career and family. However, work can also be a mechanism for coping and a refuge from personal distress, boredom and meaninglessness. It cam be the primary means through which people feel useful in society and life and develop a sense of identity.

Burn out is physiological state of stress affecting both managers and their staff. Burn out is most likely to affect the best, the brightest and the most highly motivated. People who are susceptible to burn out are those who set high personal goals and achievements. Burn out can be minimized or avoided through stress management strategies at the organizational and individual level.

Raitano and Kleiner (2004) identify three ways of alleviating stress in the workplace: primary, secondary and tertiary. Primary prevention is the elimination or reduction of factors that promote distress. Although not exclusive, such methods are job design (redesign), participant management, and flexible hours. Secondary methods involve moderating the stress response itself, relaxation training and physical exercise are examples. Employer-sponsored aerobic exercise sessions and relaxation sessions can assist. Tertiary prevention is the attempt to minimize or cope with excessive distress from inadequately controlled stressors and inadequately controlled or moderated stress responses. This includes intervention programmes to minimize drug abuse or alcohol abuse.

Stress and personality

Stress that is attributed to pressure is highly related to individual personalities. Certain personality characteristics predispose individuals to experience more or less stress than their peers with the result that some people will handle pressure better than others. The tolerance for stress will also differ according to the stressor.

Introverted people tend to be less sociable and may take longer to form relationships with people. In these instances a promotion may trigger a stress reaction for a period of time if it results in a job that involves working with different people. The additional responsibility is not the problem, just the act of being placed in unknown company.

Extroverts are people who need other people for various reasons. They work well in jobs requiring the establishment of interpersonal relationships. If they are confined to a lonely job they can become stressed.

The rigidly structured individual is security oriented and afraid to take risks. They are stressed by anything that upsets their routine. They are uneasy in implementing new ideas or solutions that have not been tested.

The hard-driving, work-oriented individual is stress prone. They compulsively push activities to capacity and are extremely performance conscious and goal oriented. They seek honour and recognition but rarely achieve self-confidence as they are always looking at acquiring ever-increasing skills. This stress-prone individual's outlook causes continuous work overload.

The stress reducer may be as serious as the stress prone about getting the job done, but will seldom become impatient. They are less competitive and less likely to be driven by the clock. They work without agitation and find time for fun and leisure. Aware of capabilities and confident about themselves, they lead a fuller, less stressful, richer life than their stress-prone counterpart.

Risk avoiders are excessively careful. They are afraid of making decisions as this threatens their security. They experience constant inner tensions through feelings of inadequacy and dependency. Restrictive in innovative thinking, they avoid exploring new ideas. They will also avoid transfers or promotions, clinging to positions that have given them security and success in the past.

Flexible people usually have healthy, mature egos and can adapt to changing situations, whilst tolerating a high degree of stress. Challenges may be seen as stressors, but this will not impede their ability to cope.

Individuals who have a high self-esteem can deal with stress and frustration more easily. Faced with a pressure situation, performance is likely to improve. There is a strong sense of confidence in their ability to conform and optimism in their approach to performance. Individuals with low self-esteem will be overwhelmed and show a sharp decrease in performance if stress is applied. This is particularly true if stress is associated with a new job.

TYPE A AND TYPE B BEHAVIOURS

Type A individuals

Type A individuals have behaviours that are typical of many managers and senior executives. Type A personalities are extremely competitive, constantly struggling with the environment at work, in sport and at social functions. They focus upon gaining power, recognition, money and possessions in a short period of time, and portray excessive strivings for achievement. Sometimes this is accompanied by underlying feelings of hostility towards others, whom they consider to be roadblocks. The hostility may be subtle or undetected until people stand in their way.

Type A individuals are fast talking, having a sense of urgency concerning time. They thrive on deadlines, create them if they are not set and become impatient if goals and objectives are not achieved. Their work habits and their interpersonal relationships are critical in contributing to the fact that Type A personalities are three times more likely to develop cardiac disease or hypertension than Type B personalities.

Whilst Type A personalities are outwardly confident and self-assured, they can have an underlying insecurity. They may overreact to situations and can be hypercritical both of themselves (to themselves) and of others.

Type A managers or those managing Type A people need to manage their own or other's stress inducing activities and lifestyle actively so as to reduce the risk of illness without sacrificing drive and enthusiasm.

Type B individuals

In contrast, Type B personalities have an easy-going relaxed approach to life. They hold a rational approach to achievement and recognition. They experience positive interpersonal relations and maintain a balance between work and other events. They rarely have desires to become materialistic.

Stress management techniques

Professional and personal relationships are among the most useful weapons against the distress of work and people's demands. Effective listening skills, seeking advice, information and feedback and encouraging input from others can make decision making less reactive and crisis oriented. Truth and honesty are important in working relationships as mixed messages or inaccuracies can be stressful to deal with. Supportive working relationships also reduce work stress. The social support offered by the relationships has a buffering effect upon the job demands, providing psychological and emotional support for the individual's well-being.

Personal planning processes can help achievement-oriented individuals. The analysis of an individual's strengths and weaknesses and the periodic reassessment of their vocational, societal and personal goals and aspirations may allow more realistic goal horizons to be set.

Good time-management skills and knowledge of personal body clocks are also a means of reducing the negative impact of stress and increasing an individual's sense of well-being. Where possible the most demanding parts of the job should be handled during the high part of the daily cycle when the individual is most alert; whilst the less important events should be scheduled in the lower part of the cycle.

Preventative stress management strategies can also be employed in the work environment. By altering, modifying or eliminating unnecessary or unreasonable organizational demands, managers can reduce stress in the workplace. Secondly, coping skills aimed at improving the individual's response to and management of organizational demands should be offered.

Inappropriate work and physical demands can be prevented by job redesign, flexible work schedules and family-friendly work policies, provision for adequate career development and the design of the physical work settings. Role and interpersonal demands can be prevented from being stressors by team-building, providing social support, goal-setting programmes and role analysis techniques.

Individual stressor demands can be controlled by the individual managing their perceptions of stress, and by managing their work environment and lifestyle. Individuals should also have access to physical and emotional outlets such as sporting activities, exercise routines and interpersonal relationships. Counselling and psychotherapy may also be needed. Meditation, corporate opportunities for physical activity and rest, progressive relaxation techniques and moderation in diet and drinking alcohol will also help alleviate stress.

Conclusion

The ability to manage the well-being of individuals who work in the information service is important from a duty of care perspective as well as from a motivational viewpoint. It is an important management role to ensure that the physical setting, health and safety practices, work relationships and job structures do not create unnecessary stress for individuals. The ability to assist individuals manage their responses to stress and to minimize the stressors in the workplace will also result in a happier and more productive workforce.

References

Raitano, Robert E. and Kleiner, Brian H. (2004), 'Stress management: Stressors, diagnosis, and prevention measures', *Management Research*, vol. 27, no. 4/5, pp. 32–9.

20 *Career Planning and Personal Development*

Career planning and personal development are two strategies by which the information service can sustain and increase the contributions of individuals and prepare them for their future in the knowledge age. By planning their career and lifestyle, knowing themselves better and managing their personal self and image, individuals can be better equipped to cope with the changing world.

Personal development strategies should extend individuals' capacities and utilize their maximum capabilities so that there is:

- improved personal performance and relationships;
- increased job satisfaction; and
- improved quality of life.

These strategies need not be limited to the workplace. As a responsible corporate citizen, the information service can provide lifestyle training and access to counselling services to assist individuals manage and balance their lifestyle and can engender a sense of well-being.

Career planning

With the rapid and ongoing development of new technologies, the library and information services environment is characterized by fast-paced changing landscapes where new and emerging skills are a continued necessity. Career planning is a joint effort involving the organization, management and the individual. The information service can provide the structure, career path opportunities and climate to encourage career planning and personal development. The information services manager has a responsibility to ensure appropriate assignments, coaching and counselling to assist individuals in the realistic planning and attainment of their career objectives. They can develop the talents of their people by providing encouragement and support to extend the boundaries of personal growth and development. As part of the appraisal system they can assist individuals choose goals that can stretch them and help identify the means to attain them. From a professional point of view the manager can act as a role model, providing personal and professional qualities that individuals may strive to achieve.

The individual also has to accept responsibility for their growth and development. This includes identifying their long-term career plans and seeking assistance from the organization's training resources and development programmes. Action plans can be developed to assist in career planning by:

- identifying critical achievements in their work and personal lifestyle;
- producing an inventory of their current skills and knowledge together with their anticipated future needs (a 'where am I now?' analysis);
- identifying the ideal job and lifestyle position ('where do I want to get to?');
- defining the opportunities, constraints and critical success factors in achieving the ideal position ('how can I get there?'); and
- determining the strategies, qualifications and skills necessary to achieve the ideal position ('what will I do?').

In addition, individuals will look for evidence of organizational direction and career path opportunities when determining where their own future lies. The motivation for successful career and personal development can be damaged if an individual perceives a lack of progress in their chosen career path, or, if there is a lack of challenge in the current position and no foreseeable prospect of change. The lack of a foreseeable career path for a person within any organization is increasingly becoming an issue. Business reengineering and downsizing has invariably cut into the mid-level management positions that previously created the career opportunities.

Career development is also affected when there is a conflict of interest between personal loyalty, professional loyalty and/or organizational loyalty, since failure to reconcile loyalty dilemmas can cause stress and a feeling of futility or confusion. Problems with immediate supervisors can also lead to a sense of frustration in career progression. Mentors can provide encouragement and support in these cases. Mentors can also help to develop people's talents and often open doors to the future.

Lifestyle planning

Lifestyle planning includes making the most efficient and effective use of personal time at the operational (daily) and strategic (long-term) levels. Operational planning incorporates balancing the competing interests of work, home, family and relationships, travel time, personal fitness and other interests such as hobbies and cultural activities. Strategic planning includes longer-term personal goals, career development and retirement planning. Balance in lifestyle and making efficient use of time may include options such as working part time, or telecommuting from home.

Self-management of lifestyle begins with the individuals knowing or finding out more about themselves. This is done by critically analysing personal strengths and weaknesses, assets and liabilities. The mind map exercise can help as it allows the participant to identify and map out the important areas of their life as branches out of a central trunk. Each major branch indicates a significant personal development or lifestyle issue that influences their life. This can be further divided into more specific issues.

A mix of concrete and abstract issues can be used. For example, concrete issues may be work, home, religion, relationships, travel plans, training and development. Abstract issues may be the future, missing items in the lifestyle, things to avoid. Each of the branches is then colour coded as follows:

- areas to develop further;
- dissatisfiers; and
- satisfiers.

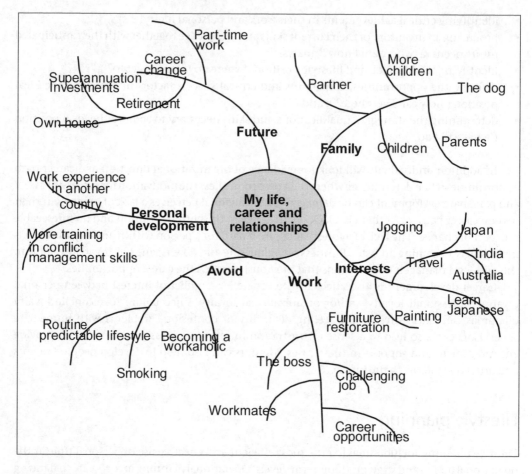

Figure 20.1 Mind map

Mind maps assist in creating a more balanced lifestyle as they identify:

* those areas that are going well (satisfiers) and those of concern (dissatisfiers);
* areas to develop; and
* areas of intense activity and those that are lacking in activity.

Self-management

Managers devote many hours to managing organizations and others to achieve corporate objectives, but rarely is time given to managing themselves and their own personal image. Managing oneself involves:

* valuing personal time, effort and energy;
* acting confidently and believing in personal talents and skills to achieve goals;
* saying no at times;
* deciding on a preferred future and taking ownership and responsibility for the outcomes; and

- learning from the past rather than regretting it.

  Individuals may also review:

- their successes to reinforce their self-esteem;
- personal motives to question their true direction;
- their lifestyle balance to allow time for personal needs such as daily exercise and the enjoyment of simple things; and
- sources of personal conflict at work, in the home, and elsewhere to create a more positive attitude and reduce tension.

PERSONAL IMAGE

The management of personal image is important if individuals are to be confident and have positive attitudes towards themselves. Image is a communication tool. It conveys an impression and message to others. If team members project an image of being confident, approachable and successful, that image will be reinforced to others.

Individuals should be encouraged to identify and manage the image that they feel most comfortable with. This includes identifying the message that the person wishes to communicate about themselves and reinforcing this. The image can be likened to a human package. It is communicated through mannerisms, appearance, dress, movement, speech patterns and personality. Facial expressions, posture and eye contact provide important information for others to judge levels of confidence. The sound, quality, intensity, rate and inflection of speech also project a powerful image. The ways in which people stand, sit and move influence others' first impressions.

Professional development and training

ENSURING COMMITMENT

Organizational support for professional development and training is demonstrated through executive commitment and recognition that this is an important investment for the future of the organization. Adequate funding is also necessary which can be further reinforced by opportunities for development and training being actively promoted and built into performance management systems.

Unfortunately during times of economic pressure, the training budget is often the first to be cut, although this represents a false economy. It is essential that all staff are adequately trained so that they have the skills and knowledge to carry out their tasks. Knowledgeable staff project a professional image as they have an in-depth understanding of the products and services that can be provided.

EFFECTIVE DESIGN OF PROFESSIONAL DEVELOPMENT AND TRAINING PROGRAMMES

An effective professional development or training programme satisfies both the knowledge and skill requirements of the individual participants and the business direction of the organization. The programme content must be relevant, understandable, easily absorbed, and associated with the work or professional environment. Learning materials should be varied in order to avoid boredom.

If the professional development or training programme is being designed in-house, a combination of didactic and experiential methods is necessary. Didactic training methods include lectures, visual aids, demonstration and panel discussion. Experiential methods of training can be provided through field trips, structured discussion, brainstorming, case studies, role playing, sensitivity training and encounter training. Adults learn in significantly different ways, testing new concepts and behaviours against what they have previously learnt. Participants should be encouraged to re-examine past experiences in the light of new information and experiences.

Where an attitudinal or behavioural change is required, efforts to change the participants' behaviour should be incorporated into the training programme. Simulation, group and individual participation, role play and case discussion should be incorporated in order to create the desired behaviour and provide immediate feedback on the success or failure of that behaviour to participants.

The potential use of new skills, knowledge or behaviour influences the type of professional development or training programme to be provided. If the planned outcome is that of increased knowledge, there is generally less need for discovery learning. If the learning is to be applied in an innovative way, then more experience-based learning is needed. If the desired outcome is to have frequent learning-on-the-job applications or it is to be used in an operating mode there needs to be more experiential learning. Retention is another aspect to consider. The longer the participants need to retain what is learnt in the training programme, the more experiential the training programme needs to be.

REINFORCING THE PROFESSIONAL DEVELOPMENT AND TRAINING PROGRAMME

A good professional development and training programme provides enthusiasm where individuals will want to demonstrate their newly acquired knowledge, skills or behaviours. This can be assisted through active support and involvement in the workplace. An example is where the immediate supervisor holds pre- and post-training meetings with the participant(s) to determine the purpose of the training programme, to set individual goals and objectives of the training session(s), to look at ways in which the newly acquired behaviour can be reinforced back in the workplace, and, to evaluate the outcomes of the training programme.

The work environment provides the greatest continuing opportunity for professional development and job-related learning. This includes job rotation, secondments and the capacity to act in higher-level positions that can be undertaken in conjunction with other courses, seminars, conferences and other training activities to reinforce the individual's effective use of their newly acquired knowledge, skills and competencies on the job.

Performance reviews also provide a method of career counselling and encouragement for staff members to plan for their future. They allow the supervisor and individual to set mutual longer-term goals for the future and outcomes to be achieved during the following year. The opportunity to sit down and plan individual strategies to achieve the information service's objectives can result in more rational and consistent goal-setting down the line.

EVALUATING THE PROFESSIONAL DEVELOPMENT AND TRAINING PROGRAMME

At the end of any formal professional development or training programme a review may be held between the organizer, the manager, the presenter (if it is a course) and participants to gather information and evaluate the training session. It is preferable for this to be done whilst the programme is still fresh in everyone's mind. Items for review may include the pace of the training session, problems with materials, groups, the presenter and general housekeeping issues.

The evaluation process is a mechanism for the reappraisal of needs and interests. It is an information-gathering and decision-making process. The evaluation should be confined to the outcome of the training process and not any other outside factor that could influence a change in behaviour.

Conclusion

Career planning, professional development and training involve an investment by the individual and the organization. Development opportunities to learn new skills through conferences and work experience can fill knowledge and skills gaps needed in the knowledge age. A good training programme will result in newly acquired knowledge, skills or behaviours. It should also enthuse participants to want to master these new 'tools' and to practise them in the workplace. For the newly acquired knowledge, skills or behaviour to be locked in, they must be applied back on the job. There must be active support and involvement in the workplace for this to happen. The immediate supervisor should be involved in pre-training and post-training meetings with the participant(s) to determine the purpose of the training programme, to set individual goals and objectives of the training session(s), to look at ways in which the newly acquired behaviour can be reinforced back in the workplace, and, to evaluate the outcomes of the training programme.

Lifestyle planning acknowledges that work cannot be considered in isolation of other influencing factors. It incorporates balancing the competing interests of work, home, family and relationships, travel time, personal fitness and other interests such as hobbies and cultural activities to create a holistic approach to life.

In concentrating on providing opportunities for the development of others as significant management task, it is sometimes easy to neglect personal professional and development needs. Self-management is not an act of self-indulgence, it is an important part of self-development. It includes paying attention to self-image, keeping abreast of change in the external environment and career planning.

Further reading

Ashcroft, Linda (2004), 'Developing competencies, critical analysis and personal transferable skills in future information professionals', *Library Review*, vol. 52, no. 2, pp. 82–8.

Gibson, Simon (2002–3), 'Coaching', *Business Review*, vol. 5, no. 2, Summer–Autumn, pp. 59–66.

McDermott, Lynda (2001), 'Developing the new young managers', *Training and Development*, vol. 55, no. 10, Feb., pp. 42–8.

Munro, Andrew (2005), *Practical succession management: How to future-proof your organisation*, Aldershot, UK: Ashgate.

Raddon, Rosemary (2005), *Your career, your life*, Aldershot, UK: Ashgate.

21 *Managing Expertise and Generation Gaps*

Information services are made up of people whose ages, functions and purposes differ. There can also be differentiations in qualifications and expertise in the subject specialization, media and the technology involved. In addition, most information services operate in organizations where further differentiations of task and perspective occur. These differentiations can be a source of conflict. The recognition that sources of conflict in organizations are often related to roles, specializations and generation outlook, rather than individuals, can assist in maintaining good personal relationships between people whose roles are in conflict.

Differentiation is demonstrated in the organization structure and in job descriptions. It is also seen in the social roles of employees, the distribution of power, control and reward systems and the communication process. Differentiation leads to the rise of subcultures and the presence of different values not just between departments, but also between specialist teams and individuals. It may also lead to intergroup conflict.

Differentiation through specialization

Differences in values occur between specialists and other staff in the organization through varying work emphases, codes of ethics, tasks, work orientations, training standards, identities and sources of motivation. These affect the way individuals view each other and have implications for the management of expertise.

Why differentiation occurs

VALUES

People with different roles, expertise and functions will place a different emphasis and value on priorities, time horizons and outlook. Whilst all might have a customer focus and are of equal value to the organization, their own values pertaining to their roles and expertise within the organization will differ. For example differences in values often occur between people with a specialist and administrative background, or between people with a strategic focus and those providing technical support. This may cause each to view the other with suspicion.

Some of the differences occur because people in one work group do not fully understand the roles and functions of the other work groups. They are not aware of each other's contribution to the organization. They only see the others' roles in the areas of work that immediately affect them or where the work unit boundaries overlap. Often people with different role functions will

Element	Traditional or organizational view	Specialist or expert view
Outlook	Mistrusts haste	Demands immediacy
Boundary considerations	Relies on boundaries	Ignores boundaries
Dependencies	Relies on dependencies	Values independence
Knowledge and information sharing	Trained to consider risk, confidentiality and the 'need to know'	Values openness and curiosity
Energy	Conserves energy	Exploits energy
Task environment	Mono-tasking, highly focused	Multi-tasking
Respect	Respect based on status and performance	Respect based on peers' review of performance
Trust	Guarded, distrust in others, judgmental	Confides, gives trust and knows how to authenticate people's trustworthiness
Values	Values standardized procedures and a single or best way of doing things	Values questions and new ways of doing things
Problem solving	Reactive – uses economic rationalism	Proactive – uses innovative thinking
Preferred work environment	Predictable, controlled	Challenging
Work orientation	Power	Learning

Figure 21.1 Differences in outlook between organizational and specialist staff

be physically separated from each other, which will further reinforce their differences. Despite the advantages of email, geographic isolation means that there is a lack of spontaneous face-to-face communication where personal alliances and understanding can be established. Motives for actions will also differ. For example, finance or administrative staff may value their ability to make savings in expenditure for the organization, whilst the front line or service delivery personnel may wish for more money to increase their opportunities for customer service delivery.

THE TASK ENVIRONMENT

Information services staff work in teams as archivists, librarians, telecommunications providers and have a strong identity with the work unit. This is the result of differentiation in tasks within information centres, individuals' dependence upon each other to get things done and, often, the physical separation of each component of the service. For example, computing centres, libraries and records management functions are often housed in purpose-built accommodation and may be separate from each other and from the rest of the organization. As a result, information service staff may be perceived as being 'different' by administrators in the rest of the organization who work to preserve the organization's hierarchy.

OUTLOOK

By their nature, most people working in information services are cosmopolitan people. Their strong sense of expertise and specialization in their areas results in the view that they are specialists working for an organization. They often have a low identity with any one particular organization as their career development lies within their area of expertise. In comparison, administrators are local people. They are primarily organization people, who just happen to be in the role of an administrator. Often, they are trained internally by the organization and judged accordingly. Their career development lies in promotion up the organization's hierarchy. This often leads to conflicts of goals arising between information services staff and administrators.

ASSESSMENT

The standard of training for specialists in information services and their subsequent expertise and competence is often set by the various professional associations. Their professional peers will also judge their ongoing performance. In addition to this, information service personnel have to conform to internal organizational standards. Their annual performance appraisal will be usually based on the achievement of the organizational objectives and standards rather than their professional ones. If the values and norms differ widely between the two, the individual could experience a role conflict situation. This could ultimately affect their motivation.

Organizations and peers frequently recognize and acknowledge a different set of achievements. Peers may recognize achievement through the delivery of papers at conferences, publishing on the Internet or in professional journals. This may not be valued to the same degree by the employing organization. The recognition of achievement within the organization may be more aligned to the organization's own objectives and values.

CULTURE

The various specialists that are found in information services have their own culture. They use particular terminologies linked to their specialist areas, display symbols such as their diplomas and degrees, and often hold the norms and values of their professional association. The use of certain terms or phrases may be threatening to others if they are uncertain of their meaning. Likewise, many tasks are specific to their roles. The terminology used to describe the tasks and the reasons for doing them may differ from other parts of the organization. This can lead to a misunderstanding of the reasons for certain tasks and perceptions that some information service personnel are too highly paid.

MOTIVATION

The strong sense of identity within the various specialists in information services leads to other behaviours and attitudes. Motivation is often found in the value of the service rather than in professional gain. Information service personnel will often require a high degree of freedom and autonomy in their areas of work. This is partly due to their physical separation from the rest of the organization and also to the nature of their tasks.

CAREER DEVELOPMENT

The difference in outlook between the various specialists in information services has implications for their career development, training and reward systems. The internal career path needs may differ between specialists, and with the rest of the organization. Usually the only avenues of promotion within organizations are to managerial positions. This may be contrary to the needs of the specialist who will find the additional administrative responsibilities unwelcome. Managers need to develop career paths for specialists in information services who wish to continue working in their area of expertise but require more responsibility and, recognition and rewards for their achievements.

REWARD SYSTEMS

Reward systems will also differ for the different types of staff employed in information services. Specialist staff can be motivated by improved work conditions, opportunities for professional contact and autonomy in the workplace, rather than by money or status.

The information services manager should be aware of differences in values between specialist staff and staff in other parts of the organization. They may need occasionally to explain these differences in order to minimize conflict. Within their own staff hierarchy, the information services manager should minimize conflict through open communication and the provision of appropriate career development, staff training and reward systems.

Generation gaps

Generations comprise a group of people who can be demographically identified by biological trends and who have shared experiences. Different generations exhibit broad characteristics brought about by external environmental experiences that lead to differences in priorities, in views on leadership and in expectations and attitudes in life and the workplace. Generation gaps explain these dissimilarities. Whilst these characteristics are highly generalized in their use, they are helpful in giving an insight into differing opinions, behaviours, motivational needs and values of both staff and clientele. Although there are minor differences in interpretations of the dates, the generations comprise the:

- Silent Generation – born between World War I and World War II;
- Baby Boomers – born between 1945 and 1965;
- Generation X – born between 1965 and 1980;
- Generation Y – born in the 1980s and 1990s; and
- Generation Z – born in the late 1990s and 2000s.

SILENT GENERATION

About to retire from the workforce, this generation experienced the austerity years of the depression and war that disrupted family life and career paths. Predominantly the workforce was comprised of males and there was life-long allegiance to the organization.

Levy et al. (2005, p. 7) found the Silent Generation to be:

- traditionalists with high respect for position power;
- uncomfortable with change, preferring consistency;
- exhibit strong loyalty and have a 'job for life' expectation;
- historically focused, relying on experience to guide decision making;
- disciplined and modest in their approach to life; and

- slow adopters of technology.

BABY BOOMERS

Baby Boomers grew up in a post-war era of expansion and prosperity. They have a strong sense of generational identity and are characterized as being materialistic and interested in physical objects such as home ownership and consumer goods.

They are the first generation where access to a tertiary education was inexpensive and widespread. In the workplace they have witnessed major transformations, including the transition from a pre-technology world to a digital era; although not all have successfully made this transition. In contrast to Generation X, Baby Boomers grew up with an ethos for the need to remain with the employer, even if they were unhappy.

Levy et al. (2005, p. 7) list the characteristics of Baby Boomers as follows:

- viewing work from a process orientated perspective;
- valuing company commitment and loyalty;
- believing in sacrifice in order to achieve success;
- valuing teamwork and group discussion;
- believing achievement comes after 'paying dues';
- seeking long-term employment but don't expect a 'job for life'; and
- ambitious at work and in personal life, and status orientated.

GENERATION X

Unlike their stereotype definition portrayed in the media, Generation Xers are not lazy and have had to overcome an era of downsizing in organizations where mid-level management career opportunities vanished. Generation X also witnessed the socio-economic impact of an unprecedented number of women entering the paid workforce in an era where there were increasingly flexible and varied gender roles for women. Offsetting this, the spread of the Internet created new industries and new technology-related job opportunities.

Generation Xers are less concerned with the trappings of success and more environmentally, economically and socially conscious than previous generations. They care about the quality of their future and that of the earth and environment. In caring about their future, exercise and having a healthy body and mind is important, therefore they look for balance in lifestyle and leisure time. Financial and emotional security is important. They have good work ethics and company loyalty, as long as it is reciprocal. Generation X is not afraid to challenge authority in a changing world of diminishing resources.

Levy et al. (2005, p. 7) summarize these characteristics as:

- independent and resourceful with free agent approach to careers;
- accepting of change and comfortable with diversity;
- having high expectations of work/life balance;
- they 'want it now'; and
- technology literate and life-long learners.

Levy et al. (2005, p. 16) found that Generation X individuals believe high performance in their organization is directly linked to the quality of the organization's leadership. On a personal level, they are convinced that their career progress will be directly affected by the quality of the leadership they demonstrate and consequently development of leadership skills is critical to them. Levy goes on to say that they want to be challenged in a meaningful way and they need a sense of ownership and engagement if they are to perform to their potential. They need to be inspired to lift their performance above the ordinary. They also believe that the more opportunity they have to learn and develop, the more they will achieve for the organization.

On their views on management and leadership, Levy et al. (2005, p. 16) found that Generation X individuals identify a difference between management (which they see as technical and task focused) and leadership (which they see as creating a sense of purpose, inspiration and alignment). They are convinced that those in management positions need leadership skills and the greater leadership capacity they have, the more effective they will be as a manager. They look to managers for leadership skills such as strategic thinking, motivation, effective communication, constructive conflict management and team building. They appreciate managers with strong coaching and mentoring capability. They do not see the manager and the leader as separate; they see them as integrated in one person.

GENERATION Y

As children of the Baby Boomers, this generation holds political and social values closer to the Baby Boomers than Generation X. While some were born in a pre-digital era, most Generation Y members take the widespread use of digital technology for granted. They are a techno-savvy generation; being the first to grow up immersed in a digital and Internet-driven world. Globalization in the economy and communications has also assisted this generation to be much more tolerant towards multiculturalism and internationalism than previous generations.

Generation Y exhibits strong people skills and a desire to influence and change the world for others and themselves. Whilst they have mostly been fairly sheltered in their upbringing, they have experience early pressures for success in their education and work. Their appreciation of their skills can lead to them being considered self-centred. They tend to be ambivalent towards authority, seeing it as something to work around rather than against.

Levy et al. (2005, p. 7) found Generation Y to be:

- self-reliant and independent with a desire for freedom and flexibility;
- entrepreneurial thinkers comfortable with change and diversity;
- technology and media 'savvy';
- placing high value on education and skill development;
- relishing responsibility and wanting to play meaningful roles;
- believing that social responsibility is a business imperative; and
- desirous of collaboration.

Levy et al. (2005, p. 16) found that for Generation Y, ownership, engagement and learning were important leadership factors. They strongly held the view that personalized leadership made the difference in encouraging them to go the 'extra mile' for the organization. Generation Y saw leadership in those that gave them scope, autonomy and opportunity, rather than those who would give them direction, regulation and commands.

The increasing stratification of wealth in many societies has lead to an increase in the societal differences between poor and rich members of this generation. Those who have had the opportunity of a good education are savvy consumers, conscious of money and its impact on life.

GENERATION Z

Generation Z is expected to be the most technologically advanced generation yet (Levy et al., 2005, p. 7). Whilst not yet in the workforce, they are predicted to spend longer living with their parents and to marry much later than previous generations.

Developing the common good

The differentiations in expectation and values within information services and with the parent organization brought on by differences in age groups and specialization need to be managed so that the competitive elements foster rather than hinder the organization's objectives. The information services manager will need to identify ways to motivate individuals of different generations and those who are specialists in their field, whilst still maintaining the organization's competitiveness. The value of the specialist expertise should be recognized and balanced against the strengths that others can offer, such as their internal knowledge of the history of the organization.

Goals should be set that encourage specialists to look further than their area of expertise. Differences in values, and the reasons for these, should be openly explored and discussed. A greater understanding of the differences in values, attitudes and behaviour will help reduce the barriers of acceptance. Role conflict between specialist groups should be recognized for what it is rather than as a personal issue.

References

Levy, Lester et al. (2005), *The generation mirage? A pilot study into the perceptions of leadership by Generation X and Y*, Auckland, NZ: Hudson.

Further reading

Coupland, Douglas (1991), *Generation X: Tales for an accelerated culture*, New York: St Martin's Press.
Crawford, Tom (2005), *Employer branding*, Aldershot, UK: Ashgate.
Howe, Neil and Strauss, William (1991), *Generations: The history of America's future, 1584–2060*, New York: Morrow.
Sheahan, Peter (2005), *Generation Y: Thriving and surviving with Generation Y at work*, Prahran, Aus: Hardie Grant.

VI Governance and Accountability

The theme for Part VI is effecting good corporate governance. Rapid transformations in science and technology, business and society present choices and dilemmas that if addressed incorrectly can have far-reaching and detrimental consequences. This means that the correct decision must be made that is inclusive of all matters. Good governance and accountability stem from having good practices and processes in place.

Along with customer satisfaction and profitability, public and private sector organizations are being judged on the manner in which they encourage sustainable development, demonstrate social leadership and corporate ethics. Chapter 22 explains the concept of good governance and how this can be reinforced through ethical behaviour and codes of conduct. It also considers the need to ensure sustainability in decision making, programmes and projects as well as the need to manage the many different forms of capital.

Accountability and influence are at the core of governance practices. Chapter 23 explains how accountability and influence can be affected by power and identifies how individuals often acquire power within organizations. The chapter also considers how influence is used to get things done and how power can be institutionalized in authority. Finally the power–authority continuum is extended to the process of delegation, whereby authority can be distributed throughout the information service so that others may share the work and responsibilities.

Transparency is also an important component of good governance. Transparency can be assisted through open decision making and communications, the theme of Chapter 24. This chapter acknowledges that decisions are influenced by perceptions, emotions and intuition and that the potential for these to provide a biased viewpoint needs to be taken into consideration. Chapter 24 explores the appropriateness of different decision-making styles.

Communication is the vehicle through which decisions and policies that are critical to good governance are made and conveyed within the organization and externally. Chapter 24 identifies how governance can be managed through effective communications including reports and meetings.

An important part of the governance process is to ensure a return on investment and that the organization is performing to expectation. Chapter 25 considers the management issues associated with projects to ensure that they deliver the return on investment for the organization. It also provides details on how the return on investment for information products and services can be enhanced and strategies for charging for information products and services. Chapter 25 also provides strategies for measuring and evaluating performance. It describes the performance evaluation process and how performance can be measured in different work units. This requires consideration of outputs and outcomes, quality and value, cause and effect. Information has specific qualities that make the measurement of its value more difficult. Different mechanisms for measuring its value are explored. The chapter also includes examples of performance indicators that can be used in information services and identifies some criteria for performance.

Chapter 26 identifies major risks that can affect information services. The chapter advocates that a business perspective should be taken for each; including the need to plan according to the event and its impact on the business of the organization.

Chapter 27 addresses the issue of security. The objective of security measures is to preserve the confidentiality, integrity and availability of information. Responsibility for this is found at all levels of the organization. The chapter identifies different security threats and how these can be overcome through the appropriate management of people, information, physical environment and the technology. The choice of security level is a business issue. It also addresses access controls and lists other good management practices that maintain the integrity, availability and confidentiality of information. Chapter 27 also considers business continuity issues and treats disaster recovery as a component of business continuity.

The trend, adopted by market-oriented governments and large corporate entities, towards the outsourcing of all but their core business activities can significantly impact upon the way in which managers manage the provision of services and utilize their human resources. Chapter 28 explores the issues surrounding outsourcing, including decisions on what can be outsourced, what should remain in-house and the pros and cons of outsourcing. The outsourcing process is described in detail, covering determining the right objectives and strategy, determining what to outsource, assessing the benefits, determining the risks, selection of the vendor, negotiating the contract, structuring the relationship and managing the risks.

PLANNING AND MANAGING FOR TRANSFORMATION

CREATING THE RIGHT CORPORATE ENVIRONMENT

TRANSFORMING THE CORPORATE ENVIRONMENT

MANAGING YOURSELF AND OTHERS

MANAGING IN A DYNAMIC ENVIRONMENT

EPILOGUE

POSITIONING TO EXCEL IN SERVICE DELIVERY

GOVERNANCE AND ACCOUNTABILITY

PART VI – GOVERNANCE AND ACCOUNTABILITY

22. **Corporate governance**
Management oversight – roles and responsibilities; Corporate governance principles; Ethics; Code of conduct; Sustainability; Managing different forms of capital

23. **Accountability and influence**
Understanding the use of power; Influence; Authority; Delegation

24. **Encouraging transparency**
Making the right decision; Understanding perceptions, intuition and emotions; Decision-making styles; Organizational communications

25. **Measuring benefits and performance**
Management oversight – roles and responsibilities; Benefits evaluation; Adding value as a return on investment; Pricing information; Performance evaluation; Performance indicators

26. **Risk management**
Management oversight – roles and responsibilities; Sources of risk; Managing risk

27. **Security**
Management oversight – roles and responsibilities; Confidentiality, integrity and availability; Planning; Risk and vulnerability analysis; Management; Access control; Disaster recovery; Business continuity; Maintaining and testing; Compliance

28. **Outsourcing**
Making the outsourcing decision; Benefits of outsourcing; Managing the outsourcing decision; Managing the outsourcing process

Figure PVI.1   Governance and accountability

22 *Corporate Governance*

Corporate governance is far more than complying with a legal and regulatory regime. It is a future-shaping activity, in which directions are set and managed, and decisions made with sustainability, ethics and integrity in mind. Corporate governance is about choice and influence in actions and decision making: choices that can lead to effective and ineffective impacts and consequences, or sustainable and unsustainable futures; as well as using or misusing power to influence outcomes, or doing the right thing versus the wrong thing.

Corporate governance comprises the systems, structures, practices, procedures and corporate culture that organizations have in place to minimize risks and exposures and optimize performance and accountability. Examples of these include putting rigorous corporate governance principles in place, having a visible code of conduct, utilizing independent audit practices, establishing a sound system for risk oversight and management, managing for sustainability and for different forms of capital. To maintain the integrity of these systems, structures, policies, practices and procedures, it is necessary for them to be reviewed for their effectiveness at least annually.

Uncertainty about the future and growing domains of inconceivability in the external environment present complex dilemmas in decision making; where the impact of making the wrong judgment can be devastating for employees, the organization or the broader community. Good corporate governance structures can help to ensure the correct and sensitive resolution of such complex problems and proposals to ensure sustainability and value for today and the future. This does not mean that executive management has to be an expert on each and every issue that arises. Rather it is knowing when to seek independent expertise and professional advice to supplement their collective knowledge and expertise.

Management oversight – roles and responsibilities

Effective corporate governance is a value-added activity that is the responsibility of everyone in the organization. It enhances the increasing importance of corporate reputation and provides a level of confidence for customers and stakeholders in the ability of the organization to:

* achieve excellence and quality of output;
* embrace a sustainable future;
* meet its corporate and legislative responsibilities; and
* meet the ultimate accountability requirements.

The Chief Executive is ultimately accountable for the organization's reputation, decision making, compliance, direction and outcomes. This involves establishing a sound foundation through their leadership style and ethical behaviours, instituting and maintaining the right corporate culture, making sure that different forms of capital are identified and managed in a sustainable manner, and ensuring that effective organizational structures, oversight entities and systems are in place to ensure good corporate governance.

Senior management has a responsibility for upholding and reinforcing the desired corporate culture, ensuring the integrity of governance systems, structures, policies, practices and procedures, that staff are aware of and understand the policies and procedures, that value is added when duties are discharged, that rights are recognized and acknowledged, and that adequate procedures and practices are in place to support good governance and responsible decision making. Individuals are accountable for their own ethics and integrity in outlook, practices and decision making, as well as ensuring that they follow the correct procedures and practices.

Corporate governance principles

The Australian Stock Exchange Corporate Governance Council has identified ten principles for good corporate governance that have been adapted to meet the needs of information services:

- establishing sound foundations for the management and oversight roles of senior management and other oversight entities that may include boards and committees;
- structuring to add value, by ensuring that there is an effective composition, size, balance and commitment of skills, experience and independence to discharge adequately responsibilities and duties appropriate to the nature of the operations today and for the future;
- promoting integrity, ethical and responsible decision making amongst those who can influence strategy and financial performance;
- safeguarding integrity in financial and other reporting, with independent verification to ensure that there is accountability in the seeking and use of financial resources;
- maintaining a corporate culture, practices and procedures so that there is timely, factual, objective and balanced disclosure of all material matters concerning the organization;
- respecting the rights of all stakeholders, including the community as a whole, and ensuring that these are clearly recognized and upheld;
- recognizing that every business decision has an element of uncertainty and carries a risk that can be managed through effective oversight and internal control;
- having formal mechanisms such as a balance of skills, competencies, experience and expertise, and continuing professional development that lead to enhanced management skills and effectiveness in keeping pace with inconceivability in the external environment and other aspects that governance of an information service in the knowledge age requires;
- ensuring that the level and composition of remuneration is sufficient and reasonable to attract the skills and expertise necessary to achieve the performance expected, and that the relationship between the remuneration and performance is defined and executed; and
- recognizing the impact of actions and decisions on the legal obligations and interest of all stakeholders.

Ethics

Public and social accountability is based on the notions of legitimacy, fairness and ethics. As part of the quest for quality management, standards for ethics and integrity are also important in the pursuit of excellence. They are also the centrepiece of good corporate governance. Ethical standards define what is right and wrong in terms of the behaviour of individuals towards others, and how those in a position to influence materially the integrity, strategy and operations of the information service should operate. Executive management has a responsibility to set standards and demonstrate by example issues such as honesty, fairness and equity, respect and integrity, and accountability.

The nature of the activities of information services means that people are privy to insider information and other commercial and personal information, either directly or indirectly, that could be used for personal gain. A clearly articulated policy can assist individuals to deal with ethical problems and conflicts of interest. Ethical policies also guide the necessary behaviour standards and practices to maintain confidence in the integrity of the information service. They often form the basis of a code of conduct.

Ethics are generally based upon three principles. These are:

- utilitarian principles, such as the greatest good for the greatest number and responsible care, and accountability in the use of resources;
- individual rights, or respect and protection of the basic rights of individuals such as the right to privacy, to free speech and to due process; and
- justice, where fair and impartial rules are imposed and enforced on everyone to ensure the equitable distribution of costs and benefits.

Code of conduct

Good corporate governance ultimately requires people to act with integrity with today and the future in mind. Whilst societal values, the justice and political systems provide the broad framework within which ethical values operate, ethical behaviour and integrity is also interpreted according to individual values, culture and experience. What may be considered ethical behaviour to one person could be considered inappropriate to another. A code of conduct sets the boundaries and individual responsibilities for what is considered to be ethical behaviour in situations where personal values systems can differ.

A code of conduct recognizes that most people want to do the right thing, but that certain environments present opportunities for temptation and/or material gain. The code is particularly useful in environments where there are financial functions, intense competition, opportunities for insider trading or conflict-of-interest situations to occur. In dealing with issues related to codes of conduct, perception is just as important as reality. Safeguarding corporate reputation and integrity requires the use of the test as to whether it could normally be perceived that an advantage was taken or that a conflict of interest arose out of a situation.

The Australian Stock Exchange Corporate Governance Council identifies several areas for inclusion in a code of conduct that has been adapted as follows to meet the needs of information services:

- conflicts of interest – managing situations where the interest of a private individual (who may or may not be an employee) or group interferes with or appears to interfere with the interests of the information service or organization as a whole. An example might be where a member of staff has a strong religious convictions and attempts to influence the selection policy of a library;

- corporate opportunities – preventing employees or stakeholders from taking advantage of property, information or position, or opportunities arising from these, for personal gain or to compete within the organization. Examples include where a manager attempts to influence the selection of a candidate who is a close friend for a position, or where a senior executive accepts the offer of hospitality such as a free overseas trip from a supplier;
- privacy and confidentiality – restricting the use of non-public information except where disclosure is authorized or legally mandated. The right to know principle is appropriate here. Even when there may be no harm intended, or intention of disclosure to a third party or for personal gain, the act of unnecessarily accessing personal information from a system is in breach of confidentiality. For example, unauthorized access to the personnel record of an individual or tracking their choice of websites out of personal interest can constitute a breach;
- fair dealing – by all employees with the information service's customers, suppliers, competitors and employees. For example the provision of preferential treatment to certain customers at the detriment of others, or favouring one supplier over another because they have the best festive season parties;
- use of the information service's assets – protecting and ensuring the efficient use of assets for legitimate business purposes. Acceptable use is appropriate here. For example, the use of corporate time and equipment quickly to undertake electronic banking may be more productive for the information service and individuals than their visiting a bank. However, the continuous use of electronic devices for gaming purposes during work time would not be considered to be a legitimate or efficient use;
- compliance with laws and regulations – active promotion of compliance. Examples here include compliance with occupational, health and safety regulations, equal employment opportunity awards, consumer protection regulations, corporate taxation and financial reporting requirements, and environmental laws; and
- encouraging the reporting of unlawful/unethical behaviour – active promotion of ethical behaviour and protection for those who report violations in good faith. Whilst confidentiality may not always be guaranteed, it is important to develop a culture where inappropriate behaviour is not condoned, that appropriate action will be taken when reports are received, that employees are enabled to disclose potential misconduct without fear of retribution, and that exposure is considered an important obligation to maintain an ethical corporate culture.

The presence of a code of conduct does not in itself ensure good corporate governance. An understanding of the contents and what constitutes compliance is necessary for all employees and key stakeholders. The objectives and content of the code of conduct should be readily available on the corporate intranet, visibly promoted on a regular basis and explained to new employees as part of the induction process. Compliance with the code of conduct should be continuously monitored by management, and any departures quickly dealt with.

Sustainability

Sustainability is relevant to information services management in two ways. It needs to be incorporated into core values and taken into account in ensuring effective governance and decision making within the information service and, secondly, sustainability issues need to be considered and incorporated into information service delivery. The 1992 Earth Summit in Rio de Janeiro popularized the term 'sustainable development' as a means to make decisions and carry out programmes and projects in a manner that maximizes benefits to the natural environment and humans and their cultures and communities, while maintaining or enhancing financial viability.

From a management perspective, sustainability is a holistic process and includes incorporating a whole of life approach, balancing short-term needs with society's long-term interests, as well as ensuring that resources are used no faster than they are renewed. The latter is known as living within the carrying capacity and can be applied to intangible items such as education and skills development or developing trust and respect in people, as well as the tangible environment of water facilities and ecosystems. Sustainable organizations and communities invest in and take good care of all their capital assets so that benefits accrue for themselves and others, now and in the future. They look at the entire enterprise, process or acquisition from a 'cradle to the grave' perspective in terms of total cost of ownership, or input, throughput and output to determine inefficiencies or waste.

The Sustainability Reporting Programme identifies the following basic principles for sustainability:

- concern for the well-being of future generations;
- awareness of the multi-dimensional impacts of any decision (broadly categorized as economic, environmental, social); and
- the need for balance among the different dimensions across sectors (e.g. mining, manufacturing, transportation), themes (climate change, community cohesion, natural resource management) and scale (local, regional, national, international).

The Sustainability Now website presents a holistic view of managing in a way that meets the needs of the present without compromising the ability of future generations to meet their own needs. The principles it espouses include:

- systems thinking – acknowledging the fact that seemingly discrete projects and activities are in fact a part of many interacting or interdependent social, ecological, and economic systems that together form one complex global system;
- temporal and spatial scales – assessing the environmental, social and economic impacts of our actions over varying scales of space and time;
- risk, uncertainty and the precautionary principle – identifying and actively managing risk and uncertainty; recognizing the value and limitations of both quantitative risk analyses and subjective risk perception in situations characterized by significant uncertainty;
- values-focused thinking – developing alternative solutions to problems based on human needs and values and evaluating these options on the basis of those values;
- engagement and integration – engaging stakeholders and forming integrated design and consultation teams at the onset of appropriate projects to take advantage of a pooled body of knowledge to help define and solve the issues at hand;
- equity and disparity – ensuring that the equity and disparity of current and future generations have been considered and that a fair and consensus-seeking process is in place to ensure that the benefits and costs are distributed fairly among various stakeholders;

- efficiency – seeking to maximize the contribution of well-being of humans and ecosystems while minimizing the stress on people and ecosystems, seeking win-win solutions and clarifying irreducible trade-offs; and
- process and practicality – applying sustainability as a dynamic process rather than a static end point. The scope for living sustainably in the context of changing technology and human values is enormous.

In a practical sense sustainability can be achieved through:

- policies and processes that reduce energy usage, waste and costs;
- managing the organization's reputation as a good community citizen by building social capital;
- respecting and taking care of its employees and families through family-friendly practices;
- embedding a culture, values and mindset of sustainability in all its forms;
- building a capacity of organizational learning to avoid mistakes and look for innovation; and
- taking an integrated approach to sustainability, rather than treating each element of sustainability as a discrete item to be managed in isolation.

Managing different forms of capital

Capital is a resource that, managed sustainably and effectively, is a source of wealth and value. Traditional management concentrated on managing human and financial resources from an internal perspective of assets and liabilities for the organization. The knowledge age is witnessing a growing acceptance that many different forms of capital exist that need to be governed to add value today and for the future; not just from a governance perspective but with the view that organizations can create worth for themselves and society by better managing these. Increasingly organizational performance is being judged on the way in which it recognizes and takes care of a wide range of capital items, including intellectual, client, social and natural capital.

BUILT CAPITAL

Built capital includes buildings, equipment, vehicles, information and communications technology (ICT) and infrastructure. Managing built assets is akin to good asset management of tangible assets, which includes maximizing the return on investment and reducing future resource requirements by prolonging the asset's life or strengthening its disposal value.

CLIENT CAPITAL

Client capital is the value that results from the relationship that an organization has with its clients. Increasingly organizations are recognizing the importance of customer relationship management in retaining their clients who are in the position of exercising choice in who they deal with. ICT is proving an asset in enabling organizations to add value to the customer and enhance the relationship by tailoring products and services to meet individual needs any time, any place.

FINANCIAL CAPITAL

Managing financial capital includes managing the growth, investment and financial value of the organization, maximizing its wealth and the value of its assets in the market place, ensuring its capacity and capability to make a profit, and fund its acquisitions and liabilities.

HUMAN CAPITAL

Having an appreciation for the importance of people's personal skills and abilities is a significant part of managing human capital. The success of organizations in the knowledge age is due to the collective worth of their people's aptitudes, talents, experiences, education, know-how, skills sets, imaginations, thoughts, intelligence and capabilities. How these are encouraged and applied will determine the extent to which they add value and bring innovation and achievement to the organization.

Managing human capital also includes concern for the health and well-being of individuals. This includes their physical and mental health; so employing healthy lifestyle programmes or sponsoring lunchtime keep-fit activities help support the well-being of this important capital source.

INTELLECTUAL CAPITAL

Intellectual capital consists of knowledge, intelligence and ideas in an organization and the unique processes and intellectual assets that an organization holds. Its management and protection is increasingly important in the knowledge age. Intellectual capital is reinforced through policies and practices that encourage creativity and innovation. Whilst intellectual capital that resides in people's heads cannot be protected, once it is applied it can be protected through intellectual property rights that include patents, copyright and other forms of legal protection.

NATURAL CAPITAL

Managing natural capital places importance on the value of the ecological carrying capacity and sustainability of the natural environment. It includes consideration for the sustainability of natural resources in choosing alternatives for transport and managing water and energy consumption in the workplace. Natural capital consists of:

- those things that are taken out of nature and used e.g. water, plants and animals, oils, gas, minerals and wood;
- ecosystems that are the natural processes which communities rely upon such as wetlands that enable water filtration and provide a buffer for flooding, carbon dioxide–oxygen exchanges, and the fertility of soils; and
- aesthetics or the beauty of nature that contribute to the general quality of life e.g. providing flowers and plants in the workplace, positioning windows to reveal a pleasing view, or providing an outside courtyard where people can relax during a break.

Preventing pollution and managing wastes in an ecologically sound manner are two other examples of investing in natural capital.

SOCIAL CAPITAL

Social capital is concerned with connections and relationships within a community. This might be within an organization, a community of practice or a local community. From a management perspective, this means managing and valuing the interpersonal and institutional relationships and norms that an organization has internally and with the external environment. For example, its abilities to build relationships, cooperation and trust, influence and show leadership that adds value to organizational processes and outcomes, or which shapes the quality and quantity of its interactions with society for improved community productivity and well-being.

Developing a social capital programme might include forming relationships with or sponsoring local community groups, supporting an employee volunteer program, encouraging corporate family days where members of the family can visit on site, or encouraging membership and corporate connections with communities of practice in relevant research fields.

Conclusion

The capacity to govern effectively is derived from human will and choice, either as an individual or as a group. Corporate governance requires sound management practices that provide effective oversight, promote integrity, enable transparency in decision making, add value in all processes, manage risk and enable the capacity to make the right decisions. This is sustained through a code of conduct and corporate culture philosophy that is inclusive and upholds ethics and integrity in decision making.

Coexisting with corporate governance principles are the management concepts of sustainability and managing different forms of capital. In keeping with the need for balance and concerns for the future, organizations that exhibit good corporate governance characteristics invest in and take good care of all their capital assets so that benefits accrue for themselves and others, now and in the future.

References

Australian Stock Exchange Corporate Governance Council (2003), *Principles of good corporate governance and best practice recommendations*, March, available at www.shareholder.com, accessed 4 March 2005.

Sustainability Reporting Programme, available at http://www.sustreport.org/business/report.org/intro_lg.html, accessed 20 June 2005.

Sustainability Now, available at http://www.sustainability.ca/index/report/intro_lg.html, accessed 20 June 2005.

Further reading

Das Gupta, Ananda (2004), *Human values in management*, Aldershot, UK: Ashgate.

Davies, Adrian (2005), *The practice of corporate governance*, Aldershot, UK: Ashgate.

Fishel, David (2003), *The book of the board: Effective governance of non-profit organisations*, Leichardt, Aus: Federation Press.

Laszlo, Charles (2003), *The sustainable company: How to create lasting value through social and environmental performance*, Washington, DC: Island Press.

23 *Accountability and Influence*

Power and authority are behavioural processes that are manifested in influence and determine the way in which governance is acted out. Power is the ability to influence others. It is legitimized in authority. Power may be sought and used by individuals or groups, particularly in times of change. The quest for power can lead to healthy and productive competitive outcomes or it can result in disruptive, selfish or harmful behaviours, where the outcomes are not as beneficial.

Authority is institutionalized power. It is based on position, personal characteristics, expertise and knowledge and the situation. Authority can be delegated by giving responsibility and authority to others to execute a job. However, the manager or persons involved in the act of delegation are still accountable for the outcomes.

Understanding the use of power

Power has a classical double meaning of:

- the ability to influence the activities of individuals, groups, organizations, societies and nations; and
- determining who gets what, when and how.

This is because power is the capacity or potential of one unit to influence or elicit compliance in another in relation to behaviour or attitude. This may be willing or unwilling, conscious or unconscious compliance. Whilst an individual or group can have the capacity and potential for power, they may never use it.

The use of the word 'power' often has negative connotations. This is the result of many people associating power with its abuse rather than its ethical use. A test of good governance is to avoid the abuse of power. This requires a good understanding of the various power sources and how to use these effectively to persuade and influence ethical outcomes rather than control people and situations for personal gain.

POWER BASES

The acquisition and use of power is a natural process within organizations. French and Raven (1959) have defined five sources of power: three are derived from organizational sources whilst the other two are derived from personal sources. Reward, coercive and legitimate powers are the three power bases that are derived from positions within the organization. Expert and referent power sources are personal power sources.

Reward power

Reward power stems from the ability of an individual to provide tangible rewards in return for certain outcomes. People will comply with the requests of others if this will result in a positive benefit. The power base is contingent on the individual perceiving that:

- the person has sufficient authority to be able to offer rewards; and
- the reward is perceived to be a benefit.

The requests should also be perceived to be feasible, proper and ethical, and the incentive sufficiently attractive and at a level that could not be attained by another less costly course of action. For instance, if an assistant records manager asked a staff member to work late for an hour one night in exchange for two hours off during the following day, the request would be considered in the light of whether:

- the person had the authority to grant the two hours off, or even to ask the person to stay behind in the first place;
- the staff roster situation and personal workload made it feasible to take the two hours off the next day;
- the activities already planned for that night were of more importance; and
- someone else was available and prepared to work late.

Coercive power

Coercive power is the extent to which a manager can manipulate or control other people. It is a power based upon fear. Coercive power was a factor of traditional management styles where autocracy prevailed. Today it is recognized that coercive power is used in very extreme circumstances and can result in hostility, resentment and aggression as well as erode the manager's referent power. Coercion and punishment are only effective when applied in a small way and in legitimate circumstances.

Legitimate power

Legitimate power is the power based upon position and is found in authority. For example, the request of the finance manager for the information services manager to submit their budget papers by the end of the month. Requests using legitimate power are usually made politely, confidently and clearly, with their underlying reasons explained. From a governance perspective a non-legitimate use of power may be a request to delete certain documents from a file.

Expert power

Expert power is based on the possession of knowledge, experience or judgment that other individuals do not have, but respect or need. Most lecturers demonstrate the possession of expert power over their students. However, possession of expertise is not sufficient for managers or lecturers to influence people. It is also necessary for individuals to recognize the manager's or lecturer's expertise and perceive them to be a credible source of information.

Expert power is demonstrated through the display of certificates or awards on office walls; by acting confidently and decisively in a crisis; by keeping informed and informing others of emerging technology issues, by presenting papers at conferences, and by maintaining personal credibility.

Referent power

Referent power is developed out of a person's admiration for another and their desire to model their behaviour on that person's attributes. Role models and mentors have referent power as they engender a feeling of personal alignment, affection, loyalty and admiration on behalf of the subject. Referent power is often based upon an individual's personal characteristics. An information services manager is likely to build referent power if they are articulate, show consideration for individual needs and feelings, encourage and develop individuals, and if they exhibit ethical behaviour.

ACQUIRING POWER

Individuals often acquire power within organizations through:

- developing a sense of obligation in others;
- building a reputation as an 'expert' in certain matters;
- fostering others' unconscious identification with them or their ideas; and
- maintaining the belief that others are dependent upon them.

Managers who are ethical in acquiring power are sensitive to what others consider to be legitimate behaviour in acquiring and using power and seek to use it to effect positive outcomes. They recognize that power is an essential management tool. They have a good understanding of the various types of power and its effects on different people. They develop expertise in using different types of power in order that the correct type can be used in the right circumstances to achieve the information service's and the parent organization's objectives. They exercise restraint and self-control to ensure that power is not abused or used impulsively.

COUNTER POWER

Power sources can be neutralized by counter power. Individuals may influence others by exercising a restraint on the use of power. An example of counter power is where employees engage the services of an outside body to negotiate on their behalf their working conditions with management, or where a group of individuals may try to neutralize a negative influence within the organization.

Influence

Influence is the action that creates a behavioural response to the exercise of power. When power sources are activated they are influential in that they get someone to do something in a required way. Influence is important in that it can assist or distort the governance process.

There are many uses of influence within organizations. One of the most common forms of influence is the legitimate request. When an officer in the records management section is asked to check the location of a file, the officer will normally comply. The officer sees the request is made within a work role setting and is legitimate.

Rational persuasion is used to persuade another party that the proposals or decisions are justified and that they will be successful. It incorporates a logical argument in which a party is convinced of the need to change their mind or that the suggested behaviour is the best outcome for all. Rational persuasion is reliant on the party having some knowledge or perception of the issue as the persuader does not have any tangible controls on the outcomes.

Rational faith is based upon expert power, where a person's credibility or expertise is sufficient to influence the other party to take a particular course of action. An example of rational faith is where an employee uses a particular database that has been recommended by the librarian or research officer. The employee may not be aware of the contents of the database, but will use it on the recommendation of the librarian.

Indoctrination establishes certain values and beliefs in people that lead to behaviours that support the organizational objectives. The induction process is a form of indoctrination.

Information distortion influences a person's impression and attitudes as it limits or censors the information that they receive. The target person is influenced without being aware of it. Information distortion takes place when reports are edited or when information is withheld from those who need it. A similar form of distortion occurs in situational engineering, where a physical or social situation is manipulated.

Authority

Authority is institutionalized power. Whilst authority is based upon formal position and legitimacy, its acceptance is governed by the use of factors such as compliance, leadership and expertise. Authority can be gained from position, personal characteristics, expertise and knowledge, and the situation.

POSITION

This is the part of authority that is conferred upon individuals because they occupy a particular position, such as the Chairperson of the Board of Directors or Chief Executive Officer. The position and title are approximately indicative of the relative standing of the position holder's authority compared to other individuals, even though it may not be a specific measure of the exact degree of authority. The true extent of the position holder's authority is measured by the scope and range of their activities within the organization.

PERSONAL CHARACTERISTICS

Personal characteristics such as vision exhibited by leaders in getting others to do things are a part of authority. Domination, physical disposition and certain personality traits are also used to gain authority.

EXPERTISE AND KNOWLEDGE

A person's specialist knowledge and expertise can confer a degree of authority over those not having the same level of knowledge or expertise to make a decision or solve a problem. This is known as authority of knowledge or expertise. It can be independent of level or position, for example a person's knowledge or expertise in a particular information system may provide them with a higher degree of authority over its future management than others who have not been exposed to the system.

SITUATION

Finally, authority can exist in a given context, specific as to time and place and determined by the elements of the situation. As an example, an individual who, upon witnessing a fire in a storage room or taking a bomb threat call may with their first reactions initiate a course of events that may not occur given a normal situation. The situation therefore provokes leadership behaviour and the acceptance of responsibility on behalf of an individual, who, though not in a position of authority, assumes authority in that particular situation by issuing orders.

Delegation

Delegation is the organizational process by which authority is distributed throughout the information service so that others may share work and responsibilities and contribute to the governance process. The distribution of authority through the delegation process does not occur automatically; it occurs by deliberate design. Delegation is a three-stage process:

- an individual is given responsibility for a task, such as to write a report or to manage a work unit;
- secondly, they are given the authority to do the job. They may also be given the necessary position power needed to execute the job;
- finally, they are required to be responsible for their actions and outcomes.

Whilst the information services manager may give authority to an individual to achieve certain outcomes, the manager is still in possession of their own authority over the situation. They have neither more nor less authority than they did before they delegated it. The same thing is true of responsibility and accountability that is central to good governance. No matter how much authority or responsibility the manager delegates, he or she still retains ultimate accountability for the outcomes and results within the information service.

The individual who has been given authority must recognize the fact that they will be judged by their manager on the quality of their performance. They are still responsible and accountable to their manager. By accepting authority, people denote their acceptance of responsibility and accountability.

BENEFITS OF DELEGATION

Delegation improves decision quality and acceptance. It can lessen the load of higher levels of management and allows for quicker responses. Since the delegate is often closer to the point of action and has more specific information than the manager, it allows for a better decision in less time.

It is also a form of job enrichment and an effective method of managerial development and training, providing for internal promotion and career paths within the information service. Individual's jobs become more meaningful and challenging, leading to increased levels of motivation. In situations where organizational levels are being flattened and career paths restricted, delegation serves as one way in which employees can be extended and given further responsibility.

Whilst most people will welcome delegation there may also be some resistance. Some individuals do not wish for any more authority or responsibility, or do not wish to increase their already demanding workload. Others may lack self-confidence or have a low personal need for achievement. The amount of delegation that will be acceptable will vary according to the manager, the individual and the situation.

Unfortunately, some managers do not delegate. A failure or reluctance to delegate is caused by a number of reasons. They may feel insecure or do not know what to do. They may lack confidence in individuals being able to perform the task, although it could be argued that this is evidence that their training and staff development programmes are not effective. Their insecurity may be further aggravated by a feeling that their people have the potential to do a better job than themselves. They may also have a desire to maintain absolute control over the operations of the workplace.

Delegation, like other processes, can be learned. The most basic principle to effective delegation is the willingness by managers to give their people real freedom to accomplish their delegated tasks. Managers have to accept that there are several ways of handling a problem and that their own way is not necessarily the one that others would choose.

Individuals may make errors, but they need to be allowed to develop their own solutions and learn from their mistakes. Improved communication and understanding between managers and their people can also overcome barriers to delegation. Knowing the strengths, weaknesses and preferences of their people enables managers to decide which tasks can more realistically be delegated to whom.

The delegation process can be enhanced if the individual completely understands their responsibilities and role expectations, and is given sufficient authority to carry out their tasks. Their responsibilities and limits of discretion should be well defined. Assistance in the forms of psychological support, advice, technical information, should be provided and feedback given at regular intervals. The individual should be willing to accept their responsibilities and be encouraged to act on their own and make use of their newly acquired authority.

Conclusion

Power and authority are inextricably linked and central to the effectiveness of transparency in decisions and good governance. Power is the ability to influence others, which is legitimized in authority. Delegation allows the giving of responsibility and authority to others. Like politics, power can have negative and positive connotations. It can be abused as well as used effectively to persuade and influence outcomes.

References

French, J.R.P., and Raven, B. (1959), 'The bases of social power', in *Studies in Social Power*, D. Cartwright (ed.), Ann Arbor, MI: Institute for Social Research.

Further reading

Kakabadse, Andrew et al. (2004), *Working in organisations*, Aldershot, UK: Ashgate.

24 *Encouraging Transparency*

Transparency in governance processes is achieved through open and participative decision making, as well as having a culture where executive management is approachable, open to all suggestions and ideas, provides clarity on issues and fosters strong communications across the organization and with its stakeholders. Openness includes candid and honest discussion leading up to when decisions are taken so that a comprehensive view is formed of the issues being considered, as well as frankness about the decision itself.

Encouraging transparency involves ensuring that there is no confusion about why and when actions or decisions are being taken, that people are clear about the ramifications of the actions or decision and about the actions or decisions themselves. Whilst today's environment is fast paced and actions or decisions need to be made quickly, individual styles differ. Some people seem to act quickly, whilst others always appear more hesitant. Much of this has to do with personal decision-making styles which are linked to individual thought systems.

People's perceptions of situations, past experience and emotions also influence decision making.

Making the right decision

Decisions that are made within information services have multiple impacts: some being strategic and concern transformational change with long-term implications, others being operational or tactical, affecting and effected by groups or individuals. Certain decisions will be based on simple and well-defined facts whilst others will involve complex and ill-defined situations. Making the right decision and communicating this within the organization and to key stakeholders is an important component of good governance.

Corporate governance and decision making are linked in two ways: the organizational processes and culture that support ethical and accountable corporate governance guide decision making, whilst at the same time, making the right decision is a factor of good corporate governance.

PARTICIPATIVE DECISION MAKING

Modern management techniques encourage the use of participative decision making, acknowledging that higher-quality decisions and greater transparency results from these practices. Participative decision making allows people to bring multiple views, aspects and knowledge of the subject area, different abilities, interests and skills, as well as freedom of thought to the decision-making environment. This type of decision making is most successful in open organizations and where individuals possess the knowledge and abilities that enable them to make informed decisions.

Participative decision making is also useful for resolving differences in transformational environments. The sharing of norms and values and the communication processes involved can positively influence the motivation of employees, minimize conflict, clarify issues of concern and result in less resistance to the planned changes. By involving groups rather than individuals in the decision-making process there is likely to be more acceptance of risk with the feeling that there is safety in numbers. Equally, the people directly concerned should be involved as they are immediately affected and have the most practical knowledge of day-to-day operations.

Transparency also includes ensuring a duty of care, precision and truth. Where tough decisions are needed, participative decision making should not be used as an excuse for stalling the decision or as a substitution for individual action. Likewise the failure to make a decision and indecision are equally ineffective. In these instances it is important that the most sensible and implemental decision is made.

Understanding perceptions, intuition and emotions

Many decisions are influenced by perception, intuition and emotion that can skew truth and objectivity. From a management perspective, the need to deal with perceptions is as real as the need to deal with facts. Perceptions are formed from personal experience, knowledge, discussions and conversation that sometimes can be incorrect or misconstrued. Likewise, an individual's perception or interpretation of an issue can be influenced by past experiences that may not be entirely relevant to the case in point, or they may be correctly influenced by variables that are not widely known to others which could lead to their choice of actions being questioned and affect others' evaluation of the outcome of their decision.

Intuition influences decision making in that it involves abstract thoughts that are not associated with concrete evidence but are based on individual instinct or apprehension. Often the words 'sixth sense' or 'gut feeling' are applied to the phenomenon of adding a further dimension to the five conventional senses that are used by individuals.

Decision making is also an emotional process. What may appear to be a small decision taken at one level may be considered to have significant emotional consequences at another. For example, decisions on eligibility for car parking spaces or mobile phones may seem to be routine by senior management but attach considerable emotional importance to those who do not qualify. Feelings of self-worth, biases and experiences also affect the emotional processing of decision making. Emotions are involved in diagnosing and defining the problem, in selecting acceptable solutions and in the implementation of the solution.

Decision-making styles

RIGHT AND LEFT BRAIN HEMISPHERES

Various decision-making styles can be found amongst people. One explanation for the different personal attributes and decision styles of individuals can be found in the way in which they use the human brain. The human brain can be divided into two halves. Looking down on the top of the exposed brain two hemispheres are present, the left and the right. The left brain controls the right-hand side of the body and the right brain the left side.

The right and left hemispheres have different thinking styles. The left brain in most people is particularly involved in thinking activities that use language, logic, analysis, reason and mathematical ability. It is also associated with awareness of detail, recognition and classification of problems and optimizing results over time. The right hemisphere is more associated with pictorial, image thinking, spatial awareness, creative ability and intuitive thinking. The right, it is argued, is much better at seeing wholes. Problem solving, writing and planning require high-level left side use, whilst the right brain is particularly associated with the ability to make non-logical connections and to see overall patterns or trends. It uses intuition as the basis for decision making. The knowledge of these two different thinking styles allows individuals to recognize and value the thinking styles involved in the decision-making process.

APPROPRIATENESS OF DIFFERENT DECISION-MAKING STYLES

There are four main decision-making styles; directive, analytical, conceptual and behavioural. Often more than one decision-making style is appropriate, and managers can select the style most appropriate for the situation.

Directive style

According to Rowe (1984, p. 18) managers with a directive style are efficient and logical yet generally have a low tolerance for ambiguity and a low cognitive complexity. They are autocratic, have a high need for power and maintain tight control. They focus upon technical decisions, preferring a systematic structure. Decisions are made rapidly, with little information, usually obtained verbally, and few alternatives are considered. Only short-range, internal factors are usually considered.

Analytical style

Analytical managers have a greater tolerance for ambiguity than do directive managers, but require control over decision making. As their decisions are based on careful analysis, they require more information and consider more alternatives. They are careful but enjoy variety. They are able to adapt to or cope with new situations. Analytical managers are oriented to problem solving and strive for maximum output.

Conceptual style

Conceptual managers are broad in their outlook, achievement oriented and consider many alternatives. They value commitments and integrity and are creative in finding solutions. They focus on long-range issues, are future oriented and are able to negotiate effectively. They will frequently use participative decision-making techniques.

Behavioural style

The behavioural-style manager is concerned for the organization and development of people. They communicate easily, show empathy and tend to be persuasive. Their focus is short or medium range. They use limited data as their emphasis is on decision making through people.

Organizational communications

FORMAL AND INFORMAL CHANNELS OF COMMUNICATION

Transparency and openness in organizations are dependent on good communications for clarity and comprehensiveness. Communication is the process through which the thoughts, processes, ideals and decisions of management and governance functions are transferred and adopted by others. The extent to which formal and informal channels of communication are used within information services depends upon the complexity and stability of the environment, and the size, nature and corporate culture of the parent organization.

Increasingly, formal and informal communications are conveyed through electronic means. Collaborative information and communications technology (ICT) tools enable individuals and groups to see and hear each other, work on shared documents, and witness changes as they occur. This speeds up not only the process of communication, but also the reaction. Messages are conveyed and received instantaneously so the message that is conveyed needs to be the correct one.

Rapidly changing environments require rapid communication with less time for formalized procedures. In contrast, bureaucratic-type structures create situations where procedures and regulations are followed and communication is much more formal.

Formal channels of communication

Formal communications are often used by management to inform people of significant corporate issues and to provide answers to routine questions. They convey factual information and explanation without the emotional perspectives often found in informal communication. Intranets and email are often used as vehicles for formal communications. Formal communication can also be oral. Enterprise collaboration tools, meetings, appraisal interviews and formal discussions or conversations are all used to convey important messages. Formal communication should be open and timely in order to engage trust and keep people informed of important events that may affect them.

Informal channels of communication

Informal communication occurs as part of the social relationship of people. It is not confined to hierarchies, work relationships or work practices. Informal communication supplements formal communication; in the absence of good official communication, informal communication may supplant it. Informal communication channels distribute information that may not have been communicated officially.

The 'grapevine' and chat groups are widely recognized forms of informal communication. Both are fast, highly selective and discriminating. They provide management with insights into employee attitudes, help spread useful information and act as a safety valve for employee emotions. Both have positive and negative implications. Whilst rumour and/or hostility may psychologically help people by releasing emotions, they can be disturbing to others. They may also spread false rumours. This can be a problem where there is no permanent membership and so cannot be controlled.

STRUCTURED AND UNSTRUCTURED COMMUNICATIONS

Communication within organizations moves along a continuum from unstructured to semi structured to structured communication. Unstructured communication is difficult to predict in terms of frequency, process and information that is shared. It includes the use of emails, calendering and scheduling tools, instant messaging and chat groups. Unstructured information does not conform to defined formats or protocols.

Semi structured information can be based on structured processes but the content or threads of discussion may still be unpredictable. In the case of online forums or shared work spaces there can be distributed authorship. Committee meetings held in person or through video, web or audio conferencing tools are other examples of semi structured communication environments. Inter-organizational business processes are examples of structured communications where the information and processes are formalized and predictable, usually conforming to defined standards for data interchange.

REPORTS

Reports are part of the governance process. They formally bring matters to the attention of executive management and stakeholders upon which informed decisions can be made. In order to convey appropriate decision-making information or account for their actions, managers write or commission annual reports, monthly or quarterly reports, reports relating to specific issues, submissions and budget papers.

Regular reports provide continuous feedback to senior management. They often contain statistical information, analysis of trends and reports on activities. Issues of concern can be raised through these reports for further action. Regular reports usually follow a specific format that is established by the parent organization.

Regular reports can be supplemented by reports on specific issues. These can include papers for discussion and/or action, requests for the introduction of additional services or changes in service level, requests for changes in policy or reports relating to future planning. Reports such as these are compiled on a less regular basis and vary in length. They begin with a summary of the reasons for the report and contain details of background, progress to date, legal or resource implications and recommendations. Specific reports are either commissioned or written by in-house specialists. They use corporate data and data from external sources. They are written for senior management so that appropriate action can be authorized and taken.

Budgets are a form of report in that they identify the requirement for, and proposed use of funds. They communicate the need for funding, priority services and major areas of expenditure to senior management, employees and stakeholders.

MEETINGS

Meetings, whether attended in person, through video, web or audio conferencing tools or online via enterprise collaboration tools, assist the governance process as they bring together a group of people with a common interest to accomplish a goal. Participants in meetings use communication skills to share knowledge and experiences, to plan and make decisions, to solve problems, to negotiate and evaluate, to consult and to disseminate information.

Meetings are important components in ensuring transparency in decision making. Handled effectively and efficiently, a meeting will result in creative thinking, multiple thought input, enhanced group cohesiveness, commitment to the outcome, cooperation and better decision making. Handled ineffectively or inefficiently a meeting can waste time, stifle creativity and foster aggressiveness, or result in attacks on others. This can lead to a breakdown in communications between the participants, that in turn creates more problems.

Purposes of meetings

Meetings are a useful tool where decisions require judgment rather than calculations or expertise, or when a pooling of ideas improves the chances of a good decision. They can increase collaboration between work units and be used to ensure that everyone has a shared understanding of issues. Meetings are also helpful where it is necessary to get the participants' acceptance of the decision. Meetings should not be called to solve routine problems, neither are they useful as a vehicle for briefing individuals about issues upon which they have little control or that are unrelated to work. Intranets and electronic collaboration tools can be more efficient mechanisms to use in these circumstances. Figure 24.1 explains some of the purposes and types of meetings that can be held in information services.

Framework for effective meetings

Meetings can be scheduled or unscheduled, held in person or through electronic collaborative work tools. They can also be scheduled on a regular or irregular basis. The agenda should communicate a well-defined purpose for the meeting and a sense of direction for the participants. It should prepare participants for the tasks that they need to accomplish during the meeting and afterwards. The agenda should provide details of date, time and place of the meeting. Time refers to both the starting and ending time as open-ended meetings invite time-wasting procedures. A time may also be set for each item on the agenda. It is also useful to label agenda items according to their desired outcome, for example, 'for discussion', 'for endorsement', 'for information'.

The agenda should be circulated to participants in advance to allow time for reading, research and consultation with others. Background material such as reports, statistics, and proposals should be distributed with the agenda. To ensure that the meeting is effective and productive, participants should be:

- stakeholders in the decision-making process;
- individuals that can contribute through relevant knowledge or appropriate level of expertise; or
- individuals that can communicate and contribute to the meeting in a positive, creative and open fashion.

The ideal number of participants in a meeting is between four and eight. If too many people attend, or if those who are not directly involved in the agenda issues attend, there is a risk of too much time being spent on explaining the background. Agenda issues may also become sidetracked. Likewise, if the wrong people attend they can stifle creativity and waste their own and others' time.

The role of the chairperson is to keep the pace of the meeting brisk. They should ensure that participants do not waffle or get sidetracked onto issues not relevant to the agenda. The chairperson should facilitate open communication and dissipate potential personality problems to make it easy for all participants to put their point of view. Individuals should not be allowed to dominate meetings. The chairperson should have knowledge of group dynamics in order

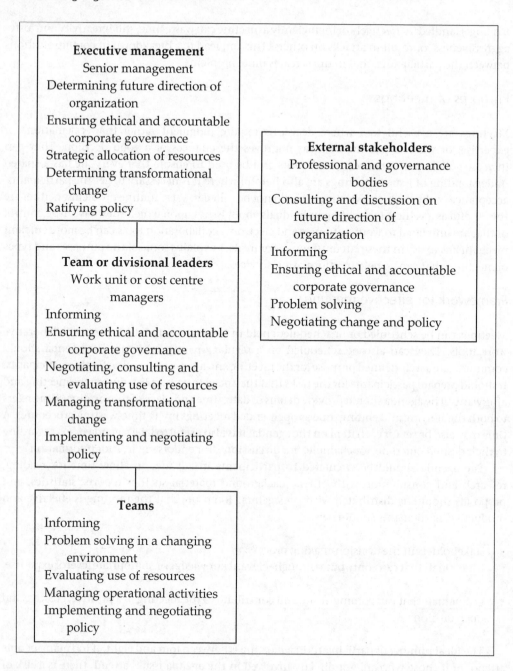

Figure 24.1 Examples of meetings held in information services

to steer the participants in a creative fashion to the desired outcome. A skilled chairperson is able to persuade participants to think again and get proposals accepted where less experienced colleagues may fail.

The chairperson should ensure that all decisions made at the meeting are recorded, together with details as to who is responsible for follow-up actions, what these actions are and when they should take place.

The meeting environment

It is important that meetings are held in non-threatening environments. If people from different organizations or work units are meeting in person, it is often best that this be on neutral territory. Physical features of the room and seating arrangements can affect the outcome of the meeting. A round or oval table is better for problem solving and group discussion. Participants should be comfortably seated in a business-like manner with room to move and the ability to clearly see all members. People likely to be in conflict or confrontation with each other should not be placed opposite each other. There should be no noise distractions or interruptions although, in the case of long meetings, breaks should be scheduled with refreshments of non-alcoholic beverages. The size of the room should give the impression of being comfortably full but not crowded. Large premises are threatening and stifle discussion.

Conclusion

Transparency in governance processes is achieved through making the right decision, as well as having a culture that is open and accountable. Participative decision making is favoured as a means of encouraging input and transparency to decisions. Generally the additional cost of participative decision making in terms of staff time is offset by the benefits that arise from the commitment to the decision and the greater creativity that arises from a wider range of options arising from the participative process.

Communications in organizations can take many forms: formal and informal, structured and unstructured. All of which serve a purpose in encouraging suggestions and ideas, lessening confusion and providing clarity on issues, and enabling discussion and decision making across the organization and with its stakeholders.

References

Rowe, A.J. (1984), *Managerial decision making (Modules in Management)*, Chicago, IL: Science Research Associates.

Further reading

Hammond, John et.al. (1998), 'The hidden traps in decision making', *Harvard Business Review*, Sept./Oct., pp. 47–58.

Quirke, Bill (2000), *Making the connections: Using internal communication to turn strategy into action*, Aldershot, UK: Ashgate.

Ruff, Peter and Aziz, Khalid (2004), *Managing communications in a crisis*, Aldershot, UK: Ashgate.

25 *Measuring Benefits and Performance*

A measure of success in the knowledge age is the extent to which an organization adds value through innovation, inventive systems and processes and the exploitation of knowledge and information. Equally an important component of good governance is in ensuring that the information service is delivering valued products and services to its customers and stakeholders commensurate to the investment that is being made and that its performance is measured and evaluated. This includes identifying how well the information service is using its resources by relating the outcomes and outputs to the investment in the assets.

Benefits evaluation can be a powerful tool in generating commitment to libraries and information services as it enables the understanding of intangible benefits that are more difficult to measure.

Performance is related to value in that poor performance gives little or no value to the user. However, value is also related to the exchange factor in that often people do not value anything that is free. The provision of information and related services comes at a cost, some of which may be subsidized. Calculating the level of subsidy in prices and costs is quite complex and involves consideration additional to just economic and financial costing models.

Management oversight – roles and responsibilities

Barton (2004, p. 140) states that for performance assessment to fulfil its potential as a management tool, it must be embedded within the management culture of the library and its parent organization. She quotes Lakos (2002) as defining a culture of assessment as an organizational environment in which decisions are based on facts, research and analysis, where services are planned and delivered to maximize positive outcomes and impacts for customers and stakeholders, and where staff care to know what results they produce and how those results relate to customers' expectations.

Johannsen (2004) observes that the focus has shifted from an external focus on society to an internal focus on the library itself. There has also been a similar shift from the user as a citizen with rights to the user as a customer with individual preferences and needs that can be observed. Ingrained in this shift are the values of competitiveness, economy, efficiency, enthusiasm, flexibility, honesty, innovation, professionalism, quality, reliability, responsibility, responsiveness, user orientation and work environment.

Benefits evaluation

The need to articulate, evaluate and realize the benefits and costs of libraries and information services is becoming increasingly important in gaining political and public support for new and existing initiatives that are competing with other demands in the public and private sectors. Some of this need arises from the unfortunate fact that corporate memories retain recollections of spectacular failures or underperformance with greater clarity than outstanding successes that by their nature are quickly and seamlessly integrated into daily routines, practices and processes. A second reason is that many of the important benefits are intangible or difficult to quantify in a material sense. Yet as Sumsion et al. (2003, p. 13) point out, knowledge of appropriate cost (and benefit) is an essential ingredient in management's decision making.

Sumsion et al. (2003, p. 14) identify that economic aspects are only one part of the equation. Values such as learning, education, information, culture, social and community impact, as well as recreation also contribute a beneficial return on the investment. However, the development of social capital, increased levels of innovative thinking and small incremental efficiency gains are difficult to quantify when compared with tangible outputs such as an increased number of transactions. As organizations move from information provision and interactive services to more high-value transformational outcomes through the exploitation of knowledge and information and information and communications technology (ICT) the span and level of sophistication of benefits evaluation and realisation increases, see Figures 25.1 and 25.2.

These benefits arise:

- for the organization in increased organizational performance through efficiencies and productivity gains, more reliable knowledge and information for better decision making, increased global competitiveness, increased revenue, growth in intellectual capital and renewed investor interest;
- for the customer in quality customer service, convenience and choice through multiple delivery channels; direct cost savings, efficiencies in interactions, more accessible information for better decision making, and personalized, customized and integrated services available anywhere at any time;
- as political benefits which include increased trust and citizen engagement, increased transparency and accountability in elected governments; as well as,
- for society in terms of enhanced quality of life, increased knowledge and skills, greater community cohesiveness and enhanced community development, increased social capital and sustainability.

Sumsion et al. (2003, p. 14) consider the benefits of public libraries on the basis of 'public' or 'merit goods' and 'private goods'. They explain that the benefits of 'merit goods' extend beyond the individual user to society in general. 'Merit goods' promote causes such as education, culture, informed citizenship, social inclusion and equality of opportunity – which extend beyond leisure use. Positive externalities arise where a better-informed and educated clientele enjoys external benefits that affect others beyond the individual user. The acquisition of a commodity can provide external benefits to others besides the acquirer. We all benefit when ignorance is reduced.

In support of the 'private goods' argument, they identify that borrowing from a library is an economic alternative to buying and owning as a private person. They provide a formula for the economic value as follows:

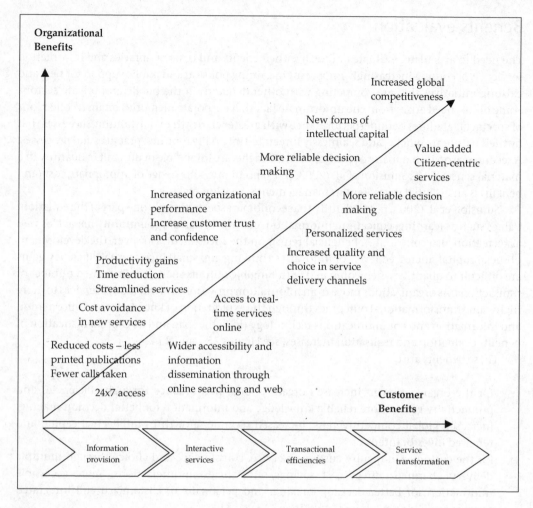

Figure 25.1 Organizational and customer benefits realization model

Value of benefits = $f(C\text{-}L)(N)$
Where
C = cost of commercial alternative;
L = charge made by the library (0 if free); and,
N = number of users (or audiences).

Adding value as a return on investment

The linkages between adding value through the delivery of quality and innovative information products and services and a return on investment are similar to the linkages between corporate governance and decision making. Adding value through knowledge, processes and innovation can lead to an increased return on the investment; whilst at the same time, the need to add value is a fundamental requirement in ensuring that practices and procedures deliver a return on investment as part of good corporate governance.

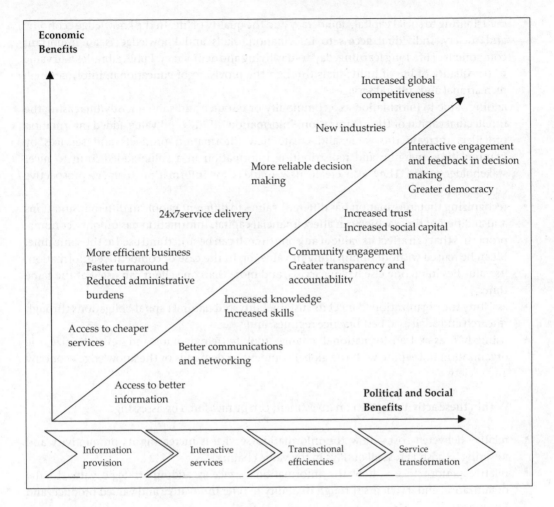

Figure 25.2 Economic, social and political benefits realization model

There are many different ways of valuing and measuring this. The following provides insight into different mechanisms that can be used within information services to determine whether value is being added and if there is a return on the investment.

PERFORMANCE AND VALUE

Information services contribute to organizational performance and transformation, sustainability, and different forms of capital through the following activities:

- assisting the parent organization increase or maintain its financial capital, competitiveness and market share by adding value to the amount and quality of knowledge and innovation within the organization. For example, in acquiring, organizing and disseminating accurate and timely information to retain its client capital, assist new product development and to make it successful against its competitors;

- contributing to social capital, democracy and the quality of life. In the knowledge economy and society, individual access to information, skills and knowledge is an important component of life-long learning, day-to-day living and democracy. Public libraries add value to the quality of life of individuals through the provision of educational, informational, recreational and cultural services;
- adding value to information as a commodity or resource and subsequently increasing the intellectual capital of the organization. Information utilities and value added information providers increase the value and create new information products and services by manipulating, merging and redistributing information in a value added form to meet stakeholder needs. They also create new markets for information to meet prospective customer needs.
- recognizing that information has different values to different people in different situations and at different times which can affect financial capital. Information has unique economic properties that can affect its value at any one time. It can be stored and used at the same time. It can be reused without diminishing in value, or, in the case of competitive information, its value lies in no one else having access, and more than one client can use it at the same time;
- assisting the organization to meet its sustainability and natural capital obligations through research and advice on best practice regimes; and
- using ICT as a transformational change tool to reinvigorate and revolutionize the organization in keeping with the global competitive demands of the knowledge economy and society.

Within these activities return on investment can be measured by assessing:

- relative delivered cost – how the information service is increasing its productivity and lowering its costs across all outlays in the value chain;
- relative performance – how the information service is adding strategic value to the organization and its clients through its ability to offer innovative and valued products and services; and
- financial savings – how the information service is delivering savings to the organization.

The return on investment for information products and services is also enhanced by:

- adding other information to the original information;
- reprocessing and repackaging the information to meet market or customer demands;
- making information more accessible to customers; and
- refining the information to meet individual needs.

The above points are regarded as enhancements to the value chain. However, information by itself is not necessarily useful. If it is not used, for example it sits unused within an information system because people do not know of its existence, or, it is not useful to clients or the business because it does not meet their needs, then it has no value to the organization. Burk and Horton (1988) have suggested five ways in which the performance and value of information may be measured:

- quality of the information itself – accuracy, comprehensiveness, credibility and currency;

- quality of the information holdings – accessibility, adaptability, ease of use, format;
- impact upon productivity – greater returns, improvement in decision making, more efficient operations;
- impact on organizational effectiveness – new markets, improved customer satisfaction, meeting goals and objectives; and
- impact on financial position – cost savings, creation of new assets, improved profits.

They also go on to rank or rate the information resource according to its:

- effectiveness in supporting the activity it was designed to support;
- strategic importance of the information resource (or service) to the activities of the parent organization; and
- strategic importance of the activities being supported to the parent organization.

These generic measurements of performance and value for the information resource may also be applied to measure the value and performance of the individual work units within the information service as well as to the information service as a whole.

BALANCED SCORECARD

Missingham (2005) also includes the balanced scorecard methodology in her research into the value of libraries over the past decade. She notes that this tool, developed by Kaplan and Norton, enables clarification of the organization's vision, defining expected results in terms of financial perspective (including return on capital), customer perspectives, internal business processes and learning and growth of staff. Libraries using this methodology are able to demonstrate value by linking their activities to the organization's value statements.

CONTINGENT VALUATION

Contingent valuation is an economic methodology used to estimate the value that a person places on a good or service. It is based on surveying individuals to establish value. Missingham (2005) explains that it seeks to determine:

- how much individuals would be prepared to pay, willingness to pay (WTP) in order to secure the provision of a public good; and
- how much money they are willing to accept for loss of quality of life, willingness to accept (WTA).

Applied in the information services context, the methodology enables consideration to be given to the cost implications of having or not having an information service.

Missingham (2005) quotes the British Library study of 2004 that was based on contingent valuation and assessed the value enjoyed indirectly and directly by UK citizens. Over 2,000 individuals were surveyed to assess:

- willingness to pay – asking individuals how much they are willing to pay to continue to access the service and directly measure the demand curve with a budget constraint;

- willingness to accept – asking individuals how much they are willing to accept in compensation to forgo the service and directly measure the demand curve without a budget constraint;
- investment in access – estimate of time and cost invested in accessing the service;
- cost of alternatives – costs incurred if forced to use alternatives; and
- price elasticity – change in demand with a change in price.

The study showed that the British Library generates value around 4.4 times the level of its public funding.

The ultimate criterion for assessing the quality of a service is its capability for meeting the stakeholder needs it is intending to serve, and the value of a service must ultimately be judged in terms of the beneficial effects accruing from its use as viewed by those who sustain the costs.

Pricing information

The 'user pays' environment and the recognition of the business value of information has created the need to consider the cost of information and how to apply a charge or price to information when it is transferred to another party in the form of an information product or service.

Pricing of information products and services is linked to issues such as financial management and costings of service provision, equity, the opportunity presented to do something with the information, the economic properties of information, value to the customer and willingness to pay. Sometimes avoidance costs are taken into consideration, where the cost of not having the information is factored into the equation. An example is the public utility that offers information under a 'Dial before you Dig' programmes where information about water and sewerage pipes, energy pipelines or communications cables are provided free of charge, on the basis of this being more cost effective than the cost of repairs in the event of accidental severance.

Generally the value of information to an organization can also be assessed as:

- a consumption good – where the organization sells the information as a value added product;
- a customer service good – where the organization provides information as part of its services; or
- an investment good – where the organization uses it for decision making to achieve competitive advantage.

SUBSIDIZATION

Information products and services are not free. There are costs associated with capturing or purchasing data and equipment, storage, processing, production, distribution and exchange. However, the nature of some information, particularly that which is provided as a customer service good, is that its value and optimum return on investment lies in it being fully subsidized. Subsidization is a policy decision that takes into account social or community service obligations where everyone contributes some or all of the funding of the service so that the service is delivered as:

- fully subsidized – information products and services are made available at no cost to the user. The total cost being absorbed by the information service or parent organization as part of a community service obligation;
- partially subsidized – information products and services are made available at nominal cost. The information service or its parent organization exercises partial cost recovery and funds the remainder of the costs of providing the products or services internally; or
- full cost recovery – information products and services are made available either at market rates (cost & profit) or at the rate required for total cost recovery from the customer.

CONSUMPTION GOODS

Other information products and services have a value to specific customers in that they are designed and offered to fit a specific market need. These fall into the category of a consumption good. An example is where a library may offer specific research services tied to its local history collection to architects who specialize in restoring old houses. These services can be made available on a full cost recovery basis. As a consumption good different charging strategies can be used for information products and services that are influenced by:

- product or service intensity – information products such as maps that contain very detailed information or services that are provided in depth will often command a higher price that others that have less depth or detail;
- product life of the information – information that is rare or offers a new perspective will be of greater value. The price can be set much higher than for information that is older. Out of date information has no value;
- supply time – the faster information is made available, the higher the price that can be set;
- customers' ability to pay and type of customer – organizations that rely on information products and services as a means of creating their next business advantage will recognize that information is a critical resource and will build provisions in their budgets accordingly. Clients requiring information for more personal reasons will be less willing to pay;
- medium or format – the medium or format influences the cost of dissemination of the information product or service;
- extent of the value-added processing – information that is tailored to meet specific or individual needs and is highly processed will command a higher price than a more generic information product or service; and
- intended use of the information – information that is used for commercial purposes may be priced at a higher rate than information that is used as a social good.

Performance evaluation

Performance measurement and evaluation are important management activities. They serve two purposes:

- as an assessment of how effective the information service is in its performance; and
- as an accountability factor to the stakeholders by measuring the appropriateness and efficiencies of services.

Performance evaluation is the process by which the information service determines whether it is on course for the achievement of the parent organization's objectives. The process includes:

- establishing an appropriate evaluation process;
- measuring and evaluating the performance; and
- adopting procedures for acting upon the outcomes and recommendations of the evaluation.

The establishment of the evaluation process requires the development of specific objectives and the establishment of performance indicators to measure progress. The specific objectives define the intended level and quality of the service, the outcomes to be achieved, and the timeframe and resources available to achieve the outcomes.

The timing and format of the evaluation depends upon whether management is evaluating the continuous performance of the information service as a whole, of each of the work units, or a specific project or aspect of the service. In the case of the latter, the performance of the service should be evaluated prior to and at the completion of a specific project. Finally, actions should be initiated in response to any findings or recommendations that arise out of the evaluation.

Tangible evidence of performance for information services operating within profit-making organizations is found in the extent to which they contribute to corporate competitiveness, overall profit growth, sales increase and increased return on investment. The measurements of leadership capabilities of the information services manager could include the information service's ability to:

- provide an increased level of services to meet customers' needs;
- improve and extend information systems to match the growth in the corporate demand for information; and
- maintain the competitiveness of the organization through either doing more with less, obtaining strategic information or applying innovative uses to existing technology.

In non-profit making organizations effectiveness is usually based upon comparative measures such as benchmarking, or subjective evaluations. Comparative measures are often related to budget expenditures such as cost per unit of output, or on market share ratio such as percentage of senior citizens (clients) who utilise the services of a public library.

APPROPRIATENESS

Appropriateness measures the business fit of the information service with the goals and objectives of the organization and how it meets the needs of key stakeholders. This includes the level of consistency of service with the future business direction of the organization and the extent to which it takes into account risk and other evaluation mechanisms.

OUTPUTS AND OUTCOMES

Outputs and outcomes are two of the most common means of measuring and evaluating the effectiveness and efficiency of an information service's performance. Outputs provide a simple focal point for measuring the cost effectiveness of the information service. They can be compared with inputs to measure efficiency, and with the corporate objectives to measure effectiveness.

They demonstrate value in terms of efficiency in managing human and material resources and in being financially responsible. Examples of output measures include the average number of helpdesk enquiries successfully handled by an individual within a fifteen-minute response time, or the number of missing files or records located within the organization over a period of time.

Output measures can also be used to determine how processes and services can be made more cost effective, or to benchmark services and activities against other services.

Services are evaluated or appraised through outcomes. These measure the impact of the outputs on the target market and the environment. They are the intended consequences of the information service's activities and are found in achievements such as changes in circumstances or behaviour, or benefits such as needs that are satisfied.

Impacts are a third means of measuring effectiveness. These measure what differences, positive or negative, have been made.

QUALITY AND VALUE

Tangible measures of efficiency are linked to value for money and involve the extent to which productivity is improved or duplication is lessened. Value for money also considers whether there are alternative or more sustainable mechanisms for delivering services for less costs and/or better outcomes.

However, many of the benefits of the information service are intangible. The quality of the service may be recognized by the customers and stakeholders or senior management, but it is often difficult to apply concrete measures that can be directly attributed to the information service. Sometimes an attempt is made to assume some sort of qualitative measures by applying a timescale to the quantitative measures, for example the number of enquiries or advice taking fifteen minutes or more. The assumption is that the longer the period of time taken, the more in-depth and valuable the service given. There are two problems with performance measures of this type:

- there is not necessarily a correlation between time and quality; and
- they fail to measure the impact or outcome of the advice and how it was used in the value chain.

For example, the customer may be dissatisfied with the advice but out of politeness and consideration for the staff have made them feel helpful and successful.

The measures of quality (capability) and value (benefit) that arise out of the above example are much more difficult to measure directly. Indirect measures have been used, but as Orr points out (1973, p. 320), the relationship between capability and utilization is mediated through demand, which is itself a highly complex variable.

There are three measures of performance common to all services. These are efficiency and two other aspects: 'how good is the service?' and 'how much good does it do?'. The latter can be expressed as quality and value or effectiveness and benefit. Orr (1973, p. 318) states:

If the work units that comprise the information service collectively supply pertinent and timely information in an efficient manner that enables the organization to take advantage of its competitors, it will be perceived as being a valuable asset by senior management and funded accordingly. Services that are efficient and reflect the needs of the customers are usually well supported. Customers convey positive feedback to senior management and tangible effects are felt upon the parent organization. This support is reflected in the level of funding that the information service receives. In contrast, poorly focused, inefficient information services result in disillusionment for both the staff and customers. This is manifested in a lack of commitment by customers, senior management and other stakeholders. Unless the service is refocused to meet customer needs and the quality of service improved, the information service and its level of funding will invariably decline.

CAUSE AND EFFECT

Orr (1973, p. 318) has developed four basic propositions:

- that, other things being equal, the capability of the service tends to increase as the resources devoted to it increase, but not necessarily proportionately;
- that, other things being equal, the total uses made of a service (utilization) tend to increase as its capability increases, but not necessarily proportionately;
- that, other things being equal, the beneficial effects realized from a service increase as its utilization increases, but not necessarily proportionately;
- that, other things being equal, the resources devoted to a service increase as its beneficial effects increase, but not necessarily proportionately.

The cause and effect sequence is useful in that it points out that funds invested in different services or work unit activities may not necessarily have the same impact. There are other important interactions that have just the same, if not more, effect on the services. For example, in competitive, customer-oriented environments it is quality and innovation, not quantity, that distinguishes an information service. The knowledge, creativity and resourcefulness of the staff can have more impact on the quality and value of the service than the funding level. The level of resources and funding still has some bearing upon the output and performance of the information service. Without adequate resources, the services will gradually decline. However, funds alone do not constitute a good service. The effectiveness of the information service's policies and practices, staff competence and morale, and the leadership skills of management also impact the quality of the service.

Performance indicators

A performance indicator is the formula that is used to measure progress, quality and level of service towards achieving the organization's objectives. It is the means of knowing whether a specific objective is being achieved (see Figure 25.3). However, even success in producing outputs and achieving outcomes does not call for complacency. The results should be analysed to see if there are better ways of achieving the same results at least cost.

Performance indicators combine the elements of inputs, outputs and outcomes. Generally three types of indicators are used. These are:

- workload indicators;
- efficiency indicators; and
- effectiveness indicators.

Workload indicators are output oriented. They measure the amount of work achieved against set milestones. Efficiency indicators compare resource inputs against resulting outputs.

Type of indicator	Objective	Performance indicator
Workload	To scan 2,500,000 items into an image system over a period of three months as part of the take up of a large image project	Actual work progress in terms of the number of items accurately scanned at the end of each week of the project
	To process 10,000 client requests for information per year.	Actual requests for information (reported monthly)
Efficiency	Provide a helpdesk service at a maximum cost of $100.00 per person per month	The actual cost of providing the helpdesk service (based on unit cost)
	E-business system to provide client transactions at a maximum cost of $10.00 per transaction	The actual average cost of client transactions each month (dollar value of resources used divided by total number of transactions per month)
Effectiveness	To provide information services that satisfy 90% of customer demands for information within three days.	Analysis of information services against customer demand/requests for information and time taken to provide information, summarized monthly

Figure 25.3 Examples of performance indicators in an information service

They quantify the resources used to achieve the intended outputs (services or products) so that the ratio of outputs to inputs can be determined. Effectiveness indicators measure the extent to which services achieve objectives using qualitative and quantitative indicators.

Performance indicators must be relevant to the cause and should clearly relate to the specific objectives of the service. They should be measurable. The information used must be reliable, valid and verifiable. Data collection should be accurate and unbiased, interpreted accurately, and collected in time for proper use to be made of it. It is important that the indicators are not subjective. They should be capable of being translated into meaningful information for use by those who require them.

Each indicator should be unique. It should reveal some important aspect of performance that no other indicator does. The value of the information should be weighed against the costs of the collector's and analyst's time, efforts and resources. The degree to which routine operations are impeded in collecting the data, and the acceptance levels of staff time and operating expenses should be balanced against the value of the information provided.

Taylor (1986, pp. 181–4) has defined several other qualities or attributes that can assist in producing meaningful indicators in information services. For example, the audit should be at a definable point in the process, such as the number of abstracts completed or requests for information processed. The activities should be easy to count and define. For example, enquiries can be classified as taking under one minute, one to three minutes, five to ten minutes, and so on.

A defined output should also be consistent with existing information systems and, if possible, covered by historical data. Like should be compared with like. The historical context is important as it allows for comparisons over a period of time. The output should have a terminal quality. It should be isolated and counted at the point where it changes function and status. For example, the issue of a library book changes the status of the book from an asset or library resource to a source of information, education, culture or recreation for the customer. By counting issue transaction statistics, public libraries are counting one of the sources of added value to the quality of life in their communities. The outputs are the result of a process in which value is added.

Conclusion

Ensuring the return on investment in the information service is a complex issue that is directly related to planning and managing projects to fit the business needs of the parent organization and the customers' information and service needs. It also requires consideration of how the return on investment can be increased at the different stages of the value chain, and, charging strategies for information products and services.

Information services often experience difficulty in designing quantitative and qualitative measures that prove their value as many of the benefits are intangible or linked to other outcomes for which they cannot be directly accountable. Outcomes such as the value of the service in contributing to organizational competitiveness, its social value and contribution to a community, or the creation of value-added information-based products and services can be used to measure performance and value. Other mechanisms through which the performance of the information service (and its information resource) may be valued include accuracy, comprehensiveness, accessibility, adaptability and ease of use, impact on productivity, impact on organizational effectiveness and impact on financial position.

In order to measure performance, information needs to be collected and analysed over time. The information services manager must determine what pieces of information are needed to evaluate or measure the service's performance.

References

Barton, Jane (2004) 'Measurement, management and the digital library', *Library Review*, vol. 53, no. 3, pp. 138–41.

Burk, C.F. and Horton, F.W. (1988), *Info map: A complete guide to discovering corporate resources*, New Jersey: Prentice Hall.

Johannsen, Carl Gustav (2004), 'Managing fee-based public library services: Values and practices', *Library Management*, vol. 25, no. 6/7, pp. 307–15.

Lakos, A. (2002). 'Culture of assessment as a catalyst for organizational change in libraries', Proceedings of the 4th Northumbria International Conference on Performance Measurement in Libraries and Information Services, 12–16 August 2001, Washington, DC: ARL.

Missingham, Roxanne (2005), 'Libraries and economic value: A review of recent studies', *Performance Measurement and Metrics*, vol. 6, no. 3, pp. 142–58.

Orr, R.H. (1973), 'Measuring the goodness of library services: A general framework for considering quantitative measures', *Journal of Documentation*, vol. 29, no. 3, Sept., pp. 315–22.

Sumsion, John et al. (2003), 'Estimating the economic value of library benefits', *Performance Measurement and Metrics*, vol. 4, no. 1, pp. 13–27.

Taylor, R.S. (1986), *Value added processes in information systems*, New Jersey: Ablex.

Further reading

British Library (2004), *Measuring our value*, London, British Library, available at www.bl.uk.

Codling, Sylvia (1998), *Benchmarking*, Aldershot, UK: Gower.

Holt, G and Elliot, D. (1998), 'Proving your library's worth: A test case', *Library Journal*, vol. 123, no. 18, pp. 42–4.

Kaplan, R.S. and Norton, D.P. (1996), *The balanced scorecard: Translating strategy into action*, Boston, MA: Harvard Business School.

Kingma, B.R. (2000), *The economics of information: A guide to economic and cost-benefit analysis for information professionals*, 2nd edn, London, UK: Libraries Unlimited.

McCallum, I. and Quinn, S. (2004), 'Valuing libraries', *Australian Library Journal*, vol. 53, no. 1, pp. 55–69.

Niven, Paul R. (2005), *Balanced scorecard diagnostics: Maintaining maximum performance*, New Jersey: John Wiley.

Rowley, J. (1997), 'Principles of price and pricing policy for the information marketplace', *Library Review*, vol. 46, no. 3/4, pp. 179–89.

Sumsion, John et al. (2002), 'The economic value of book borrowing from public libraries: An optimisation model', *Journal of Documentation*, vol. 58, no. 6 . pp. 662–83.

26 *Risk Management*

Risk management comprises the identification and mitigation of risks that might affect an organization or activity. Risk management is not an excuse for curtailing freedom, for not being prepared to take a chance, or a reason for not being innovation or risk taking. In fact the greatest risk is to do nothing and therefore risk nothing. Innovation, progress and opportunities to create the next advantage all involve some elements of risk.

Risks surround us, they are in abundance and there for the taking. Those who do not take risks achieve nothing. The challenge is to identify potential risks and proceed to manage them in a manner that leads to a successful outcome. Awareness of risks is as important as managing the risks themselves. It is far better to be aware of all possible and probable risks than to progress in ignorance. There is a difference between taking a risk avoidance approach in which everything is slowed down such that progress and initiatives are stifled, or progressing proposals with eyes open, knowing the potential and possible risks to look for.

Management oversight – roles and responsibilities

As risk management is both a corporate governance and strategic management issue, executive management should hold the ultimate accountability for risk management issues, even though risk management specialists may be employed within the organization. Executive management should set the strategic risk management policies, including setting the desired levels of risk tolerance, as well as providing oversight of risk management issues within the corporate environment.

Line managers and specialist risk managers (where they exist) should identify and monitor possible and potential risks, instigate control and mitigation practices for these risks and ensure regular reporting to executive management on these issues.

Risks can occur from internal and external sources. The complexity of the environment and potential for sudden and serious risks to emerge means that external risks are likely to be more damaging and threaten the livelihood of the organization than those that are initiated from within, such as through innovation. The nature of risk is that any member of staff can be in a position to identify risks, either through observation, through conversations with stakeholders such as suppliers, union representatives, customers, or in coming into contact with other external intelligence sources. The best way to manage this environment is to ensure that systems, practices and processes are in place such that make the management of risk an integral part of the planning and management process and general culture of the organization.

Sources of risk

Major risks that can affect libraries and information services include:

- fraud, theft or misappropriation – this can be financially detrimental to the information service and its parent organization or result in a loss of clients if their relationships with the organization are affected. If the fraudulent person is a member of the information service's staff, this can have an adverse affect on the morale and levels of trust amongst staff members;
- security violations and computer crime – these can result in the loss of competitive information or severely affect the operations of the organization's systems through the use of logic bombs, computer viruses, etc.;
- inappropriate use of computer systems – the sending of inappropriate email or text messages or inappropriate access to pornographic or other unsuitable websites can be extremely upsetting and damaging to recipients, expose the organization to litigation, as well as tarnishing the reputation of the organization and being a misuse of employer's assets;
- technology change – that renders practices and processes, products and services obsolete overnight;
- inefficiency and waste – these lead to high costs, low profitability and low productivity;
- legal exposure – this includes breaches of contract, statutory breaches or where adverse legal action is financially and organizationally debilitating;
- loss of public reputation, image or regard for corporate citizenship – the loss of an organization's reputation or image can severely affect its standing in the market;
- lack of contingency planning and business continuity strategies – may result in the information service or its parent organization being unable to continue its business activities during times of degraded conditions. Common causes for business interruption include interruption of power supply, electrical surges or spikes that damage equipment, industrial action or denial of service attacks through the Internet;
- loss of key staff and expertise – this can leave the information service or its parent organization vulnerable in terms of a loss of business knowledge and expertise if there had been poor succession planning. It may also result in an organization's intellectual property being transferred to a competitor;
- public liability – especially where inappropriate or incorrect advice or information is provided by inexperienced personnel which can have financial, legal, duty of care and image implications for the information service or its parent organization;
- property damage – this may inhibit the operations of the information service and its parent organization if access and movement within the organization's building are restricted;
- unlawful acts, arson, vandalism and terrorism – as well as the potential for property damage, acts of vandalism or terrorism can have a major impact on the safety and psychological well-being of staff;
- occupational health and safety issues – an unsafe workplace not only exposes staff to health and safety risks, there is an adverse effect on the morale and productivity of staff. Apart from the fact that this can expose the organization to the threat of litigation, there is a duty of care perspective that needs to be taken seriously. The use of information and communications technology (ICT) equipment such as screens and mobile telephones have been identified as possible sources of radiation that may be a health hazard to users over a long period of time;
- other workplace issues – such as enterprise bargaining disputes, claims of sexual harassment, inappropriate skill mixes, cultural or religious conflicts or language difficulties;
- equipment breakdown or down time – especially where there are mission-critical operations that require a 24x7 always on operating environment;

- poorly maintained or inappropriate equipment or infrastructure – this includes ageing equipment infrastructure that leads to breakdowns or superseded equipment that no longer fits the purpose and needs updating;
- financial exposures – such as bad debts, exchange rate movements, inadequate costing systems or incorrect budget controls;
- natural and manmade disasters – these include damage through earthquakes or weather events, fire, exposure to long-term hazards and pollution, or pandemics that affect operational capabilities; and
- political risks – such as a change of government that brings a new political agenda, loss of a significant corporate champion for the information service, or changing community expectations that require the rethinking of funding or service delivery strategies.

Managing risk

Risk management involves the establishment of the context for risks, identification of risk, analysing the probability of it occurring and the magnitude of the potential risk, evaluating and prioritizing risks, introducing appropriate strategies to treat or manage the risks and monitoring and reviewing risks.

ESTABLISHING THE CONTEXT

Establishing the contextural environment in which risks may occur draws upon much of the information obtained through the strategic planning process; for this identifies the issues in the organization's strategic and operational environment from which risks may arise. Strategic audits, strengths, weaknesses, opportunities and threats (SWOT) analysis, desired future business direction, stakeholder interests, capability profiles, present levels of resources and organizational capability and scenario planning activities can all feed into this activity. It is against this present and future context that risk tolerances and limits are set and possible and probable risks are evaluated. For example, a highly innovative entity where being first to market is of critical importance in a fast-moving environment will have a higher tolerance for risk and evaluate risks accordingly, than a more conservative organization, such as an accounting firm, where corporate reputation and knowledge of the most recent company and taxation regulations and legislation is used as a differentiating factor. Determining the criteria against which risk is to be evaluated is part of the process of establishing the contextual environment in which risk management takes place.

IDENTIFYING RISKS

The second stage in the risk management process is to identify the risks that need to be managed. This requires consideration of all aspects of both the internal and external environments, including the strategic influences identified in the chapter of the same name. As previously identified, unidentified risks pose a major threat to an organization, so it is important to ensure that all sources of risk are identified in the first instance. This is an instance where more is better, leaving the formal risk evaluation and prioritization process to determine which risks are given more attention.

In addition to drawing on the strategic planning process as a source for identifying risks, risks can also be identified through audits, brainstorming, personal experience, focus group discussion and surveys. Communication is extremely important in order to identify risks and to explain risk management strategies to those affected. Different stakeholders will have different perceptions of the likelihood and severity of the risk, so communication with all stakeholders will provide a richer picture of the potential and probable risks than taking a narrower approach.

Once risks have been identified, it is necessary to identify when, why, where, how are the risks likely to occur and who might be involved. The sources, consequences and potential costs of each risk should be calculated. These can be tabulated in a spreadsheet, but if a more serious or comprehensive approach is required, then a commercial risk management product should be used to guide the risk management processes. Accountability mechanisms and control processes should also be incorporated against each risk.

ANALYSING RISKS

Once risks have been identified, the next stage is to analyse the risks according to the likelihood of the event and the magnitude of the associated consequences. Together these provide an indication of the level of risk.

Business Excellence Australia have identified descriptors to assess the likelihood of risk:

Likelihood	Event occurrence	Event timing
Almost certain	The event will occur in most circumstances	Will occur once a year or more frequently
Likely	The event will probably occur at least once	Will occur once every three years
Possible	The event might occur at some time	Will occur once every ten years
Unlikely	The event is not expected to occur	Will occur once every thirty years
Rare	The event may occur only in exceptional circumstances	Will occur once every one hundred years
Very rare	The event may occur only in highly exceptional circumstances	Will occur once every three hundred years
Almost incredible	The probability of this event is highly unlikely	Will occur once every thousand years

Figure 26.1 Likelihood of events

Adapted from Business Excellence Australia (n.d.), *Introduction to risk management*, Sydney, Aus: Standards Australia International Limited.

The consequences of risk can be determined by evaluating the potential effect, fallout or outcome of the risk on the organization and its operations. Generally these are considered to be extreme, critical, major, minor or insignificant as per the following:

Consequence	Effect, fallout, outcome
Extreme	An extreme incident that would affect the organization's survival or would result in extensive long term adverse impacts on the organization, the community and/or its environment.
Critical	A significant incident that would compromise the operations of the organization and have a long term detrimental effect on the organization, the community and/or its environment.
Major	A significant incident that would have a serious impact on the operations of the organization and require remedial action within the organization, the community and/or its environment
Minor	A localized incident that would have short term disruption or detrimental impact on the organization, the community and/or its environment.
Insignificant	A minor incident with no lasting detrimental effect or impact on the organization, the community and/or its environment.

Figure 26.2　Consequences of events

The level of risk is determined by plotting the likelihood of the risk against the consequence as follows:

Risk	Consequence				
Likelihood	Insignificant	Minor	Major	Critical	Extreme
Almost certain	Medium	Serious	High	High	High
Likely	Medium	Medium	Serious	High	High
Possible	Low	Medium	Serious	Serious	High
Unlikely	Low	Low	Medium	Medium	Serious
Rare	Low	Low	Medium	Medium	Serious
Very rare	Low	Low	Medium	Medium	Serious
Almost incredible	Low	Low	Medium	Medium	Serious

Figure 26.3　Level of risk

EVALUATING AND PRIORITIZING RISKS

Risks are evaluated according to whether they are high, serious, medium or low, following which they are prioritized. Using the identified sources of risks for libraries and information services above, Figure 26.4 provides an example of how risks can be evaluated and prioritized. In evaluating risks the degree of control over the risk, the cost impact, benefits and opportunities should be considered, against the already established criteria.

Risk source	Likelihood of risk	Consequence of risk	Risk level	Priority
Fraud, theft or misappropriation	Possible	Minor	Medium	5
Security violations and computer crime	Possible	Major	Serious	1
Inappropriate use of computer systems	Possible	Major	Serious	2
Technology change	Likely	Major	Serious	2
Inefficiency and waste	Likely	Insignificant	Medium	6
Legal exposures	Possible	Major	Serious	3
Loss of public reputation, image or regard for corporate citizenship	Unlikely	Major	Medium	4
Lack of contingency planning and business continuity strategies	Possible	Major	Serious	1
Loss of key staff and expertise	Likely	Minor	Medium	4
Public liability	Unlikely	Major	Medium	5
Property damage	Rare	Major	Medium	5
Unlawful acts, arson, vandalism and terrorism	Very rare	Major	Medium	5
Occupational health and safety issues	Possible	Minor	Medium	4
Other workplace issues	Possible	Minor	Medium	4
Equipment breakdown or down time	Likely	Major	Serious	1
Poorly maintained or inappropriate equipment or infrastructure	Possible	Major	Serious	2
Financial exposures	Unlikely	Minor	Low	7
Natural and manmade disasters	Possible	Major	Serious	3
Political risks	Possible	Minor	Medium	6

Figure 26.4   Evaluation and prioritization of risks in libraries and information services

TREATING AND MANAGING RISKS

After deciding on priorities the risks need to be treated within the context of the strategic direction and operations of the organization. Risk treatment strategies can include:

* avoiding the risk by not proceeding with the activity or choosing alternative paths that have less or more acceptable risks attached;
* reducing the likelihood of the risk through risk mitigation strategies;
* transferring the risk, in full or in part, to another party, such as underwriting or taking out insurance on the risk and eventuality of an outcome; or
* choosing to retain the risk.

MONITORING AND REVIEWING RISKS

Few risks remain static so it is important that risks and the effectiveness of their treatment are monitored on a continuous basis. Changing circumstances can affect the likelihood and consequences of the risk. For example, the likelihood of risk of a pandemic or terrorist attack causing significant disruption is significantly higher today than ten years ago. In addition, the effectiveness, suitability and costs of risk treatment measures can vary and need to be continually assessed.

Conclusion

Taking risks is an ordinary everyday occurrence and is a necessary feature of progressing new ideas, creativity and innovation. Risk management is a process for identifying risks and making informed decisions about courses of action that balance the risks with the outcomes. Tolerance for risk will differ across organizations dependent upon their business objectives and the environment in which they operate.

References

Business Excellence Australia (n.d.), *Introduction to risk management*, Sydney, Aus: Standards Australia International Limited.

Further reading

Wilding, Edward (2005), *Information risk and security: How to protect your corporate assets*, Aldershot, UK: Ashgate.

27 *Security*

Information security has become an integral part of life. It is also a business management and governance matter rather than a technical issue, as proper security ultimately results in minimizing business damage. Effective security cannot exist just through funding allocations. It must be an adopted state of mind by employees and contractors of the organization, infused into the corporate culture and made a natural way of life.

Organizations today must deal with a multitude of security risks. Terrorist attacks, fires, floods and other disasters can destroy critical information and its associated infrastructure; but in this uncertain world, the physical security and safety of staff is increasingly becoming a priority. The objectives of information security management are to ensure confidentiality, integrity and availability of information and resources.

Management oversight – roles and responsibilities

Responsibility for security can be found at all levels. The Chief Executive is ultimately accountable for the confidentiality, integrity and availability of the organization's information resource and systems and for the physical safety of their staff. Executive management has a responsibility for establishing a security-conscious corporate culture that makes effective security a way of life, for ensuring that there are appropriate standards, policies and procedures on security that reflect the level of risk within the organization, that there is appropriate funding and priority given to security, disaster recovery and business continuity strategies, that staff are aware of and understand the policies and procedures, and that adequate security procedures and practices are in place to manage the risk. Individuals are responsible for ensuring that they follow the correct procedures and practices and maintain a vigilant eye for possible intended or accidental breaches. The information services staff and line managers or team leaders are responsible for systematic testing of strategies to ensure that all of the correct procedures and practices are in place and followed.

Confidentiality, integrity and availability

Ensuring the confidentiality of information includes protecting privacy, commercial and competitive information from unauthorized access and use, and ensuring that information is accessible only to those authorized to have use.

Maintaining the integrity of information relies upon the ability to protect it from unauthorized manipulation or processing, as well as safeguarding the accuracy and completeness of information and processing methods.

The continued availability of information ensures that authorized users have access to information and associated assets when required. This requires mechanisms to ensure that the information is resilient, backed up and that steps are in place to restore and maintain access levels quickly in times of degraded activity. The testing of data recovery should be performed on a periodic basis to confirm that the backup process is effective and that correct and usable information is available.

Planning

Security should be planned and managed through a security strategy that is aligned to agreed critical business objectives, functions and processes, infrastructure and resources, and risks and scenarios. This should be supported by a series of general and application controls that either:

- prevent threats; or
- detect and control the effects of damage if it takes place.

The security strategy should encompass human, natural environment and political components, as well as the built environment, hardware and software failures, as the strength of the security chain is determined by its weakness link.

EXECUTIVE COMMITMENT

The first task in undertaking a security strategy is gaining executive management's support and commitment to the strategy and its degree of specification and adherence to international standards. International standards advocate the world's best practices that are very appropriate for some organizations, but can be too onerous for others. The level of detail and implementation chosen should be commensurate with the business objectives, functions and processes, criticality of infrastructure and resources, and risks and scenarios. This is because:

- security strategies can be time consuming and expensive to implement;
- they have considerable impact on the day-to-day operations of the organization; and
- physical, people, information security issues are one of the biggest risks to organizations today and should not be underestimated.

CHOOSING THE RIGHT SECURITY LEVEL

The choice of security level is a business and risk management issue. The requirement for an appropriate level of control ought to be balanced against the need to make information easily available for decision making. The level of security should take into account:

- the type of business and its operating environment;
- the level of business risk;
- ease of use;
- the relative cost;
- feasibility; and
- availability of skills and resources.

The level of risk can be calculated according to the amount of damage or loss that could result due to a security exposure, multiplied by the probability (or frequency) that this may occur. Modern technology environments encourage access to systems from widely dispersed work stations or personal computers. Security features need to control unauthorized access without introducing barriers to legitimate use.

Security features can be expensive in terms of the capital costs for the security devices, additional costs for encryption facilities in messaging and telecommunications and labour costs in maintaining security. The level of security should match the level of risk. It is not cost effective to introduce a higher level of security than is necessary. In fact this could lead to a loss in productivity for the organization.

The level of security should be chosen to be feasible and practical. It ought not to inhibit work or information flows to the extent that it is detrimental to the organization's activities. It must also match the organization's level of expertise and resources.

Risk and vulnerability analysis

An important task in developing a security strategy is to assess the level of risk and potential threats to the organization and its vulnerability to these risks. The level of risk is influenced by the type of organization, the external environment, its business and its objectives. An organization that operates in a highly competitive environment, depends upon large scale information processing and access for its business, or manages a large proportion of personal or commercially sensitive information will have a higher security risk than an organization in a more stable and less sensitive environment. For example, the need for confidentiality, integrity and availability of systems in the banking or airline industry is much higher than in a public library system. In security, a compromise should not be entertained. Best practice should be implemented commensurate with the level of risk.

Threats to security can be found in human error or deliberate human intervention, natural and political disasters, hardware and software failures. Examples of human error include incorrect keying of input data, errors in program development or maintenance, or operator error.

Security can be deliberately violated through:

- unauthorized access – access to critical information or systems with or without causing damage;
- damaging information – by damaging, contaminating, destroying, erasing, manipulating or rendering information meaningless; and
- fraud – manipulating data to obtain a financial or other advantage.

Natural and political disasters include earthquake, flood, fire, industrial sabotage, terrorism and war. These have the potential to threaten, either partially or totally, access to information and the functioning of the supporting technology. They can also severely degrade the functionality of the organization. Hardware and software failures include power failure, failure of equipment, network failure, or systems malfunction. These can lead to loss of information and functionality for the organization.

The most prevalent security vulnerabilities or points of failure can be avoided by adhering to international security standards and having good information and communications technology (ICT) security, people and asset management practices in place. Most common vulnerabilities arise from virus, worm or Trojan infection, insider theft of proprietary or commercial in-confidence information, private information abuse or fraud, degraded performance through external attack, and laptop theft. Statistics also show that organized crime is much less likely than internal management and employees to pose a threat of theft, fraud and abuse.

Management

Security is achieved through the appropriate management of people, information, physical environment (including buildings), specific library collections and the technology (including networks and systems). The following provides some of the mechanisms used in security management.

PEOPLE MANAGEMENT

People are often a source of security violations. The security risks are found in human error, asset misappropriation and theft, fraud, loss of key staff with in-depth knowledge of competitive information, or the misuse of information and facilities. Apart from deliberate actions, an unfortunate aspect of security violations is that a considerable number are unintended. Security violations often occur through ignorance and negligence of following proper procedures.

Security should be addressed in the recruitment stage and monitored through the individual's life with the organization. Everyone must be made aware of information security threats, the importance of maintaining proper security and backup controls, and be equipped to support the organization's security practices and procedures during their work.

If the parent organization continually deals with sensitive information or operates in a highly competitive environment, all new personnel must be screened before being appointed. All employees and third parties utilizing the organization's information and supporting technical infrastructure ought to sign a confidentiality (non-disclosure) agreement with the organization that extends beyond their employment period. Employees and third parties should be advised in writing of their rights and restrictions of levels of access, the security requirements of the organization, and the appropriate disciplinary action if these security requirements are breached.

Authentication, identity and access management policies and processes should also be in place to determine those who should legitimately be given access and what access rights they should have. Authentication practices enable the users to be positively identified using two or three factor authentication processes that might include a combination of user ID in smart card, biometric or token form, password or other factor known only to the user, and a user ID. Identity management and single sign-on systems provide a centralized view of users and their access across multiple subsystems.

The main fraud mitigation techniques include having codes of conduct and fraud policies in place and ensuring that all staff are familiar with these, maintaining a fraud awareness and incident management programme and having a fraud response plan. All security breaches should be investigated and counter measures taken to ensure that similar breaches do not reoccur.

With all instances of risk through human intervention, a corporate culture that encourages teamwork and collaboration and values ethics and integrity, so that temptation is minimized, is a valuable strategy in avoiding opportunities for security breaches.

INFORMATION SECURITY

Information has varying levels of sensitivity and criticality and is protected through classification schemes for the data and information itself, as well as an identity and access management regime that ensures that 'those who can have access do, and that those who should not have access do not'. Some information may require an additional level of security protection or special handling such as intrusion and change protection devices; examples being some types of personal information or commercially sensitive information. Information classification systems can be used to define an appropriate set of security protection levels and to communicate the need for special handling requirements to users. Information that is classified as high security will require specialized storage and restricted access and circulation provisions.

Information security policies and procedures should relate to information in electronic and hard copy form. Documents, paper records or microfiche are at risk of security breaches as much as information stored in electronic form.

SPECIFIC COLLECTIONS

Libraries and archives face particular risks in terms of physical security and wilful or accidental damage to their collections. This risk increases where there is open access to the collection. Damage can occur at both the collection level and the item level through:

* theft of an item of stock (such as a journal or DVD);
* wilful damage to an item or part of an item of stock (such as the cutting out of an journal article or picture in a book);
* accidental damage (such as warping of a CD left out in a hot car, or a pet or small child chewing a book); or
* fire, storm or other damage.

Many libraries have installed security devices that either scan clients as they exit the premises, or provide videotape footage of movements within the building in order to minimize this type of damage. Libraries that house valuable and unique collections such as national libraries must weigh accessibility and ease of access against the security of the collections. Archives and other institutions that house critical collections in paper or electronic form may require special climatic or security surroundings that physically control humidity or extract oxygen from the air in the event of fire.

PHYSICAL ENVIRONMENT

Critical or sensitive business activities should be housed in secure areas. They can be protected from unauthorized access, damage and interference by a defined security perimeter with appropriate entry and exit controls and security barriers.

Information and communications technology should be physically protected from security threats and environmental hazards. The physical environment that houses the supporting ICT such as file servers, mainframes and network controllers should have hazard detection and suppression controls that minimize risk from damage through explosion, fire, water or other natural disasters. Support facilities such as power supply and cabling infrastructure must also be well protected. A battery-based or independent uninterruptive power supply ought to be installed to provide continuous operations in the case of a total or partial power failure. Equipment (including work stations) should also be protected against power spikes and lightning. Advanced planning should take into account future requirements so as to ensure the availability of adequate capacity and resources.

Physical access to storage locations may be restricted to minimize the risk of disgruntled employees or competitors destroying original and backup copies of information and software programs. A clear-desk policy can be in place to reduce the risk of unauthorized access to information sabotage or damage.

All staff should be aware of the procedures to be undertaken in the case of earthquake, fire, bomb threat or terrorist attack in the form of chemical or biological agent or hostage situation. The need for evacuation will differ according to circumstance. In the case of earthquake or bomb threat the safest place may be inside the building, away from windows and protected by a strong structure. Wardens should be appointed and evacuation procedures in the event of fire clearly displayed. In the case of bomb threat all staff should be issued with a list of questions to ask the caller in order to locate the bomb and assess the situation. Where appropriate, mail should be screened before opening and procedures put in place to deal with any suspected contamination.

INFORMATION AND COMMUNICATIONS TECHNOLOGY

As well as twenty-four-hour physical protection and fault detection, ICT should also be protected against loss, damage and interruption to business activities or wire tapping. These should be continually reviewed in line with changing security, environmental and operational risks. Firewalls and other network perimeter security devices and procedures should also protect against viruses, spam, intrusion devices and denial of service attacks. Disks should be scanned before being introduced or exported from organizational equipment. Virus and other intrusion detection software ought to be installed on all personal computers, updated at least daily and used as a matter of course. Only authorized software should be used, and the downloading of information or software programs from remote sources should be controlled to minimize the risk of spyware and other adverse types of software being unknowingly installed.

Good asset management should be in place with regular audits performed. Tangible assets should be assigned an asset or inventory number and labelled with the number. The asset register or inventory should maintain a record of all assets, the asset or inventory number and the name of the person to whom they are allocated. This should include all hardware and software, mobile devices, and random checks should be made to ensure that all loaded software is legitimate and where necessary licensed.

GOOD HOUSEKEEPING PRACTICES

In addition to the specific security requirements mentioned above, good housekeeping practices and routines maintain the integrity, availability and confidentiality of information. These include (but are not restricted to):

- maintaining and periodically revising security plans so that they remain relevant to the level of risk, are complete, and reflect the current business environment;
- a regularly maintained backup copy of critical information and software stored off site;
- a register of security incidents to enable the organization to review regularly all security incidents and identify commonalities to improve the approach to security;
- controlled access to networks and systems by third parties;

- instilling norms of ethical behaviour amongst employees;
- accountability procedures for all assets;
- protection from the introduction of software containing viruses and other programs that can make unauthorized or unknown modifications to either the software or information; and
- the continuous monitoring of equipment performance.

Access control

Access to information and its supporting technologies should be controlled to prevent unauthorized use or access.

AUTHORIZING USE OF ORGANIZATIONAL-WIDE NETWORKS AND SYSTEMS

There should be formal policies and procedures that control and document the allocation of access, from the initial register and management of new users, management of user privileges and passwords, to the deregistration of users who no longer need access to services. The allocation of privileged access that allows users to override systems controls should be on a very restricted basis. Teleworkers and other remote users will require special considerations for logging, access and control.

NETWORK AND COMPUTER ACCESS CONTROL

To prevent unauthorized network or computer access, technology facilities that service multiple clients must be capable of:

- identifying and verifying the identity, terminal and location of each user;
- recording successful and unsuccessful accesses;
- providing a password management system to allocate, check, maintain and prompt the user to change quality passwords;
- restricting the access times and connection times of users where appropriate, or when not in use through time-out controls and automatic log offs;
- providing enhanced user authentication facilities such as dial-back, smart card tokens or key-based encryption; and
- automatically disabling or disconnecting users when a small number of consecutive incorrect passwords are entered.

Access to network addresses, controls and configuration files must be managed in a secure and controlled manner.

APPLICATION ACCESS CONTROL

Logical access can be used to control access to applications and information residing on computers. These should be protected from any utility software that may be capable of overriding the application, and should not compromise the security of other systems.

Access to systems administration menus and critical system files must be restricted so that only authorized personnel are able to access these to maintain authority and user-level controls.

There should be a period review of users' access permissions to ensure that access permissions continue to be valid. Audit trails should be designed to track access and changes to applications and the information in order to confirm that any changes are valid and authorized.

PHYSICAL ACCESS

Access to rooms housing equipment should be strictly controlled. The employees and visitors must be appropriately identified. Proximity devices, badges or other means of identification should be worn at all times, registers (either electronic or manual) need to be kept for when people enter and leave, and, closed circuit monitors should be actively monitored by security personnel.

INFORMATION ACCESS AND PRIVACY CONSIDERATIONS

The protection of an individual's personal information is a democratic right. Privacy and data protection can be safeguarded through legislation. Where this is absent, the organization can develop its own code of conduct that:

- guards against the indiscriminate collection and use of personal information;
- ensures confidentiality in its information practices;
- provides individuals with the right to view their personal records, to challenge and have corrected (or noted) any incorrect personal information about themselves; and
- holds executive management accountable for the security and use of personal information that is in the possession of the organization.

Disaster recovery

In the event of a major outage (failure or disaster), disaster recovery and business continuity plans protect critical business processes from their adverse effects. The emphasis for the information services is on protecting and ensuring the continuity of access to information and its supporting technologies. However, other business aspects such as alternative sites for the total business operations must be considered.

Disaster recovery should take a business perspective. It should:

- highlight preventative actions that may be taken;
- seek to minimize the impact of the disaster on the information service, the parent organization and its clients; and
- improve the organization's ability to recover efficiently and effectively.

IMPACT ANALYSIS

Before designing the disaster recovery plan an impact analysis should be undertaken. This describes the types of events that may cause an outage and analyses their impact on the business. The impact analysis links the development of the disaster recovery plan to the business needs of the organization. It also identifies the priorities within the business operations, so that critical processes can be restored first. The business impacts include:

- loss of business opportunities;
- likelihood of penalty clauses in contracts that may be affected by the outage, such as penalty fees for delaying the completion of a project or late payment;
- loss of important material; and
- impact on staff, customers, stakeholders and executive management.

THE DISASTER RECOVERY PLAN

The disaster recovery plan is part of the business continuity management process. It specifies how an organization will maintain its information services necessary for its business operations in the face of an outage or disaster. The disaster recovery plan has four components:

- emergency plan – this specifies the type of emergency and the actions to be taken that fit the emergency situation;
- backup plan – this specifies the facilities required (including data restoration, disks, computing equipment, telecommunications and networks, work stations) as a recovery site and to maintain operations;
- recovery plan – this specifies how the processing will be restored, including the responsibilities of individuals and a priority list for the retrieval of important material; and
- test plan – this specifies the frequency and manner in which the components of the disaster recovery plan will be tested.

DISASTER RECOVERY SITE

Arrangements need to be made for alternatives for a recovery site. The alternatives for a recovery site can be:

- backup facilities that are owned by the parent organization – if the organization operates out of a number of geographic locations, a site (or a number of sites) can act as the backup facility for others;
- right of access to facilities offered by organizations that specialize in providing disaster recovery sites – the organization may undertake a contract with a specialist organization for the use of a mobile, hot or cold site as a contingency measure. A hot site is a facility that operates equipment compatible with the organization. A cold site is a building that is designed so that it is able to accept equipment at short notice; or,
- facilities at another establishment – a reciprocal agreement may be undertaken with an organization that operates compatible equipment for each to act as recovery sites.

MANAGING THE RECOVERY

The recovery plan should be regularly updated, known and understood. Executive management must know how it will be managed and in what order so that business processes can be restored as quickly as possible. The recovery plan should be maintained in paper as well as electronic form, and copies stored off site, such as in bank vaults, the recovery site and the homes of executive management and key staff members. As the recovery plan will include sensitive and competitive information, it should be secured off site.

A consolidated contact list should be maintained. This should contain the names, addresses, contact numbers and responsibilities of the people required to implement the recovery process. The contact list should be stored alongside the recovery plan.

In addition to the people directly involved in the recovery process, the contact list should also include details of suppliers, vendor contacts, business partners such as electronic trading partners and key customers. One of the first management tasks will be to advise those on the contact list of the event and the actions taken to restore business processes to normality.

Disaster recovery plans assist the organization restore and recover its business, either on or off site, following an outage or other security incident.

Business continuity

Business continuity differs from disaster recovery in that it is more comprehensive and provides alternatives for all resources and activities so that critical business functions can continue. Disaster recovery only considers the loss of computer-related and network facilities and provides alternatives for data processing at other locations. It does not cover issues such as the requirement for office space or alternative work facilities, emergency telephone systems, operational facilities to support staff who may be disoriented by the changes or the business impact associated with the inability of customers to access services.

Business continuity management counteracts interruptions to business activities and protects critical business processes so that there is an interrupted availability of all key resources supporting essential business functions. It addresses business scenarios. For example:

- planning for known events such as the continuity of operations at the end of an outsourcing contract, whilst the service provision is either being transferred to another vendor, or being brought back in house; or
- what to do when the information-related facilities are still working, but employees of the information service or parent organization are denied access to the building because of an incident.

Business continuity requires a process and programme to be developed and maintained for the availability of processes and resources in order to ensure the continued achievement of critical objectives in the event of an emergency or disaster. This also includes the speedy restoration of critical business processes and services in the event of a serious business interruption. The processes will differ according the event and level of risk. For example, the strategy to maintain business operations in the aftermath of a terrorist bombing of the office building in which the organization operates will differ from the strategy to maintain business operations during a period of industrial unrest that causes the supply of power to be continually interrupted.

Business continuity is a continuous and ever changing process that needs the support of executive management in order to ensure that the necessary permanent funding and availability of backup infrastructure, recovery strategies, training, testing and revision are in place to cover present day and emerging risk situations.

Maintaining and testing

The efficiency and effectiveness of the security controls can only be achieved if they are maintained. The security strategy should be tested through regular audits, monitoring and critical incidence reproduction. There should also be regular awareness and training programmes for all staff that incorporates human, natural environment and political components, as well as the built environment, hardware and software failures, and there should be regular rehearsal and systematic testing of strategies and plans.

Compliance

Finally there will be legal and regulatory compliance issues to be managed. These include privacy protection, adherence to software licensing conditions and other intellectual property rights protection, records and data protection evidence, audit considerations, securing of forensic evidence so that it is admissible in court, and telecommunications interception rights.

Conclusion

In an increasingly uncertain world, security, disaster recovery and business continuity are ever more necessary and complex. Everyone has an important role in ensuring confidentiality, integrity and availability of information, and a duty of care for the physical safety of themselves and others.

The overriding factor in the management of security is that it should be managed in accordance with the level of risk and potential threats to the organization. The requirement for a high-level of security should also be balanced against the need to make information available for decision making. Ultimately, the choice is a management rather than a technical issue.

Risk management and business continuity strategies are proactive management strategies for the identification and management of risk and for ensuring the continuity of access to information in a working environment that may be operating under degraded conditions.

Further reading

Callan, James (2002), *How to keep operating in a crisis: Managing a business in a major catastrophe*, Aldershot, UK: Ashgate.

Saint-Germain, René (2005), 'Information security management best practice based on ISO/IEC 17799', *Information Management Journal*, vol. 39, issue 4, July/Aug., pp. 60–66.

Schlicke, Priscilla (1998), 'Disasters: Prevention, rescue and recovery', *Handbook of library and information management*, Ray Prytherch (ed.), Aldershot, UK: Gower.

Wilding, Edward (2005), *Information risk and security: How to protect your corporate assets*, Aldershot, UK: Ashgate.

28 *Outsourcing*

Outsourcing is the contracting out of services to a third party (the vendor or service provider or partner) to manage on the organization's behalf. It is a means through which the market can be tested under competition policy; or where the organization can divest itself of underperforming corporate assets, increase its flexibility, offer difficult to deliver services, or concentrate its activities on its core business. Outsourcing is also used to overcome continuing capital and operational budget restrictions and reduce overhead costs, to focus on customers and improve service levels, to gain access to changing expertise and know-how, improve security and manage the complexities of continuously developing technology directions. In most instances it involves the transfer of ownership and responsibility for assets (including the people) from the organization (the client) to the vendor. In all instances accountability is paramount.

Information and communications technology (ICT) and its related areas are one of the most accepted areas where outsourcing occurs. As market-oriented governments and large corporate entities outsource many of their ICT business activities, there are significant impacts upon the way in which information services managers manage the provision of ICT and related information services and utilize their human resources. In an outsourced or market testing environment, the manager's role is no longer that of managing a workforce that delivers the services. Rather the manager's role changes to one of contract management, purchasing services and putting processes in place in which the organization and the outsource provider can work cooperatively and productively together in order to get the best out of the relationship. This involves a role in contract administration and performance review to ensure that the outsourced or contracted out service meets the specified service levels and customer needs. For whilst functions and activities can be outsourced, business responsibility for the functions and activities cannot. If the outsourcer is unable to perform, for whatever reasons, it is the organization that bears the consequences and the resulting regulatory, customer or brand damage.

Outsourcing also requires an understanding that the outsourced provider operates in a commercial environment and needs to make a profit, as well as being flexible and prepared to consider innovative approaches to the way in which business is conducted and services delivered.

Any functions or activities that are repetitive, frequent or take place in bulk and do not involve a competitive edge can be outsourced or contracted out. Aside from ICT, common functions and services that are outsourced include corporate services such as payroll processing, human resource services, debt collecting, freight operations and call centres. Traditionally, the decision to outsource is based on the vendor's ability to offer economies of scale or specialization at a higher level than that achievable by the organization itself. Partnering, in which both parties leverage their competitive advantage in the market place through each other, is another way of managing service delivery.

Ball (2003) also includes difficult to deliver services as contenders for outsourcing. He cites examples such as:

- sudden unpredictable peaks of activity or demand, where maintaining in-house staffing levels to cope with peaks may be impossible;
- the impracticability or expense of opening service points outside core hours;
- lack of in-house expertise for specialist work, such as design or health and safety; or
- poor or declining performance.

Making the outsourcing decision

Information services that have been the most successful at outsourcing are those that have invested their time and energies into making a thorough examination of their options for outsourcing and make an effort to embrace transparency on both sides of the contract. The decision as to what to outsource is a governance issue, and should be made in the context of the criticality of the service in question to the business needs of the organization, an assessment of in-house capabilities and available skills transfer and expertise, financial situation, market opportunities, business and technology direction, the rate of change and complexity in the external environment, risk factors and benefits.

Outsourcing is also a relatively long-term proposition. The length of the contract is usually between three and ten years. This is for two reasons:

- the service provider needs to be assured of a long-term contract in order to achieve a return on investment for the infrastructure they provide; and
- the initial expenses of handover and change mean that the cost savings for the organization are not realised until the third or fourth year of the contract.

Whatever the extent of the outsourcing services contract, accountability for service provision remains within the organization. The fundamental responsibility and accountability for strategic decisions relating to the quality of the end products or services still rest with management. In the end, both parties have a common goal of delivering better services.

Benefits of outsourcing

Outsourcing is often a contentious issue. The major reasons that are given for not outsourcing are:

- a fear of loss of control;
- the lack of ability to trust another party with a strategic investment;
- there is not a strong business case;
- the cost and effort of contractual negotiations give little return on the investment in time and legal representation;
- it results in constraints on flexibility; or
- concerns over vendor capabilities.

Small to medium sized enterprises, in particular, gain from outsourcing. They can enjoy access to new technologies and improved services without a major upfront capital outlay or being left with redundant equipment. They also have access to a higher level and greater range of expertise than they could afford by themselves. Existing services can be upgraded or new ones introduced to completely transform the organization's capabilities and services.

Outsourcing can reduce costs by cutting an organization's capital investment in equipment and staff. It obviates the need for debt financing of expensive ICT. It also provides a mechanism to shift technologies, take on board new technology directions, or introduce new information services cheaper and faster than if the organization was locked into an investment in its own infrastructure. Organizational change, mergers and new business or programme start-ups can also be achieved cheaper and faster.

Managing the outsourcing process

Managing the outsourcing process involves:

- determining the right objectives and strategy;
- determining what to outsource;
- assessing the benefits;
- determining the risks;
- selecting the vendor;
- structuring the relationship;
- negotiating the contract;
- managing the risks; and
- being an exceptional client.

DETERMINING THE RIGHT OBJECTIVES AND STRATEGY

An inhibiting factor to the success of outsourcing is that organizations frequently do not take the time to determine their objectives for outsourcing and develop a strategy to match. Each objective will require a different outsourcing mix and strategy, contract and management mechanisms. For example, an outsourcing strategy that is based on allowing the organization to focus on its core business will require a totally different partnership arrangement than one that is focused on a shift in technology or the sharing of risks.

DETERMINING WHAT TO OUTSOURCE

Outsourcing can be applied to any service; from window cleaning in the library to security services. Applied to ICT, outsourcing includes information technology, data centre and telecommunications network maintenance and facilities management, personal computer support, infrastructure development, systems maintenance, systems integration and systems development and design, training, end-user support, and service delivery such as the delivery of value added information products.

Within the functions of archives, records management and library services the following could also be considered for outsourcing:

- storage and retrieval of records and archives;
- delivery of specialized information services; and

- processing of journals and other stock (including accessioning, assigning the bibliographic description, binding, attachment of bar codes and radio-frequency identification (RFID) tags).

The concept of outsourcing is also being applied to business strategy and change management, business and process reengineering.

The extent of outsourcing varies and includes:

- shared services – where clients pay monthly fees for certain transactions or services. These are provided for, or run on the service provider's or vendor's systems, alongside transactions of other clients;
- remote computing – where a specific part of the vendor's installation is reserved for a particular client; and
- total outsourcing – where the service provider takes over all, or nearly all of the services and equipment.

In determining what to outsource, consideration needs to be given to understanding the key business objectives for outsourcing and the risks associated with outsourcing.

ASSESSING THE BENEFITS

The outsourcing of areas such as ICT or the storage of corporate records to a specialist in the field allows the information service and its parent organization to refocus on where it can add competitive advantage. However, this is just part of the outsourcing equation. The benefits should be assessed with other value added factors in mind. These may include financial benefits through the ability to spread the costs over a number of years, share risks or jointly developing capabilities commercially.

The benefits of outsourcing can also include

- skills and knowledge transfer;
- flexibility in the technology development and acquisition to support continued innovation;
- the migration to new ICT platforms and infrastructure at significant lesser cost than outright purchase;
- the divestment of legacy systems and other underperforming assets;
- lessening of overheads associated with storage; and
- access to new markets and services.

This can be with the view to:

- upgrading or introducing new information services to transform the organization's capabilities;
- sharing the level of risk in the introduction of new capital-intensive technologies;
- managing a new business or programme start-up; or
- increasing flexibility for handling peaks and troughs in service delivery and business cycles.

DETERMINING THE RISKS

Determining risk in outsourcing involves the identification of risk, analysing the probability of it occurring and measuring the magnitude of the potential risk. It also involves considering the impact and ease of appropriate strategies to manage or mitigate the risk. Some of the first mentioned risks below can be minimized through effective contract negotiations and by the organization putting in place appropriate risk management and risk mitigation practices and procedures. The later mentioned risks will need to be determined between the organization and the outsourcer.

Risks associated with the outsourcing process include:

- loss of expertise, key competencies and skills of staff within the information service which may have long-term corporate knowledge and financial implications;
- costs are not actually reduced, only deferred. The internal changes within the organization that are required as part of the transition process may be higher than expected, or the time spent in negotiating the contract negates any financial gain in the outsourced agreement;
- lack of contract negotiation and continued contract management skills within the organization. Similarly the purchasing of these skills may be an additional overhead for the information service;
- incorrectly and under-specified service delivery outcomes that lead to business functions not being performed. This can result in incompatible or inappropriate services being offered; leading to damage to operations, brand name, productivity, a loss of clients, failure to adhere to necessary regulatory requirements or a loss of return on investment;
- outsourcing worsens rather than fixes existing problems or inefficiencies. Problems or inefficiencies remain unsolved or become even more acute; only the responsibility for them has changed;
- poor vendor selection. This can occur either because the vendor or service provider is less competent than believed, or the coordination requirements are higher than expected. The vendor should also be financially sound, experienced and knowledgeable about the services offered;
- inadequate or unclear contracts leading to costly litigation;
- integration problems or problems in getting different contractors and/or vendors to work together or find technically sound interoperable solutions. This is often experienced in areas where the integration of systems is managed by multiple parties, the result being an increase in the complexity and overhead costs of the outsourcing project;
- lack of flexibility and responsiveness to the needs of the information service;
- continually changing service provider staff such that there is little or no understanding of the business by those delivering the service; and
- delays in project execution or completion.

Improved telecommunications and lower labour market rates have resulted in a number of outsourcing venture operations being moved offshore. This can expose the organization to a number of risks that need to be managed as part of the contract negotiations. Examples being where:

- personal information residing on databases housed offshore (or in another commercial environment) is not subjected to the same level of privacy protection as the in-house systems;

- the same levels of security over confidential or commercially sensitive information are not applied in the outsourced environment, particularly where the information resides on shared services; or
- any intellectual property rights that the organization may have are not protected in the outsourced environment.

The failure of security systems is a significant risk either on or offshore. A compromise or failure of information security involving information subject to privacy protection can cause considerable embarrassment and severely damage customer relationships and trust in the organization, whilst the loss of commercially sensitive information may set back an organization's competitive advantage for a considerable length of time.

SELECTING THE VENDOR

The selection of the vendor should be based upon:

- the vendor's credibility and capability to provide the services being outsourced;
- size and shape, including whether the vendor is able to concentrate on the information service's needs or whether it has other business interests to attend to;
- financial strength and viability to remain in business for the life of the partnership (and longer);
- proven technical and service capability and performance in similar information related environments;
- the variety of platforms offered to support the requirements of the information service and its clients;
- their ability to be controlled in terms of future direction, so that the information service shapes its future needs rather than being manipulated by the vendor;
- security and risk management issues;
- tender conformance;
- full cost of the proposal;
- the vendor's vision, strategic business direction and client relationship perspective;
- the vendor's adaptability, understanding and ability to contribute to the organization's business in a timely manner; and
- the vendor's compatibility with the organization's corporate culture.

STRUCTURING THE RELATIONSHIP

The relationship between the information service and the vendor must be a partnership of goodwill, understanding and good communication. In order to bring true value to the arrangement, there needs to be a high level of trust between the partners and a cultural fit between the organization and the service provider. Many outsourcing arrangements fail to achieve their full potential because of poor communications and information flows, poor access to the right people or a lack of defined contact points, and a lack of appreciation and/or follow up on divergent expectations.

A governance framework, the structure of which will be dependent upon the objective of the outsourcing exercise, needs to be in place so each party can be very clear about:

- the business objectives and requirements of the outsourcing arrangement;

- each other's expectations, roles and obligations in the partnership agreement;
- the organization's business and corporate culture;
- the distribution of risk between the parties;
- the ownership of the assets;
- the required outcomes and outputs; and
- the terms and conditions of the agreement itself.

NEGOTIATING THE CONTRACT

The contract should meet the organization's business needs and objectives rather than the vendor's. Having a defined contract is important as it is inevitable that this will be referred to in the future when matters of contention arise. A detailed specification for the outsourcing contract should be drawn up with legal advice. In addition to the items discussed in the relationship structure above, it should specify:

- the areas to be outsourced;
- the service levels required. For example, hours of operation, minimum service factors, and the penalties if these service levels are not met;
- the level of service and contribution required of the organization and its management staff;
- costs, including those for maintenance and support;
- billing and asset management issues;
- intellectual property rights and copyright, including ownership of systems and developments, data and indemnities against the intellectual property rights of third parties;
- integration procedures for systems that may now be managed across multiple parties, for example telecommunications, office and email systems and business systems;
- risk management, including data redundancy, procedures and responsibilities, distribution of risk between the parties, security, confidentiality and backup, privacy protection;
- transfer of assets, including details of assets, date of transfer, value at date of transfer, disposal of surplus assets, outstanding liabilities on assets;
- staff, including what happens to existing employees as well as continued access to the right people who know the business after the contract has been signed. The contract should specify conditions relating to staff development, transfer of staff and transfer conditions, outstanding liabilities in terms of accrued leave payments, superannuation or other contractual obligations, use of contractors, availability and costs of additional staff, backup arrangements for key or critical staff, minimum proficiencies, poaching of staff;
- disputes and damages settlements, including problem escalation procedures, formal and informal dispute resolution procedures. A third party arbitrator should be specified;
- termination clauses, back out and change requirements for both parties. Termination clauses should cover the termination of the contract in the event of a dispute or violation of the contract, and the assistance to be provided at the end of the contract life. The contract should also cover the circumstances in which the contract conditions may be altered;
- performance measures. For example, response times, turnaround time, throughput;
- review and monitoring, including third party review on physical security, disaster recovery, operations controls;
- indemnities and liabilities, including provision for indemnity insurance or other indemnity provisions against contractual default and liability provisions for the vendor or service provider; and

- other issues, including notices, relationships of parties, successors or assignments, approvals or similar actions, contract variation procedures, waivers, publicity, governing law.

This list is not comprehensive but covers the main points of the contract.

MANAGING THE RISKS

Senior management must be involved in contract negotiation and ongoing monitoring of performance levels. Legal advice should be obtained before and during the negotiation of the contract.

It is very important how the transition is managed and that thought is also given to managing the transition period at the end of the contract. The agreement should provide that on termination the service provider or vendor will assist the organization in taking back control of the service or in handing over the service to another vendor with the least possible disruption.

Whilst it is likely that the numbers of staff will be significantly reduced, the information service must be prepared to keep some expertise to oversee the contract and to evaluate performance and service delivery. As much thought should be given to the capabilities and skills of those who should remain as to the management of the staff who will transfer or leave.

Any reduction in staff within the information service may harm general morale and cause termination and severance for many employees. Change management strategies should be put in place to manage the transition stage. Whilst the service provider may hire a number of staff, others may face job loss, early retirement or significant readjustment and retraining. Staff should be kept informed of progress and likely outcomes in terms of job security at all times. There needs to be a high level of trust between the partners and a cultural fit between the organization and the service provider.

There should also be a post-implementation review to determine the effectiveness of the outsourcing process, and to provide on-going evaluation and monitoring of activities.

BEING AN EXCEPTIONAL CLIENT

Outsourcing is a client–provider relationship where there are obligations on both sides to ensure that each party is actively working to keep the affiliation on a positive footing. These obligations include:

- acting professionally and with respect for each other;
- understanding the other's business drivers as a legitimate interest;
- ensuring that reporting and other obligations are met in a timely manner;
- using agreed processes, procedures and engagement models, particularly in handling differences;
- knowing and accepting responsibilities and delivering on them;
- agreeing that when things are not working as they should, that both parties will strive to fix them; and
- systematically reviewing progress.

Conclusion

Outsourcing is a partnership between the information service, its parent organization and the third party service provider (the vendor). Whilst the emphasis in the literature and corporate environment has been associated with the outsourcing of ICT, the reasons for outsourcing, risk and contract management strategies, and, relationships issues apply equally to any outsourcing venture in the other work units that belong to the information service.

Outsourcing is a viable consideration where the goods or services can be provided more efficiently or effectively by an experienced third party. However, many decisions to outsource ICT or other services have been based upon a belief that organizations would then be able to refocus on the core business rather than being sidetracked by ICT or other issues. Outsourcing for this reason alone is short-sighted and is merely shifting responsibility for the delivery of services from an in-house source to an external source. The time, energy and expense taken in selecting the right service provider or vendor, establishing the contract conditions, and monitoring performance mean that the true benefits must come from elsewhere.

References

Ball, David (2003), 'A weighted decision matrix for outsourcing library services', *The Bottom Line*, vol. 16, no. 1, pp. 25–31.

Further reading

Geddes, Michael (2005), *Making public private partnerships work: Building relationships and understanding cultures*, Aldershot, UK: Ashgate.

Harrington, Keith (2003), 'Contracting out of a public library service: Business to be, or not to be?', *Library Management*, vol. 24, no. 4/5, pp. 187–92.

Linder, Jane C. (2004), 'Transformational outsourcing', *MIT Sloan Management Review*, Winter, pp. 45–51.

Sweetland, James H. (2001), 'Outsourcing library technical services: What we think we know, and don't know', *The Bottom Line*, vol. 14, no. 3, pp. 164–77.

PART **VII** *Positioning to Excel in Service Delivery*

The theme for Part VII is positioning the information service to excel in services that meet the right customer needs. It deals with defining and managing the end products and services that result from all of the other activities in the book. It also considers alternative strategies that can be used to deliver products and services. As a reflection of its level of importance, this part could easily be at the beginning of the book. However, it has been located towards the end of the book as it builds upon all the other practices and processes that must be in place within the information service to support service delivery.

Chapter 29 considers strategic marketing strategies to increase the competitiveness of the information service. It outlines the process of a strategic marketing exercise and explains the marketing mix, or 'the four Ps' of product, price, place and promotion in the context of information services. The chapter also outlines how markets can be divided into market segment groups of need markets, geographic markets, product markets and demographic markets. Market targeting can be undertaken through three strategies: undifferentiated marketing, differentiated marketing and concentrated marketing. Each strategy is explained drawing upon examples in information services. Customer satisfaction studies also provide an indication as to whether existing information service customers are satisfied with current services.

Underlying the marketing concept is a system of exchange. The theory behind exchange system analysis is explained in the context of information services. A further analysis that can be used in marketing is the competitive portfolio analysis. Chapter 29 explains how the product life cycle and the Boston Consulting Group's portfolio matrix can be used in a competitive portfolio analysis. A specific example of how the competitive portfolio analysis can be used in managing library stock is explained. Today, organizations are making widespread use of customer relationship management systems and tools to understand their customers' needs and behaviours in order to develop stronger relationships with them. Chapter 29 introduces some of the issues for successful customer relationship management. Finally, Chapter 29 describes the rejuvenation strategies that can be used to recover some services' lack of use over time or to stop the decline in the product life cycle.

Positioning the information service to excel requires consideration of how the corporate image is formed, managed and projected. Chapter 30 considers image analysis in the context of determining service provision. Image studies measure the perceptions that people have about the information service. Chapter 30 also looks at strategies for projecting the information service externally through communication. Information on managing the corporate image is included as well as other formal communication mechanisms, such as annual reports and submissions to outside bodies.

Whilst Chapter 29 focused on understanding customers, product preferences and the market place, Chapter 31 is concerned with ensuring quality service and service support once the customer has engaged with the information service. Chapter 31 introduces the reader to quality control and choice in service delivery. It makes the point that people have differing perceptions of quality according to how they judge it and their cultural background. The chapter lists the main determinants of quality and identifies five gaps that can cause unsuccessful service delivery. The role of quality in the value chain is covered, as is the need for continuous rather than one-off improvement.

Chapter 31 reflects a customer approach to management. It describes these in terms of 'Rs' that stand for retention, requirements, refined segmentation, etc. The chapter points out that the delivery of the service or product is only the beginning of the relationship between the organization and the customer. Choice of channels and service backup is extremely important to deliver a total quality service. Suggestions for a customer service charter are included. Finally, the chapter describes how technology can be used by organizations to retain their customers.

CREATING THE
RIGHT
CORPORATE
ENVIRONMENT

TRANSFORMING
THE CORPORATE
ENVIRONMENT

MANAGING
YOURSELF AND
OTHERS

PLANNING AND MANAGING FOR TRANSFORMATION

PART VII – POSITIONING TO EXCEL IN SERVICE DELIVERY

29. **Competitive strategies**
Strategic marketing; The marketing management process; Exchange system analysis; Competitive portfolio analysis; Diversification and service rejuvenation; Using competitive intelligence; Customer relationship management

30. **Corporate image**
Image analysis; Projecting the corporate image; Branding; Other corporate communications

31. **Ensuring service quality**
Management oversight – roles and responsibilities; Meeting customer expectations and perceptions; Designing a multi-channel service; Customer retention; Maintaining service quality; User surveys; Customer service support

MANAGING IN
A DYNAMIC
ENVIRONMENT

EPILOGUE

POSITIONING
TO EXCEL IN
SERVICE
DELIVERY

GOVERNANCE AND ACCOUNTABILITY

Figure PVII.1   Positioning to excel in service delivery

29 *Competitive Strategies*

Organizations today face many challenges and if they are to survive they must achieve three concurrent goals: customer satisfaction, market domination and increased profitability. They must not only complement existing roles, but also continually embrace opportunities and seek the next new advantage. Providing consistently higher-quality customer services and new product offerings ahead of competitors is one means of differentiating services.

Strategic marketing is part of the total planning process and assists the organization to remain competitive. Strategic marketing makes use of many of the concepts and functions of strategic planning. Strategic marketing strategies ensure viable market positions and programmes for the survival and success of the information service.

Market segments comprise individuals or groups who are actual or potential customers of the information service. Markets can be divided according to need, product, demography and geography, each market having its own particular characteristics. Market targeting involves the evaluation, selection and concentration on the desired market segments. There are three strategies for market targeting: undifferentiated marketing, differentiated marketing and concentrated marketing.

Various analyses assist marketing strategies. These are exchange system analysis, image analysis, customer satisfaction studies, competitive portfolio analysis and product life cycles. The exchange system analysis is useful as it enables the information services manager to identify what the customers are prepared to exchange for the services that the information service offers. Its importance lies in the fact that both tangible and intangible items can be identified, including the more esoteric values that the information service community may hold. This may be useful information when planning new services or in justifying existing services. Customer satisfaction studies determine whether customer expectations for services are higher or lower than those being provided. Product life cycles and product portfolio matrices help the information service to determine which areas have the potential for growth. Finally, diversification and service rejuvenation can help to instil new growth into ailing services.

Supporting these strategies are customer relationship tools that enable the information service to collect and analyse information about customers' needs and behaviours in order to develop stronger relationships with them.

Strategic marketing

In striving to invent new advantages as well as maintain competitive advantage, it is important for management to understand:

- their entire range of existing and potential services;
- where they will compete;
- the services with which they will compete now and in the future;

- their competitors' objectives, strengths and weaknesses, performance and strategies;
- changes in the market place and market space, that includes emerging technology directions;
- their customers' own business objectives and strategies; and
- how they will best deliver their services into the future.

Strategic marketing as part of the strategic management process of organizations provides this understanding. Strategies are developed that ensure viable market positions and programmes for the survival and success of the information service. Strategic marketing has been defined by Kotler et al. (1980, p. 56) as 'a managerial process of analysing market opportunities and choosing market positions, programs and controls that create and support viable businesses that serve the organization's purposes and objectives'.

The marketing management process

Kotler (1999, p. 30) has identified five basic steps in the marketing management process that can be represented as:

$$R \Rightarrow STP \Rightarrow MM \Rightarrow I \Rightarrow C$$

Where:

R = Research (i.e. market research)

STP = Segmentation, targeting and positioning

MM = Marketing mix (popularly known as the four P's, i.e. product, price, place and promotion)

I = Implementation

C = Control (getting feedback, evaluating results and revising or improving STP strategy and MM tactics).

RESEARCH

The strategic marketing process builds upon the information already obtained through the strategic audit undertaken during the strategic planning process. This includes information about the present and future environment, stakeholders, the external and internal environment, mission, programmes, and performance evaluation and review. Additional information relating to markets, customers and the resources is gathered by researching:

- the primary market for the information service;
- the major market segments in this market;
- the needs of each market segment;
- market awareness and attitude to the information service;
- how potential customers learn about the information service and make decisions to use its services;
- customer satisfaction levels;
- the major strengths and weaknesses in staff, resources, programmes, facilities, etc.;
- opportunities to increase resources;
- key customer groups of the information service;

- key customer needs to be satisfied;
- the market segments to focus on;
- major competitors; and
- the competitive benefits that can be offered to the target market through market positioning.

A SWOT analysis can also be used during this process to identify new opportunities that are in line with the objectives of the service. Other analysis tools that can be used to gather information include needs analysis, image analysis and customer satisfaction studies.

Proposed opportunities for information services are then analysed by considering market segmentations, the size and growth rate of the customer base, consumer behaviours, possible exit barriers and some forms of measuring and forecasting the attractiveness and effectiveness of the services in the future.

A new service or market opportunity is attractive if:

- it is of good size – that is, if many people would use the service;
- it has the potential for growth;
- it is cost beneficial on both a short-term and long-term basis;
- there are adequate financial and technical resources and a competent and trained staff;
- there are low exit barriers; and
- the service is in line with the information service's mission and objectives.

It may be the case that an opportunity satisfies most of these criteria, but that it has to remain dormant until financial resources or technical solutions can be found or staff trained to provide the service.

The target market, that is the particular group(s) to which the service is aimed, needs to be identified. This is followed by a process of competitive positioning. This involves researching competitors' services and the needs of the target market in order to find a market or market niche. This determines whether the information service is in a strong or weak competitive position, whether the programme is attractive and whether there is high or low alternative coverage.

Once a target market has been defined and the service's competitive position determined, a market strategy is devised. This includes the development of the marketing goals and objectives. Goals may include such aspects as increasing the quality of the information service, its participation level, or its satisfaction level. Funds need to be allocated to the marketing budget. New services that are designed to meet new markets should have the important values explained to staff before commencing the service.

Finally the market strategy is implemented and controls put into place to ensure that the information service's resources, service and objectives are correctly matched to the right markets.

MARKET SEGMENTATION

A market is a set of individuals, groups or institutions that are actual or potential customers for a product or service. Markets can be divided into groups with specific requirements; this is called market segmentation. In information services there are need markets, geographic markets, product markets and demographic markets.

Need markets

Need markets consist of individuals or groups who have similar or common needs or are seeking similar benefits. Information services are challenged with customizing services and meeting a diverse range of customer demands for services that cannot be met in a cost-effective manner through single solutions. By grouping people with similar needs, services can be more effectively planned with some level of individual customization. For example, within a public library the need market for a homebound service would be the frail, the physically impaired, those people who are convalescing at home after surgery or hospitalization, young and old patients with terminal illnesses who are living at home, elderly people who can no longer drive and for whom public transport to the information service is inaccessible, and others who would benefit for some reason to have the library service come to them. In corporate environments, customers expect quite different services to the housebound service mentioned above. Their needs include access to web services, electronic mail and enterprise collaboration tools, information in varying formats (such as electronic and printed information), personal computer and information and communications technology (ICT) systems support, and electronic document and records management services. Within these needs, as Kotler (1999, p. 26) indicates, 'there are buyers who seek a low price, others who seek high product quality, and still others who seek excellent service'.

Geographic markets

Whilst globalization and the ubiquitous use of information and communications technologies have created a worldwide footprint in the provision of information services, local or geographic markets still need consideration in planning and designing services. Geographic markets consist of those customers who live or work in a region or a particular geographic locality. Geographic markets determine the type, size and setting of the information service together with the operating hours and services offered. For example, residents living in outer metropolitan areas and who spend long hours commuting may require the public library to be open at later hours than those operating in the inner city. However, the dense population of inner cities may place more intensive demands on the service than those of outer metropolitan areas or semi-rural localities. Rural areas having isolated pockets of population may be best served by a mobile library service.

Information services serving organizations that have branch offices situated in regions or states need to consider the specific requirements of each location and develop their services accordingly. Each market has its own particular characteristics. Using the public library example, the need market for a housebound service differs from that of a geographical market requiring a mobile library service. Whilst each is served by a 'library on wheels' the library services offered to the housebound differ from those offered to people using the mobile library. This is in terms of the time, length and frequency of visits, and choice and format of material.

Product markets

Product markets are determined by a demand for a particular product or service. A product market may be those people who have a demand for remote access to electronic information services because they work away from the office. This market could be further segmented according to specific scientific or technical information requirements such as spatial information being required by field geologists.

Demographic markets

Demographic market segmentation is one of the most popular methods of distinguishing market segments in information services. These market segments have clear market needs, and information relating to these markets is usually readily available. Demographic markets may be identified by age, nationality, or physical needs such as the physically impaired, who may need specialized equipment such as large computer screens or ramp access.

CUSTOMIZING SERVICES TO MEET MARKET SEGMENTS

Markets that can be subdivided into identifiable segments or subsets may require individual marketing strategies. The information services manager should be aware of their:

* market segments' current and potential future size;
* major customers and potential customers, and their locations;
* customers' and potential customers' current levels of awareness of the range and levels of existing services;
* customers' needs and motives for using the services; and
* customers' concepts of competitive alternatives to the information service.

The strength in the market segmentation approach lies in the fact that it is based upon the customer rather than the product or service. The customer is assured of a service that satisfies as far as possible their individual needs rather than a mass-market offering. This is in line with the societal marketing concept. Such an example can be seen in a weekly storytelling session for preschool children in a public library. The session may satisfy many needs, some of which may not have been foremost in the library staff's minds when they proposed the service, but which exist all the same. These could be a need for an only child to socialize with others of its age group; a need to provide the beginnings of a lifelong association with information and the library; a need to begin the learning process through books and stories; a need for a baby sitting service; a need for the parent to get out of the house and talk to other parents; a need to promote the library to children of all ages; or a need for recreational activities. In this example, the storytelling session satisfies up to seven diverse needs of parents, library staff and preschool children.

MARKET TARGETING

Market targeting involves the evaluation, selection and concentration on specific market segments. There are three strategies for doing this: undifferentiated marketing, differentiated marketing and concentrated marketing.

Undifferentiated marketing

In undifferentiated or mass marketing the information service focuses upon the needs that are common to all people. Services are provided that appeal to the broadest number of customers. In concentrating on these basic services, the information service attempts to achieve excellence.

Undifferentiated marketing is often pursued in times of financial constraint, when additional or specialist services are curtailed, and basic services consolidated. Costs associated with providing specialist services can be saved, but whether this is an effective strategy is debatable.

Differentiated marketing

In differentiated marketing the information service decides to operate in at least two segments of a market and designs separate services and programmes for each. In a large corporate organization this could mean differentiating services to research and development staff and to executive management. A variety of programmes to suit the diverse needs of different information service customers is provided. The aim of this approach is to provide services catering for specific needs that strengthen the information service's overall identity within the organization and increase its use. However, there are costs associated with this. Specialist services may involve additional staff with specialized skills and expertise, administrative and promotional costs.

In differentiated marketing some information services may be heavily promoted, these are called saturate segments. Others may be designated as hold segments. In this case services are offered but not heavily promoted.

Concentrated marketing

Concentrated or niche marketing occurs when the information service concentrates upon a small number of submarkets. Instead of spreading itself thinly, being all things to all people, the information service provides in-depth services in a few areas, serving a smaller percentage of the market place. It purposely determines a small number of target markets and sets out to concentrate on these. As a result, it achieves a strong market position through its detailed knowledge of its market segments' needs and its subsequent reputation.

A concentrated marketing strategy may also be used when establishing a new information service. After determining several target markets and having regard for financial resources and the level of staff expertise, it may be considered prudent to concentrate upon providing a few market segments with a quality service, rather than to spread the market base too thinly.

The establishment of a new information service requires procedures to be put into place, staff to be trained, policies and routines to be established. These initial activities are time and energy consuming. If too wide a market base is selected in the initial establishment phase, it may be difficult to provide a high-quality service. As an initial favourable impression is critical to the future of the information service, quality rather than quantity becomes a factor in service provision. Later, when all operations are running smoothly, a decision can be made on whether to broaden the service or product base. This called a segment 'roll out' strategy.

No one strategy is superior to the others. In adopting a particular target strategy, the information services manager must base their decision upon the type of information service; the financial, technical, human and information resources available; the availability of competitive services; customer and potential customer needs, and the types of services having the potential to be offered. The information services manager must then decide which strategy is the most attractive given the constraints and opportunities of the information service's external environment, and its own strengths and weaknesses.

MARKETING MIX

A marketing mix is a key part of the marketing strategy. A four-factor classification called 'the four Ps' has been defined by McCarthy (1971, p. 44). These are product, price, place and promotion.

- product – refers to the quality, design, features and branding of information services and involves the special features offered, the way they are offered and level of service provision. The driving force is customer value;
- price – relates to whether a direct fee is attached to the service such as a debit to the cost centre or payment for an online search or a photocopy. There may be price modifiers such as discounts or community service obligation allowances. The driving force is the cost to the customer;
- place – concerns the logistical provision of the service, coverage and locations of service points in the market place and multi-channel management in the market space. The driving force is customer convenience; and
- promotion – involves the advertising and publicity campaigns, the message communicated, the media used and the timing of such. Promotional campaigns should be realistic and affordable. The driving force is the preferred means of communication to the customer.

Kotler (1999, p. 95) suggests the addition of two more Ps that are becoming important, especially in global marketing. They are:

- politics – political activity such as laws or trade embargos; and
- public opinion – new moods and attitudes that can affect their interest in certain products and services.

IMPLEMENTATION

Having completed the strategic planning component of marketing, the information service must determine how products and services will be distributed and promoted. This will include choice of delivery channels that are considered in full in the chapter on ensuring service quality.

CONTROL

Customer satisfaction studies

Customer satisfaction studies provide an indication as to whether existing information service customers are satisfied with current services. Customer satisfaction studies are a marketing tool as they can be used as an argument to maintain existing funding levels if the results are good, or for increased funding if the results show that customer expectations for services are higher than those provided.

The results of the customer satisfaction study can be plotted onto the matrix graph according to their performance rating and importance (see Figure 29.1). This will determine which services need improved performance and which services should be discontinued. Services falling in quadrant A are important services that are being well provided. Services in quadrant B have possibly too high a performance level for their importance. The information service staff can afford to pay less attention to these services.

	Low-level performance	Level of performance in service offering	High-level performance
Extremely important		**D.** Service is important / Level of performance is low / Information service needs to concentrate on services in this area	**A.** Level of performance is high / Service is important / Information service should maintain current position
Importance of service		**C.** Low priority / Service fair / Service may be abandoned	**B.** Service is less important / Level of performance is high – possible overkill / Information service can afford to pay less attention to these services
Less important			

Figure 29.1   Matrix graph to determine services

Services that fall into quadrant C have only a low priority and performance is deemed as low. These services can be the first to be abandoned if resources are few, in order to concentrate on those services in quadrant D. Quadrant D includes those services that are acknowledged to be important, but where the information service is performing badly. This is the area where resources need to be concentrated.

Exchange system analysis

Underlying the marketing concept is a system of exchange. The potential for exchange exists when two or more parties possess something of value that may be exchanged. This may be goods, services, money, a favour or goodwill. The simplest exchange is between two parties, and such an exchange may be seen in a public library where a customer exchanges money for access to a computer. Government departments may provide information services in exchange for monies received from rates and taxes. There is no direct exchange between the customer and the department as the rates or taxes that fund the service are paid to the revenue collecting agency of the government in power. Information service staff also exchange their knowledge and expertise, time and energy in return for salaries and other fringe benefits from the employing organization.

Multiple-party exchanges occur when three or more parties are involved in exchanging something of value. In the case of the storytelling session example in the public library, the parents require that their children meet others of the same age, engage in a learning process and be happy. They are exchanging their time for social and educational processes for their children. They also require that the library staff are friendly and that the library is clean and safe. In this instance they are exchanging monies paid in rates for services and safety. The children who attend want to have fun, maybe learn something and therefore obtain their parents' approval. They are exchanging their time for their parent's love and acceptance. The public library, in holding the storytelling sessions, wishes to promote the library as a fun place and as a life-long institution for information and self-education. The storytelling session must meet all of these needs in the exchange process.

Competitive portfolio analysis

The product life cycle and the product portfolio matrix are used to make strategic marketing decisions as part of the competitive portfolio analysis. Whilst they are based upon products rather than services, their general concepts can be used to distinguish which services have potential for growth and which are at the end of their useful life. In addition to ensuring that the information services remain current, knowledge of the growth and decline of services affect tasks and activities, budget allocations, technology use, staff levels and the future direction of the information service.

PRODUCT LIFE CYCLE

The product life cycle is based upon the concept that products or services, like living things, have a finite life span. The basic proposition is that market growth and competitive characteristics change from one stage of the product life cycle to the next. These changes have important implications for marketing and planning strategies.

The introductory stage of an information service is usually marked by slow growth in use, heavy advertising and promotion. Staff must develop the service to suit customer needs, and much enthusiasm is needed. In the growth stage, there is an increase in use of the service that is still promoted quite heavily, and staff may have to finetune the service further to suit customer needs. The maturity stage is characterized by such services being seen as standard, a slowdown in growth and the spending of less time and money on advertising. In the decline stage, fewer people use the service, it is often superseded by other more appropriate services or deemed to have a low priority and plans are made to terminate it. Information technology shortens the life cycles of information services with many services quickly becoming obsolete as new applications emerge.

The life cycle concept has some drawbacks. Sometimes the stages in the life cycle cannot be clearly separated and may be difficult to distinguish. For information services, the maturity stage is the dominant stage and most services fall into this category. It is often difficult to predict when the next stage of the life cycle begins or how long it will last. Rejuvenation strategies may be used to stop the decline in the life cycle.

PRODUCT PORTFOLIO MATRIX

Whilst the product-service life cycle focuses upon growth dynamics, the product portfolio matrix emphasized market growth (attractiveness) and relative competitive position (strength) of products or services. As information services become more competitive the significance of the product (service) portfolio matrix increases.

The most widely used matrix is that developed by the Boston Consulting Group. Known as the BCG portfolio matrix, it classifies each business unit according to its potential for growth and its relative competitive position. In the information service, work units may be substituted for business units. The BCG matrix classifies products, services or markets into four groups and uses circles, with areas proportional to the sales volumes for each, to give a visual image of an organization's current products. In information services, usage rates could be substituted for sales volumes to provide an image of its current services (see Figure 29.2).

According to the BCG matrix, products that have a high market share and high growth (stars) are roughly self-sufficient in terms of cash flow. They have the highest profit margins. These are the important information products or services and should be expanded if possible. Eventually the 'stars' become 'cash cows' as they reach the maturity stage of the product or service.

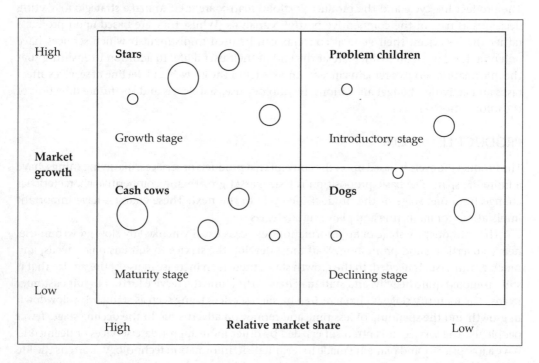

Figure 29.2 The Boston Consulting Group portfolio matrix

'Cash cows' are valuable assets; they have a high share in a low growth market. As products they generate more cash than is necessary to maintain a market position and should be protected at all costs. In information services, 'cash cows' would equate to the established products or services that have a high rate of usage and little competition. 'Cash cow' services maintain the value image of the information service and help to ensure its continued success and survival.

'Dogs' are products with low market share and slow growth. Their outlook for the future is usually bleak. 'Dogs' in information services comprise the information products or services that are declining in use and can often be superseded by new and better services. Alternatively, they are services that have failed to reach their potential.

'Problem children' are products with high growth potential but low market share. They require large net cash outflows if their market share is to be maintained or increased. If successful these products become the new 'stars' that in the future become 'cash cows'. If unsuccessful they become 'dogs'. In information services, 'problem children' usually equate to new services that require fairly large funding allocations for their establishment and promotion. They may also be services that do not perform well. There can be a variety of reasons for their poor performance; they may have been inadequately managed, or have had inappropriate marketing strategies applied to them.

The information service can determine its information products' and services' use and standing by displaying these on the product portfolio matrix. They should also be linked to the product or service life cycle and its associated marketing and planning strategies.

The BCG matrix is useful in that it recognizes that products and services have differential growth rates and emphasizes the relative share of market held by products and services in the same stage of growth.

USE OF THE COMPETITIVE PORTFOLIO ANALYSIS IN MANAGING LIBRARY STOCK

The BCG portfolio matrix is an important tool for assessing the quality of stock in a library or information centre. 'Best sellers' are 'stars'. They become 'cash cows' when their original price has been justified by their large issue rate, by their use in strategic decision making or when their presence creates an image of the library or information centre having good, current stock. 'Dogs' are stock that no one wants. All libraries and information centres have some 'dogs'; the result of a mistake in stock selection, when the market for an item has been misjudged, or the blurb was misleading. 'Problem children' comprise the stock that contains valuable information but is often overlooked by customers or library staff because of format, appearance, or lack of knowledge of the contents. 'Problem children' stock can become 'stars' through education of library staff or promotions that draw attention to such stock in interesting ways. If left alone they become 'dogs'.

Diversification and service rejuvenation

There comes a time when it appears that an information service can no longer expand its services in its basic market. Growth has stabilized through the market being saturated and, if growth is to continue, new services or markets must be sought. The information service has four options at this stage:

- to remain in a stable situation and to accept the status quo;
- to look for new markets;
- to diversify into new areas; or
- to provide new services to its existing markets.

Changes in consumer behaviour, competitor behaviour, technology or government policies may also influence the information service to adopt one of the above strategies. Rejuvenation strategies can overcome some lack of use of services, or, stop the decline in the product life cycle. Lazer et al. (1984, pp. 21–8) have identified four rejuvenation strategies:

- recapturing strategies – attempts to revive the old market by concentrating on previous and existing customers without modifying the service, for example using displays and promotions that focus attention on existing services;
- redesigning strategies – marketing a modified version of a service that has been declining or has previously been abandoned. The original reasons for customer rejection may no

longer prevail and it may be possible to rekindle interest among present customers, such as releasing a classic film on DVDs;

- recasting strategies – marketing a modified service to new customers, where the object is to capitalize on existing strengths and experience, although some adjustments to the service and market have to take place. For example recasting storytelling sessions in public libraries from being aimed at preschoolers to being used as bibliotherapy with the aged; and

- refocusing strategies – marketing an abandoned or declining service to new customers. For example marketing an archive or local history collection, which may have been established through legislation or demand for school project material, to the local newspaper for a series of articles on local identities or places of interest. Such a strategy may result in greater usage of the service by the general public.

The information service's decision to rejuvenate or diversify services should be based upon its resource requirements and capabilities. The potential of the rejuvenated or diversified services to contribute to the profile and value of the information service, the cost involved and predicted extended life span on a cost-benefit basis must also be assessed. In selecting the most appropriate strategy, the extent of service modification and degree of marketing effort needed to stimulate demand need to be evaluated.

Using competitive intelligence

Competitive intelligence supports management's role in managing customers, competition and change in order for the information service and its parent organization to remain competitive in its environment. It:

- provides an early warning of developments in the external environment, in particular the industry, technology, economic or legislative change, that could adversely affect the business success of the organization;

- identifies new product, process or collaborative opportunities to create new markets and business opportunities; and

- creates an early understanding of the competitive environment so that surprises can be eliminated or their impact lessened by allowing a longer time and better opportunity to respond.

Competitive intelligence gathering is not spying or undertaking industrial espionage. Good intelligence gathering is based on information that can be obtained from sources through legal and ethical means. Published sources of competitive information include information on web pages, trade publications (electronic and hard copy), market analysts' reports, aerial photographs, job advertisements, government reports and filings. Other information can be obtained through the continuous monitoring and surveillance of competitor actions for key events or changes, the following of leads, checking of sources and the surfacing of ideas. The art is in knowing what information is relevant, where to find it legally and how to convert it into intelligence for the basis of future management decisions and actions.

Competitive intelligence involves obtaining information about:

- which competitors are vulnerable;

- which competitors are likely to make moves that could endanger the organization's position in the market; and
- the requirements of the competitor's customers.

Breeding (2000) identified several problems that users of competitive intelligence (CI) have with the information that they receive from the process. These include shallowness, credibility, timeliness, focus, providers, quantity, and information sharing. Breeding goes on to say that

> *if CI providers are consulted late in the decision making process, shallow and poorly focused information is often the result. If sufficient time is not taken for analysis then the reports are often information-based rather than intelligence-based. In addition, the sheer quantity of information contained within the reports often overwhelms the reader.*

Customer relationship management

Customer relationship management (CRM) has been variously described as a corporate philosophy, strategy or tool. The objective is to focus on and learn more about customers' needs and behaviours in order to develop stronger relationships with them. It helps organizations use ICT and people's knowledge to gain insight into the behaviours of customers and the value of those customers, and builds on the marketing strategies previously discussed. CRM brings together information about customers, sales, marketing effectiveness, responsiveness and market trends and enables the information service to:

- provide a better customer service;
- enable a better overall customer experience;
- understand how customers define quality;
- identify potential problems quickly, and correct service deficiencies before major problems occur;
- make multi-service channels more efficient;
- introduce and cross-sell information services and products more effectively;
- simplify marketing and service processes;
- discover more customers; and
- increase customer use of information services and products.

To be beneficial, the CRM strategy needs to be thought through, so that it does not result in a flood of unorganized, ad hoc information. It should be given a business rather than an ICT focus. The information service needs to decide the business objective for needing insight into the behaviours of customers and the value of those customers, what kind of customer information is required, where the data and information are captured and stored, and how they will be used. Business objectives might be to improve customer support, to increase service performance or to improve the marketing effectiveness of the information service. The information service should also learn how to use the information to develop and prioritize tailored customer offerings.

Sources of information will be found in all of the multi-service channels, i.e. mobile, websites, portals, shop fronts, call centres, fax services and include information collected on:

- responses to advertising campaigns;

- transactions data, e.g. multiple-channel analysis of fax, web, face-to-face, kiosk services, letters, phone;
- account information;
- customer service and support data, e.g. service requests, complaints, information returns; and
- demographic data, e.g. usage habits.

It is important that a complete 360-degree picture of the customer or potential customer is built up, with everyone that interfaces with the customer being trained and confident in adding to, analysing and using the CRM data, as well as understanding its value and use as a business intelligence tool.

Conclusion

Marketing is often mistaken for promotion. Marketing includes consideration of promotion strategies but it is more closely aligned to strategic planning. Marketing strategies ensure viable market positions and programs that meet the objectives of the parent organization, customer information needs and ultimately, contribute to the success of the information service.

Marketing strategies and customer relationship management tools enable the information service to prioritize and make informed decisions about the continuation of existing services and proposals for new or extended services. The bottom line considerations in this decision-making process are the business fit, customer needs and long-term sustainability. Any proposals for new services or extending existing services to new markets must be in line with the information service's objectives. Sufficient expertise, human, technical and financial resources should be available to support such services.

References

Breeding, B. (2000), 'CI and KM convergence: A case study at Shell Services International', *Competitive Intelligence Review*, vol. 11, no. 4, pp. 12–24.

Kotler, Philip (1999), *Kotler on marketing: How to create, win and dominate markets*, London, UK: Simon & Schuster.

Kotler, P., FitzRoy, P. and Shaw, R. (1980), *Australian marketing management*, Sydney, Aus: Prentice Hall.

Lazer, W., Luqmani, M. and Quraeshi, Z. (1984), 'Product rejuvenation strategies', *Business Horizons*, Nov.–Dec., pp. 21–8.

McCarthy, E.J. (1971), *Basic Marketing: a managerial approach*, 4th edn, Homewood, IL: Irwin.

Further reading

Adeyoyin, Samuel Olu (2005), 'Strategic planning for marketing library services', *Library Management*, vol. 26, no. 8/9, pp. 494–508.

Calvert, Philip and Pope, Adam, (2005), 'Telephone survey research for library managers', *Library Management*, vol. 26, no. 3, pp. 139–52.

Cook, Sarah (2004), *Measuring customer service effectiveness*, Aldershot, UK: Ashgate.

Hill, Nigel and Alexander, Jim (2000), *Handbook of customer satisfaction and loyalty measurement*, 2nd edn, Aldershot, UK: Gower.

Murphy, Christopher (2005), *Competitive intelligence: Gathering, analysing and putting it to work*, Aldershot, UK: Ashgate.

30 *Corporate Image*

The management of the information service's corporate image and selling the message and benefits of what the information can contribute and deliver is extremely important. For if the perceptions of the information service differ from reality then:

- the quality and value of the information service may be underestimated;
- the information service may be missing part of its market share; and
- the wrong impression of the service could be projected.

Image analysis is closely related to the issues discussed in the previous chapter. It assists in determining the information service's image to the funding and governing bodies, and its customers. This includes taking account of the image being portrayed in the market place and market space. As a result of the image analysis certain market strategies may need to be undertaken. In addition, the ability to create the right understanding of the value of the information service and manage the communication with the external environment is as important as managing the communication internally. For this is the essential mechanism of projecting and maintaining the importance and benefit of the organization in the eyes of key stakeholders.

Image analysis

Image studies measure the perceptions that people hold about an information service. They determine what people respond to, which may not necessarily be the same as what the information service really does. All information services need a positive image in order to attract funds, potential staff members and clients. However, the image differs according to particular groups, their main interests and the way in which they perceive the services offered. Senior management may view an information service according to its return on investment; which is often different to the clients who are the recipients of the services.

The information service's customers and stakeholders can have multiple attitudes, some of which will be positive, whilst others may be negative. There may also be a different image being projected in the traditional market place to that of the market space. Different sectors of the information service's community or target audience should be surveyed in order to determine its image and profile in terms of service provision. This includes surveying stakeholders, clients and non-clients regarding their attitudes and awareness, interest and desires in an effort to ascertain a spectrum of responses within each dimension. This can be done by asking simple questions about familiarity with services and how favourably the services are received. The survey questionnaire should indicate the sector of the target audience to which the respondent belongs so that an analysis can be made of the views of different client groups. The responses can then be plotted on an image matrix.

In the image matrix (Figure 30.1) quadrants B, C and D indicate the need for some development in the information service's image about the services offered. To do this, the information services manager needs to have a mental picture of what the image should be. This should be based on the strategic direction of the information service. This is then compared with the existing image of the information service. The image gap is the difference between the desired and actual images.

	B. Good position, but awareness of services is not high Information service needs to promote its activities	**A.** Good position Information service should seek to maintain this position
Favourable attitude		
Attitude towards the service	**D.** Bad position Information service needs to rebuild its image and increase its profile	**C.** Bad position Information service needs to rebuild its image and correct its profile
Unfavourable attitude		
	Low level of familiarity	**Familiarity with information service**	High level of familiarity

Figure 30.1 Matrix graph of information service's image

It may not be necessary to target all sectors of the target audience in trying to change the information service's image. The matrix graph identifies both those groups most in need of targeting and those groups for whom the information service's current image should be maintained in its present position. Changes in image may be to make the information service appear to be more efficient or relevant to corporate objectives, or more responsive to certain customer sectors. Alternatively, a sector of the client base may have unrealistic expectations of the types of services that should be offered. In which case this sector requires re-educating about the services that can be realistically delivered within the operational and budgetary framework. The reality–expectations gap is the difference between the level of an adequate service and the level of a service to meet real expectations.

Projecting the corporate image

An important aspect of the boundary-spanning role of the information services manager is to manage and project the corporate image. The corporate image is the set of beliefs, ideas and impressions that individuals have about an organization. Managing and projecting the corporate image comprises the following activities: identifying the target audience, determining the communication objectives, designing the message for both the market place and the market space, selecting the communication channels, allocating the budget, managing the process and measuring the results.

TARGET AUDIENCE

The target audience consists of the people or organizations towards which the information service needs to project a favourable image. This is with the objective of building an awareness of the services provided and increasing market share, ensuring the continuation of funds or simply communicating the image of a valued and quality service. The target audience for the information service can include all or any of the following; current and prospective customers, senior management in the parent organization, other information services, suppliers, professional bodies and other stakeholders.

DETERMINING THE COMMUNICATION OBJECTIVES

Having identified the target audience, it is important to establish how familiar the target audience is with all aspects of the information service as well as the value they place on it and the benefits they perceive arise out of it. This provides information for the image gap analysis, that is, the difference between the desired image that the information service wishes to project and the current image that it is projecting. It also identifies the gap between the target audience's awareness of the information services offered and those provided, and their perception of the quality of the information service as compared with that provided.

The next stage is to determine the required audience response in relation to the results of the image gap analysis. This may be to change the customers' attitude to the information service, to alert customers to services that could fill latent needs, to provide a better understanding of the benefits and opportunities presented by the information service, or to engender the understanding and support of senior management and other stakeholders to ensure that the information service continues to receive adequate financial support and conviction.

DESIGNING THE MESSAGE AND SELECTING THE COMMUNICATION CHANNELS

The aim is to design a positive message about the benefits and service offerings of the information service. There are many different messages and communication channels that can be used, including:

- web presence and other electronic media such as television;
  email or SMS messaging to those who wish to opt in to the service;
- personal communication, e.g. word of mouth recommendations, personal representation;
- print, e.g. a brochure or strategy report;

- oral, e.g. a description of the services that the information service offers being played whilst a person is 'on hold' on the telephone;
- multimedia or video presentation aimed at a particular audience; or
- advertisement in the local press or public area.

The choice and mix of the messages and communication channels will depend upon the purpose of the message and the target audience in both the market place and market space. Increasingly the need is towards an integrated approach to delivering the message across all communication channels, rather than planning the use of each communication channel separately.

In addition to the above, the physical surroundings of the information service will also create an atmosphere or image. The choice of colours, type of office furniture, wall decorations, floor coverings and spaciousness of the surroundings will communicate an image about the information service.

The house style of the information service's reports and stationery also communicate a corporate image. The house style should also be continued and included in any multimedia presentations and other information published in electronic form.

Colour and style in the physical surroundings and in the house style are also important. Colour exerts a powerful influence on the mind and emotions. Each colour has a symbology of its own:

- red – energy and vitality;
- orange – excitement, creativity, self-confidence;
- yellow – clarity;
- green – balance and harmony, wealth; and
- blue – power.

The way in which information service staff interact with customers and stakeholders will also project an image of the information service. The image conveyed should be friendly, welcoming and helpful, although in some environments a more formal approach may be necessary. Interaction includes the way in which individuals answer the telephone, and the articulation and wording of the greeting on the telephone answering machine. If music (rather than information about the information service) is used for the 'on hold' interval whilst people are waiting on the telephone, the choice of music will influence the person's perception of the information service.

ALLOCATING THE BUDGET

Not all of the strategies for managing and promoting the information service's image cost money. A proportion of the image promotion rests with the information services manager and their staff projecting a positive image and 'selling' the service in their interaction with customers, senior management and other stakeholders. Budget allocation for the more formal mechanisms of promoting the information service's image should be based upon the specific objectives, the tasks to be performed to achieve the objectives, and the costs of performing the tasks.

MANAGING THE PROCESS

The wide range of communication tools and messages make it imperative that these be coordinated to ensure consistency. Coordination is also required to ensure that the correct message is sent through the correct medium and communication channel to reach the correct target audience.

MEASURING RESULTS

To measure the results of the promotion, the information services manager will require feedback from the target audience. This will involve talking to or surveying the target audience about how they feel about the service, what level of awareness they have of the information service, and any other information that provides feedback on the communication objective.

Branding

Branding is associated with image building, market positioning and creating a value proposition. Kotler (1999, p. 55) identifies the main steps in developing a strong brand:

- develop the value proposition – by choosing a broad positioning, specific positioning, value positioning, or the total value proposition for the product or service; and
- build the brand – by choosing a brand name, developing rich associations and promises for the brand name, and manage all the customers' brand contacts so that they meet or exceed the customers' expectations associated with the brand.

Kotler (1999, p. 58) identifies sources for positioning that can be used:

- attribute positioning – using a special feature such as national library or archive service, or a website dedicated to a specific purpose or campaign;
- benefits positioning – offering a specific benefit such as extended opening hours;
- use/application positioning – the product or service is positioned as the best in a certain application such as a national collection of indigenous art, culture, literature, etc.;
- user positioning – the product or service is positioned in terms of a target user group such as a specific information service to scientists or a patient care information system for health professionals;
- competitor positioning – the product or service suggests its superiority or difference from a competitor's product such as 'service is our strength' or 'the emotionally intelligent organization'; and
- quality/price positioning – the product or service is positioned at a certain quality and price level such as free lending services in public libraries.

Brand names carry associations. Kotler (1999, p. 64) suggests that they should:

- suggest something about the product or service's benefits;
- suggest product or service qualities such as action or colour;
- be easy to pronounce, recognize and remember;
- be distinctive; and

- should not carry poor meanings in other countries, languages and cultures.

Kotler (1999, p. 65) also indicates that brand names should communicate meaning in order to build a rich set of associations for the brand. These can include:

- the ability to trigger in the customer's mind certain attributes or qualities;
- the suggestion of benefits, not just features;
- connoting values that the organization holds dear;
- exhibiting personality traits; and
- suggestions of the kinds of people who may buy or use the brand.

Brands can be strengthened or projected through the use of a symbol, slogan or colour.

Other corporate communications

ANNUAL REPORTS

At the end of the calendar or financial year, managers are often required to produce an annual report for the information service or provide copy for the parent organization's annual report. Sometimes they need to do both. The annual report serves several purposes. It can be used:

- to provide an account of the information service's activities for the year;
- to achieve a better understanding of the value, issues, benefits and opportunities presented by the information service;
- as a source of information about the information service. It may contain information about key managerial positions, holders of such positions and their qualifications, an organizational chart, mission statement and corporate objectives;
- as a source of information for benchmarking or comparative purposes, as it often contains statistical data;
- as a public relations exercise in that the achievements of the year are reported;
- to account for the use of resources;
- to highlight problems that prevent the information service from carrying out all of its activities;
- to reconcile the use of funds, staff, etc. (inputs) against activities (outputs); and
- to measure the organization's level of performance.

Annual reports are posted to the Internet and therefore available to other related organizations. The format, design and presentation of the report either electronically or as hard copy are powerful mechanisms to project the information service's image. It will send a message about the organization's culture and its willingness to make an impressionable image on stakeholders. For example, some organizations' annual reports are flamboyant or sophisticated and considerable prestige is attached to their contents and format. Others are very formal. Some are very plain as they are only seen as an operational requirement to report on activities once a year.

SUBMISSIONS TO OUTSIDE BODIES

Managers and in-house specialists may also draft submissions to government bodies and other organizations relating to external issues. These submissions can be either reactive to external impacts on their services or functions, or proactive in terms of positioning the information service or its parent organization in the external environment. Examples are a submission on the implications of proposed changes to copyright legislation or a submission that suggests new ways of providing electronic services to the community.

The information services manager, or their staff, will usually draft the submission on behalf of the parent organization. In this case, the submission may need to be ratified by senior management before being forwarded to the appropriate body.

Conclusion

Managing the corporate image of the information service is a vital leadership role, as perceptions of service availability and delivery are as important as reality. The ability to communicate the desired message and obtain information from the external environment is of equal importance to the ability to communicate and obtain information within the organization. Image studies assist in identifying and managing perceptions of stakeholders.

References

Kotler, Philip (1999), *Kotler on marketing: How to create, win and dominate markets*, London, UK: Simon & Schuster.

Further reading

Carter-Silk, Alex (2005), *Brand protection: Understanding and managing threats to your brand*, Aldershot, UK: Ashgate.

Hannington, Terry (2004), *How to measure and manage your corporate reputation*, Aldershot, UK: Ashgate.

Thompson, Marjorie and Whates, Peter (2005), *Communicating corporate social responsibility*, Aldershot, UK: Ashgate.

31 *Ensuring Service Quality*

Service quality in the design and delivery of the service or product is an excellent way to differentiate an organization's offerings and competitively position it as a leader in both the market place and market space. However, design and delivery are only part of the equation. Ensuring that the service support programmes encourage the continual use of the service or product is of equal importance, particularly in relation to customer retention. Maintaining market position is also essential and the information service should consistently offer high-quality, customer-focused services or products that meet current and emerging needs as well as presenting choices in the delivery of these services or products through a multi-channel approach. The emphasis in all of the above being on the customer, rather than on the products or services.

Information services are in the business of delivering services to customers who are already exposed to retail and business experiences that offer seamless, ongoing and personalized interactions in an always on, anywhere, any time world. These retail and business experiences increase the expectations of what can be delivered. In this connected world, information and communications technology (ICT) can be used to enhance the relationship between the information service and the customer. It can be used to deliver the multi-channel approach and new business advantages that enhance customer relationships through the use of value added services.

An important component of quality is to get the steps in the value chain, right first time every time. If any part of the process falls down, then the remaining processes in the value chain will build upon an inferior product or service. Differentiation at the end of the value chain can be what distinguishes one product or service from another in terms of quality.

Customer expectations and perceptions of quality often vary as this is based upon an individual judgment, so the manager must understand both their customer needs and perceptions of quality. There are also cultural differences in customer expectations and perceptions of quality, which impact on the service delivery. Gaps in service delivery can influence the perception of the level of quality offered in products or services. Customers also judge quality according to certain determinants of service quality.

Management oversight – roles and responsibilities

The bottom line of the customer-focused approach is valuing the customer. This service philosophy is reinforced through management fostering a culture that is service driven and oriented to customer needs. It is incumbent on senior management demonstrating a commitment to quality by making it a self-sustaining way of life within the organization.

Quality control should be a regular item on the agenda of senior management meetings. This serves two purposes. It sends a message about the level of senior management commitment to quality and the value that it places on quality goods and services. It also allows senior management to review progress and evaluate performance. The agenda items should cover customer and stakeholder relationships, a review of quality initiatives and programmes, identification of service delivery gaps and the strategies to close these, and a general evaluation of the current levels of service delivery.

The information services manager needs to target customer requirements in terms of quality information products and services and set realistic expectations of the choice of channels and services at levels that can be achieved. In the drive for efficiency, there is often the temptation to put choices and quality specifications in second place. This is false economy.

All employees should be given responsibility for quality and be made accountable for the quality of their individual output. They should be aware of the products, services and channels offered by the information service and its parent organization, and make an effort to understand their customers' needs. Individuals should be given training and skills development opportunities in quality management, measuring customer satisfaction and in any additional areas that may be needed to improve the service they deliver.

Meeting customer expectations and perceptions

To be in tune with customer needs and what they value in terms of choice and type of service requires the ability to listen to customers, to identify their requirements, and to suggest improvements for current information products and services. It is also important to maintain a total service focus in meeting the needs of the customer as this can be important in creating a win-win situation. The total service focus makes it easier and more efficient for the customer as they have to deal with fewer organizations; it also lessens the interface between competitive entities and the customer, resulting in a significant business advantage to the service provider.

MEETING EXPECTATIONS OF QUALITY

Customer expectations and perceptions of quality often vary as this is based upon an individual judgment. Quality control is an internal process management issue, being an important part of the value chain. However, it is judged externally by customers and stakeholders who only see the outputs or outcomes of the internal processes. For example, quality is judged in terms of:

- timeliness of service delivery – in responding to requests for information, files, helpdesk queries or the ordering and supply of new equipment;
- a well-designed product or service – that fits the purpose for use and is superior to others in the market place and market space;
- a product that does not break down or a service that is not suspended and which is easy to use;
- value for money; and
- courteous, knowledgeable and accurate staff who know their products and services.

Expectations and perceptions of quality can also differ from a cultural viewpoint. For example:

- in Germany, the dominant element of quality is an acceptance of standards;
- in Japan, quality is measured through the pursuit of perfection;
- in France, quality is viewed as luxury;

- in the United States of America, quality means 'it works'; and
- in Australia, quality is found in the relationship between the customer and the provider of the product or service.

As a consequence, the delivery of information services may subtly differ between countries in the quest for a quality service or information product.

MEETING EXPECTATIONS OF CHOICE

Customers of information services vary, which is why having choices in service delivery is important. For example, the customers of a public library will be a cross-section of people who vary in age, interests and lifestyle. They may include local business entities, schoolchildren and tertiary students, the aged and those whose primary language is not English. The staff and elected members of the local authority may also be customers of the library. To meet these divergent interests, multiple services and choices in delivery channels will be necessary.

The primary customers of an information service in a small entrepreneurial organization will be the management and employees of the organization. The information service will manage the information systems, keep the corporate records and deliver research services in such a manner so as to assist the management and employees maintain the parent organization's competitiveness. A secondary role may be to disseminate information about the organization's products to the external customers of the entrepreneurial organization. Immediacy and creativity in service delivery will be important for the service to be responsive to the young and innovative corporate environment.

Ensuring service quality based on expectations of choice requires considerations of customer:

- reach – numbers of people to be served and location, geographic dispersement, reliability and ease of access to technology, e.g. broadband and the Internet;
- demographics – language and cultural differences, stage of life that may influence the design and numbers of service channels offered;
- frequency of interactions – average size and duration of interaction;
- expectations – convenience and speed, customer habits, preferred mode of interaction; and
- skills and capabilities – familiarity with services, ability to learn new ways of accessing services, need for personal support and advice.

MEETING EXPECTATIONS OF NEED

The availability of multiple service delivery channels means that libraries and information services can start to tailor services according to each service delivery channel in a manner that can further meet the customers' expectations and needs. To do so requires a knowledge of how people with different needs communicate and use different channels; with the view to designing the channels to meet the method of communication, needs and activities. Figure 31.1 explains how different needs and activities can be met through various channel types.

Need	Activity	Channel type
I just want to do it	Transactions, order, renew, access information	Web services, email, SMS, key pad/ touch phone transactions
How do I do it	Immediate assistance, quick answers	Call centres, frequently asked questions (FAQ), web services
Relate to me	In-depth discussion, knowledgeable advice	Over the counter service, phone calls

Figure 31.1 Meeting needs and activities through different channel types

Designing a multi-channel service

In acknowledgment of the diversity of customer demographics, expectations and needs, organizations are embracing a multi-channel approach to service delivery. ICT is also driving this approach in that its ubiquitous presence is increasing customer anticipations of service offerings across multi-access channels. For example, a large proportion of the Generation X and Y population now use mobile devices as the preferred or only means of communication. This always on, instantaneous, anywhere, any time environment has implications for not just designing services to meet the small screen environment, but also in terms of responsiveness to enquiries. For example, whilst email conventions consider a twenty-four-hour response time as acceptable practice, short messaging service (SMS) conventions have expectations of an immediate response.

Designing and implementing a multi-channel strategy is quite complex, so it is essential to have an effective change management plan to engage stakeholders and drive long-term behavioural changes. The costs and benefits of a multi-channel approach can be difficult to calculate, especially if there is seen to be duplication of services. The key is to design the strategy around well-defined customer groups and transaction volume and complexity, rather than the products or services. This means having a well-defined customer value proposition for each channel. For example, transactions that are high in complexity but low in volume often fall into the 'relate to me' category and should be designed in a manner where human judgment and professional expertise can be provided, i.e. utilizing on-call and on-site services. High-volume transactions with little complexity fall into the 'I just want to do it' category and can be delivered utilizing on-mobile and online services.

To maximize efficiencies and ensure consistency of a 'brand' it is essential to have a common channel management framework across functional groups. Different channel types offer different features and qualities and will attract different users, but it is important that there be a common experience across each channel. This includes common terminology, consistency in service offerings, and a common look and feel. It is also essential that back-end processes support front-end customer requirements, and that careful attention is paid to the integration points with internal systems.

Channel types	Attributes
On mobile – SMS, video, graphics to mobile phones, PDAs, other portable devices	Anywhere, any time, instantaneous, convenience, reach, two-way communication, habit
Online – websites, portals, virtual communities, email	Speed, 24x7, self-service, convenience, reach, cost efficiency, record keeping
On site – shopfronts, meetings	Security, high touch, habit, identification
On paper – letters, brochures, books, journals, fax	Convenience, record keeping, reach, tradition
On call – call centres, IVR, voice recognition	Convenience, two-way communication, reliability, cost, speed, self service, habit
On air – radio, television	Speed, 24x7, reach

Figure 31.2 Channel types and their attributes

Customer retention

An important strategy to achieve a high customer focus and retention rate is to concentrate on the 'Rs':

- retention – the information service must develop services and strategies that keep the right customers from defecting to competitive services, or from ceasing to use services. This is sometimes known as 'stickiness'. Customers are retained through adding value and quality to standard products and services;
- requirements – different customers have different requirements and the important part of service delivery is to tailor services to meet customer requirements;
- refined segmentation – all information services have limited resources. By understanding customer preferences, a more refined segmentation can be achieved. This allows each segment to be serviced in a cost-effective manner that is valued by the customer;
- reach – different customers need to be reached in different ways. These may be reflected by offering different channels for the delivery or dissemination of information;
- response – customers will also respond differently to different messages about services and products. Messages should be tailored and disseminated in a manner that communicates the right message to the right customer group;
- relationship – the relationship between the customer and the organization delivering the service is very important. Value can be added through having knowledgeable staff who make an effort to understand their customers' needs and provide individual attention;
- receptiveness – to build a true commitment to customer service, the information service must be receptive to feedback from customers and stakeholders about its services and product. A culture should be fostered that regards complaints as valuable information about systems failures rather than as an annoyance. Formal suggestions and complaint procedures should be in place. The information service should also act on the feedback to improve quality or overcome shortfalls;

- regular consultation – consultation with customers to establish their service and product requirements can be achieved through focus groups, surveys, interviews and forums; and
- review – the customer approach to management requires a formal planning cycle of review, design, implementation and improvement of systems. Complaints and service difficulties should be regularly analysed to identify recurrent problems.

Maintaining service quality

Parasuraman, et al. (1985) have developed a service-quality model that highlights the main requirements for delivering the expected service quality. The model identifies five gaps that cause unsuccessful service delivery:

- the gap between customer expectation and management perception. Management does not always perceive correctly what customers want or how customers judge the service components;
- the gap between management perception and service quality specification. Management might not set quality standards or very clear ones. They might be clear but unrealistic, or they might be clear and realistic but management might not be fully committed to enforcing this quality level;
- the gap between service quality specifications and service delivery. This includes factors such as poorly trained or under-resourced staff, low morale, equipment breakdown or drives for efficiency at the expense of customer satisfaction;
- the gap between service delivery and external communications. Through advertising or promotions, customer expectations may be driven to a higher level of service delivery than can actually be delivered; and
- the gap between the perceived service and expected service. This gap results when one or more of the previous gaps occurs.

Parasuraman et al. (1985) have also developed a list of the main determinants of service quality. These include:

- access – the service is easy to obtain in convenient locations at convenient times with little waiting;
- communication – the service is described accurately in the customer's language;
- competence – the employees possess the required skill and knowledge;
- courtesy – the employees are friendly, respectful and considerate;
- credibility – the organization and employees are trustworthy and have the customer's best interests at heart;
- reliability – the service is performed with consistency and accuracy;
- responsiveness – the employees respond quickly and creatively to customers' requests and problems;
- security – the service is free from danger, risk or doubt;
- tangibles – the service tangibles correctly project the service quality; and
- understanding or knowing the customer – the employees make an effort to understand the customer's needs and provide individual attention.

Whilst these determinants are fundamental to good service delivery, ICT has increased customer expectations for customised and seamless service delivery. Figure 31.3 illustrates the differences in customer orientation and service delivery between traditional thinking organizations and organizations that successful embrace a customer-focused approach to meet the knowledge age environment.

Service-delivery focus	Traditional organizations	Knowledge age organizations
Customer	Invisible	Core
Organization	Silo	Networked
Prioritization	Arms' length	Interdependent
Services	Silo specific	Seamless, customer focused
Channels	Discrete	Optimized
Technologies	Independent	Inter-operable
Access experience	Channel specific	Consistent across channels
Service delivery collaboration	Silo and independent	Networked and ubiquitous

Figure 31.3 Differences in service delivery focus between traditional organizations and knowledge age organizations

ICT offers opportunities to offer quality and customised services to customers through a channel of their choice, e.g. over the counter, over the phone (mobile or fixed), through websites. However, whilst potential savings in operational costs in the introduction of computer-generated solutions are appealing, these need to be countered with the reality that demand for these services and customer expectations of response times and ability to solve the problem is also increasing.

QUALITY AND THE VALUE CHAIN

An important component of quality is to get the steps in the product or service development process, the value chain, right first time every time. The value chain is the chain of activities through which the organization transforms its input resources such as raw data or incoming correspondence into products and services that it delivers to customers. Each of the activities in the chain should build upon the value of the previous activity and contribute to the value of the final product. If any part of the process falls down, then the remaining processes in the value chain will build upon an inferior product or service. This is wasteful of resources and time. It is the quality of the total service that matters: the end product or service, and, the process that creates it.

The value chain not only leads to process improvement, it can also differentiate the product by offering an additional service. For example, raw data can be identified, captured and merged or manipulated in a series of steps to create a value-added information product. The product is marketed and can be further differentiated by offering it in either a value-added form, for example a choice of formats, or, by providing consultancy expertise to assist the customer to make the most out of the value-added information product for their purposes. The area of differentiation can be what distinguishes the product from another in terms of quality of service.

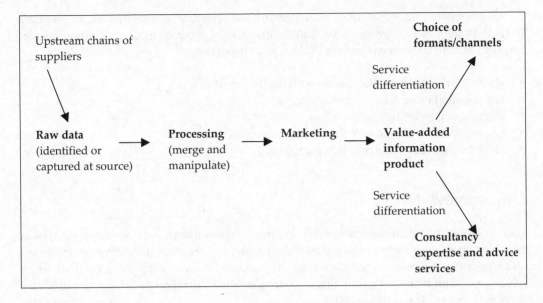

Figure 31.4 The value chain for a value-added information product

BUILDING CONTINUOUS IMPROVEMENT

Continuous improvement, 'kaizen' in Japanese, is a crucial part of both quality-based and time-based competitive strategies. The idea is that organizations can continuously improve the cost, quality and timeliness of their output by making small, incremental process improvements to achieve total service quality.

The important feature is that the improvement is built into the organization as a continuous process to which all staff have a sense of ownership and pride in improvements, rather than it being subject to a one-off improvement strategy that is initiated through a consultant.

CUSTOMER SERVICE CHARTERS

Customer service charters articulate the organization's commitment to the customer. They contain statements on:

- who the customers are;
- the value that the organization places on the customer – 'the customer is the most important person to the information service';
- the relationship between the customer and the information service and how they may be expected to be treated – 'we will respect our customers' requirements of confidentiality and privacy';
- the level of service that can be expected – 'we will respond to enquiries within ten minutes of receipt of the call'; and
- the value placed on employees and their roles in customer service – 'we respect our employees and encourage them to make creative suggestions that will further improve our service'.

Understanding customer value is important in increasing service quality. In thinking insightfully about what customers are really worth, resources can be focused on attracting and keeping the right customers. Customer value can be based on:

- the total value of their relationship with the information service;
- the potential value of their relationship;
- the profitability of their relationship;
- the insights they can provide to the information service; and
- the influence they wield over other customers.

User surveys

User surveys are useful during times of change. They measure user perceptions and expectations and, over time, map their shifting priorities and preferences, thus informing policy review and service development. At the same time, they provide valuable supporting evidence when making a case for increased resourcing, or communicating the rationale for changes in library services to users (Self and Hiller, 2002).

Hiller (2002) cites the approach used by the University of Washington, where, similar to other libraries and information services, changing patterns in usage and user expectations have led to an increased emphasis on providing electronic access to full-text resources. In this instance, survey data not only informed this change in policy, but also helped to make the case for associated changes in resource allocation and to communicate the implications of the change in policy to users.

Customer service support

The delivery of a service or product to the customer is only the beginning of the relationship between the information service and the customer. What is of equal importance is the customer relationship management, service experience and service support that encourages the continual use of the service or product.

The customers' level of satisfaction or dissatisfaction with the quality and efficiency of the service experience and support will influence their perception of the product or service. Service support can be found in:

- delivery or installation – services and products should be delivered or installed at the customer's convenience. The delivery should be fast, on time and efficiently handled. For example, the opening hours for libraries and information services should be decided with customer convenience in mind, requests for paper records files to be brought up should be executed promptly, and an upgrade of software should be installed quickly out of hours or at a time when there is not an urgent deadline being met by the operator of the personal computer;
- after sales service – follow up should be made with the customer regarding the service or product. After sales service should be efficient and attentive. For example, public library staff may enquire about the success of material selected for a school project when the child returns the material; special library staff may follow up on a request for information to ensure

that no additional information is required, or the helpdesk may ring a customer to ensure that no more trouble is being experience with a laptop or other portable access device;

- complaints handling – complaints should be acted upon immediately and managed in a positive manner. Complaints should also be logged so that trends can be identified and rectified before there is an adverse effect on the product or service. This is particularly important when dealing with software;
- warranty repairs – repairs under warranty should be efficiently handled; and
- account management – the invoicing of accounts should be efficient and accurate. Account payment processes should be designed to be convenient for the customer. The account management aspect of service delivery is potentially the highest risk area in customer service. Inaccurate accounting systems that result in goods or services not being charged, undercharged or payments outstanding have a negative impact upon the cash flow and profitability of the organization. Conversely, the continued overcharging for products or services will sour customer relationships with the organization.

Conclusion

The customer approach to management is service driven, quality oriented and centred on the customer rather than the product or service. It gives high priority to the efficiency and effectiveness of product and service delivery to the customers and aims to retain their custom through excellence in customer service support and in meeting emerging needs.

Quality is an excellent variable in service delivery that can be used to distinguish the information service from its competitors. However this service-related strategy is dependent upon the information services manager being aware of customer expectations and perceptions of quality in order to tailor the services to meet their customers' quality values.

An important aspect of ensuring service quality is to get the steps right first time, and in quickly rectifying the situation when things occasionally do go wrong.

References

Hiller, S. (2002), 'Listening to our library users: 2001 survey results', *Library Directions*, Winter, pp. 2–4.

Parasuraman, A., Zeithaml, Valerie A. and Berry, Leonard L. (1985), 'A conceptual model of service quality and its implications for future research', *Journal of Marketing*, Fall, pp. 41–50.

Self, I. and Hiller, S. (2002), 'A decade of users surveys: Utilizing and assessing a standard assessment tool to measure library performance at the University of Virginia and University of Washington', Proceedings of the 4th Northumbria International Conference on Performance Measurement in Libraries and Information Services, 12–16 August 2001, Washington, DC: ARL.

Further Reading

Calvert, Philip and Pope, Adam, (2005), 'Telephone survey research for library managers', *Library Management*, vol. 26, no. 3, pp. 139–52.

Cook, Sarah (2004), *Measuring customer service effectiveness*, Aldershot, UK: Ashgate.

Gower handbook of quality management (2003), 2nd edn, Matt Seaver (ed.), Aldershot, UK: Gower.

Hernon, P. and Altman, E. (1996), *Service quality in academic libraries*, Norwood, NJ: Ablex.

Hill, Nigel and Alexander, Jim (2000), *Handbook of customer satisfaction and loyalty measurement*, 2nd edn, Aldershot, UK: Gower.

Johannsen, Carl Gustav (2004), 'Managing fee-based public library services: Values and practices', *Library Management*, vol. 25, no. 6/7, pp. 307–15.

Rowley, Jennifer (2005), 'Making sense of the quality maze: Perspectives for public and academic libraries', *Library Management*, vol. 26, no. 8/9, pp. 508–19.

Epilogue:
Achieving the Transformation
– The Final Strategy

This chapter brings together the skills and nature of work that are anticipated in achieving organizational transformation in a challenging future. It is reflective of the role of the information services manager in each of the seven parts of the book. Each part provides insight into the significant management activities that information services managers undertake to transform information services and position them at the leading and competitive edge; delivering information services to meet the strategic business objectives of the organization and outclassing others in meeting customer information needs.

Managing in a dynamic environment

Dynamic environments that are indicative of the knowledge age call for transformational change; and transformational change comes from within and from outside as organizations react to the dynamic and powerful impacts. Transformational change occurs from within through passion, enthusiasm and an internal desire to excel; utilizing challenging environments as opportunities, and viewing competition as a testing situation in which the information service can surpass others' achievements and stand out in terms of quality customer service delivery and stakeholder relationships. Transformational change also occurs in response to external stimuli, some of which may be foreseen or prepared for, whilst others create step change or call for unconventional solutions to exceptional or extraordinary problems.

Transformational change brings with it the need for innovation, quick thinking and cleverness. As organizations confront changes in the external environment that affect the very foundations of their business they need to be agile and flexible to withstand strategic shocks and to exploit the openings and opportunities that complexity and discontinuity also bring. Flexibility also extends to service delivery, where rapid advances in information and communications technology (ICT) enable choice in service delivery channels. Making this agility and flexibility possible is a key management and leadership role.

The greater focus on external contexts and relationships means that information services managers need to be good ambassadors and relationship nurturers whilst maintaining a competitive streak. They must use their networks, communicating and political roles to obtain competitive knowledge and sell the benefits of the information service within the organization, and with customers and stakeholders. They must plan, develop and drive competitive business strategies that take into account both possible and potential futures, the internal and external environments and the available resources. These environments are continually changing, so the managers and their strategies must be flexible enough to cope with changing conditions whilst still concentrating on the objectives of the information service and its organization.

The objective of the information service is to assist the parent organization to utilize its information and supporting technologies to excel in its business, which might be in creating new advantages, to increase knowledge or to enhance the quality of life. Central to this objective is the:

- alignment of the management approach of information and ICT with the corporate vision and business directions;
- building of value into the real-time corporate environment;
- use of ICT as a tool for enabling transformational change; and
- the provision of quality services that exceeds management and customer expectations.

To do this, the information services manager maximizes creativity in designing information services and products, utilizing the supporting technology in innovative ways to achieve excellence in quality customer service and a high rate of satisfaction, market domination and increased profitability for the organization or in building social capital. In this all-encompassing environment, the continual drive to excel means that they must constantly assess their own performance and that of the information service with regards to this objective.

Traditional management roles and responsibilities, skills and mindsets have been replaced by new ones. Managers are now judged on how they inspire people through passion and vision, invest in people and unlock information and ideas. Opinions are also formed about how they build an organizational capacity to create, drive and engage in change, and use ICT as a tool for productivity gains and transformational change, as well as opening up new opportunities in service delivery.

Planning and managing for transformation

Successful transformation is built upon rigorous planning and consideration of alternatives; especially those that are conceivable (may be likely), possible (likely) and probable (most likely). Planning and managing for transformational change recognizes that organizations cannot achieve everything that they would like to do in areas where they have control and that external influences will shape decisions about the future. However, the putting of energy and resources into the initial stages of the planning process is likely to reap significant dividends in the future, over leaving the future to chance or reacting to situations as they arise. In doing so, the information services manager should choose strategies and initiate new activities and services such that they meet their strategic business needs and achieve the right outcomes and the right approach.

Acknowledging the interrelationships between assets that impinge on the information service, the information services manager assumes an integrated approach to planning human, financial, knowledge and information, technology and strategic assets. They advise on how each of these assets can be leveraged to embrace the future through the strategic and effective use of information and ICT, how they can capitalize on other business environment changes, and offer added value and excellence in their provision of existing services. As an enabler of business change; the manager needs to have flexibility and agility in order to respond to changing market and environmental conditions.

The information services manager also has a strong visionary role, providing leadership in the use of information and ICT to enhance and add value to the business of the organization.

This role is carried out by shifting mindsets as to what is possible in the future, in providing new frameworks that use knowledge and information to rethink service strategies and in blending information and ICT strategy with the business strategy, creating strategic changes at a competitive pace.

Through the use of information and its associated ICT the information services manager is in a position to deliver internal efficiencies by driving down their own costs, increasing the quality and personalisation of customer quality services, and helping to achieve costs savings elsewhere. A key role is to manage knowledge, information and data in many different formats and media to support a variety of business needs, within the organization and externally to clients and other stakeholders. Highly developed communication and interpersonal skills are needed in order to make judgments, listen, evaluate, reason, reassure, appease and provide advice to peers, customers, their bosses and stakeholders in this environment.

Collectively the planning and management of all assets, human, knowledge, information, technical, capital and financial should be undertaken with the view to:

- maximizing the return on investment for the organization;
- utilizing these assets as strategic business tools to create the advantageous edge;
- enhancing competitiveness and improving customer relationships and service delivery;
- delivering positive, tangible results and outcomes;
- providing a point of differentiation in the market place or market space; and
- reducing future resource requirements by prolonging the asset's life or strengthening its disposal value.

Creating the right corporate environment

A significant role for the information services manager is to create the right corporate environment in which transformational change can occur. This involves the need to develop and align the corporate culture with the business strategy, manage political roles and ensure that policies support the strategic direction of the organization.

The phrase 'innovate or perish' is a catchphrase of the knowledge age. It is a prerequisite for organizations in a market-oriented, highly competitive environment. An important role for the information services manager is to create and shape the corporate culture so that it values creativity and supports innovation to identify and create new opportunities and to engage positively in change. As a service organization, the information service's culture needs to espouse values of excellence and quality services leading to high levels of customer satisfaction. Collaboration and teamwork are also important in excelling in service deliver, so values of belonging, openness, learning, trust, pride, respect for others' ideas and mutual support are also important. Likewise, integrity and ethical behaviour should also be included as values, particularly where the information service is dealing with commercially sensitive or personal information.

To drive transformational change within the organization and manage the increased focus on external relationships, information services managers need to be politically active and engage in business issues inside their organization and with external stakeholders. This includes being politically astute, championing relationships and being able to recognize, control and manage organizational politics for the benefit of the information service. Political behaviour can also drive change and move forward items on the corporate agenda. The information services manager must understand what the parent organization wants and position the information service to provide creative solutions to important problems.

In the policy-making role, the information services manager ensures that the policies are well planned and thought out in terms of strategic timing, costs, the issues at stake, the values and attitudes within the organization, and those of their clients and stakeholders. Their policies are future oriented and anticipate new demands and developments.

Developing a creative and innovative corporate culture calls for leadership abilities that inspire others to show ingenuity, to have originality in thought and to feel prepared and able to demonstrate inventiveness. Managers that foster innovation also show a willingness to take risks and allow their staff to make mistakes as part of the learning process. They build a corporate capacity that values and demonstrates flexibility and adaptability as a means of dealing with unstructured problems, future proofing the organization whilst creating and offering new products and services ahead of others. Knowledge, know-how, talents, skills and expertise are necessary ingredients for innovation. These can be strengthened and encouraged through the right information sharing and management practices, rewards systems and performance reviews that support and encourage ideas generation and divergent thoughts in problem solving.

Transforming the corporate environment

Transformational leadership requires proactive, visionary, entrepreneurial and risk-taking characteristics. Transformational leaders are those who look to the future for opportunities in an age of high uncertainty and fast-changing environments, yet provide a clear understanding of what their organization is trying to achieve and why. Skills in identifying external discontinuities whilst articulating and aligning the vision to the future possibilities are required. In enabling the transformation of the organization, their role is to drive the transformational agenda using ICT as the tool, enhancing information and knowledge sharing for better decision making and governance, and inspiring others to be innovative and to achieve success.

Leadership is a critical differentiating factor for survival in the knowledge age, for exploring opportunities and mapping the way in the global economy, and for building value into the organization's processes and services in the real time and always connected environment. The ability to get things done in the corporate environment and externally rests on the leaders' capacities to inspire and lead, to influence and persuade, to delegate and to involve others in decision making.

Achievements are realized through interactions between people. Leaders shape the culture and behaviours of the organization to foster interaction and collaboration. Through their own actions as role models, they demonstrate the benefits of communication, information sharing and ethical behaviour. Trust, credibility and confidence are also important leadership considerations in ensuring that people continually achieve high-level outcomes and are happy and collegiate in their work.

In creating change to capitalize on opportunities, the information services manager has to work with others to build an agile and flexible organization with the capacity and commitment to embrace and engage in continuous change. In managing (and reacting) to radical external influences and overseeing the associated and continuous internal change, there is the dual role of preparing people to withstand sudden strategic shocks by building in flexibility and adaptiveness, whilst readying people to feel comfortable with the status quo being uncertainty.

It is a management role to enable people to see and understand the big picture, where they are given a total view of the environment where turbulence is the norm and transformational change is necessary either in anticipation of, or in response to, sudden strategic shocks. Cooperation, collaboration and enthusiasm are also needed so that the organization can pull together in times of adversity.

Group and team management uses all the facilitation skills and knowledge associated in engaging change, leadership and motivation but in a wider and different capacity. In working with groups or teams and extending their performance, managers are dealing with many individuals, each with their own and the group's needs, which leads to different and complex dynamics. In the early stage of building teams, there are feelings of individual loss of independence and control that have to be recognized and managed.

It is also necessary to acknowledge that it is natural for individuals and groups to sometimes have conflicts. With this in mind, the team builder needs to be competent at recognizing and resolving conflict. The most common reasons for differences and conflict are individual dilemmas over roles that people play in groups, and the various stages of group development that can lead to emotional tension. Trust and openness are important at all stages of team development.

In building teams, the role of the manager is to facilitate the group's management of its members rather than manage the members as individuals. Over time teams will develop a culture of self-discipline. This includes the group norms and values within which they work and exercise control over individuals without harming their egos. As a team builder, the manager improves opportunities for coordination between the team members and enables the members of the team to work together to achieve a higher level of outcome. Rather than take over themselves, they empower others and encourage the leadership capacities to be shared amongst all the members of the team at different times.

To obtain the best out of people, managers must understand individual drivers to succeed and motivate accordingly. Inspirational managers ensure that they continually extend and develop individuals, coaching them to achieve greater levels as well as responding to their aspirations.

Today motivation is linked to management flexibility and compensation for working smarter rather than harder. Organizational-level motivational strategies that include flexible work arrangements and benefits, as well as actions that recognize individual differences and circumstances are likely to lead to a higher commitment to the organization. Performance-based compensation provides incentives for individual or group effort to work more cleverly and skilfully by rewarding innovation and performance. Job enrichment and job enlargement are other motivational strategies that can be explored.

Creating a sense of usefulness, belonging and achievement, having an atmosphere that welcomes and embraces challenges and is open and sharing of good and bad news, and encouraging an environment of respect are other strategies that can be put in place at the organizational level and at the individual level to increase motivation.

Conflict and change are closely related in the desire to transform organizations. It could be said that conflict is inevitable in changing environments as people adjust to change. Conflict occurs as the result of a disagreement, threat or opposition between individuals or groups, or within an individual or group that might arise out of change. Conflict also serves as a catalyst for change. In many instances conflict is a sign of a healthy organization. Conflict of a competitive nature generally leads to improved organizational performance.

The ideal is to manage conflict so that it remains healthy enough to encourage competition between individuals and groups without becoming destructive. Win-win conflict resolution strategies are the most positive ways in resolving conflict. These focus upon ends and goals, identifying the sources of conflict and then present these as problems to be solved. Participative management techniques are used in order to gain consensus and commitment to objectives.

The ability to negotiate effectively is a critical requirement in transforming organizations and occurs with varying degrees of formality. It is commonly used in the resolution of conflict and in the making and implementation of decisions. Changing environments also bring about new kinds of relationships with customers and other stakeholders, vendors, service providers and organizations operating in the same or related industries, all of which rely upon the information services manager having exceptional negotiation and networking skills.

Experienced negotiators are articulate and have great presence and self-confidence. Their self-confidence arises out of their technical knowledge of the field in which they are negotiating and in their past negotiating experience. They need to be creative, yet determined and disciplined. They also have a high level of tolerance for frustration. They are sensitive to the behaviour of others and are able to anticipate and evaluate others' responses.

Managing yourself and others

Influencing and getting things done in the corporate environment requires good interpersonal skills that include networking with people and clearly communicating across organizational boundaries and with all levels of people, internal and external to the organization. Personal networks allow information services managers to seek and provide information, to obtain support and to influence outcomes positively. Many legitimate political tactics rely upon networks. In belonging to others' networks, valuable and competitive information can be obtained.

Managing the well-being of the individuals who work in the information service is as important, if not more important, as managing the financial, technical and information resources. Managing well-being is part of the duty of care and includes assisting individuals to manage their individual vulnerabilities to stress so that they can enjoy a quality of life and function well. Stress tolerances differ between individuals, some being more able to control or manage their responses to stressors than others.

Changing circumstances, role conflict, role ambiguity, role overload and role underload all have the potential to be stressors depending upon the vulnerability of the individual. Economic and time pressures, technological change and obsolescence, faulty equipment, job insecurity or bad working relationships, can also contribute to stress. Reducing employees' vulnerabilities to stress and personal planning processes will increase individual capabilities and help to create a more productive work environment. Supportive professional and personal relationships are among the most useful weapons against the distress of work and people's demands. Effective listening skills, seeking advice, information and feedback and encouraging input from others can also make decision making less reactive and crisis oriented.

Preparing people for their future, in terms of supporting their own and organizational needs is an important management consideration in times of transformational change. Identifying and putting actions in place to achieve career and life goals through career planning and personal development are just part of the picture. In a world where individuals perform many roles and constantly juggle work and personal commitments, a total lifestyle approach is required in order to create a sense of well-being. These actions are both an individual and organizational responsibility. The organization can support training and other personal development opportunities by making available the necessary funding and attendance time. They can also provide coaching and counselling programmes to assist individuals in the realistic planning and attainment of their goals. However, individuals also have to accept responsibility for their personal growth and development, putting in place strategies to achieve their long-term career and lifestyle plans.

Organizations today comprise a mix of people with different cultural backgrounds, who belong to different age groups and who have specialized in particular subject areas or come from different career paths. Information services also comprise individuals with very different qualifications, tasks and expertise in the subject specialization, media and the technology involved. These differentiations bring different norms, perspectives and ways of working. These add to the richness of culture and ideas, but can also lead to differentiations in expectation and values within information services and be sources of conflict. Managing these differences and bringing everyone together so that the competitive elements foster rather than hinder the organization's objectives is an important management task.

The value and contribution of each of these differences should be recognized and explored, as a greater understanding of the differences in values, attitudes and behaviour will help reduce the barriers of acceptance. Recognizing that sources of conflict in organizations are often related to roles, specializations and generation outlook, rather than individuals, will also assist in maintaining good personal relationships between people whose roles are in conflict. Where role conflict exists between specialist groups, it should be recognized for what it is rather than as a personal issue.

Governance and accountability

Increased public scrutiny and the increasing involvement of the private sector in public sector service delivery are two issues driving the governance agenda. The greater emphasis on better governance is also a factor in changing environments where there are far-reaching consequences, and where ensuring ethics and integrity, making the right choices and correctly attending to and dealing with dilemmas are paramount in decision making.

Having an excellent reputation and stakeholder confidence in an organization's ability to demonstrate good corporate citizenship and achieve excellence are also important factors that determine the success of an organization. Public and private sector organizations are now judged on the manner in which they encourage sustainable development, demonstrate social leadership and corporate ethics. In this environment, good governance and accountability stem from having high-quality practices and processes in place not just for today, but for the future. This includes having a visible code of conduct, utilizing independent audit practices, establishing a sound system for risk oversight and management, managing for sustainability and for different forms of capital, as well as regularly reviewing the effectiveness of systems, structures, policies, practices and procedures.

Whilst individuals are accountable for their ethics and integrity in their actions and for following correct procedures, the environment needs to be created where managers set the example through leadership and ensure that appropriate practices and processes are in place, understood and adhered to. This includes upholding and reinforcing the desired corporate culture, ensuring the integrity of governance systems, structures, policies, practices and procedures, and that rights are recognized and acknowledged.

The exercise of power and authority assists the manager achieve accountability and to influence outcomes. The quest for power by either the manager or others can lead to healthy and productive outcomes or it can result in disruptive, selfish or harmful behaviours, where the outcomes are not as beneficial. Managing power, either on a personal basis or that of others is an important component of managing in transformational change, where changing circumstances can lead to challenges and changes in the power base of individuals.

A test of good governance is to avoid the abuse of power. This requires a good understanding of the various power sources and how to use these effectively to persuade and influence ethical outcomes rather than to control people and situations for personal gain.

Openness and participation in decision making are also important in achieving transparency and resolving differences in changing environments. Openness includes encouraging candid and honest discussion leading up to when decisions are taken so that a comprehensive view is formed of the issues being considered, as well as frankness about the decision itself. Participative decision making allows people to bring multiple views, aspects and knowledge of the subject area, as well as different abilities, interests and skills that will result in better decisions. Ensuring that there is no confusion about why and when actions or decisions are being taken, that people are clear about the ramifications of the actions or decision and about the actions or decisions themselves are important follow up tasks.

Many decisions are influenced by perception, intuition and emotion that left unrecognized can distort opinions, misconstrue facts and interfere with decisions. From a management perspective, the need to understand and deal with perceptions is as real as the need to understand and deal with reality.

Good communications are also vital in ensuring transparency and openness in organizations. Rapidly changing environments require rapid communication with less time for formalized procedures, so increasingly electronic communication channels are used that can disseminate the same message to many people at the same time.

Good governance also includes ensuring that the information service is delivering valued products and services commensurate with the investment that is being made and that its performance is measured and evaluated. This is in part a means of accountability to stakeholders, as well as ensuring that there is continuous improvement in the service fit with customer needs. In order to evaluate and measure the service's performance, appropriate information needs to be collected in a meaningful form.

Planning for adversity is the key to overcoming adversity. Risk management strategies identify the potential for adversity and put appropriate actions in place to manage the event or situation according to the probability of it occurring. In turbulent and changing environments, a major role of the manager is to anticipate, assess, manage and minimize risk. Information services have traditionally considered information security to be one of the foundation elements of risk management. Whilst information security is still a major risk management issue, there are other risk issues that should also be managed. These include theft of intellectual property rights, personal safety and occupational health and safety risks, loss of public reputation, image or regard for corporate citizenship, and loss of key staff and expertise; all of which require other risk management strategies.

Maintaining the integrity of information relies upon the ability to protect it from unauthorized manipulation or processing, as well as safeguarding the accuracy and completeness of information and processing methods. The choice of security level is a business and risk management issue. It should take into account the type of business and its operating environment, level of business risk, practical implementation considerations and relative cost.

In the event of a major outage, disaster recovery and business continuity plans protect critical business processes from adverse effects by ensuring the continuity of access to information and its supporting technologies. These plans should be regularly updated, well known and understood. Executive management must know how the situation will be managed and in what order so that business processes can be restored as quickly as possible.

Outsourcing changes the role of the information services manager from a provider of services to a purchaser of services. In achieving this transformation their attention turns to the responsibilities of relationship building with the service provider, contract management, understanding each other's business drivers, ensuring that reporting and other obligations are met in a timely manner and systematically reviewing progress. Outsourcing provides an alternative means of making customer and support services available that are not core or critical business to the information service. Common functions and services for consideration include ICT, corporate services, debt collecting, security services, storage and retrieval of records and archives and the processing of journals and other stock.

Positioning to excel in service delivery

Having:

- identified the challenges and positioned the information service through good planning to take advantage of strategic influences of the knowledge age;
- shaped the right corporate environment such that it values creativity, supports innovation and positively engages in transformational change;
- managed the well-being of themselves and others so that they can enjoy a quality of life, prepare for their future and function well; and
- ensured proper governance mechanisms including ethics and integrity in decision making, good corporate citizenship, accountability and transparency in all activities, including outsourcing arrangements;

the information services manager has one further challenge in achieving the transformation: how to position to excel in service delivery.

The bottom line for this is in meeting customer needs. It involves ensuring that the correct competitive strategies are in place to identify needs, that the correct image is projected to attract and continue to attract and retain potential and existing customers, and to ensure that service quality prevails at the initial point of contact and in all subsequent dealings.

There are many ways in which strategic marketing and competitive strategies can be used to identify the right path in transforming the organization to harness the unpredictable world ahead, to meet the challenges of the increasingly sophisticated needs of clients and to excel in service delivery. The challenge is to choose and meld the different strategies to get the right mix, to optimize competitive intelligence to advantage, to know when to diversify or rejuvenate services, and to learn more about customers' needs and behaviours.

The management of the organization's image and messages to the external environment is as important as managing the internal communications. In their boundary-spanning role, the information services manager needs to ensure that the impressions and beliefs that individuals have about the information service are the correct ones. The image of the information service is conveyed electronically in its web presence and use of other electronic media, orally through personal communication, physically through its built environment including the physical design and colours used, and by other communication mechanisms such as reports that may be in electronic or hard copy form.

The final judgment of the service is the domain of the customer. In the universal knowledge-based economy and society, libraries and information services need to meet global standards of excellence and assist their organization to compete with global best practices. Ensuring consistently higher-quality services or products than those of competitors is a primary means of satisfying customers and achieving excellence in service delivery, that in turn provides the competitive advantage. Insisting on a commitment to quality as a self-sustaining way of life within the organization requires each step in the value chain to be of high quality.

The design and delivery of the service or product to the customer is only the beginning of the relationship between the organization and the customer. Loyalty and customer retention are also key components to the service's competitive edge. Trust, choice of service channel, complaints handling, accounts management and service backup that supports the continual use of the product or service and commitment to the customer must be of equally quality.

Conclusion

The focus for managing and transforming information services to succeed in changing and competitive environments is to create a vision and inspire others to work towards the achievement of that vision. Along the way, challenges will be encountered, often on a daily basis that will require creative thinking and innovation to resolve them. Strong teamwork and an individual and corporate capacity to engage in change will help overcome many hurdles.

Information services exist to add value to the business of the organization, whether this is to ensure survival and success through continuously inventing new advantages in a global environment or to build social capital in a local community. The bottom line in adding value is transparency, sustainability, relevance and quality such that the service excels in the mind of the customer.

Index